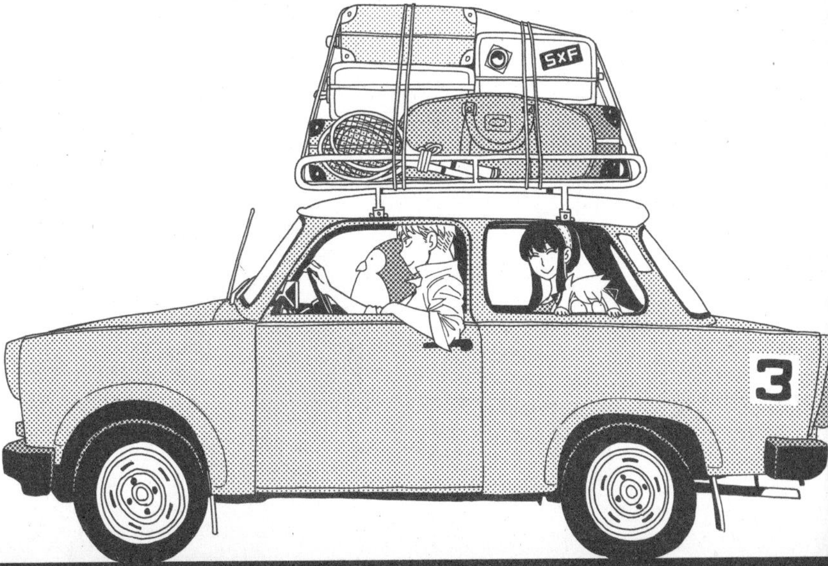
SxF
3

3

STORY AND ART BY
TATSUYA ENDO

SPY×FAMILY

SPY×FAMILY CHARACTERS

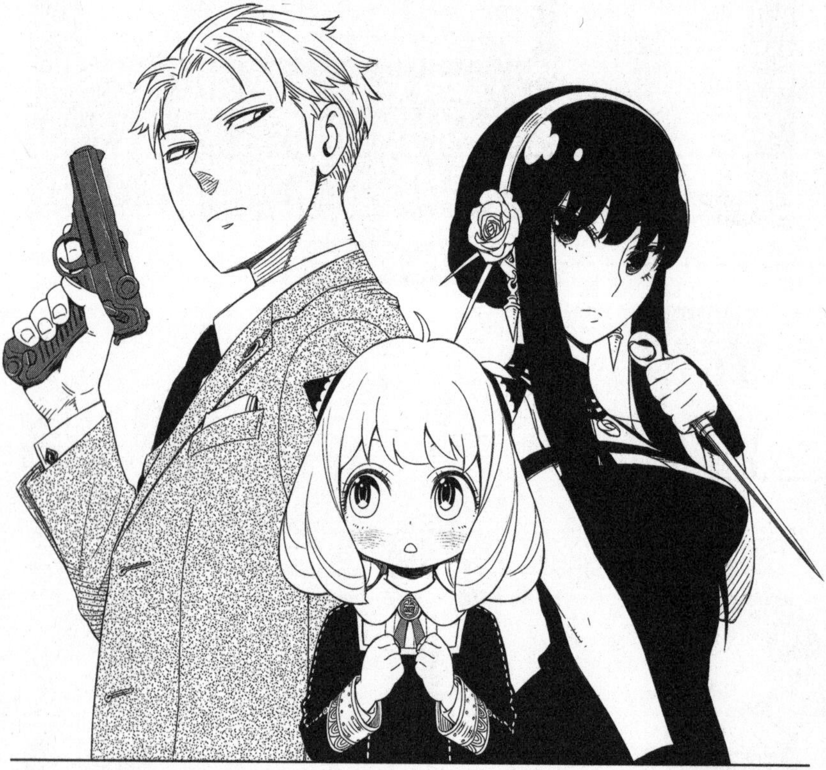

LOID FORGER

ROLE: Husband
OCCUPATION:
Psychiatrist

A spy and master of disguise covertly serving the nation of Westalis. His code name is "Twilight."

ANYA FORGER

ROLE: Daughter

A telepath whose abilities were created in an experiment conducted by a certain organization. She can read the minds of others.

YOR FORGER

ROLE: Wife
OCCUPATION:
City Hall Clerk

Lives a secret life as an assassin. Her code name is "Thorn Princess."

MISSION

OPERATION STRIX

Spy on Donovan Desmond, a dangerous figure who threatens to disrupt peace between the East and West. Must gain entry into the prestigious Eden Academy to breach the target's inner circle.

TARGET

DONOVAN DESMOND

The focus of Operation Strix. Chairman of Ostania's National Unity Party.

KEY PEOPLE

FRANKY
Intelligence asset who works with Twilight.

HENRY HENDERSON
Housemaster at Eden Academy.

BECKY BLACKWELL
Anya's friend.

DAMIAN DESMOND
Second son of Donovan Desmond.

YURI BRIAR

Yor's younger brother, a secret police officer.

STORY

Westalis secret agent Twilight receives orders to uncover the plans of Donovan Desmond, the war-mongering chairman of Ostania's National Unity Party. To do so, Twilight must pose as Loid Forger, create a fake family and enroll his child at the prestigious Eden Academy. However, by sheer coincidence, the daughter he selects from an orphanage is secretly a telepath! Also, the woman who agrees to be in a sham marriage with him is secretly an assassin!

While concealing their true identities from one another, the three manage to score Anya a spot at Eden Academy. Loid alters the school registry so that Anya is in the same class as his target's son Damian. However, angered by Damian's high-handed attitude, Anya decks him with a punch, thereby endangering Loid's mission. Worse still, Yor's brother Yuri—a member of the spy-hunting secret police—drops by for a surprise visit!

CONTENTS

SPY×FAMILY ③

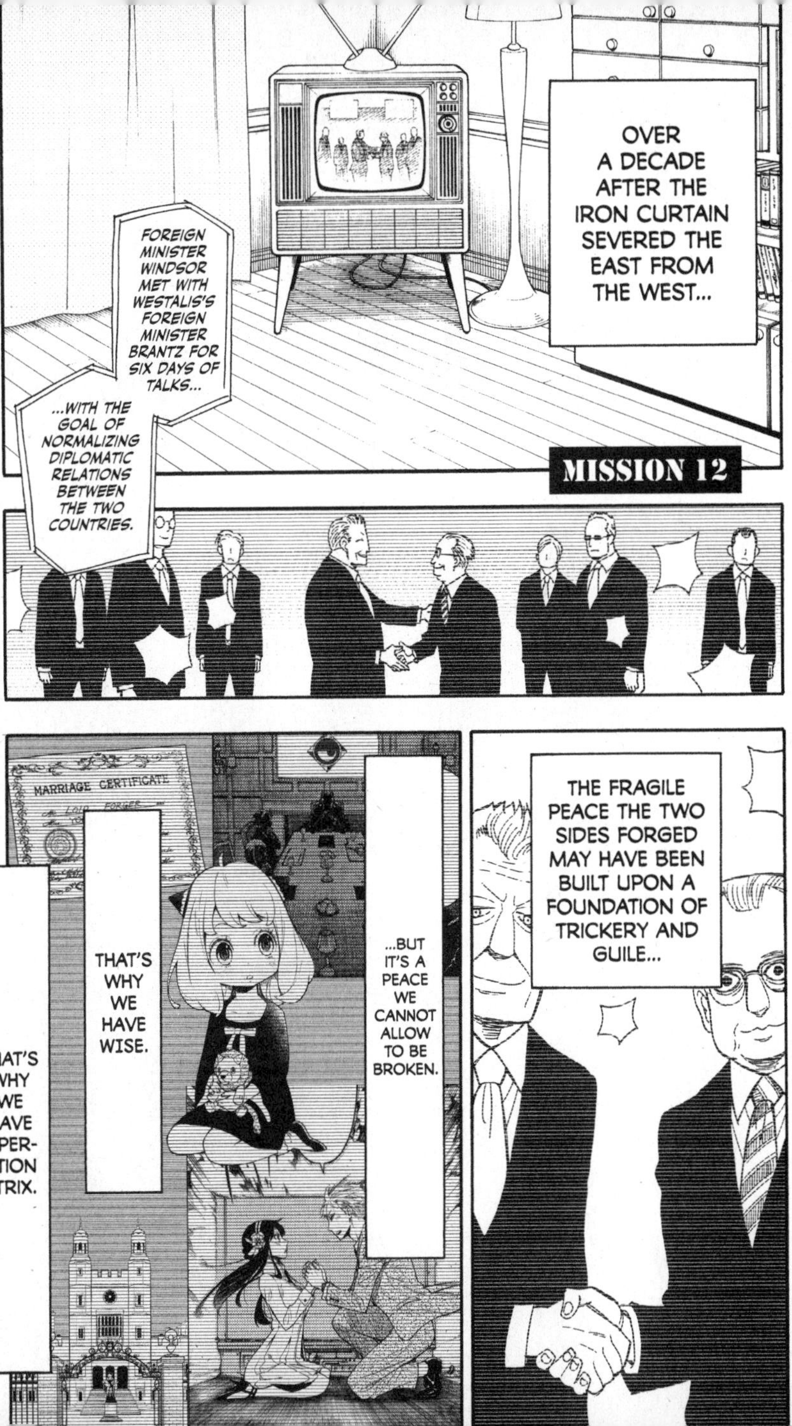
OVER A DECADE AFTER THE IRON CURTAIN SEVERED THE EAST FROM THE WEST...
FOREIGN MINISTER WINDSOR MET WITH WESTALIS'S FOREIGN MINISTER BRANTZ FOR SIX DAYS OF TALKS...
...WITH THE GOAL OF NORMALIZING DIPLOMATIC RELATIONS BETWEEN THE TWO COUNTRIES.
MISSION 12
THE FRAGILE PEACE THE TWO SIDES FORGED MAY HAVE BEEN BUILT UPON A FOUNDATION OF TRICKERY AND GUILE...
...BUT IT'S A PEACE WE CANNOT ALLOW TO BE BROKEN.
MARRIAGE CERTIFICATE
THAT'S WHY WE HAVE WISE.
THAT'S WHY WE HAVE OPERATION STRIX.

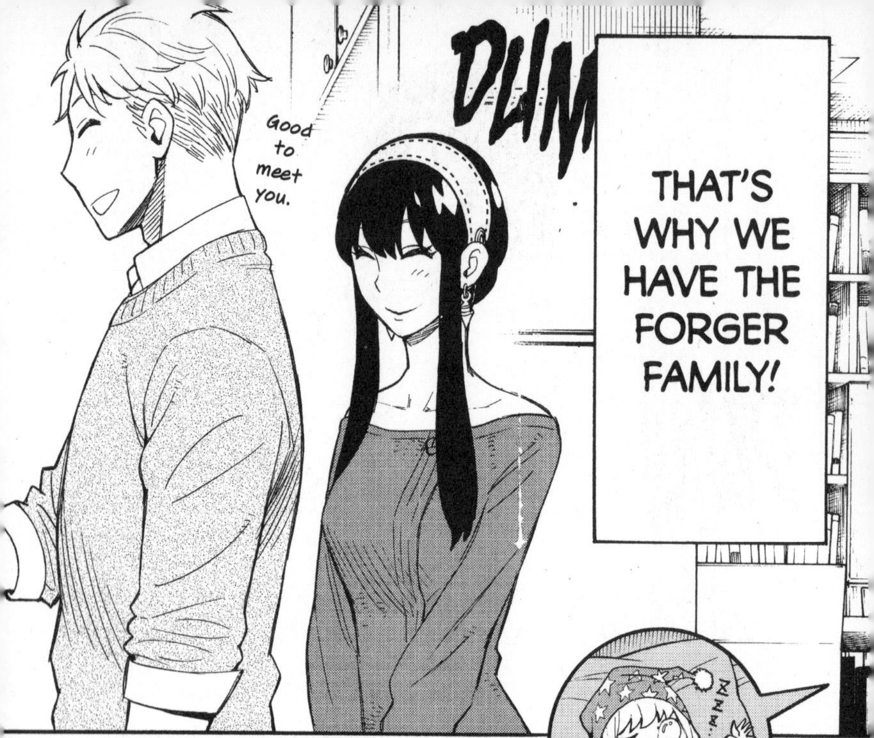
DUM
THAT'S WHY WE HAVE THE FORGER FAMILY!
Good to meet you.
ZZZ...

MISSION 12

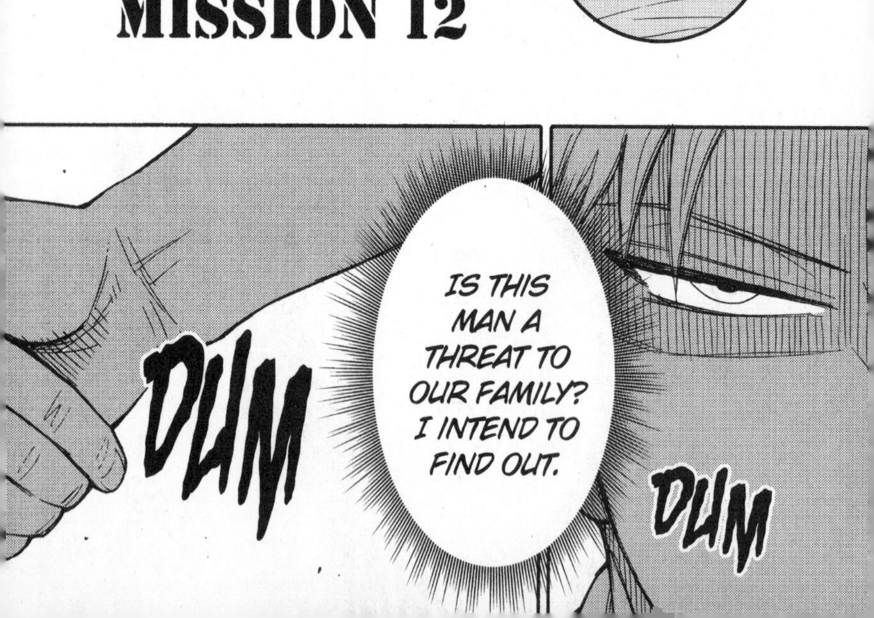
IS THIS MAN A THREAT TO OUR FAMILY? I INTEND TO FIND OUT.
DUM
DUM

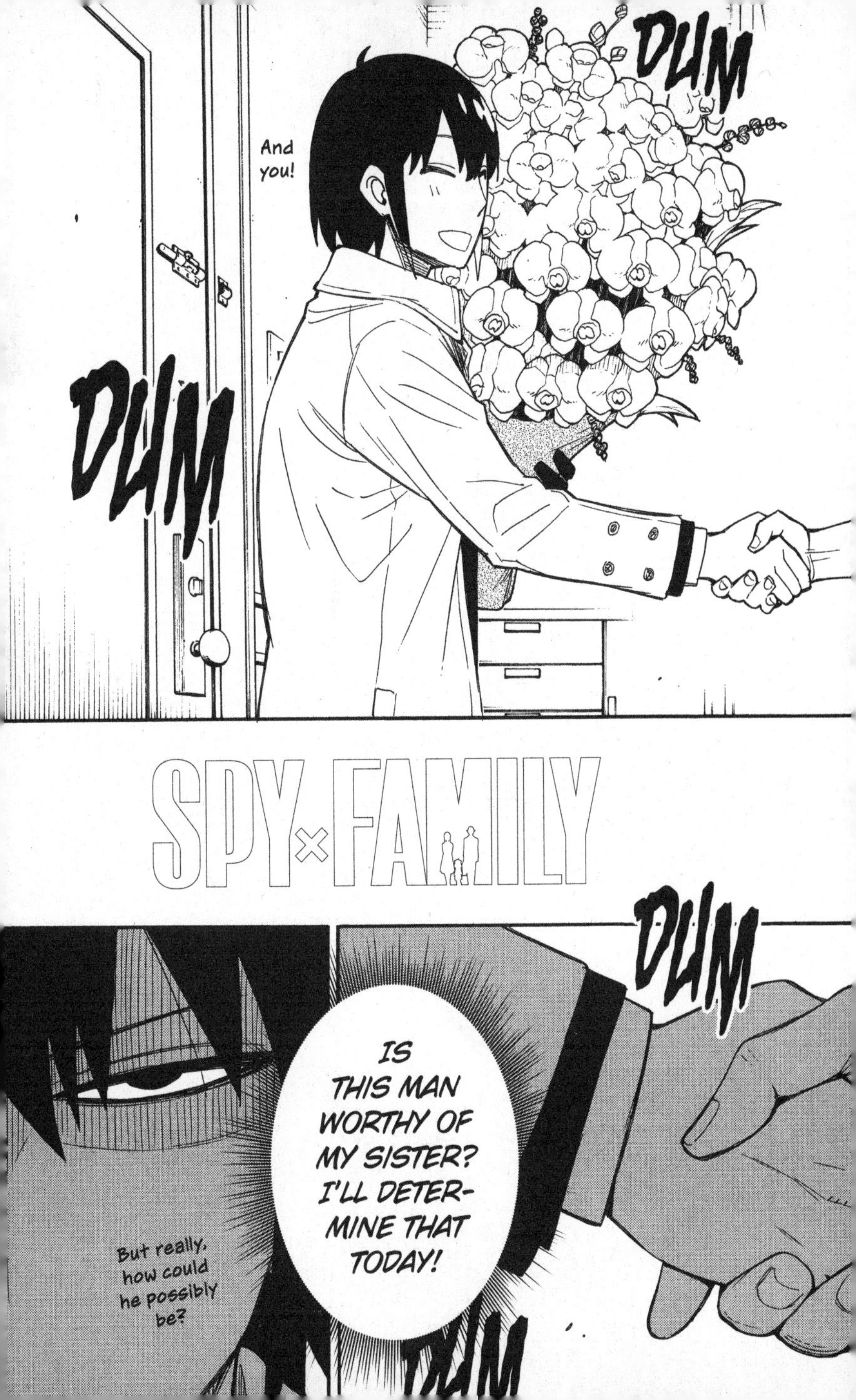
And you!
DUM
DUM
SPY×FAMILY
DUM
IS THIS MAN WORTHY OF MY SISTER? I'LL DETERMINE THAT TODAY!
But really, how could he possibly be?
THUM

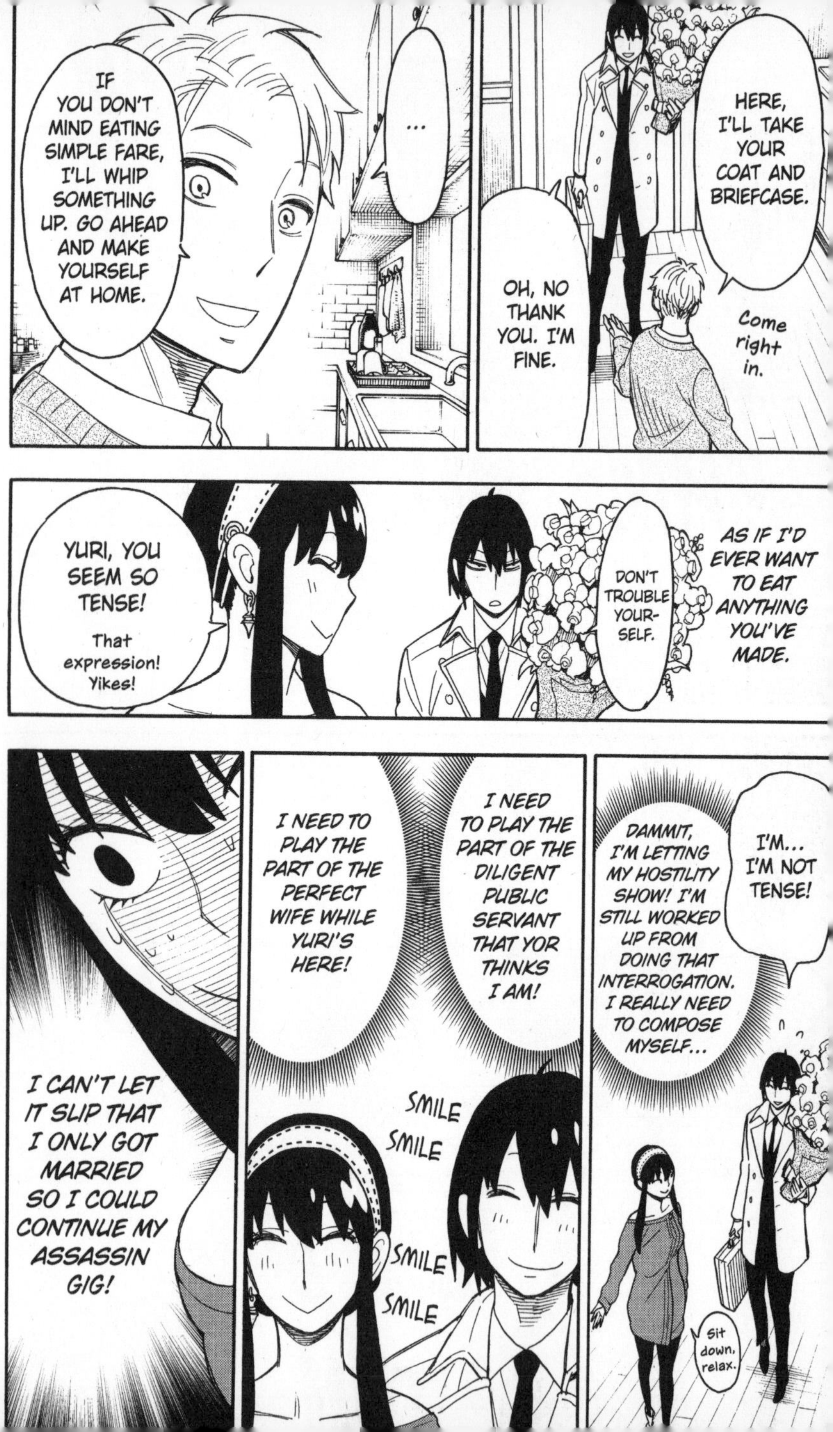
HERE, I'LL TAKE YOUR COAT AND BRIEFCASE.
Come right in.
OH, NO THANK YOU. I'M FINE.
...
IF YOU DON'T MIND EATING SIMPLE FARE, I'LL WHIP SOMETHING UP. GO AHEAD AND MAKE YOURSELF AT HOME.
AS IF I'D EVER WANT TO EAT ANYTHING YOU'VE MADE.
DON'T TROUBLE YOURSELF.
YURI, YOU SEEM SO TENSE!
That expression! Yikes!
I'M... I'M NOT TENSE!
DAMMIT, I'M LETTING MY HOSTILITY SHOW! I'M STILL WORKED UP FROM DOING THAT INTERROGATION. I REALLY NEED TO COMPOSE MYSELF...
Sit down, relax.
I NEED TO PLAY THE PART OF THE DILIGENT PUBLIC SERVANT THAT YOR THINKS I AM!
I NEED TO PLAY THE PART OF THE PERFECT WIFE WHILE YURI'S HERE!
SMILE
SMILE
SMILE
SMILE
I CAN'T LET IT SLIP THAT I ONLY GOT MARRIED SO I COULD CONTINUE MY ASSASSIN GIG!

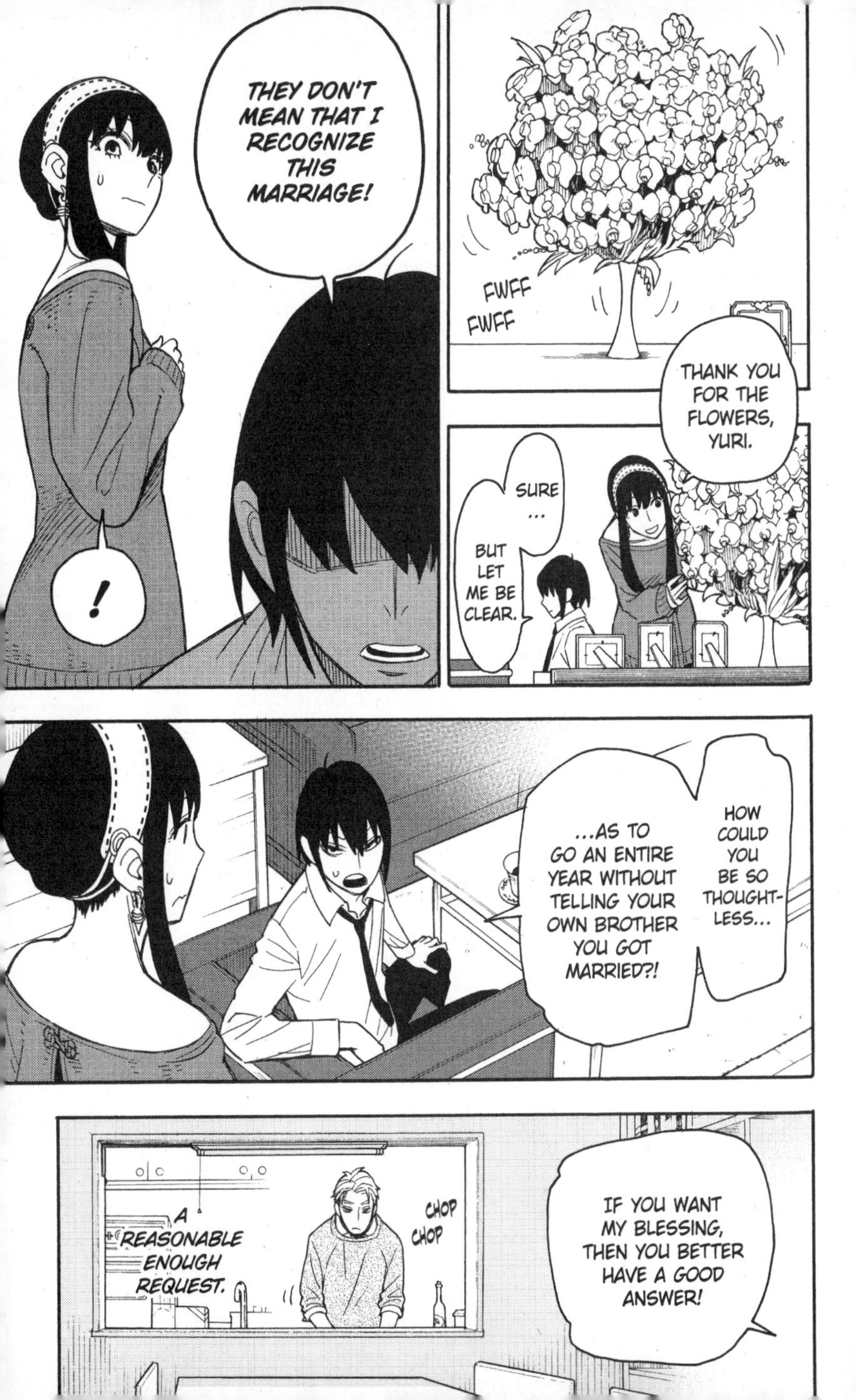
FWFF FWFF
THANK YOU FOR THE FLOWERS, YURI.
SURE...
BUT LET ME BE CLEAR.
THEY DON'T MEAN THAT I RECOGNIZE THIS MARRIAGE!
!
HOW COULD YOU BE SO THOUGHT-LESS...
...AS TO GO AN ENTIRE YEAR WITHOUT TELLING YOUR OWN BROTHER YOU GOT MARRIED?!
IF YOU WANT MY BLESSING, THEN YOU BETTER HAVE A GOOD ANSWER!
CHOP CHOP
A REASONABLE ENOUGH REQUEST.

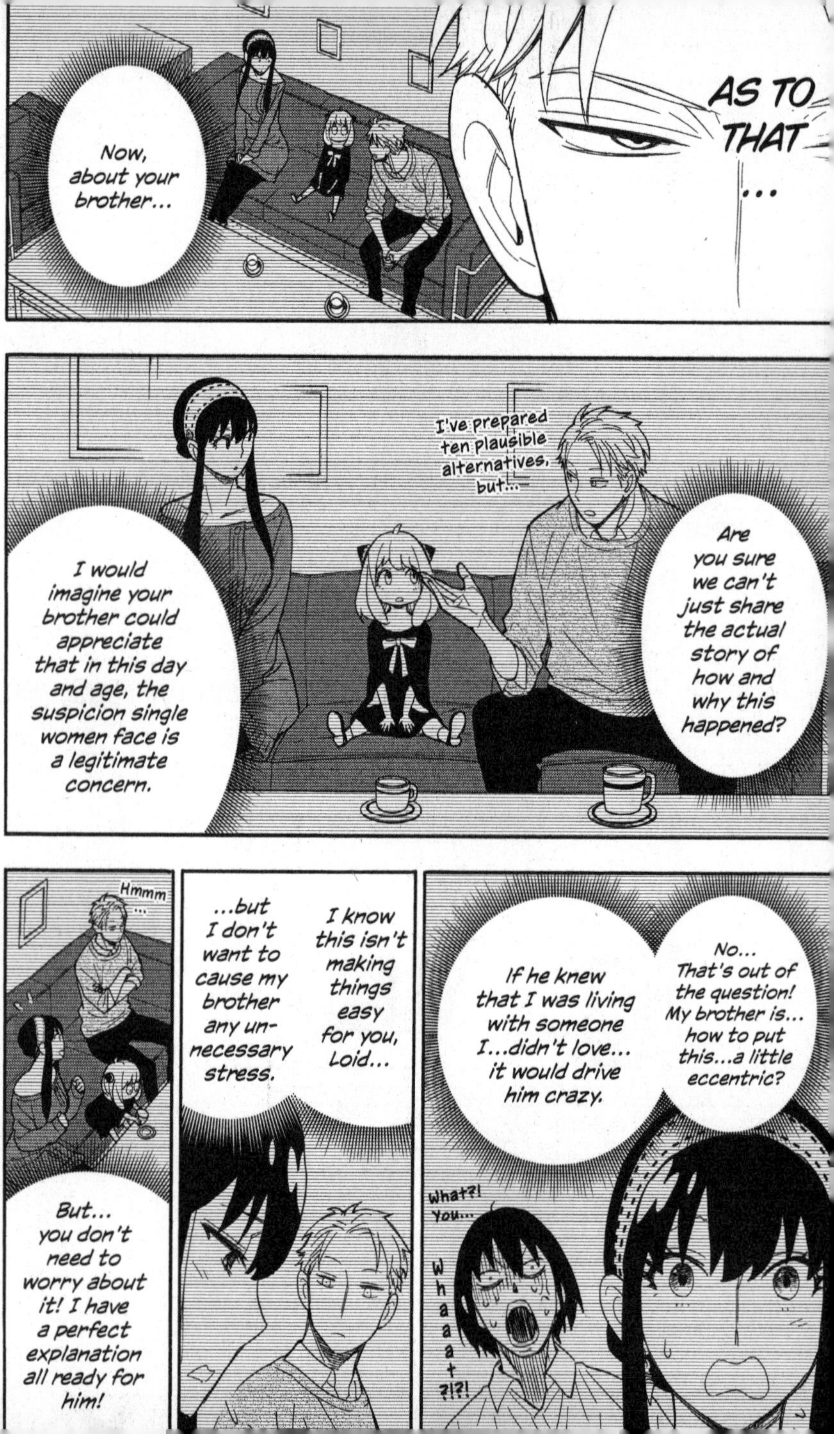
AS TO THAT ...
Now, about your brother...
Are you sure we can't just share the actual story of how and why this happened?
I've prepared ten plausible alternatives, but...
I would imagine your brother could appreciate that in this day and age, the suspicion single women face is a legitimate concern.
No... That's out of the question! My brother is... how to put this...a little eccentric?
If he knew that I was living with someone I...didn't love... it would drive him crazy.
What?! You...
Whaaaat?!?!
I know this isn't making things easy for you, Loid...
...but I don't want to cause my brother any un-necessary stress.
Hmmm...
But... you don't need to worry about it! I have a perfect explanation all ready for him!

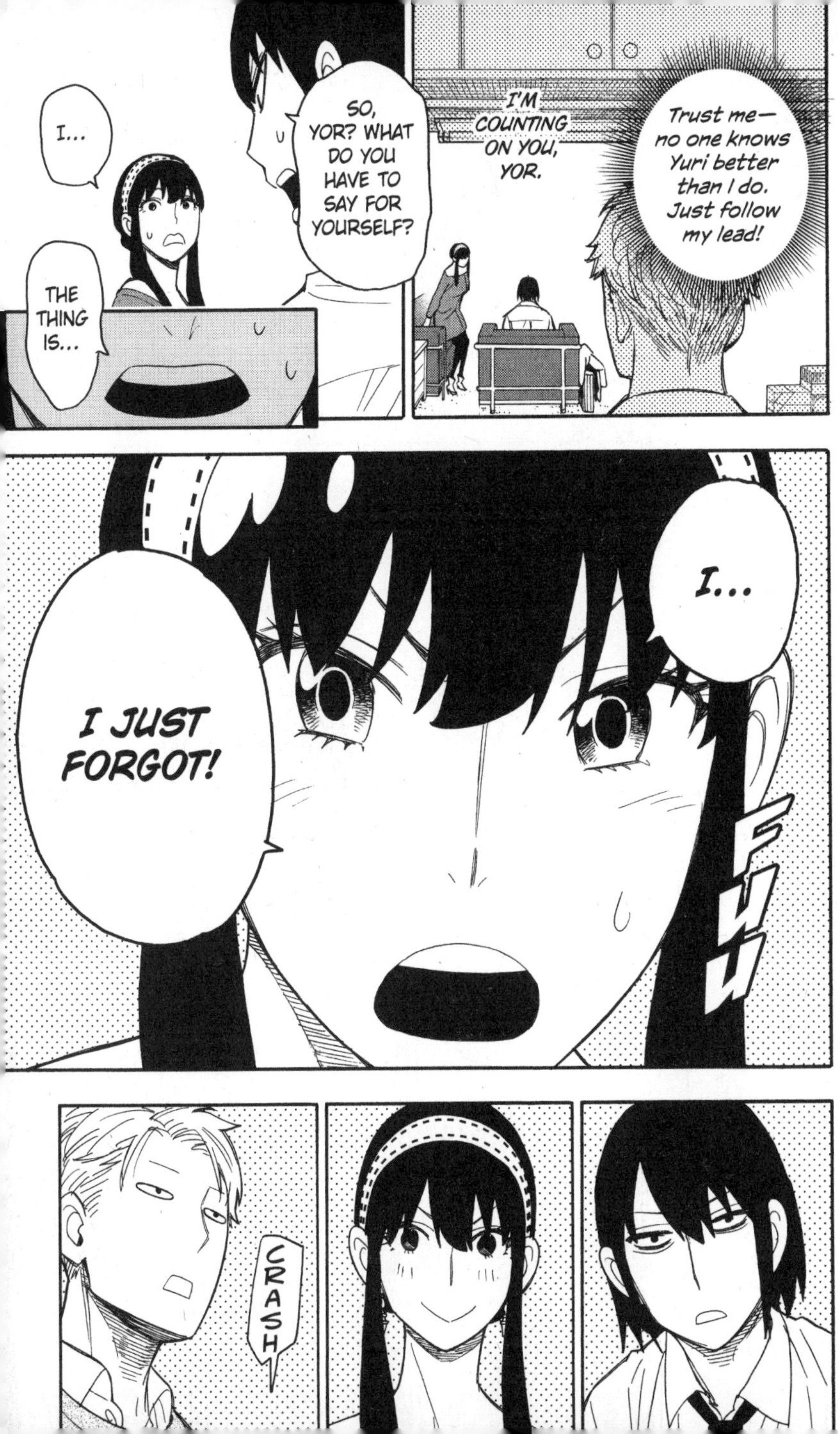
Trust me—no one knows Yuri better than I do. Just follow my lead!
I'M COUNTING ON YOU, YOR.
SO, YOR? WHAT DO YOU HAVE TO SAY FOR YOURSELF?
I...
THE THING IS...
I...
I JUST FORGOT!
FUUU
CRASH

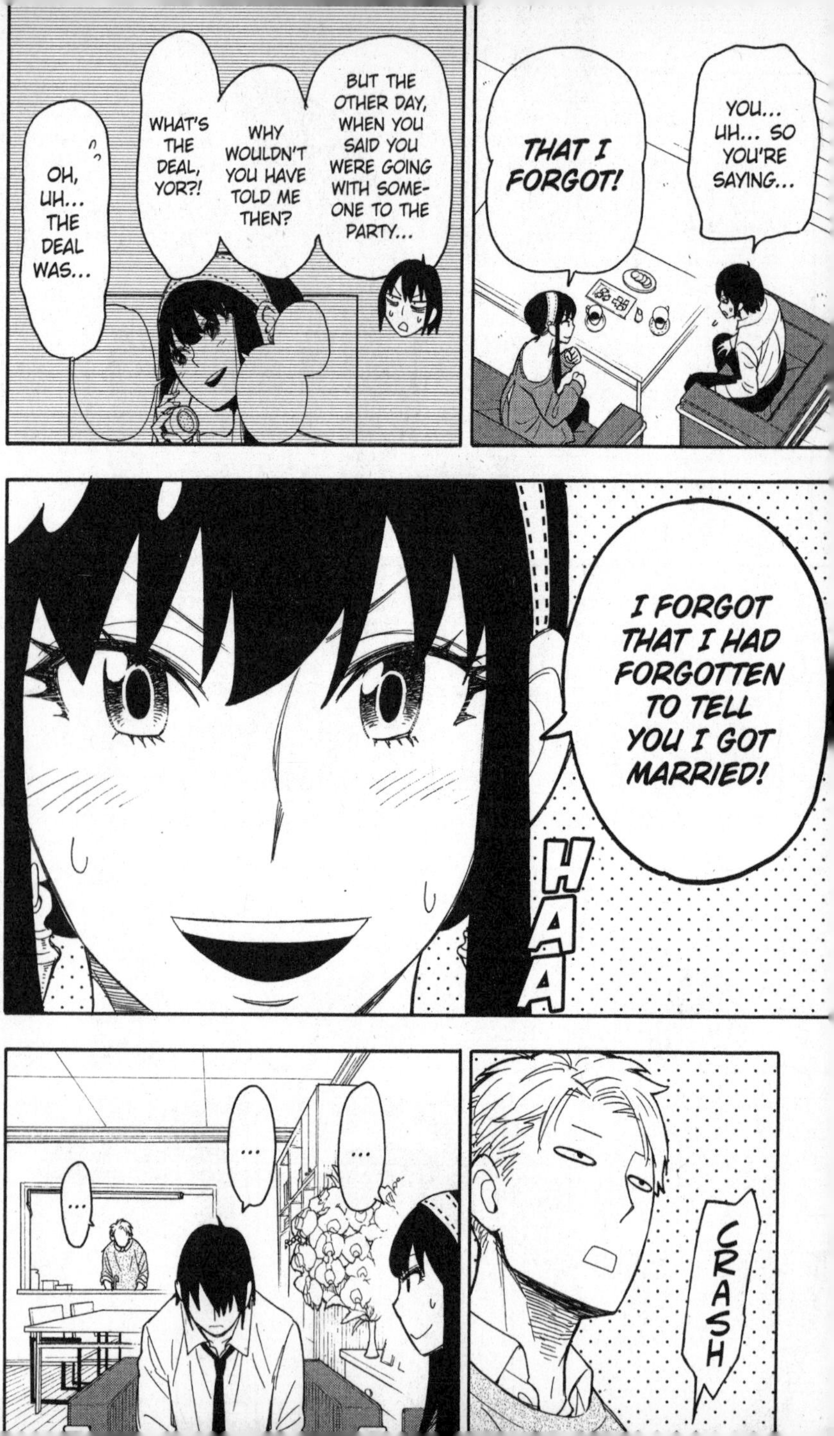
YOU... UH... SO YOU'RE SAYING...
THAT I FORGOT!
BUT THE OTHER DAY, WHEN YOU SAID YOU WERE GOING WITH SOME-ONE TO THE PARTY...
WHY WOULDN'T YOU HAVE TOLD ME THEN?
WHAT'S THE DEAL, YOR?!
OH, UH... THE DEAL WAS...
I FORGOT THAT I HAD FORGOTTEN TO TELL YOU I GOT MARRIED!
HAHA
CRASH
...
...
...

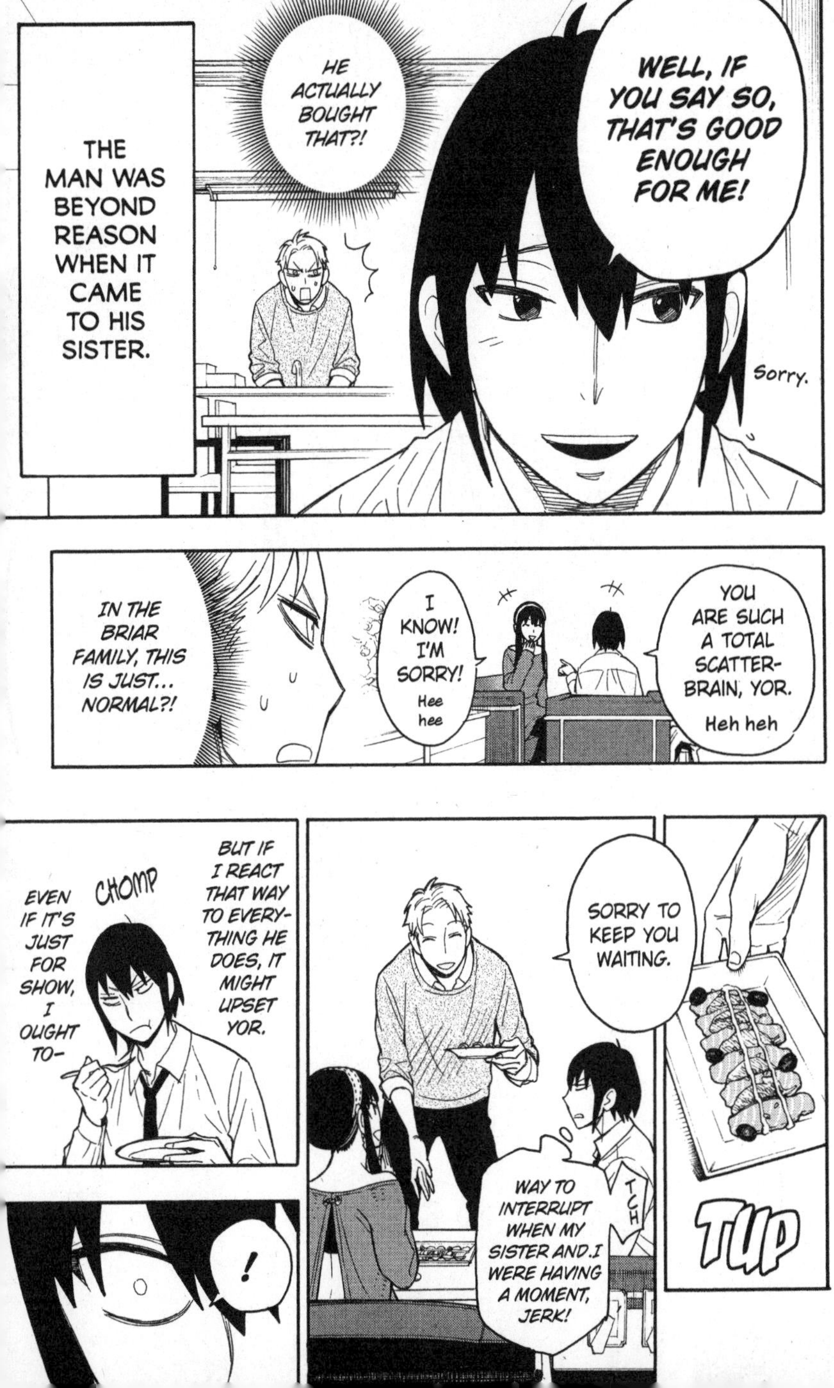
WELL, IF YOU SAY SO, THAT'S GOOD ENOUGH FOR ME!
Sorry.
HE ACTUALLY BOUGHT THAT?!
THE MAN WAS BEYOND REASON WHEN IT CAME TO HIS SISTER.
YOU ARE SUCH A TOTAL SCATTER-BRAIN, YOR.
Heh heh
I KNOW! I'M SORRY!
Hee hee
IN THE BRIAR FAMILY, THIS IS JUST... NORMAL?!
TUP
SORRY TO KEEP YOU WAITING.
TCH
WAY TO INTERRUPT WHEN MY SISTER AND I WERE HAVING A MOMENT, JERK!
BUT IF I REACT THAT WAY TO EVERYTHING HE DOES, IT MIGHT UPSET YOR.
EVEN IF IT'S JUST FOR SHOW, I OUGHT TO-
CHOMP
!

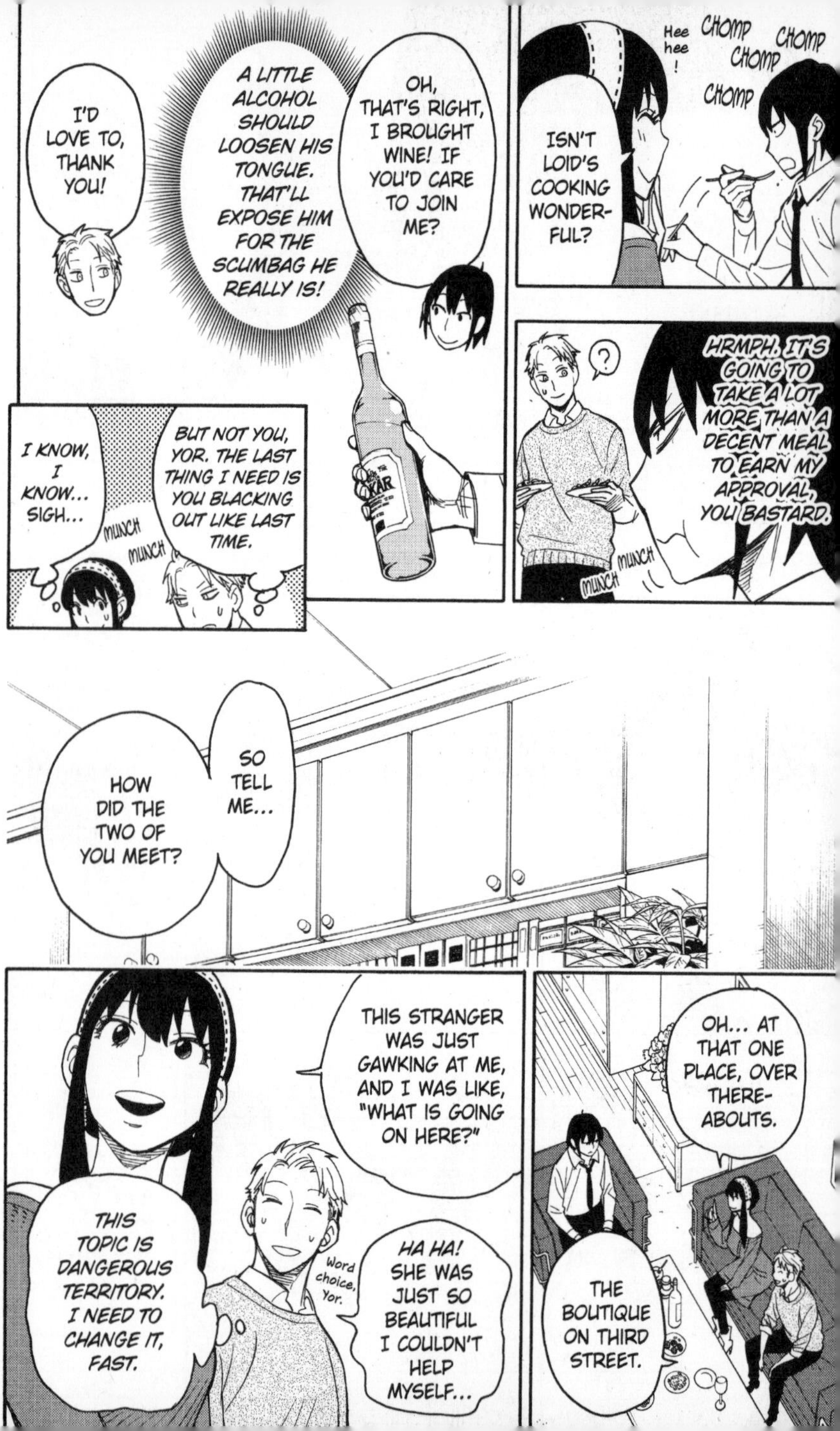
Hee hee!
CHOMP CHOMP CHOMP CHOMP
ISN'T LOID'S COOKING WONDERFUL?
?
HRMPH. IT'S GOING TO TAKE A LOT MORE THAN A DECENT MEAL TO EARN MY APPROVAL, YOU BASTARD.
MUNCH MUNCH
OH, THAT'S RIGHT, I BROUGHT WINE! IF YOU'D CARE TO JOIN ME?
A LITTLE ALCOHOL SHOULD LOOSEN HIS TONGUE. THAT'LL EXPOSE HIM FOR THE SCUMBAG HE REALLY IS!
I'D LOVE TO, THANK YOU!
BUT NOT YOU, YOR. THE LAST THING I NEED IS YOU BLACKING OUT LIKE LAST TIME.
I KNOW, I KNOW... SIGH...
MUNCH MUNCH
SO TELL ME...
HOW DID THE TWO OF YOU MEET?
OH... AT THAT ONE PLACE, OVER THERE-ABOUTS.
THE BOUTIQUE ON THIRD STREET.
THIS STRANGER WAS JUST GAWKING AT ME, AND I WAS LIKE, "WHAT IS GOING ON HERE?"
HA HA! SHE WAS JUST SO BEAUTIFUL I COULDN'T HELP MYSELF...
Word choice, Yor.
THIS TOPIC IS DANGEROUS TERRITORY. I NEED TO CHANGE IT, FAST.

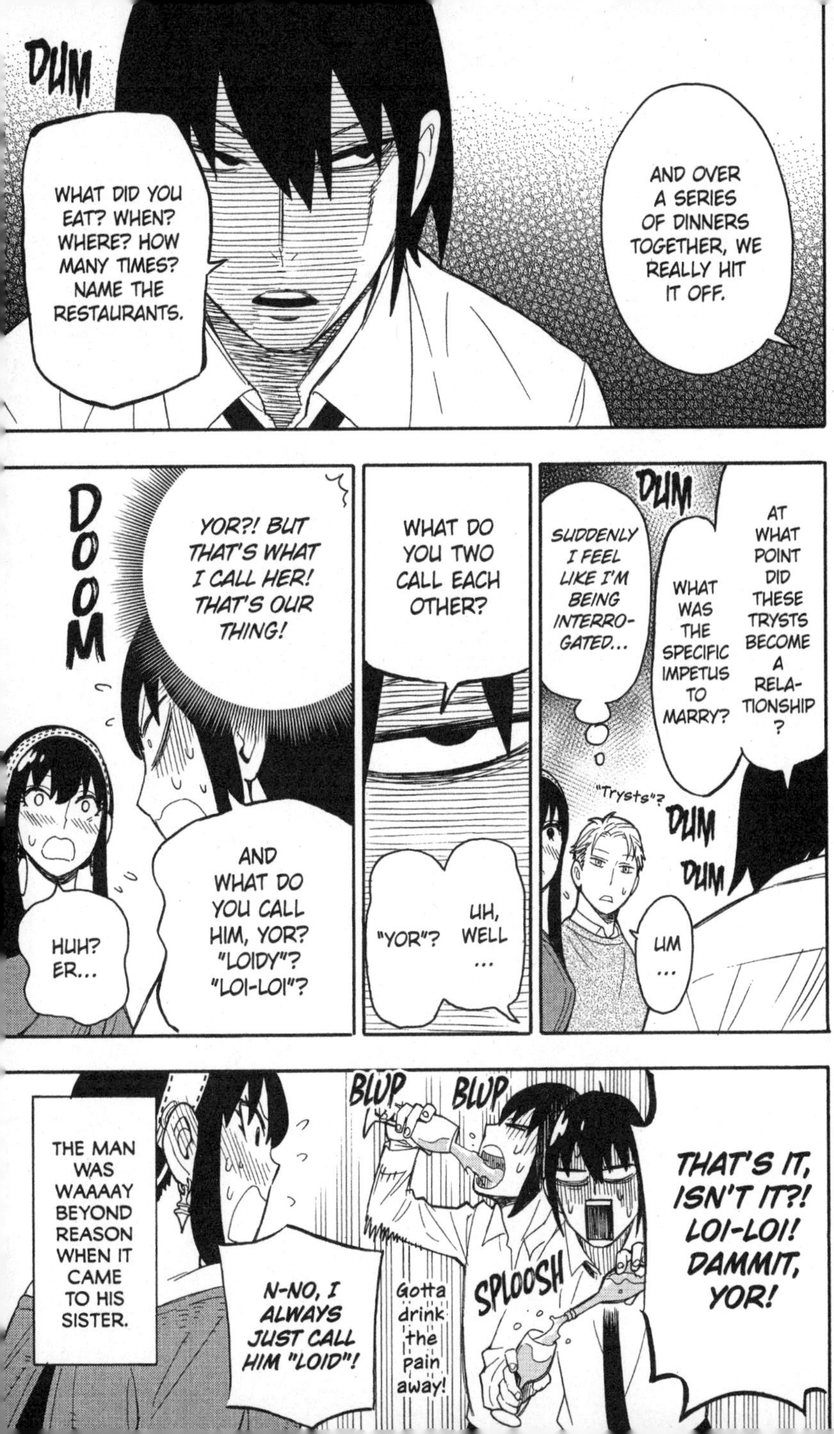

AND OVER A SERIES OF DINNERS TOGETHER, WE REALLY HIT IT OFF.
DUM
WHAT DID YOU EAT? WHEN? WHERE? HOW MANY TIMES? NAME THE RESTAURANTS.
DUM
AT WHAT POINT DID THESE TRYSTS BECOME A RELATIONSHIP?
WHAT WAS THE SPECIFIC IMPETUS TO MARRY?
SUDDENLY I FEEL LIKE I'M BEING INTERROGATED...
"Trysts"?
DUM
DUM
UM...
WHAT DO YOU TWO CALL EACH OTHER?
UH, WELL...
"YOR"?
YOR?! BUT THAT'S WHAT I CALL HER! THAT'S OUR THING!
DOOOM
AND WHAT DO YOU CALL HIM, YOR? "LOIDY"? "LOI-LOI"?
HUH? ER...
THAT'S IT, ISN'T IT?! LOI-LOI! DAMMIT, YOR!
BLUP BLUP
SPLOOSH
Gotta drink the pain away!
N-NO, I ALWAYS JUST CALL HIM "LOID"!
THE MAN WAS WAAAAY BEYOND REASON WHEN IT CAME TO HIS SISTER.

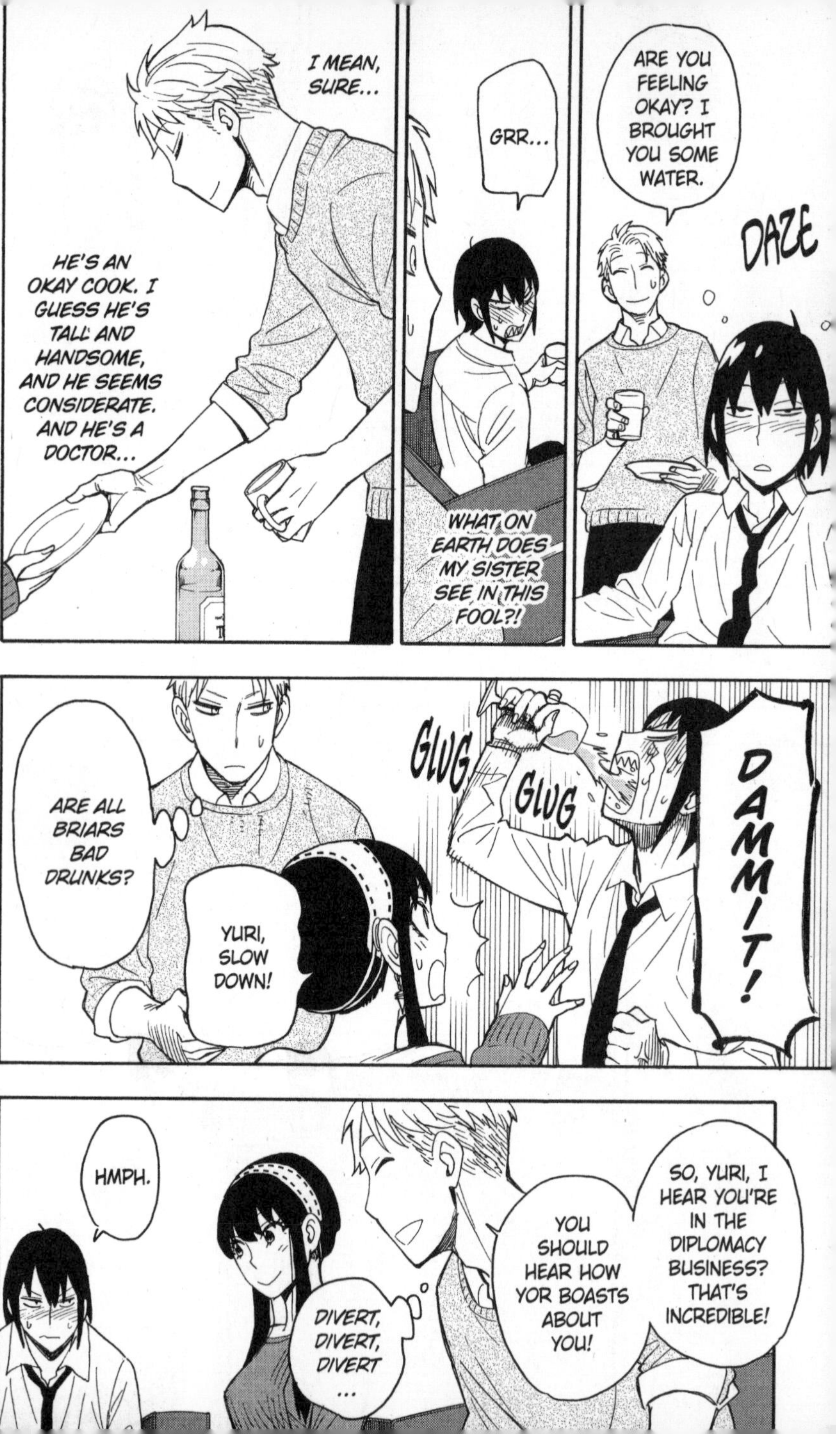
ARE YOU FEELING OKAY? I BROUGHT YOU SOME WATER.
DAZE
GRR...
WHAT ON EARTH DOES MY SISTER SEE IN THIS FOOL?!
I MEAN, SURE...
HE'S AN OKAY COOK. I GUESS HE'S TALL AND HANDSOME, AND HE SEEMS CONSIDERATE. AND HE'S A DOCTOR...
DAMMIT!
GLUG
GLUG
YURI, SLOW DOWN!
ARE ALL BRIARS BAD DRUNKS?
SO, YURI, I HEAR YOU'RE IN THE DIPLOMACY BUSINESS? THAT'S INCREDIBLE!
YOU SHOULD HEAR HOW YOR BOASTS ABOUT YOU!
DIVERT, DIVERT, DIVERT ...
HMPH.

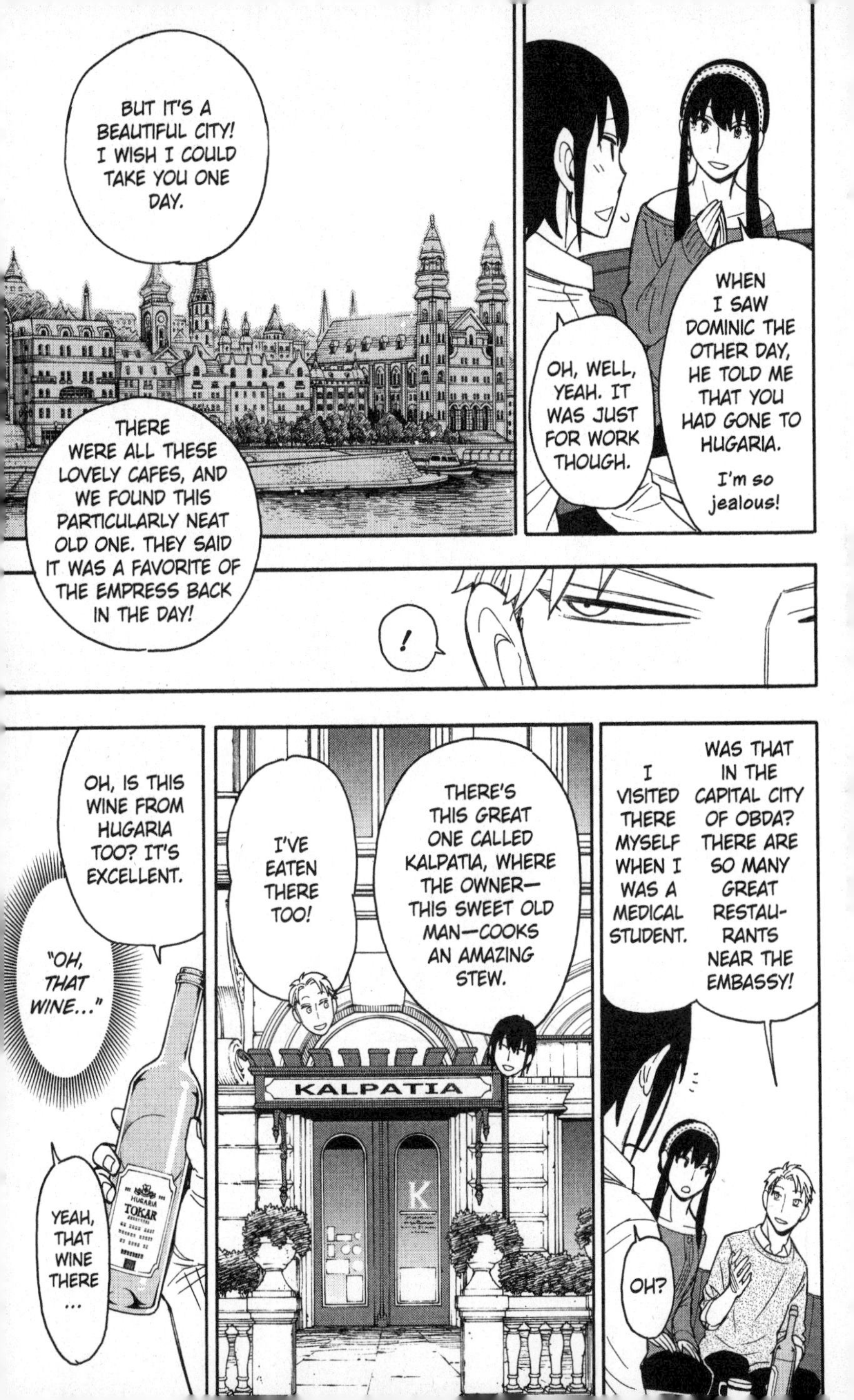
WHEN I SAW DOMINIC THE OTHER DAY, HE TOLD ME THAT YOU HAD GONE TO HUGARIA.
I'm so jealous!
OH, WELL, YEAH. IT WAS JUST FOR WORK THOUGH.
BUT IT'S A BEAUTIFUL CITY! I WISH I COULD TAKE YOU ONE DAY.
THERE WERE ALL THESE LOVELY CAFES, AND WE FOUND THIS PARTICULARLY NEAT OLD ONE. THEY SAID IT WAS A FAVORITE OF THE EMPRESS BACK IN THE DAY!
!
WAS THAT IN THE CAPITAL CITY OF OBDA? THERE ARE SO MANY GREAT RESTAURANTS NEAR THE EMBASSY!
I VISITED THERE MYSELF WHEN I WAS A MEDICAL STUDENT.
OH?
THERE'S THIS GREAT ONE CALLED KALPATIA, WHERE THE OWNER—THIS SWEET OLD MAN—COOKS AN AMAZING STEW.
I'VE EATEN THERE TOO!
KALPATIA
K
OH, IS THIS WINE FROM HUGARIA TOO? IT'S EXCELLENT.
"OH, THAT WINE..."
HUGARIA
TOKAR
YEAH, THAT WINE THERE ...

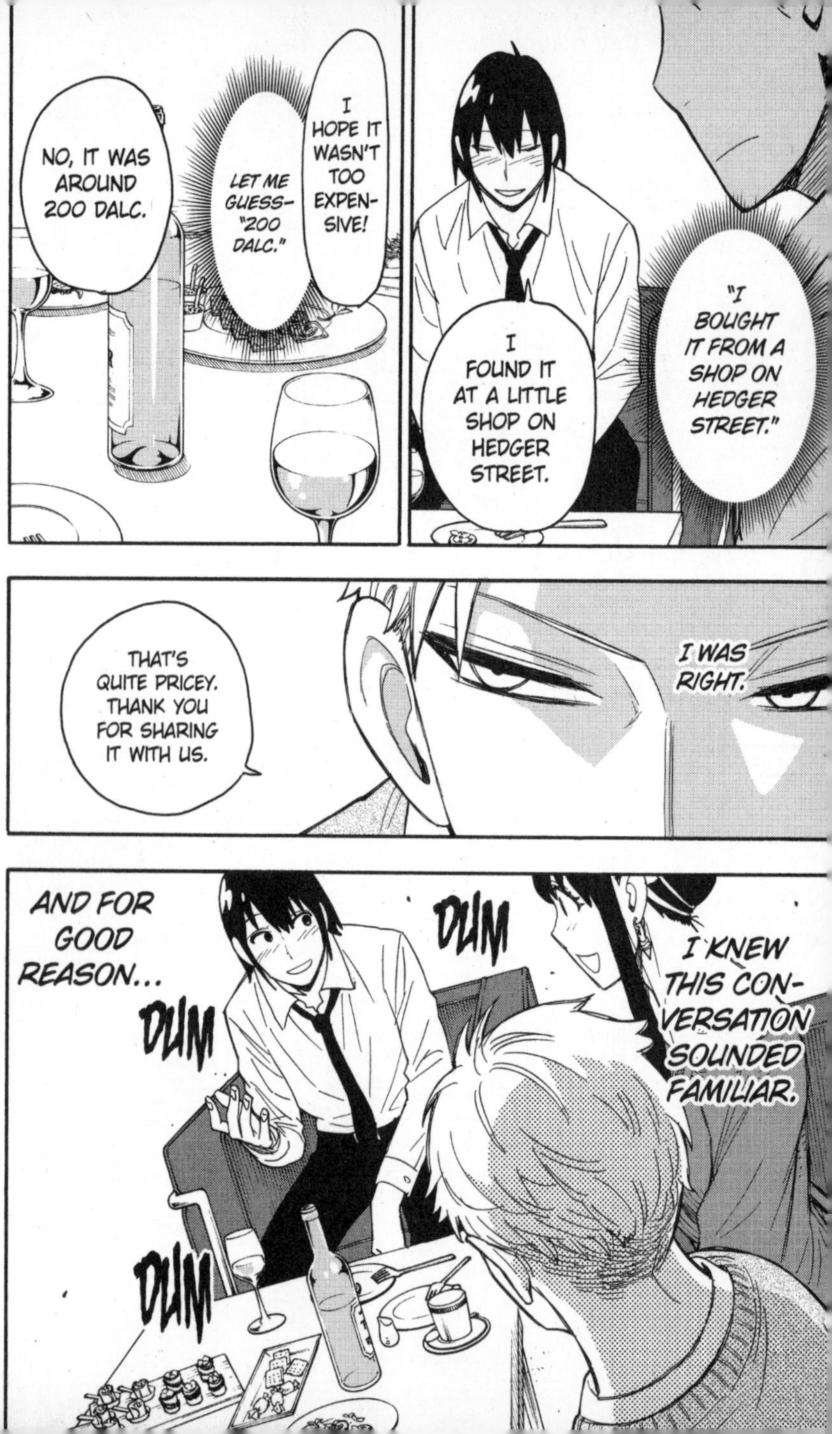
"I BOUGHT IT FROM A SHOP ON HEDGER STREET."
I FOUND IT AT A LITTLE SHOP ON HEDGER STREET.
I HOPE IT WASN'T TOO EXPEN-SIVE!
LET ME GUESS- "200 DALC."
NO, IT WAS AROUND 200 DALC.
I WAS RIGHT.
THAT'S QUITE PRICEY. THANK YOU FOR SHARING IT WITH US.
I KNEW THIS CON-VERSATION SOUNDED FAMILIAR.
DUM
AND FOR GOOD REASON...
DUM
DUM

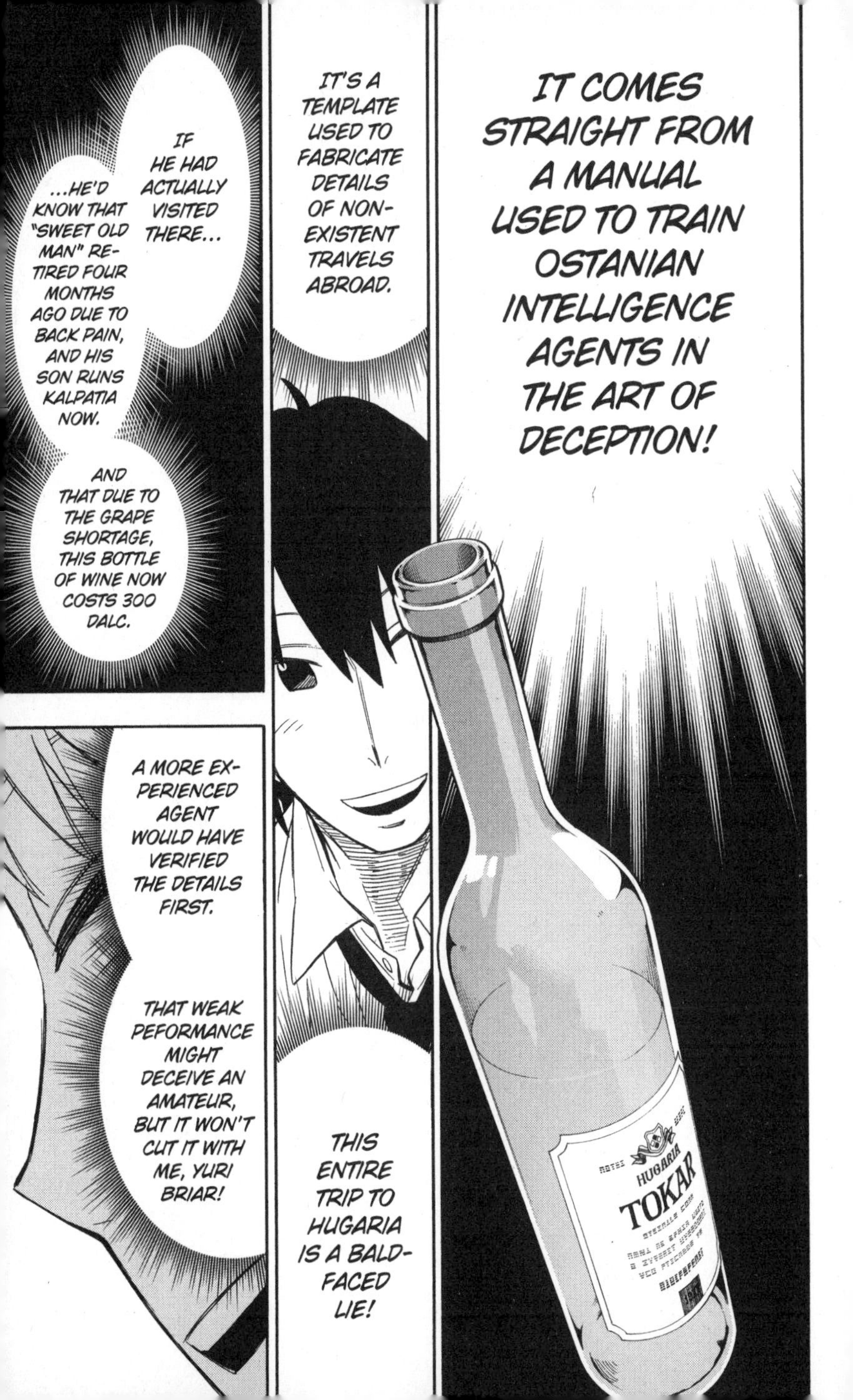
IT COMES STRAIGHT FROM A MANUAL USED TO TRAIN OSTANIAN INTELLIGENCE AGENTS IN THE ART OF DECEPTION!
HUGARIA
TOKAR
IT'S A TEMPLATE USED TO FABRICATE DETAILS OF NON-EXISTENT TRAVELS ABROAD.
THIS ENTIRE TRIP TO HUGARIA IS A BALD-FACED LIE!
IF HE HAD ACTUALLY VISITED THERE...
...HE'D KNOW THAT "SWEET OLD MAN" RE-TIRED FOUR MONTHS AGO DUE TO BACK PAIN, AND HIS SON RUNS KALPATIA NOW.
AND THAT DUE TO THE GRAPE SHORTAGE, THIS BOTTLE OF WINE NOW COSTS 300 DALC.
A MORE EX-PERIENCED AGENT WOULD HAVE VERIFIED THE DETAILS FIRST.
THAT WEAK PEFORMANCE MIGHT DECEIVE AN AMATEUR, BUT IT WON'T CUT IT WITH ME, YURI BRIAR!

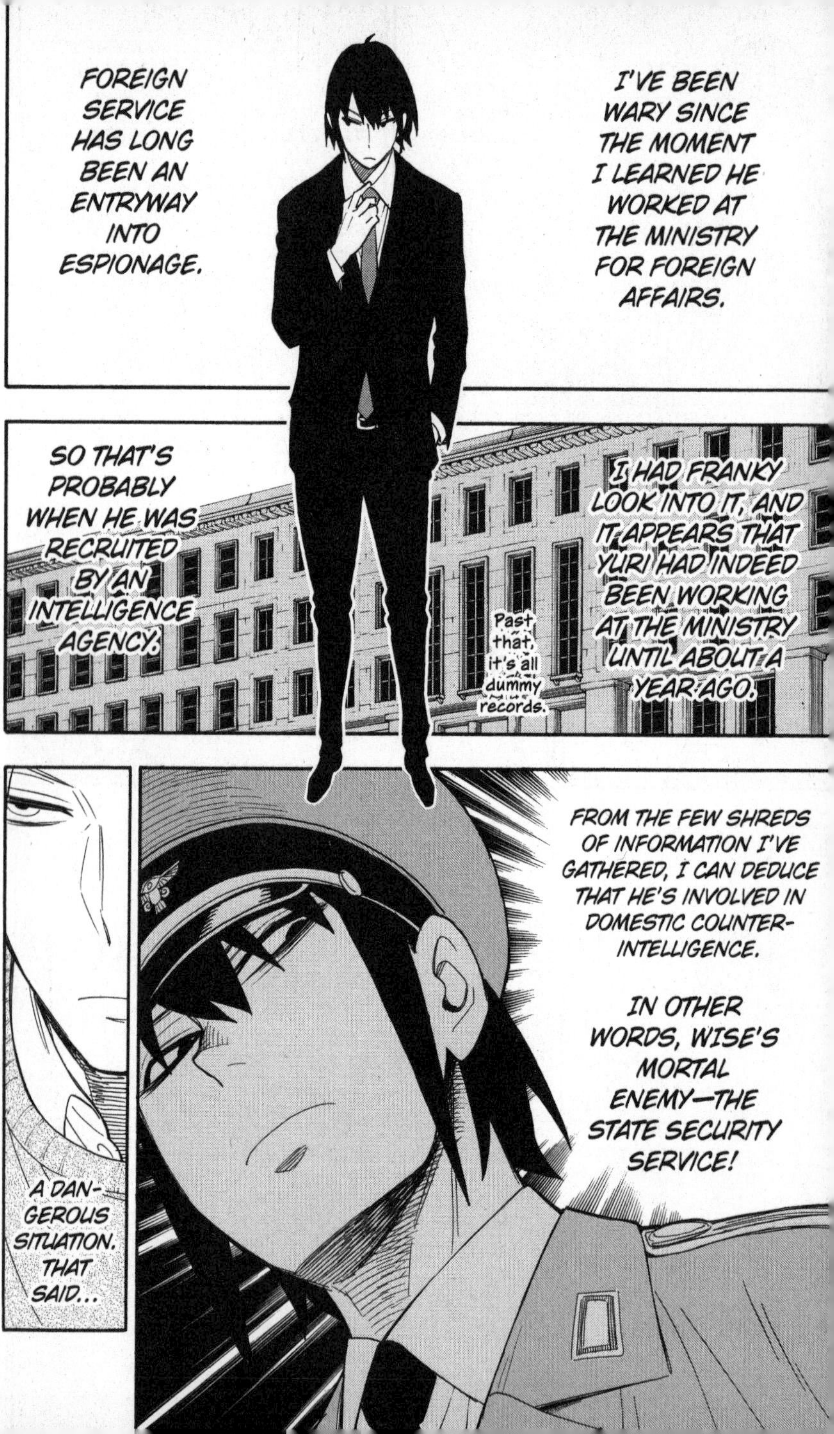
I'VE BEEN WARY SINCE THE MOMENT I LEARNED HE WORKED AT THE MINISTRY FOR FOREIGN AFFAIRS.
FOREIGN SERVICE HAS LONG BEEN AN ENTRYWAY INTO ESPIONAGE.
I HAD FRANKY LOOK INTO IT, AND IT APPEARS THAT YURI HAD INDEED BEEN WORKING AT THE MINISTRY UNTIL ABOUT A YEAR AGO.
Past that, it's all dummy records.
SO THAT'S PROBABLY WHEN HE WAS RECRUITED BY AN INTELLIGENCE AGENCY.
FROM THE FEW SHREDS OF INFORMATION I'VE GATHERED, I CAN DEDUCE THAT HE'S INVOLVED IN DOMESTIC COUNTER-INTELLIGENCE.
IN OTHER WORDS, WISE'S MORTAL ENEMY—THE STATE SECURITY SERVICE!
A DAN-GEROUS SITUATION. THAT SAID...

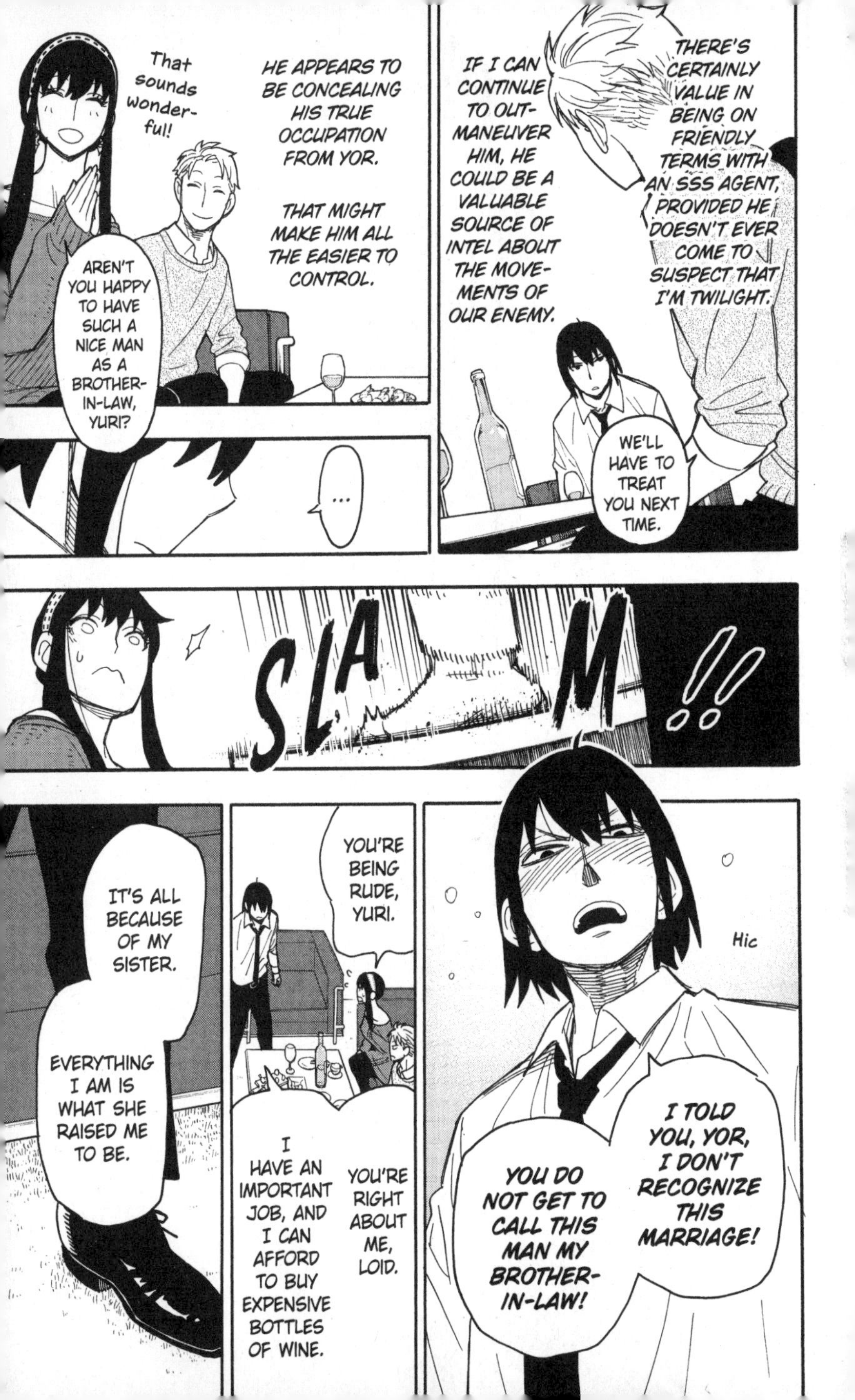
THERE'S CERTAINLY VALUE IN BEING ON FRIENDLY TERMS WITH AN SSS AGENT, PROVIDED HE DOESN'T EVER COME TO SUSPECT THAT I'M TWILIGHT.
IF I CAN CONTINUE TO OUT-MANEUVER HIM, HE COULD BE A VALUABLE SOURCE OF INTEL ABOUT THE MOVE-MENTS OF OUR ENEMY.
WE'LL HAVE TO TREAT YOU NEXT TIME.
HE APPEARS TO BE CONCEALING HIS TRUE OCCUPATION FROM YOR.
THAT MIGHT MAKE HIM ALL THE EASIER TO CONTROL.
That sounds wonder-ful!
AREN'T YOU HAPPY TO HAVE SUCH A NICE MAN AS A BROTHER-IN-LAW, YURI?
...
SLAM!!
Hic
I TOLD YOU, YOR, I DON'T RECOGNIZE THIS MARRIAGE!
YOU DO NOT GET TO CALL THIS MAN MY BROTHER-IN-LAW!
YOU'RE BEING RUDE, YURI.
YOU'RE RIGHT ABOUT ME, LOID.
I HAVE AN IMPORTANT JOB, AND I CAN AFFORD TO BUY EXPENSIVE BOTTLES OF WINE.
IT'S ALL BECAUSE OF MY SISTER.
EVERYTHING I AM IS WHAT SHE RAISED ME TO BE.

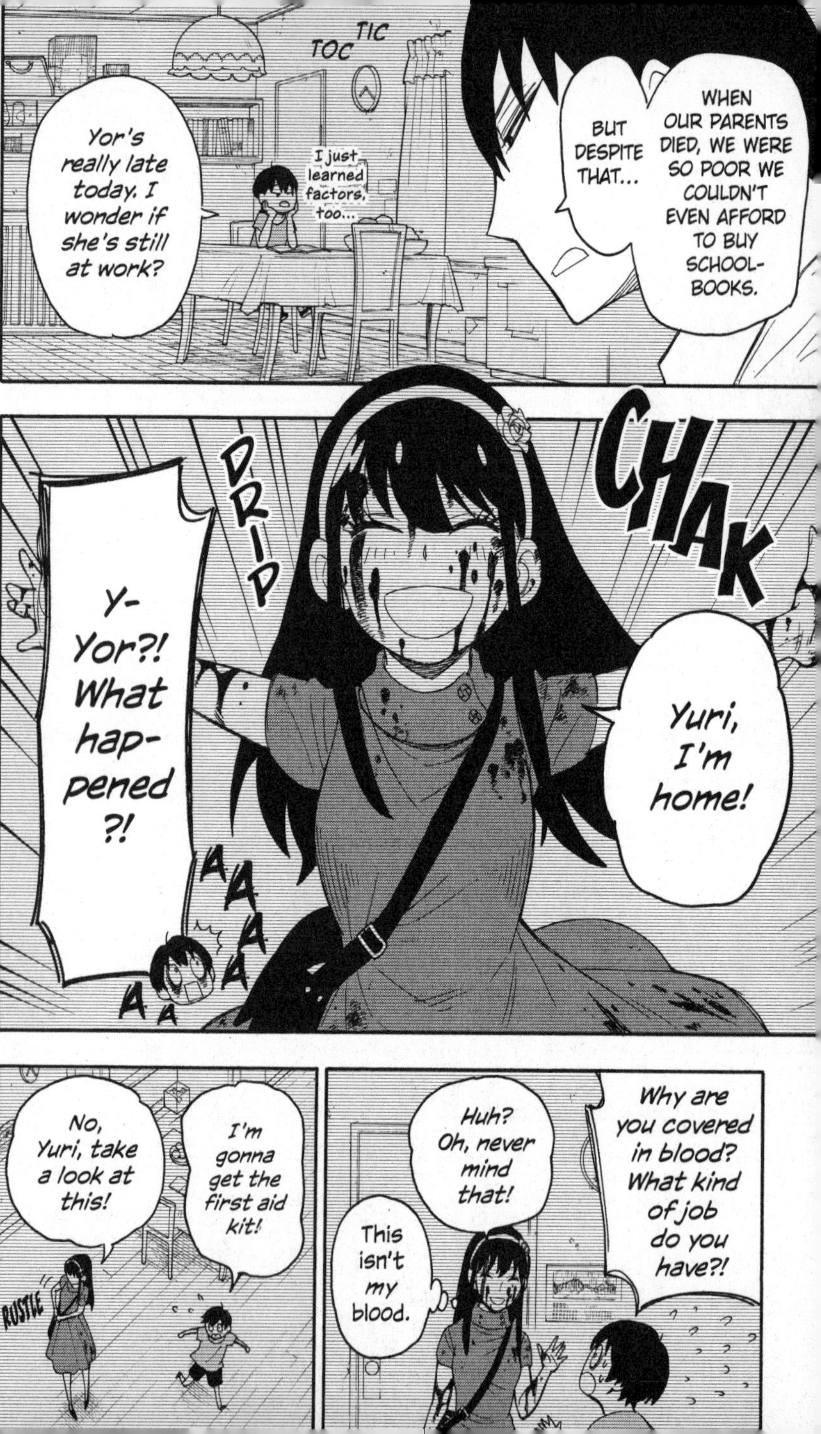
WHEN OUR PARENTS DIED, WE WERE SO POOR WE COULDN'T EVEN AFFORD TO BUY SCHOOL-BOOKS.
BUT DESPITE THAT...
TIC TOC
I just learned factors, too...
Yor's really late today. I wonder if she's still at work?
CHAK
Yuri, I'm home!
DRIP
Y-Yor?! What hap-pened?!
AAAAAAA
Why are you covered in blood? What kind of job do you have?!
Huh? Oh, never mind that!
This isn't my blood.
I'm gonna get the first aid kit!
No, Yuri, take a look at this!
RUSTLE

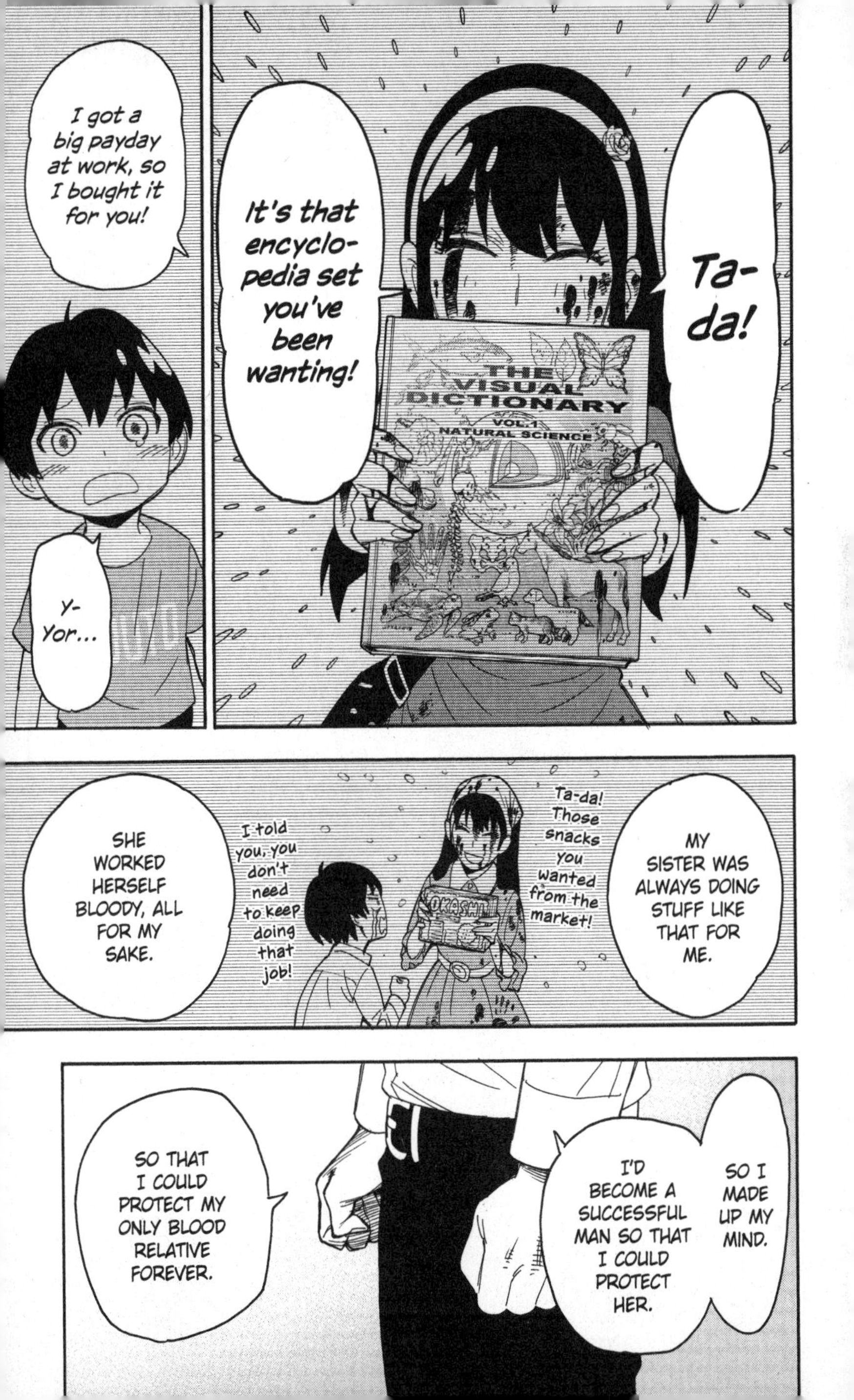
Ta-da!
It's that encyclopedia set you've been wanting!
THE VISUAL DICTIONARY
VOL.1
NATURAL SCIENCE
I got a big payday at work, so I bought it for you!
Y-Yor...
MY SISTER WAS ALWAYS DOING STUFF LIKE THAT FOR ME.
Ta-da! Those snacks you wanted from the market!
OKASHI
I told you, you don't need to keep doing that job!
SHE WORKED HERSELF BLOODY, ALL FOR MY SAKE.
SO I MADE UP MY MIND.
I'D BECOME A SUCCESSFUL MAN SO THAT I COULD PROTECT HER.
SO THAT I COULD PROTECT MY ONLY BLOOD RELATIVE FOREVER.

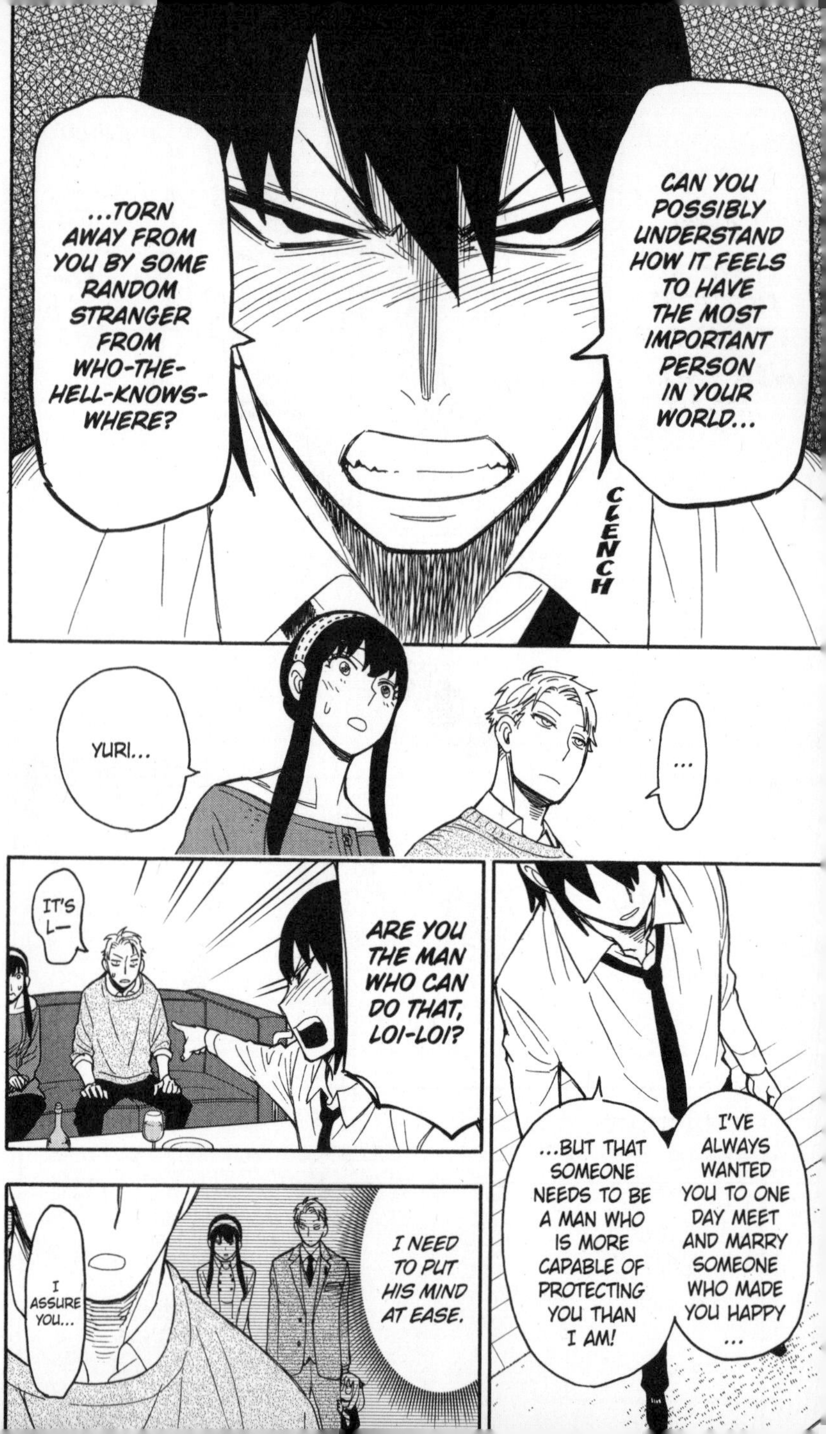
CAN YOU POSSIBLY UNDERSTAND HOW IT FEELS TO HAVE THE MOST IMPORTANT PERSON IN YOUR WORLD...
CLENCH
...TORN AWAY FROM YOU BY SOME RANDOM STRANGER FROM WHO-THE-HELL-KNOWS-WHERE?
...
YURI...
I'VE ALWAYS WANTED YOU TO ONE DAY MEET AND MARRY SOMEONE WHO MADE YOU HAPPY ...
...BUT THAT SOMEONE NEEDS TO BE A MAN WHO IS MORE CAPABLE OF PROTECTING YOU THAN I AM!
ARE YOU THE MAN WHO CAN DO THAT, LOI-LOI?
IT'S L—
I NEED TO PUT HIS MIND AT EASE.
I ASSURE YOU...

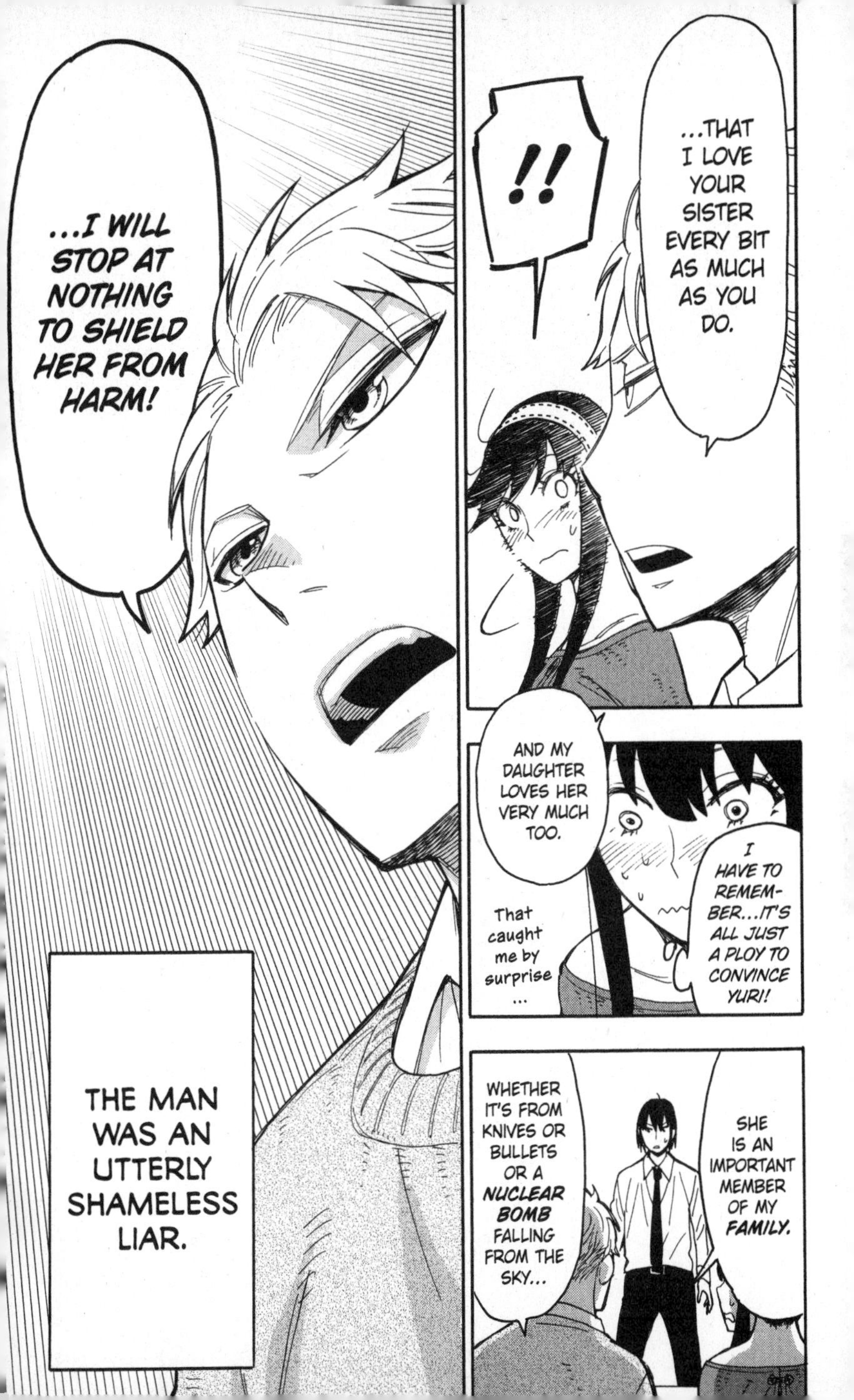
...THAT I LOVE YOUR SISTER EVERY BIT AS MUCH AS YOU DO.
!!
AND MY DAUGHTER LOVES HER VERY MUCH TOO.
I HAVE TO REMEMBER...IT'S ALL JUST A PLOY TO CONVINCE YURI!
That caught me by surprise...
SHE IS AN IMPORTANT MEMBER OF MY FAMILY.
WHETHER IT'S FROM KNIVES OR BULLETS OR A NUCLEAR BOMB FALLING FROM THE SKY...
...I WILL STOP AT NOTHING TO SHIELD HER FROM HARM!
THE MAN WAS AN UTTERLY SHAMELESS LIAR.

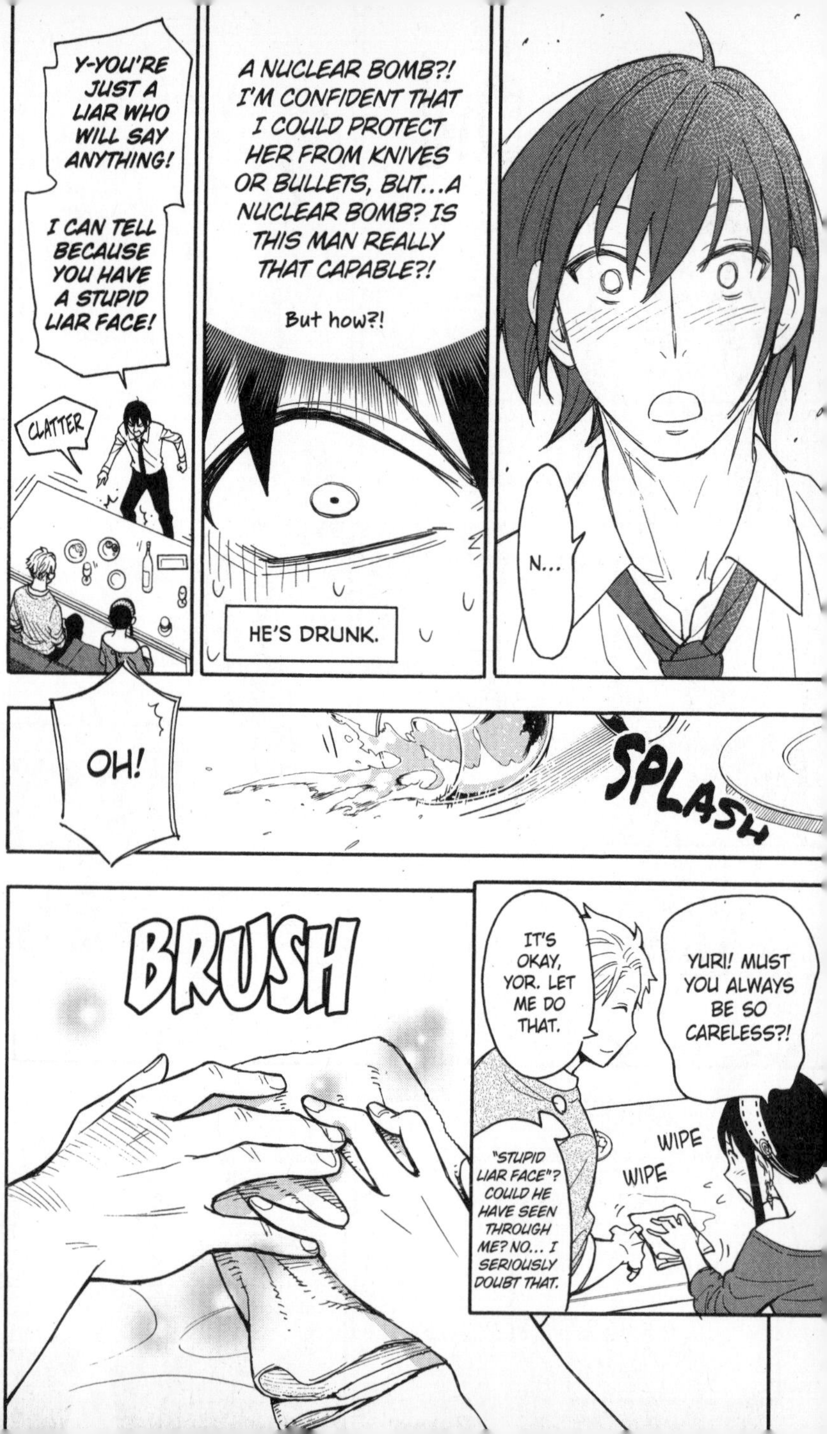
N...
A NUCLEAR BOMB?! I'M CONFIDENT THAT I COULD PROTECT HER FROM KNIVES OR BULLETS, BUT...A NUCLEAR BOMB? IS THIS MAN REALLY THAT CAPABLE?!
But how?!
HE'S DRUNK.
Y-YOU'RE JUST A LIAR WHO WILL SAY ANYTHING!
I CAN TELL BECAUSE YOU HAVE A STUPID LIAR FACE!
CLATTER
SPLASH
OH!
YURI! MUST YOU ALWAYS BE SO CARELESS?!
IT'S OKAY, YOR. LET ME DO THAT.
WIPE
WIPE
"STUPID LIAR FACE"? COULD HE HAVE SEEN THROUGH ME? NO... I SERIOUSLY DOUBT THAT.
BRUSH

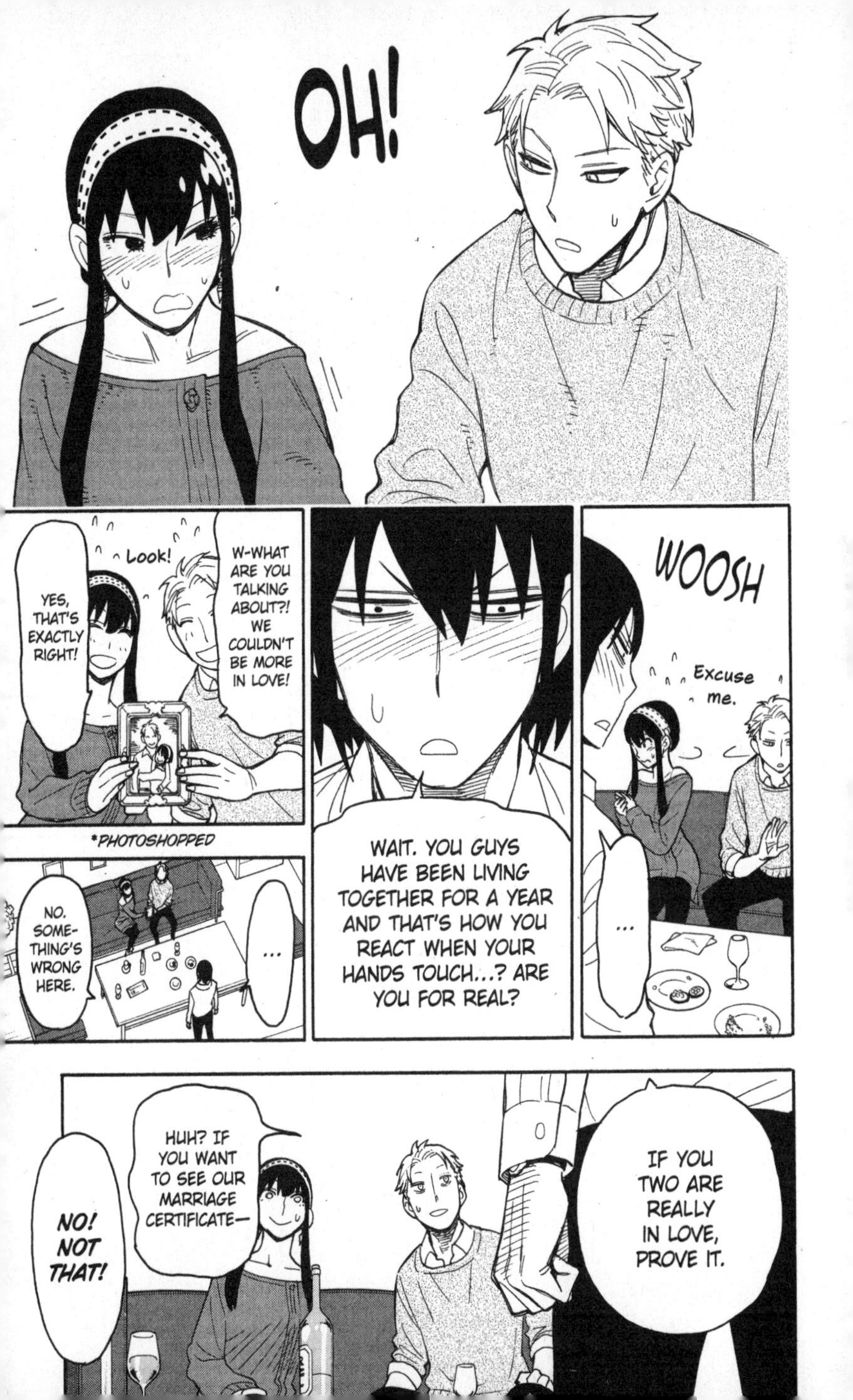
OH!
WOOSH
Excuse me.
...
WAIT. YOU GUYS HAVE BEEN LIVING TOGETHER FOR A YEAR AND THAT'S HOW YOU REACT WHEN YOUR HANDS TOUCH...? ARE YOU FOR REAL?
W-WHAT ARE YOU TALKING ABOUT?! WE COULDN'T BE MORE IN LOVE!
Look!
YES, THAT'S EXACTLY RIGHT!
*PHOTOSHOPPED
...
NO. SOMETHING'S WRONG HERE.
IF YOU TWO ARE REALLY IN LOVE, PROVE IT.
HUH? IF YOU WANT TO SEE OUR MARRIAGE CERTIFICATE—
NO! NOT THAT!

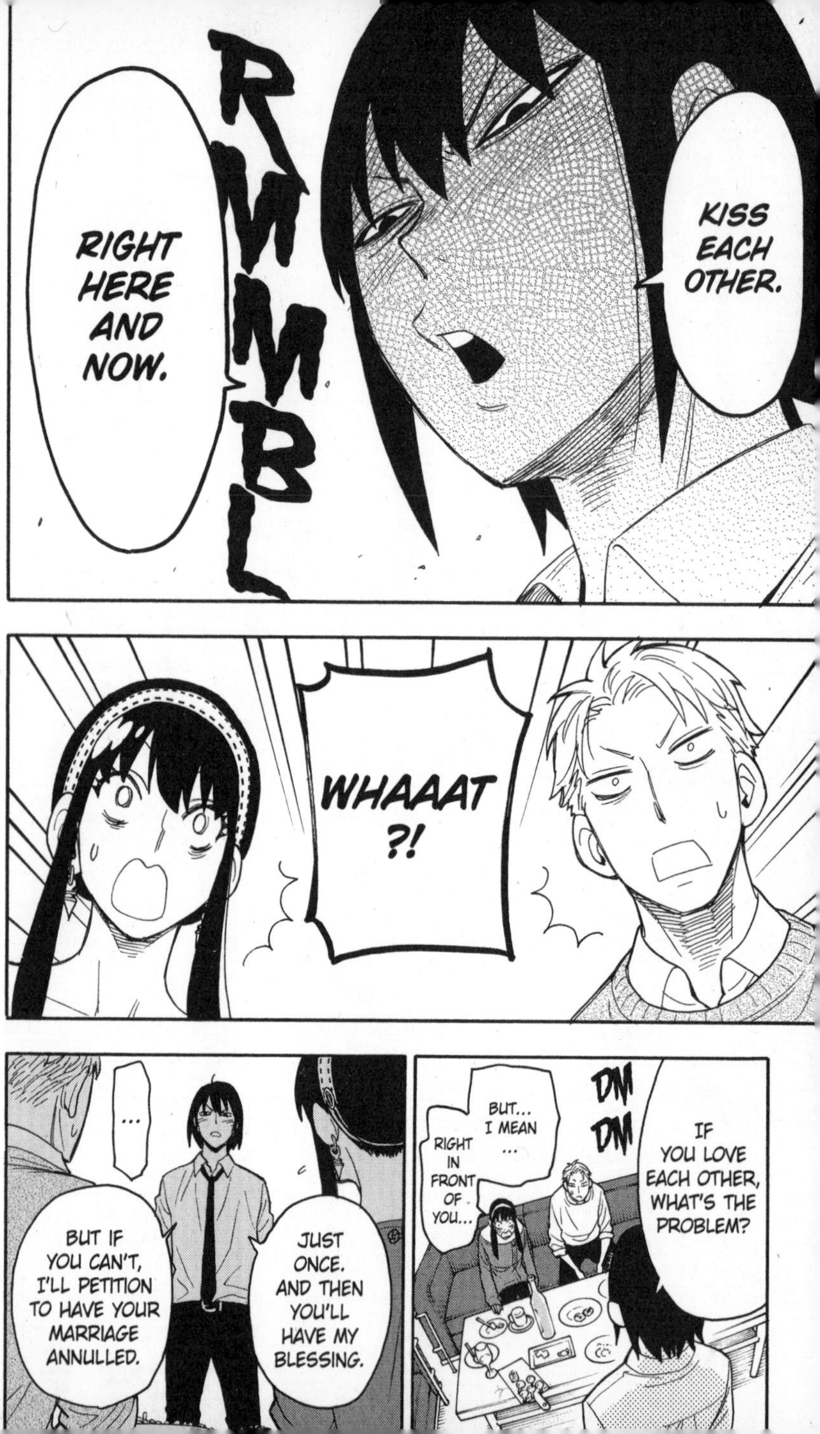
KISS EACH OTHER.
RMMBL
RIGHT HERE AND NOW.
WHAAAT?!
IF YOU LOVE EACH OTHER, WHAT'S THE PROBLEM?
DM DM
BUT... I MEAN ...
RIGHT IN FRONT OF YOU...
...
JUST ONCE. AND THEN YOU'LL HAVE MY BLESSING.
BUT IF YOU CAN'T, I'LL PETITION TO HAVE YOUR MARRIAGE ANNULLED.

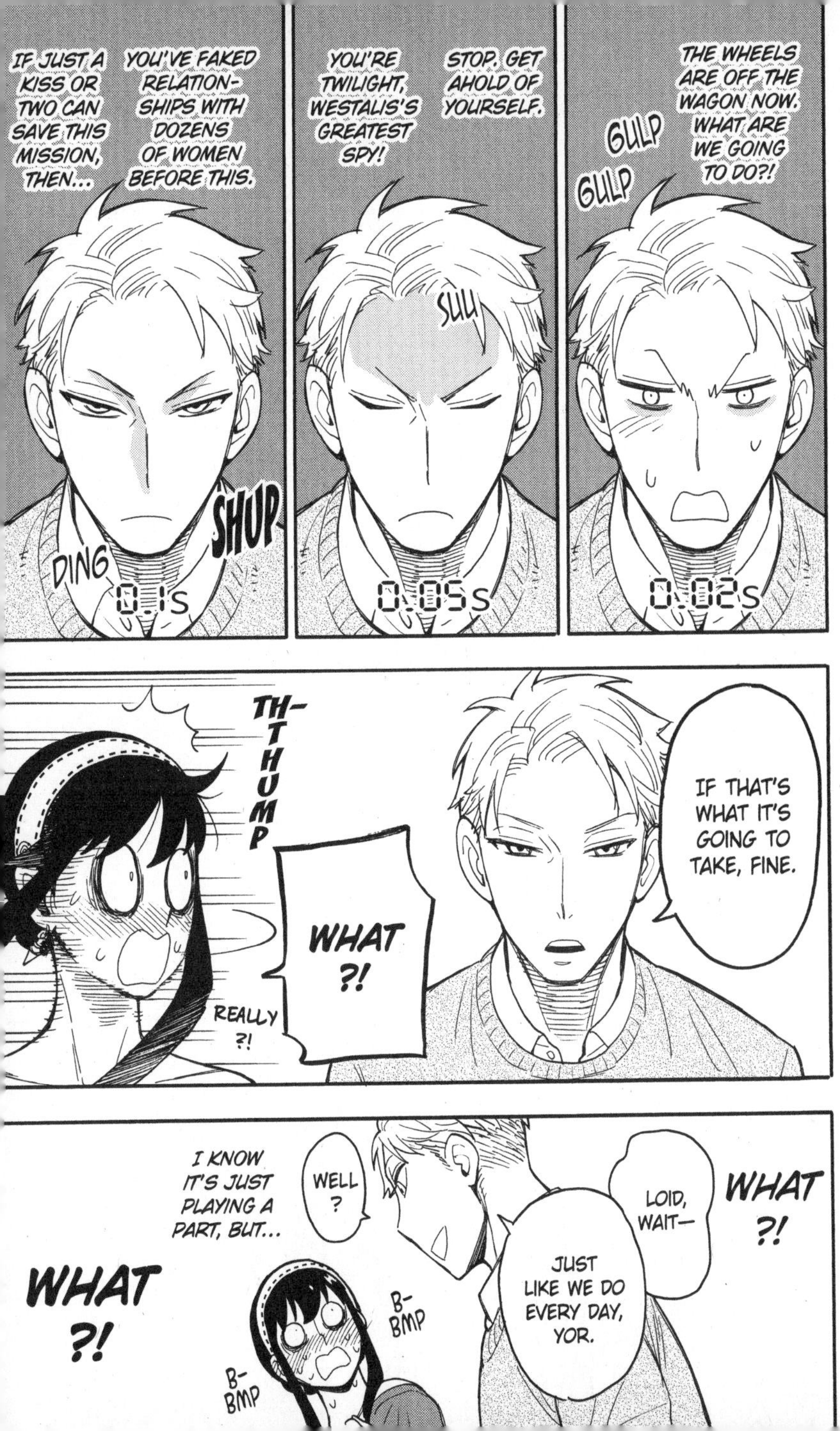
THE WHEELS ARE OFF THE WAGON NOW. WHAT ARE WE GOING TO DO?!
GULP
GULP
0.02s
STOP. GET AHOLD OF YOURSELF.
YOU'RE TWILIGHT, WESTALIS'S GREATEST SPY!
SUU
0.05s
YOU'VE FAKED RELATION-SHIPS WITH DOZENS OF WOMEN BEFORE THIS.
IF JUST A KISS OR TWO CAN SAVE THIS MISSION, THEN...
SHUP
DING
0.1s
IF THAT'S WHAT IT'S GOING TO TAKE, FINE.
TH-THUMP
WHAT?!
REALLY?!
WHAT?!
LOID, WAIT—
JUST LIKE WE DO EVERY DAY, YOR.
WELL?
I KNOW IT'S JUST PLAYING A PART, BUT...
B-BMP
B-BMP
WHAT?!

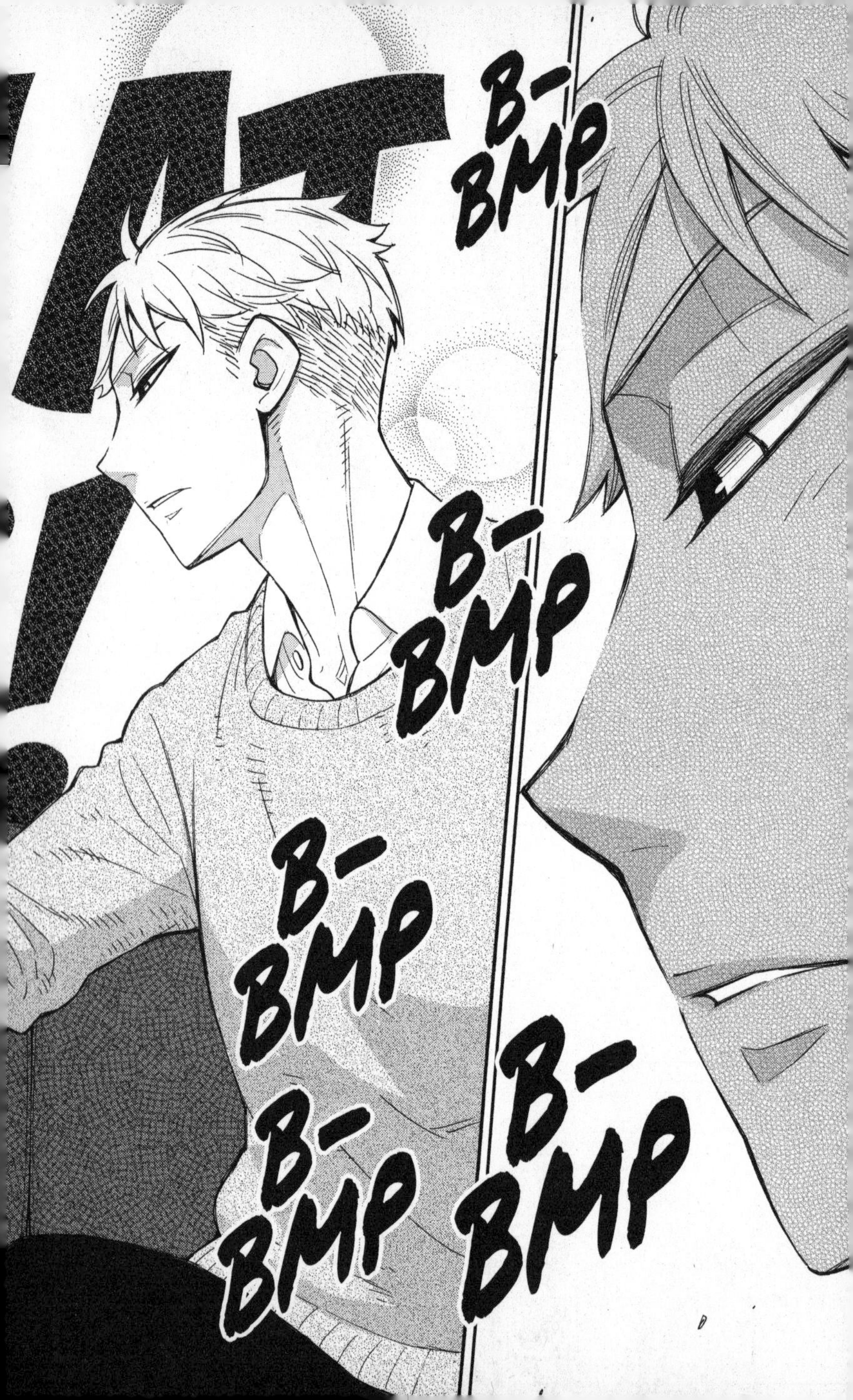
B-BMP
B-BMP
B-BMP
B-BMP
B-BMP

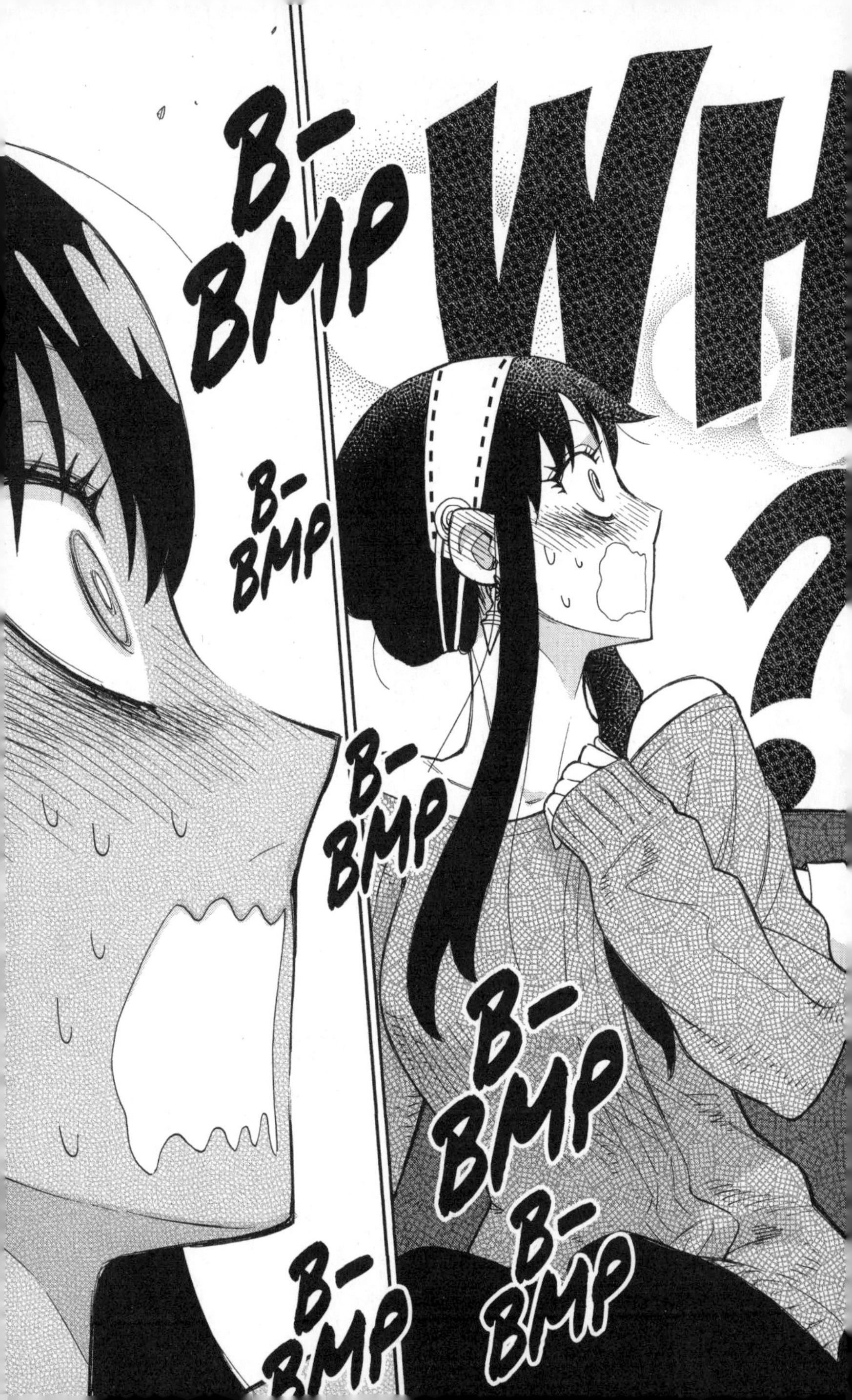
WH?
B-BMP
B-BMP
B-BMP
B-BMP
B-BMP
B-BMP

SPY×FAMILY

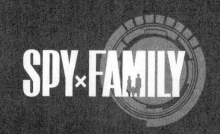

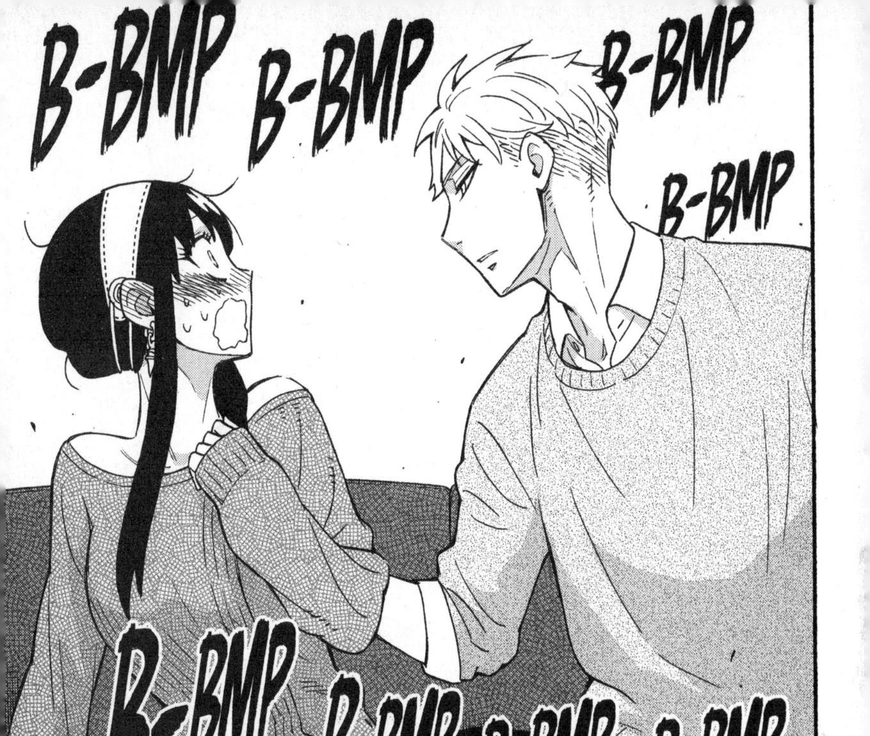
B-BMP
B-BMP
B-BMP
B-BMP
B-BMP
B-BMP
B-BMP
B-BMP

MISSION 13

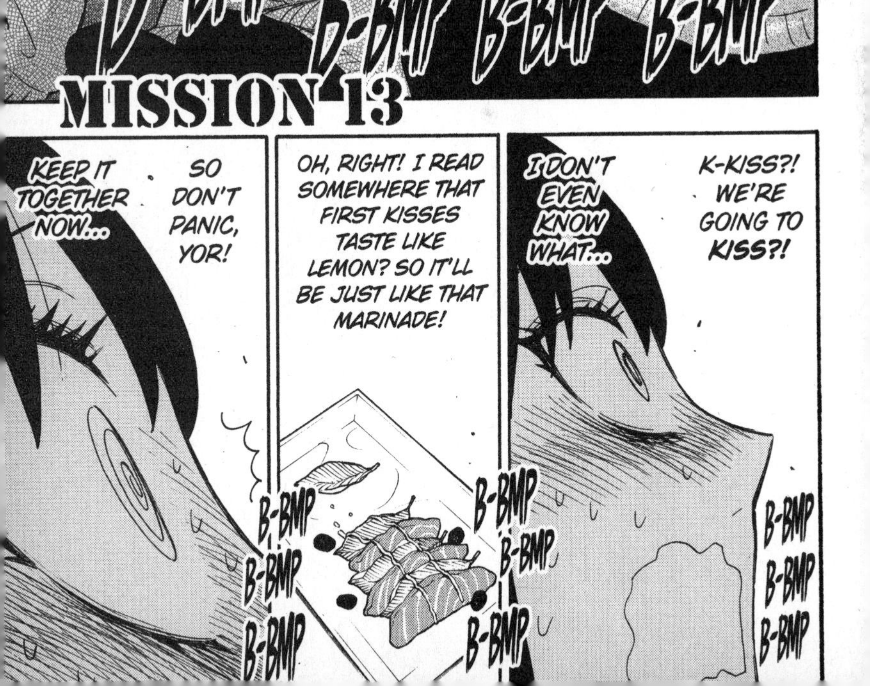
K-KISS?! WE'RE GOING TO KISS?!
I DON'T EVEN KNOW WHAT...
B-BMP
B-BMP
B-BMP
OH, RIGHT! I READ SOMEWHERE THAT FIRST KISSES TASTE LIKE LEMON? SO IT'LL BE JUST LIKE THAT MARINADE!
B-BMP
B-BMP
B-BMP
SO DON'T PANIC, YOR!
KEEP IT TOGETHER NOW...
B-BMP
B-BMP
B-BMP

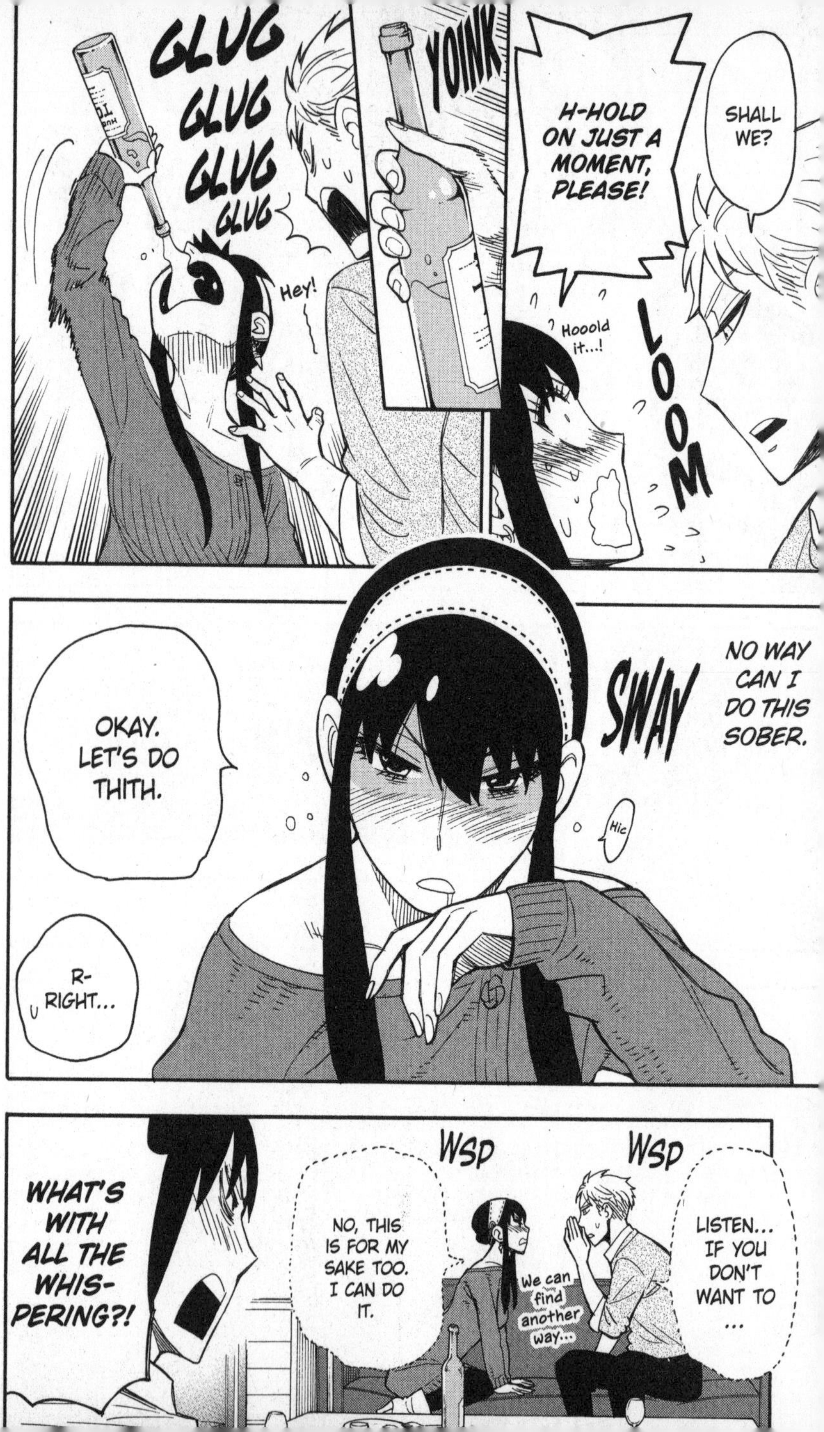
SHALL WE?
H-HOLD ON JUST A MOMENT, PLEASE!
LOOM
Hoooold it...!
YOINK
GLUG GLUG GLUG GLUG
Hey!
NO WAY CAN I DO THIS SOBER.
SWAY
Hic
OKAY. LET'S DO THITH.
R-RIGHT...
WSP
WSP
LISTEN... IF YOU DON'T WANT TO ...
We can find another way...
NO, THIS IS FOR MY SAKE TOO. I CAN DO IT.
WHAT'S WITH ALL THE WHISPERING?!

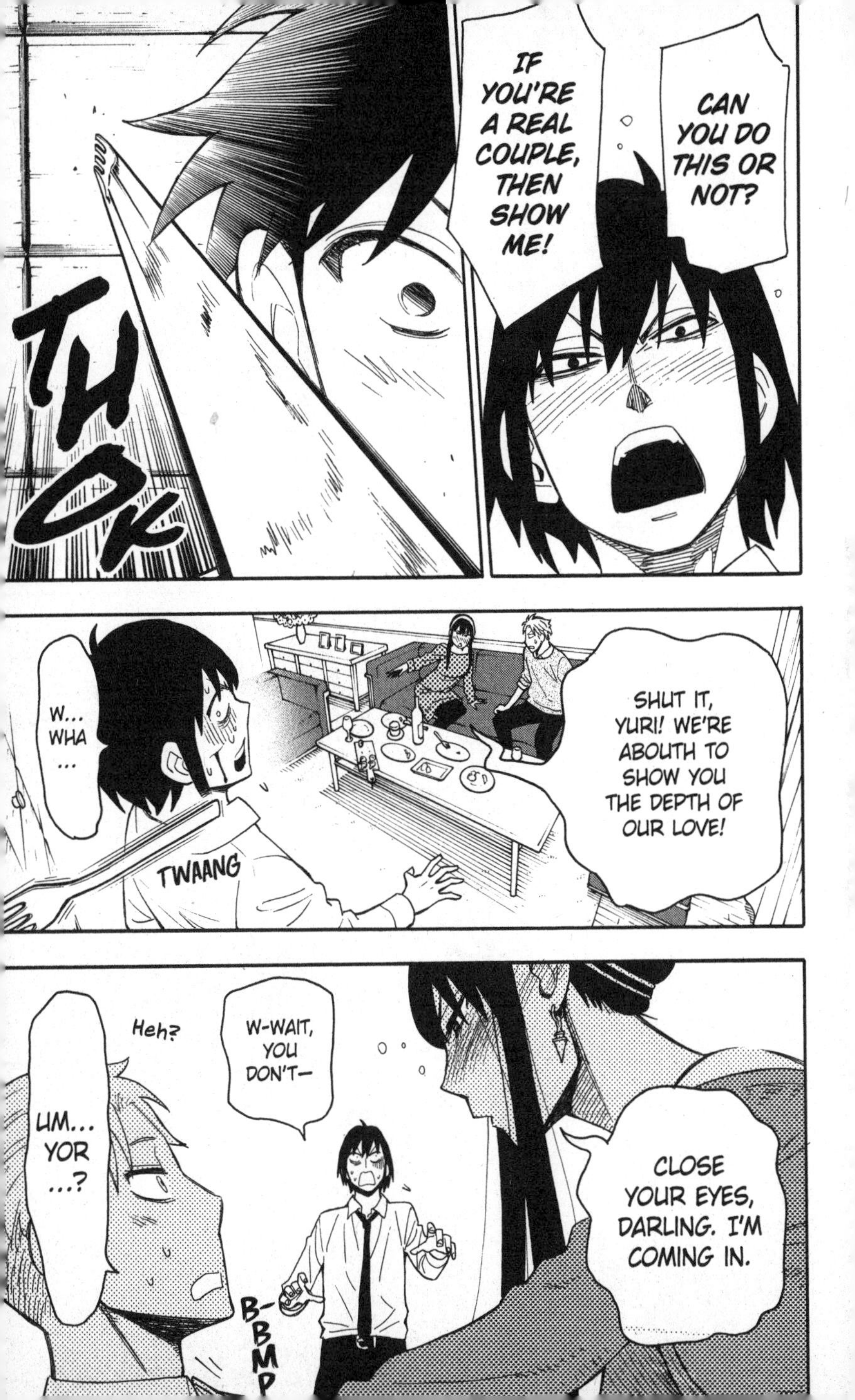
IF YOU'RE A REAL COUPLE, THEN SHOW ME!
CAN YOU DO THIS OR NOT?
THOK
SHUT IT, YURI! WE'RE ABOUTH TO SHOW YOU THE DEPTH OF OUR LOVE!
W... WHA ...
TWAANG
CLOSE YOUR EYES, DARLING. I'M COMING IN.
W-WAIT, YOU DON'T—
Heh?
UM... YOR ...?
B-BBMP

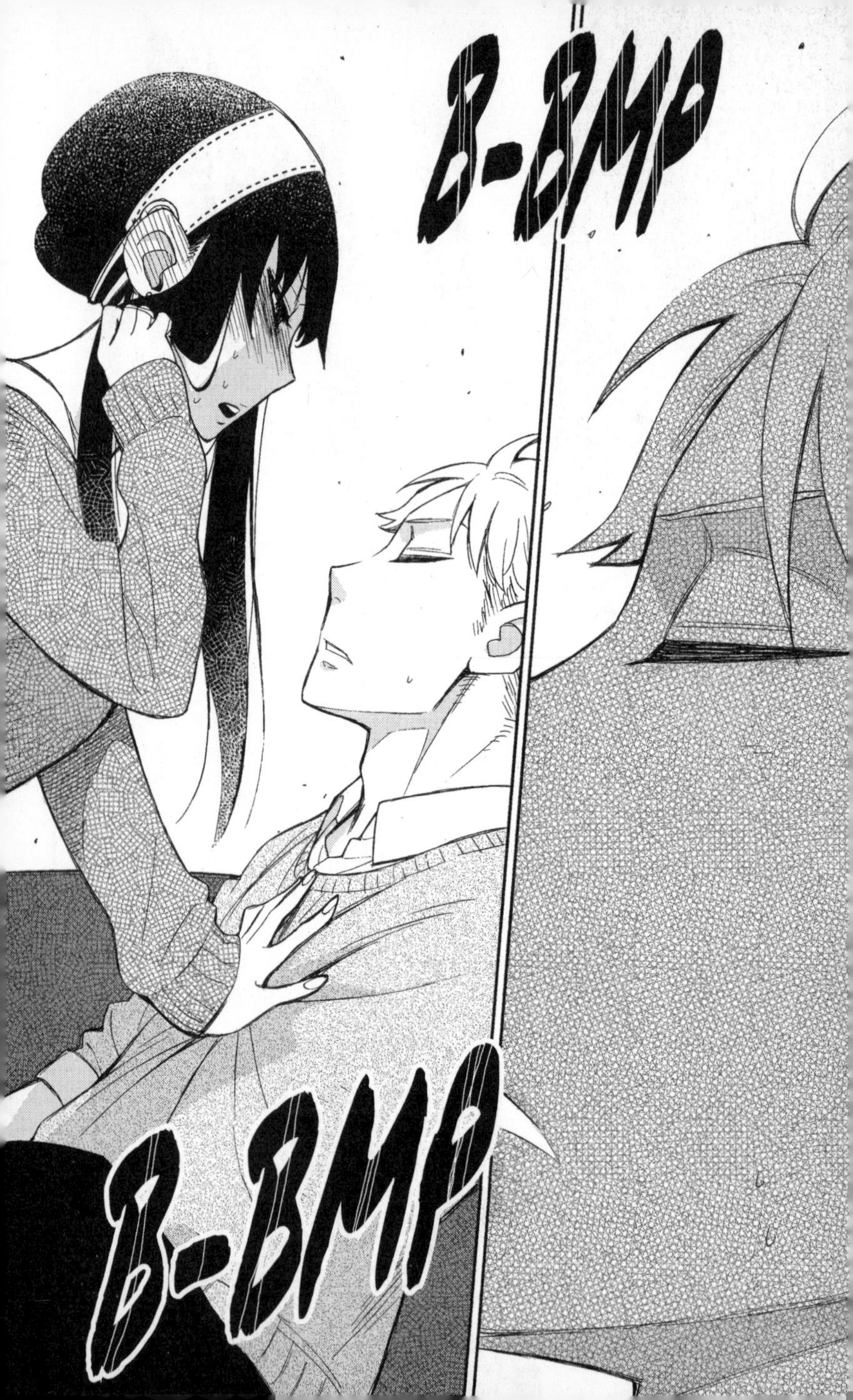
B-BMP
B-BMP

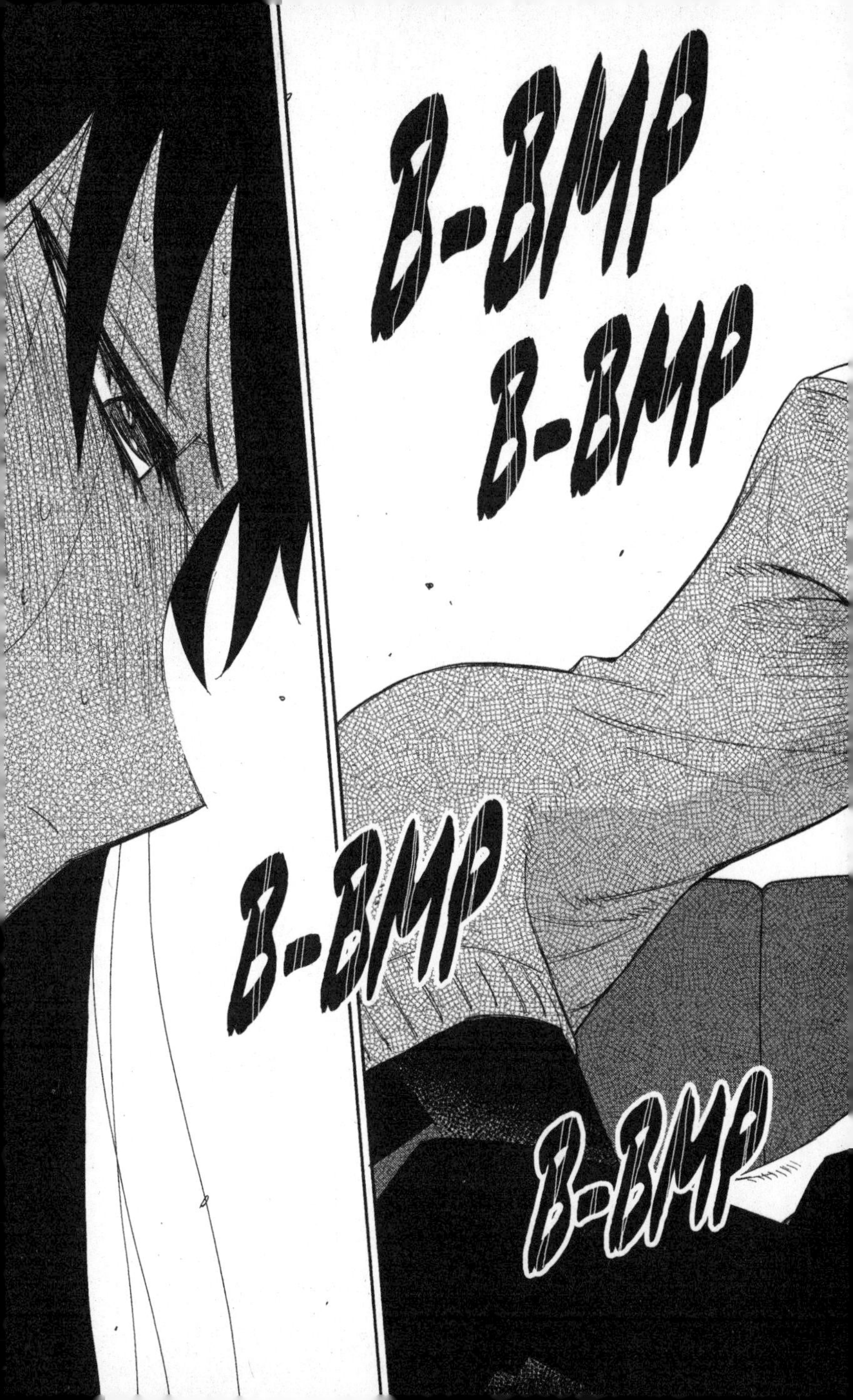
B-BMP
B-BMP
B-BMP
B-BMP

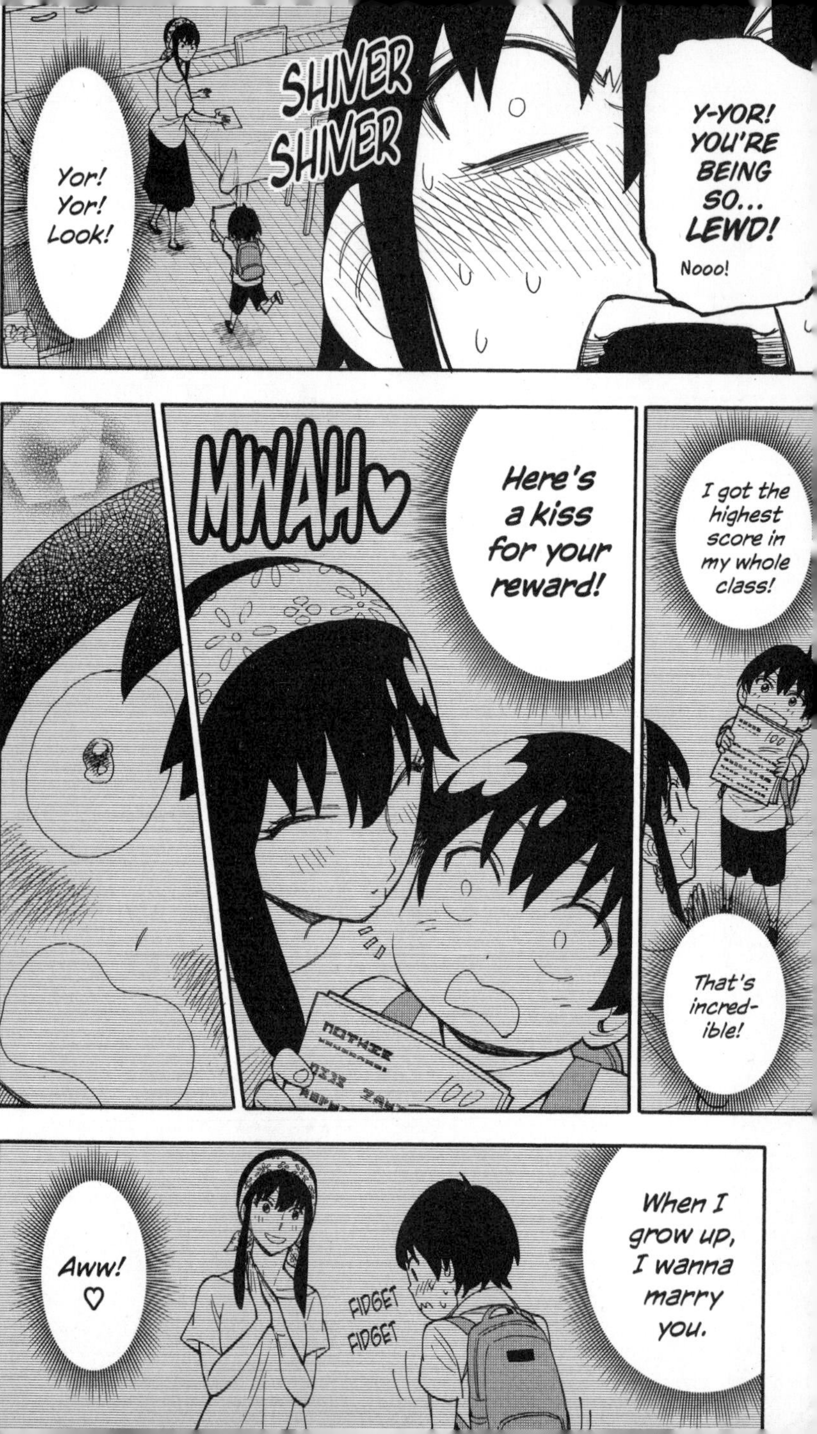
SHIVER SHIVER
Y-YOR! YOU'RE BEING SO... LEWD!
Nooo!
Yor! Yor! Look!
I got the highest score in my whole class!
That's incred-ible!
Here's a kiss for your reward!
MWAH♡
When I grow up, I wanna marry you.
FIDGET FIDGET
Aww! ♡

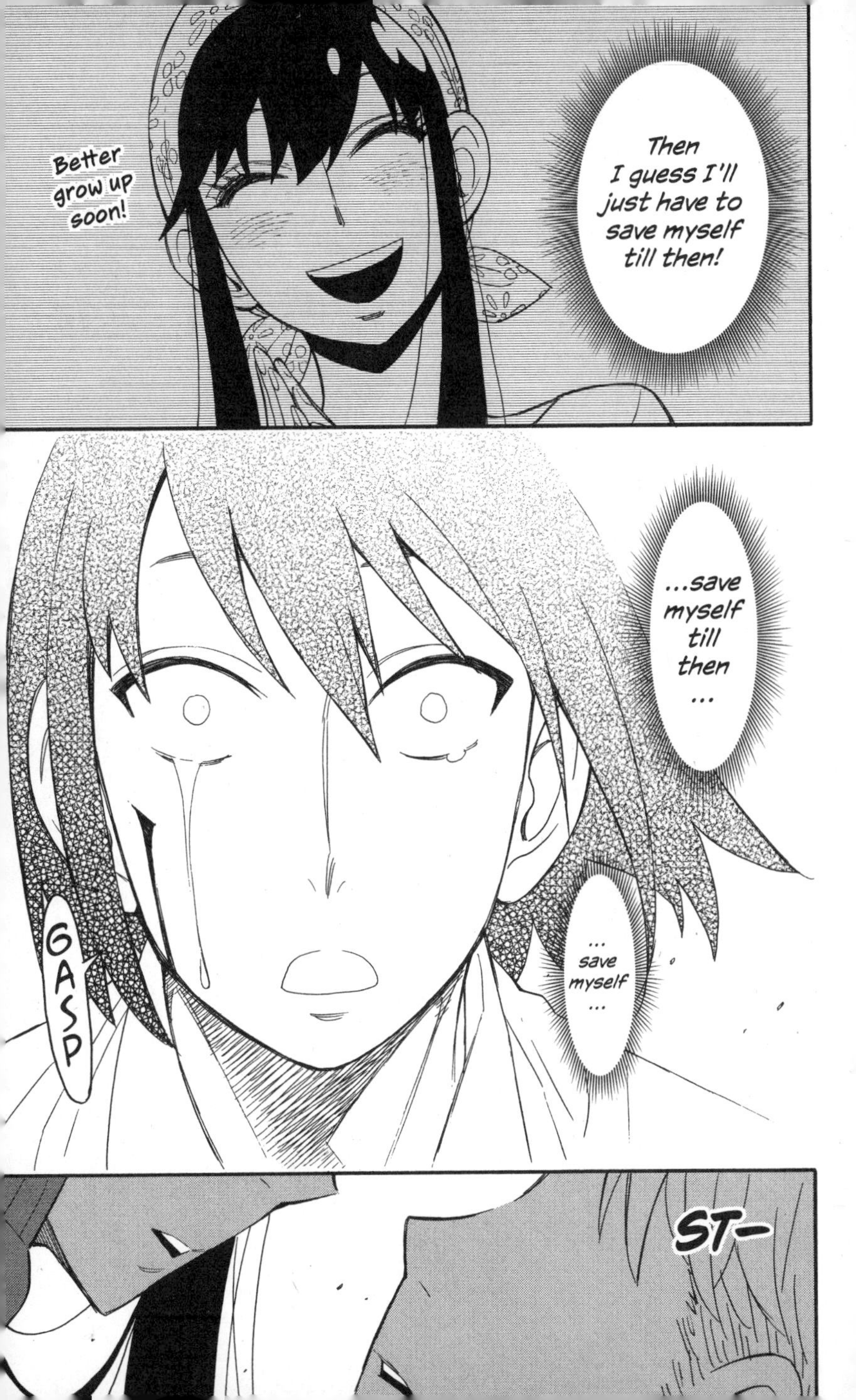
Then I guess I'll just have to save myself till then!
Better grow up soon!
...save myself till then ...
... save myself ...
GASP
ST-

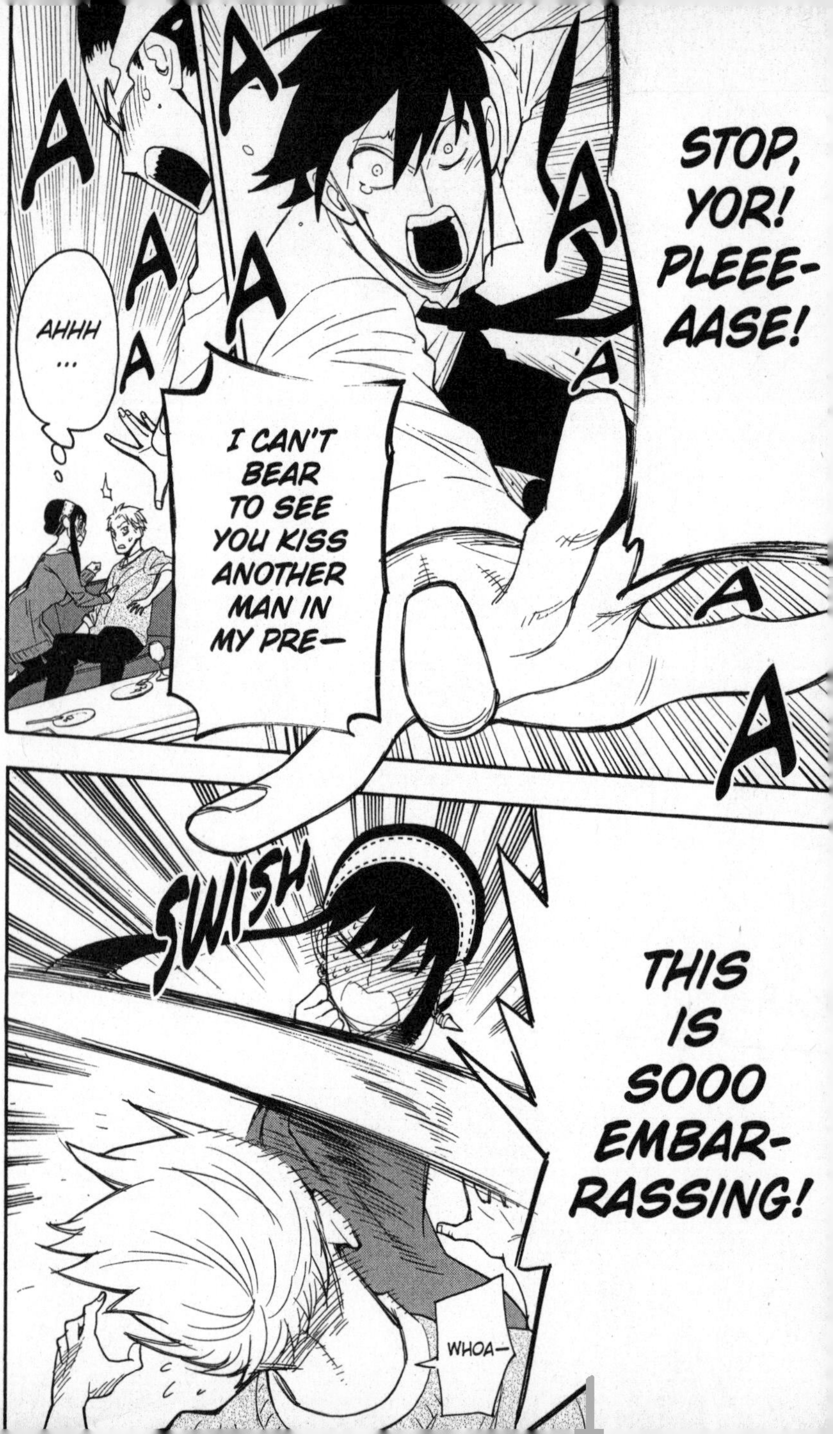
STOP, YOR! PLEEE-AASE!
AAAAAAAAAAAAA
I CAN'T BEAR TO SEE YOU KISS ANOTHER MAN IN MY PRE—
AHHH ...
THIS IS SOOO EMBAR-RASSING!
SWISH
WHOA—

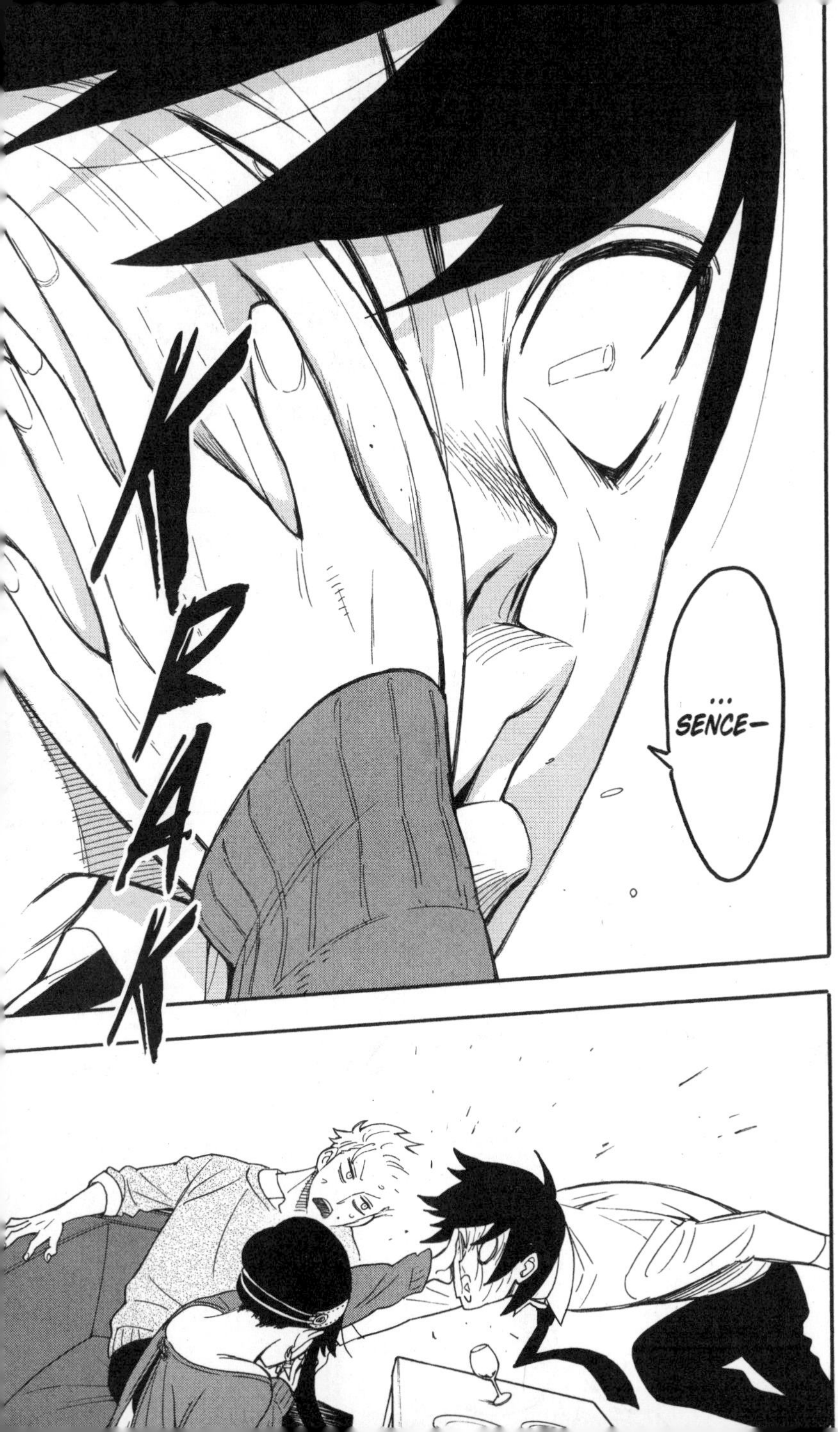
... SENCE—
KRAK

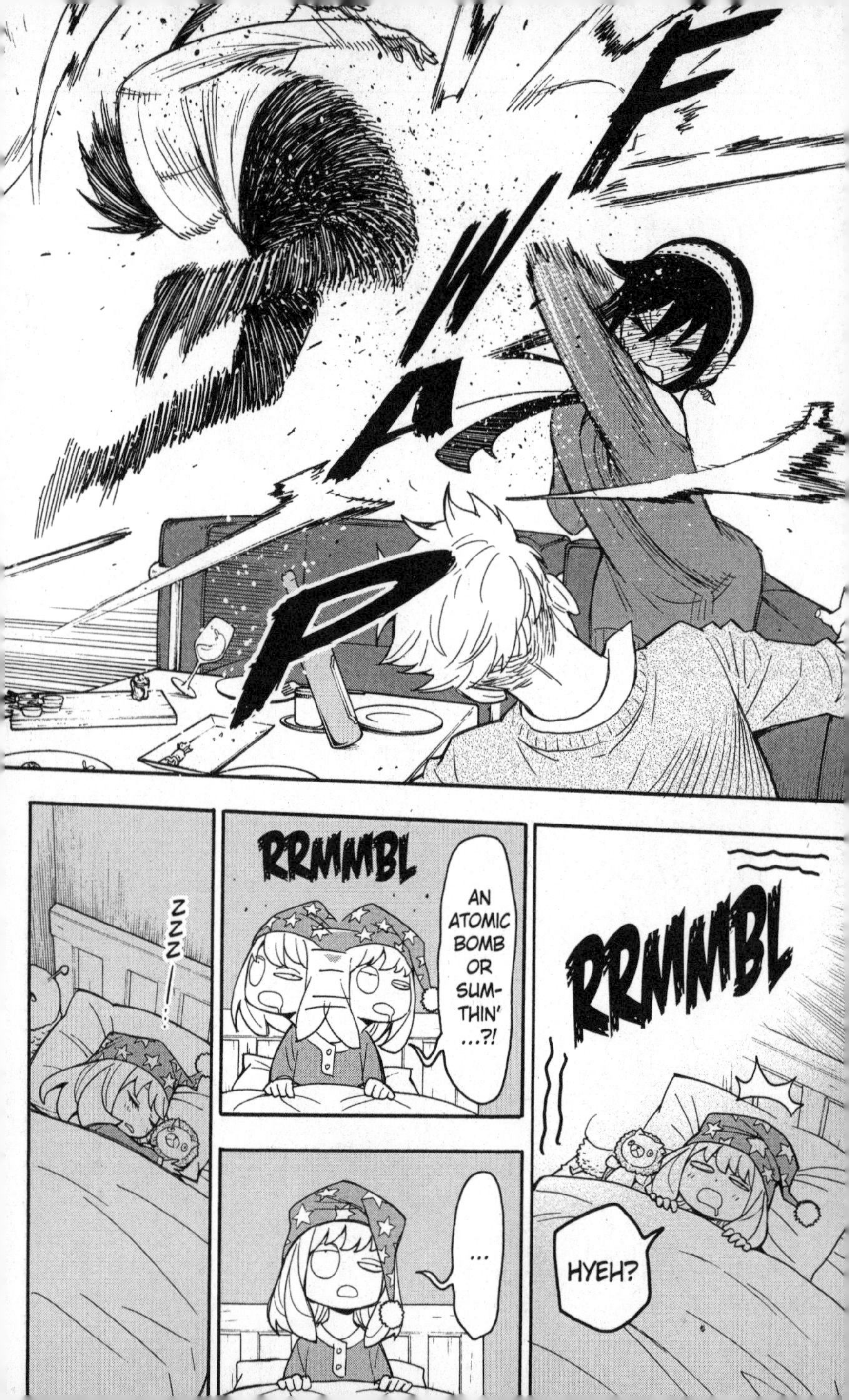
FWAP
RRMMBL
HYEH?
RRMMBL
AN ATOMIC BOMB OR SUM-THIN' ...?!
...
ZZZ......

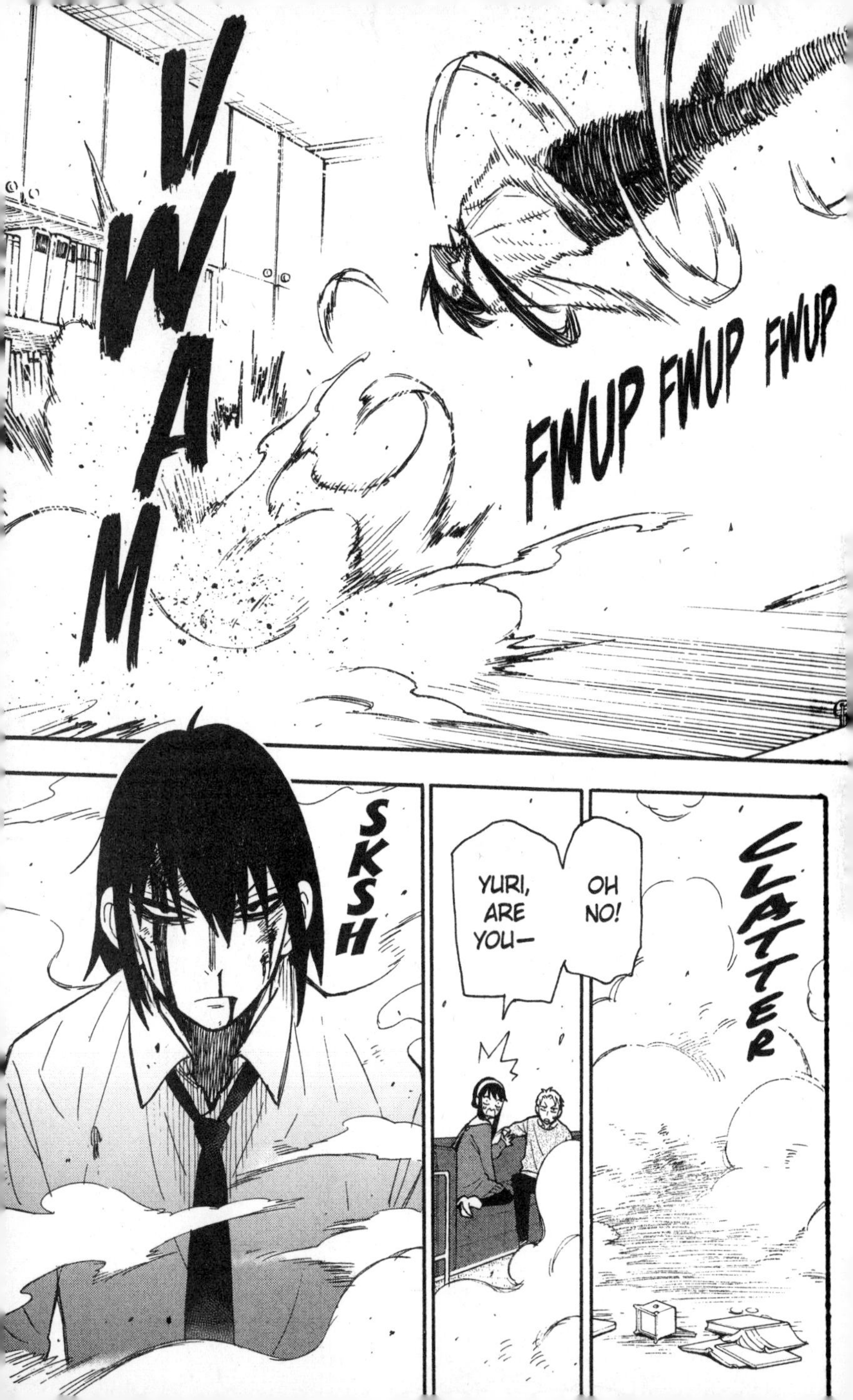
VWAM
FWUP FWUP FWUP
CLATTER
OH NO!
YURI, ARE YOU—
SKSH

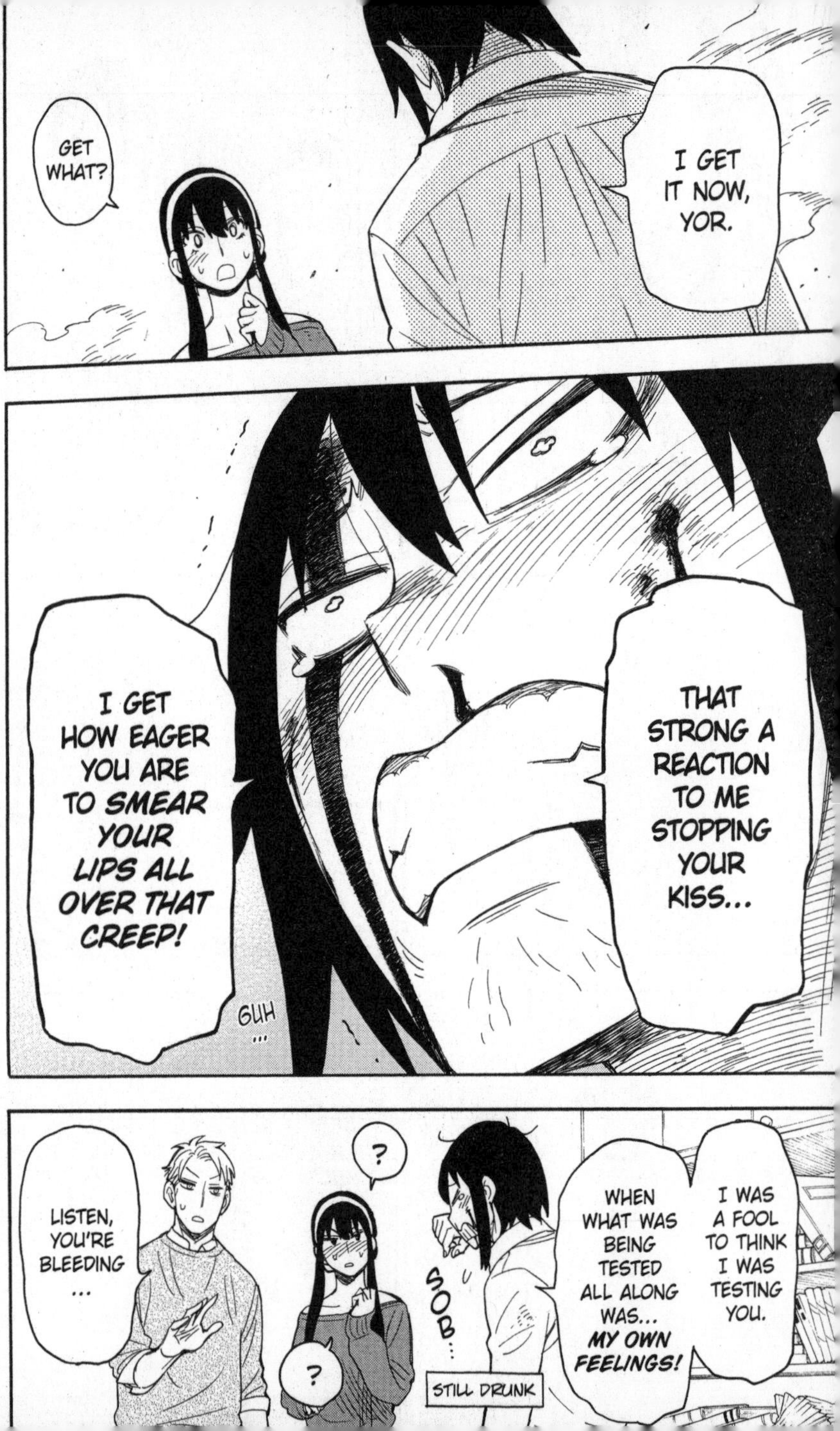
I GET IT NOW, YOR.
GET WHAT?
THAT STRONG A REACTION TO ME STOPPING YOUR KISS...
I GET HOW EAGER YOU ARE TO *SMEAR YOUR LIPS ALL OVER THAT CREEP!*
GUH ...
I WAS A FOOL TO THINK I WAS TESTING YOU.
WHEN WHAT WAS BEING TESTED ALL ALONG WAS... *MY OWN FEELINGS!*
SOB...
STILL DRUNK
?
?
LISTEN, YOU'RE BLEEDING ...

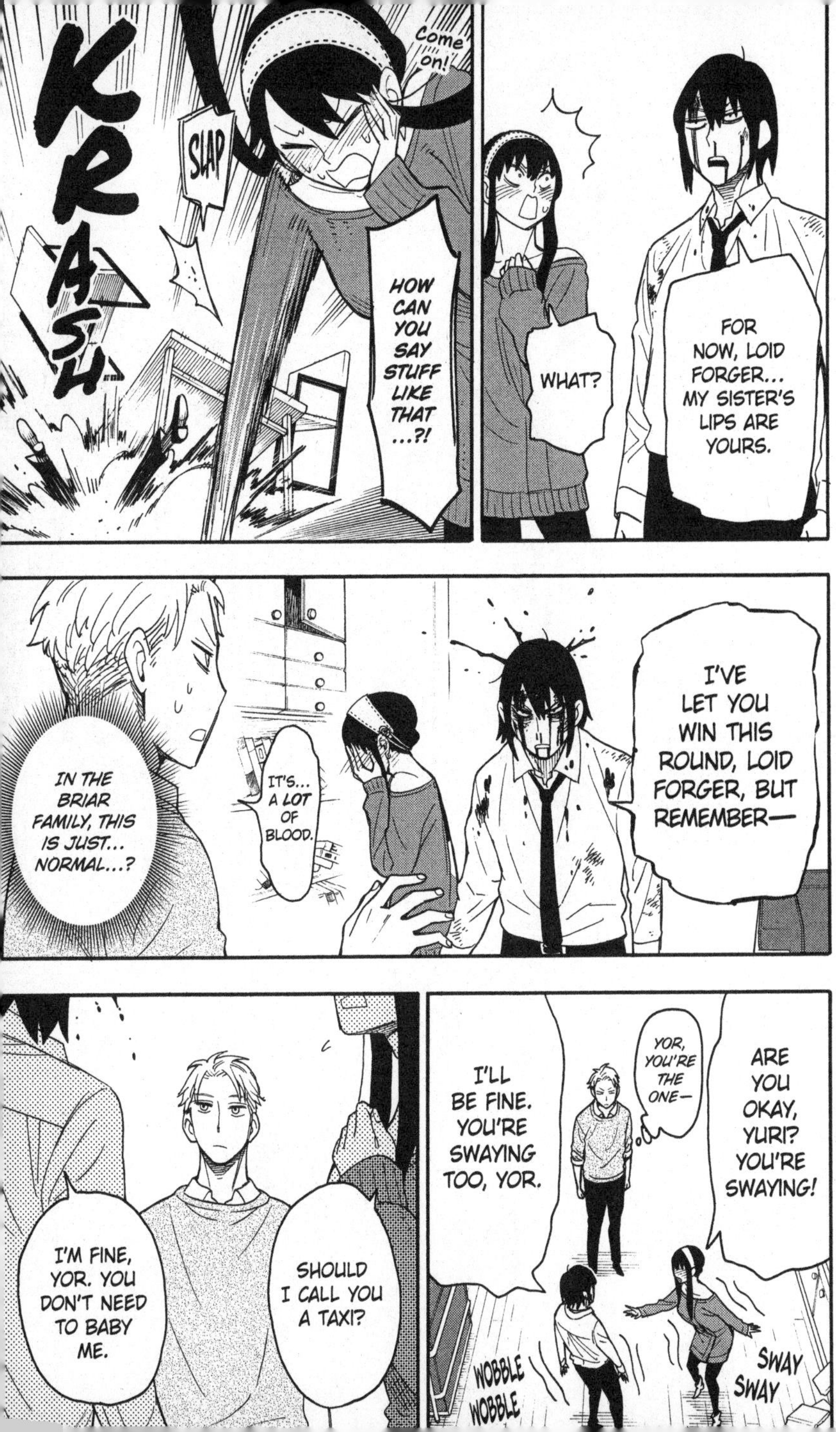
FOR NOW, LOID FORGER... MY SISTER'S LIPS ARE YOURS.
WHAT?
Come on!
SLAP
HOW CAN YOU SAY STUFF LIKE THAT...?!
KRASH
I'VE LET YOU WIN THIS ROUND, LOID FORGER, BUT REMEMBER—
IT'S... A LOT OF BLOOD.
IN THE BRIAR FAMILY, THIS IS JUST... NORMAL...?
ARE YOU OKAY, YURI? YOU'RE SWAYING!
YOR, YOU'RE THE ONE—
I'LL BE FINE. YOU'RE SWAYING TOO, YOR.
SWAY SWAY
WOBBLE WOBBLE
SHOULD I CALL YOU A TAXI?
I'M FINE, YOR. YOU DON'T NEED TO BABY ME.

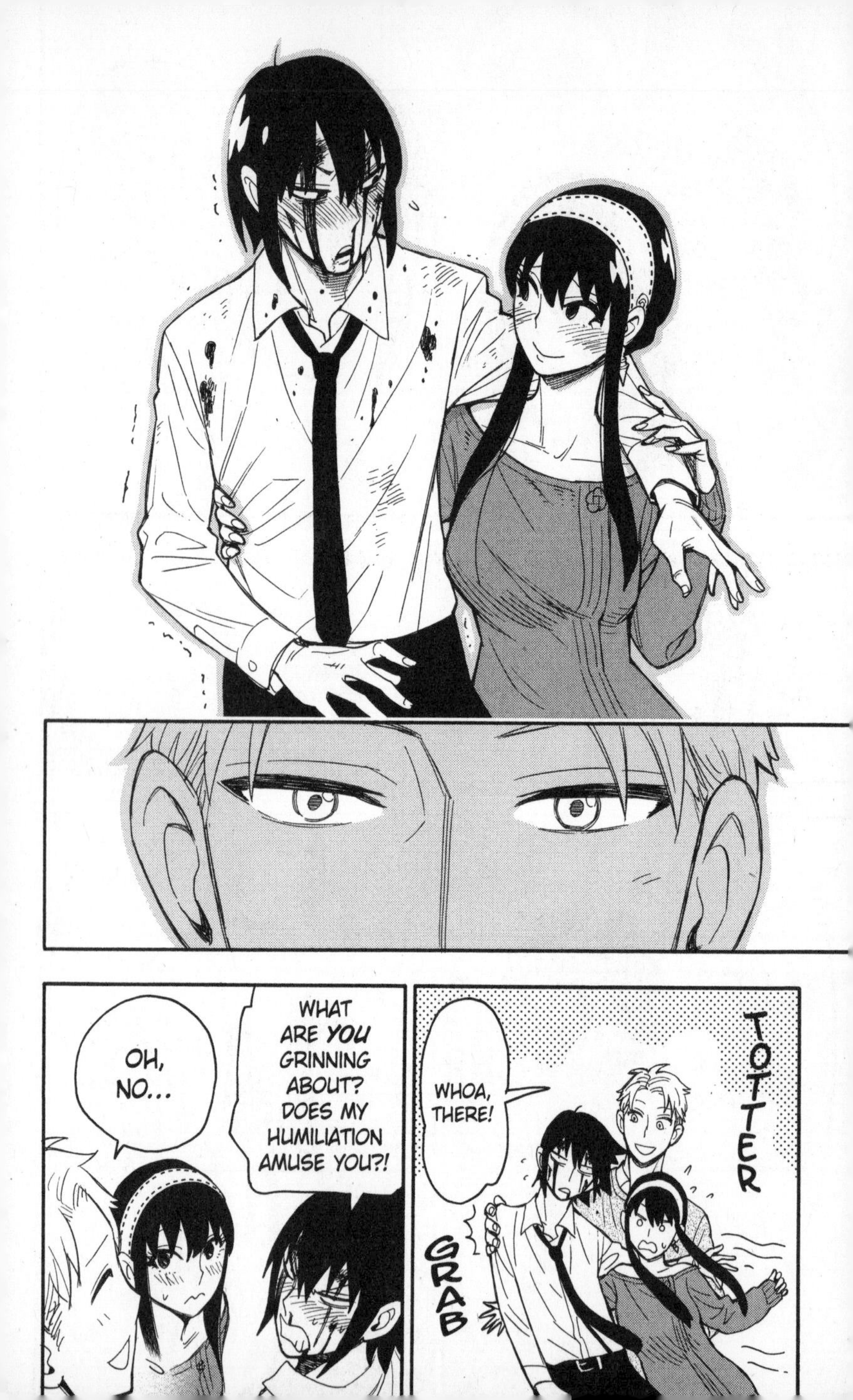
TOTTER
WHOA, THERE!
GRAB
WHAT ARE *YOU* GRINNING ABOUT? DOES MY HUMILIATION AMUSE YOU?!
OH, NO...

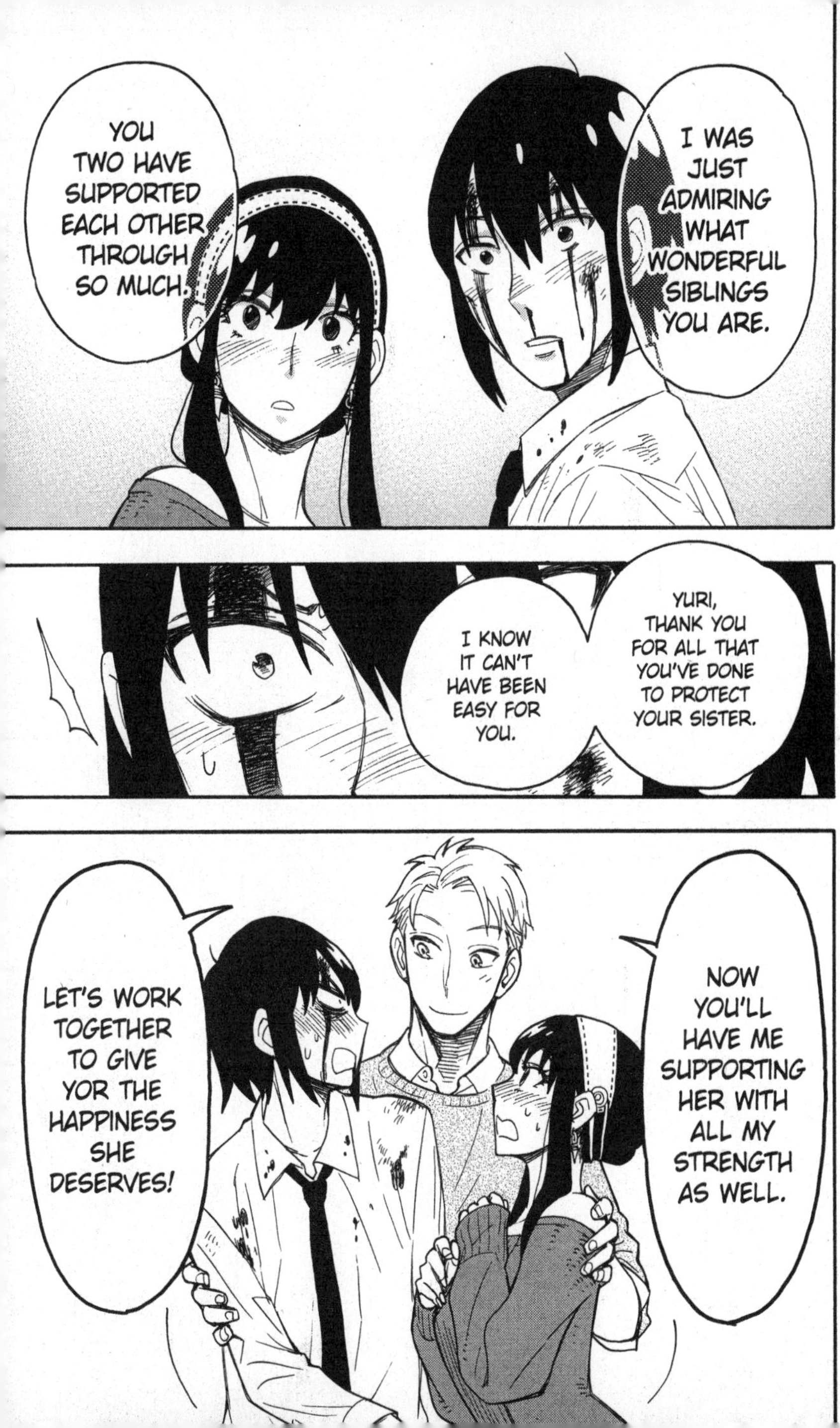
I WAS JUST ADMIRING WHAT WONDERFUL SIBLINGS YOU ARE.
YOU TWO HAVE SUPPORTED EACH OTHER THROUGH SO MUCH.
YURI, THANK YOU FOR ALL THAT YOU'VE DONE TO PROTECT YOUR SISTER.
I KNOW IT CAN'T HAVE BEEN EASY FOR YOU.
NOW YOU'LL HAVE ME SUPPORTING HER WITH ALL MY STRENGTH AS WELL.
LET'S WORK TOGETHER TO GIVE YOR THE HAPPINESS SHE DESERVES!

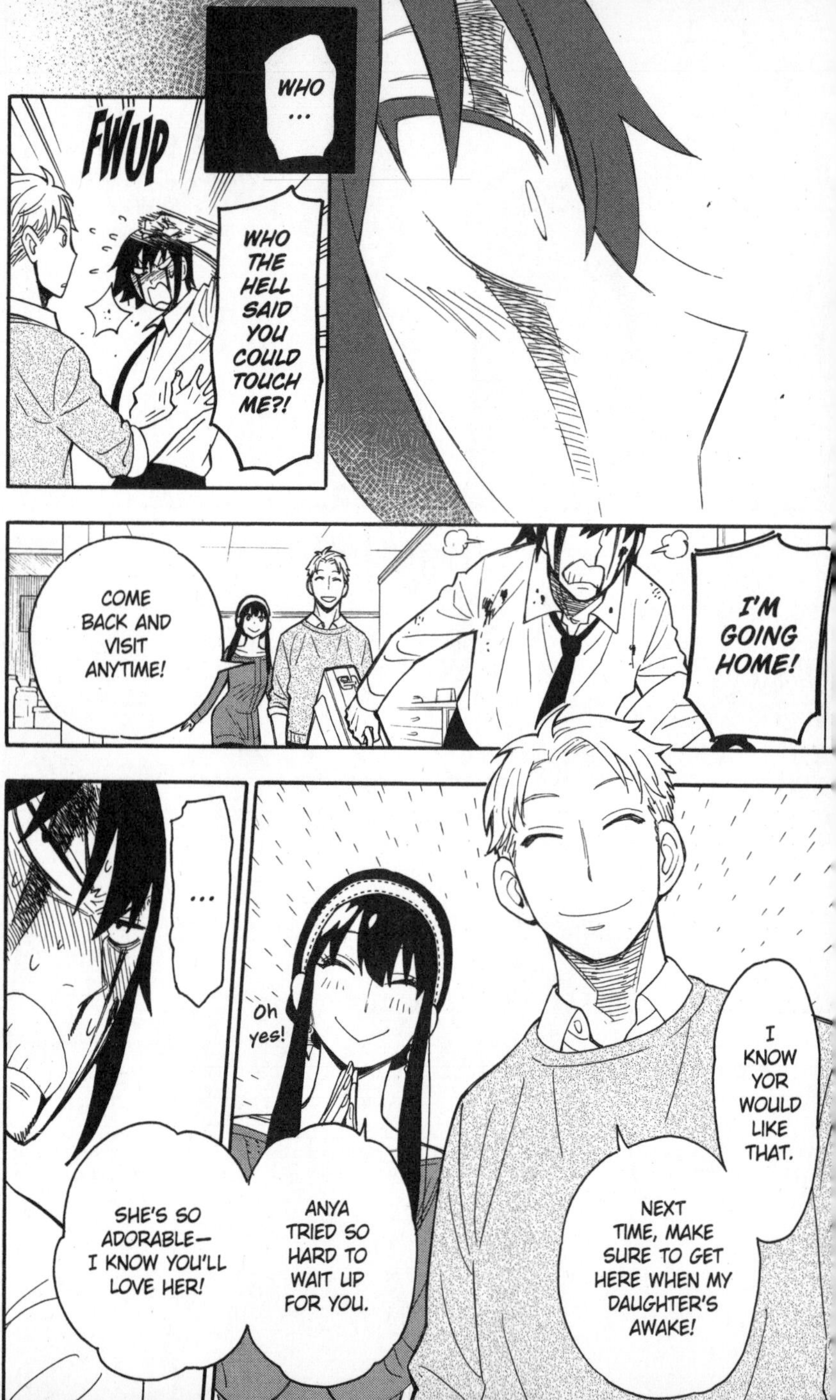
WHO ...
FWUP
WHO THE HELL SAID YOU COULD TOUCH ME?!
I'M GOING HOME!
COME BACK AND VISIT ANYTIME!
I KNOW YOR WOULD LIKE THAT.
NEXT TIME, MAKE SURE TO GET HERE WHEN MY DAUGHTER'S AWAKE!
Oh yes!
ANYA TRIED SO HARD TO WAIT UP FOR YOU.
SHE'S SO ADORABLE— I KNOW YOU'LL LOVE HER!
...

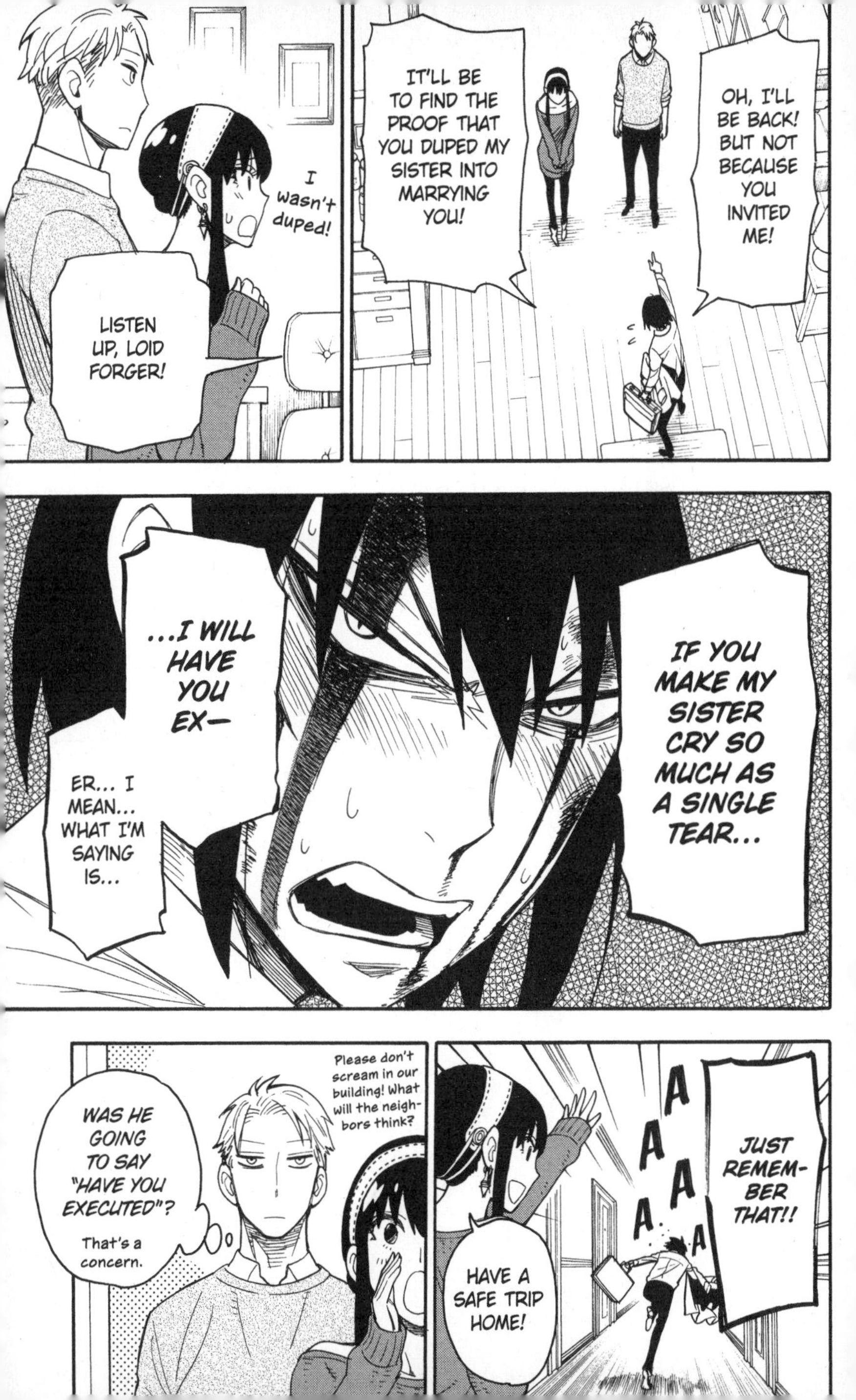
OH, I'LL BE BACK! BUT NOT BECAUSE YOU INVITED ME!
IT'LL BE TO FIND THE PROOF THAT YOU DUPED MY SISTER INTO MARRYING YOU!
I wasn't duped!
LISTEN UP, LOID FORGER!
IF YOU MAKE MY SISTER CRY SO MUCH AS A SINGLE TEAR...
...I WILL HAVE YOU EX—
ER... I MEAN... WHAT I'M SAYING IS...
JUST REMEMBER THAT!!
AAAAAAAA
HAVE A SAFE TRIP HOME!
Please don't scream in our building! What will the neighbors think?
WAS HE GOING TO SAY "HAVE YOU EXECUTED"?
That's a concern.

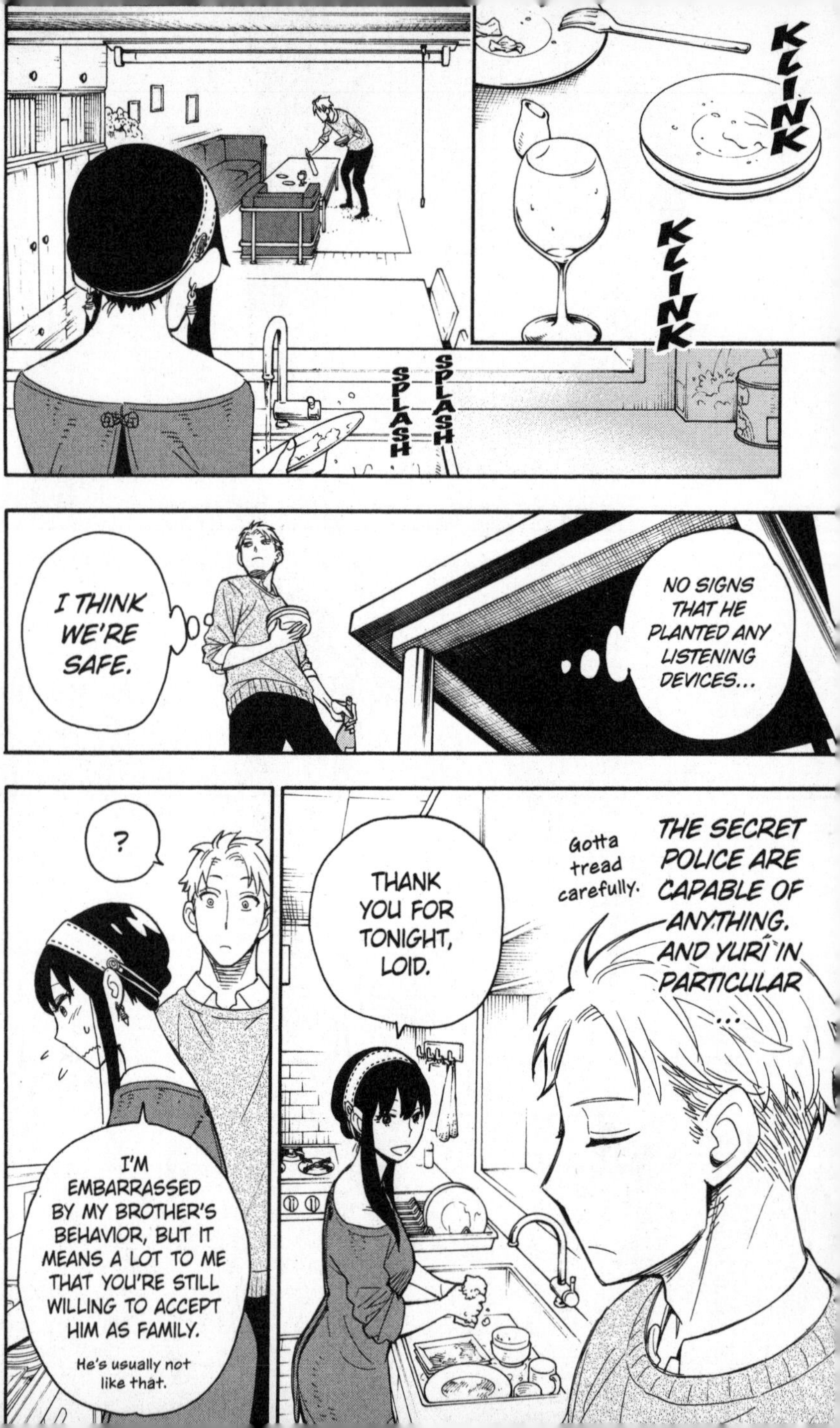
KLINK
KLINK
SPLASH
SPLASH
NO SIGNS THAT HE PLANTED ANY LISTENING DEVICES...
I THINK WE'RE SAFE.
THE SECRET POLICE ARE CAPABLE OF ANYTHING. AND YURI IN PARTICULAR...
Gotta tread carefully.
THANK YOU FOR TONIGHT, LOID.
?
I'M EMBARRASSED BY MY BROTHER'S BEHAVIOR, BUT IT MEANS A LOT TO ME THAT YOU'RE STILL WILLING TO ACCEPT HIM AS FAMILY.
He's usually not like that.

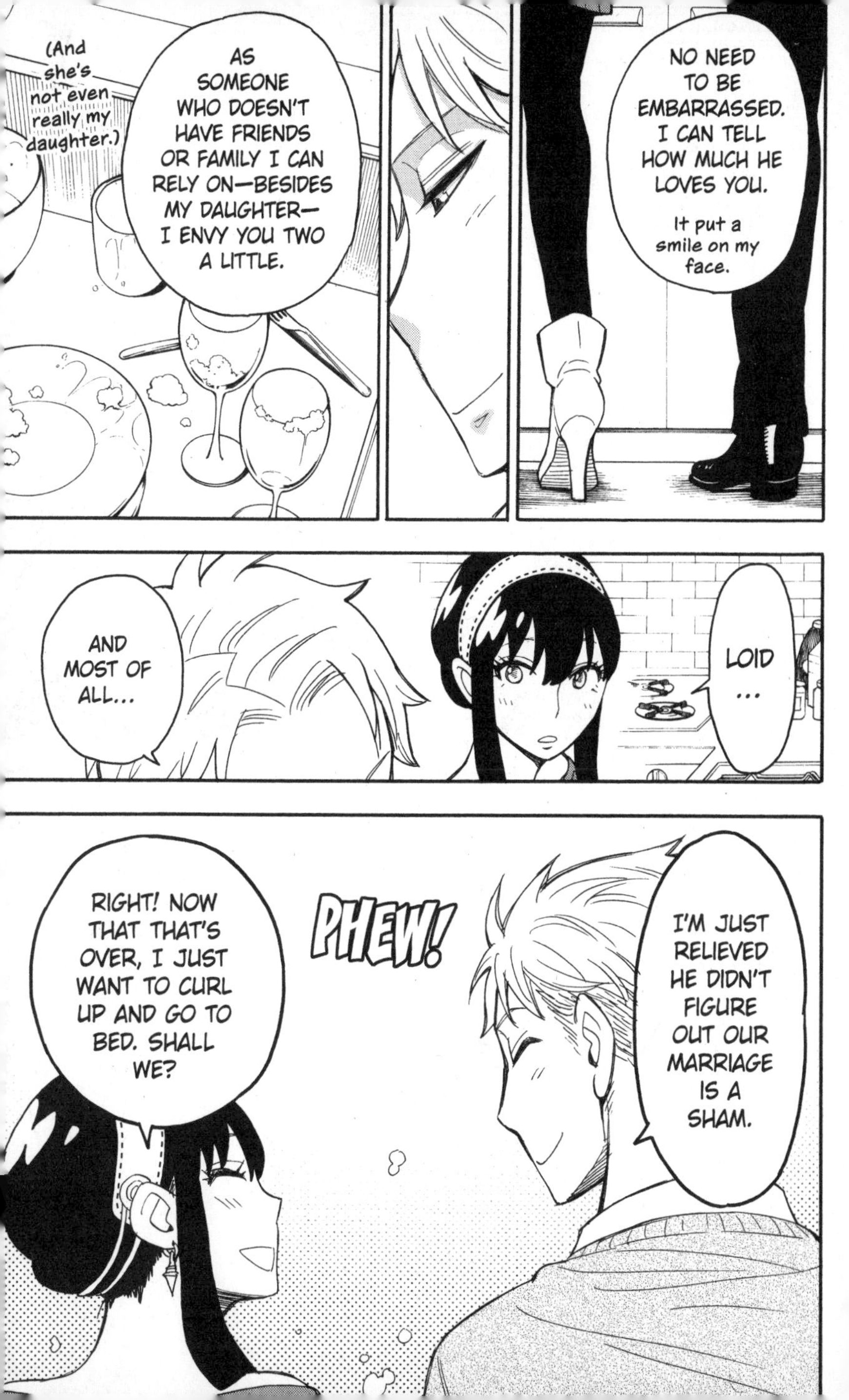
NO NEED TO BE EMBARRASSED. I CAN TELL HOW MUCH HE LOVES YOU.
It put a smile on my face.
AS SOMEONE WHO DOESN'T HAVE FRIENDS OR FAMILY I CAN RELY ON—BESIDES MY DAUGHTER—I ENVY YOU TWO A LITTLE.
(And she's not even really my daughter.)
LOID...
AND MOST OF ALL...
I'M JUST RELIEVED HE DIDN'T FIGURE OUT OUR MARRIAGE IS A SHAM.
PHEW!
RIGHT! NOW THAT THAT'S OVER, I JUST WANT TO CURL UP AND GO TO BED. SHALL WE?

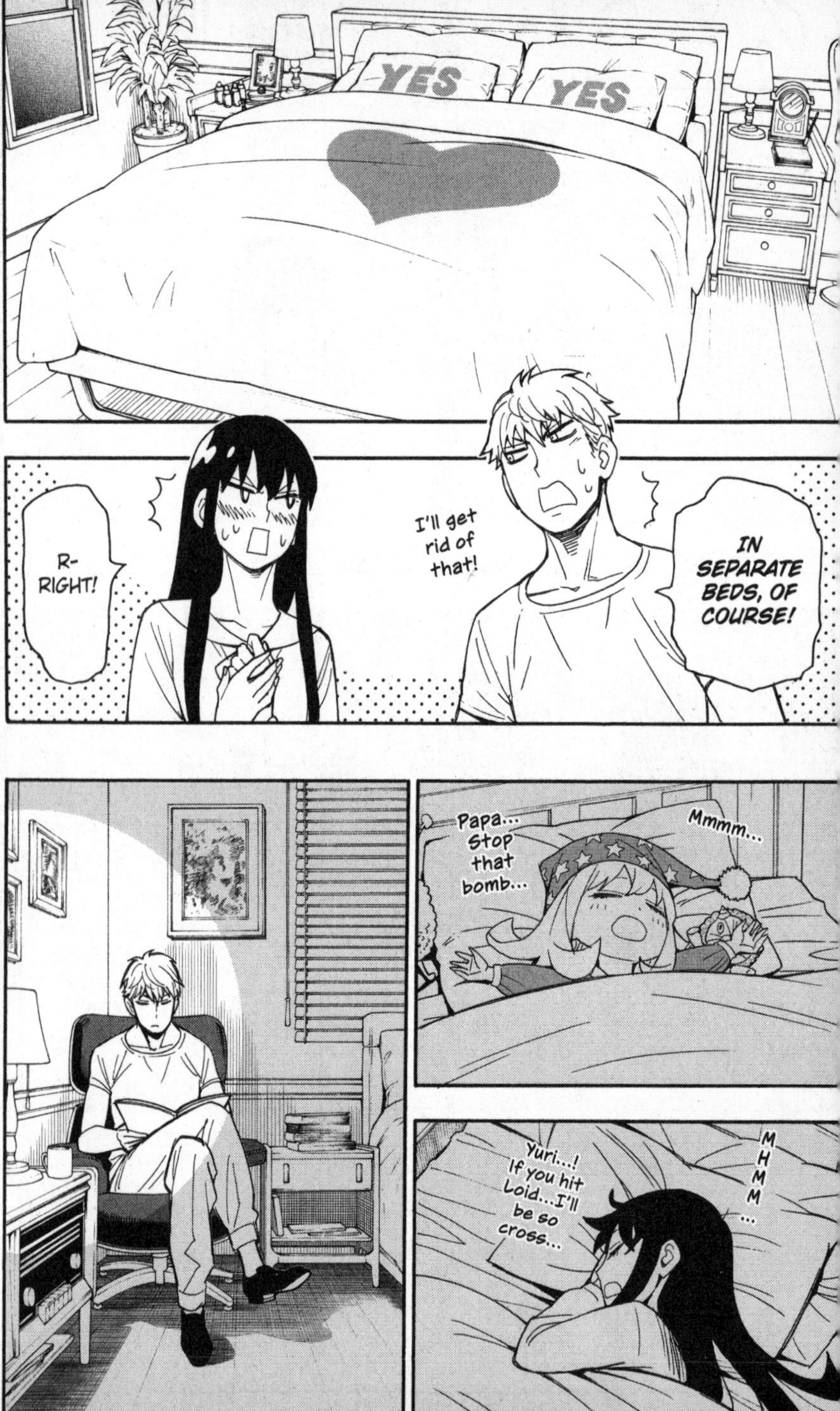
YES
YES
IN SEPARATE BEDS, OF COURSE!
I'll get rid of that!
R-RIGHT!
Mmmm...
Papa... Stop that bomb...
MHMM...
Yuri...! If you hit Loid...I'll be so cross...

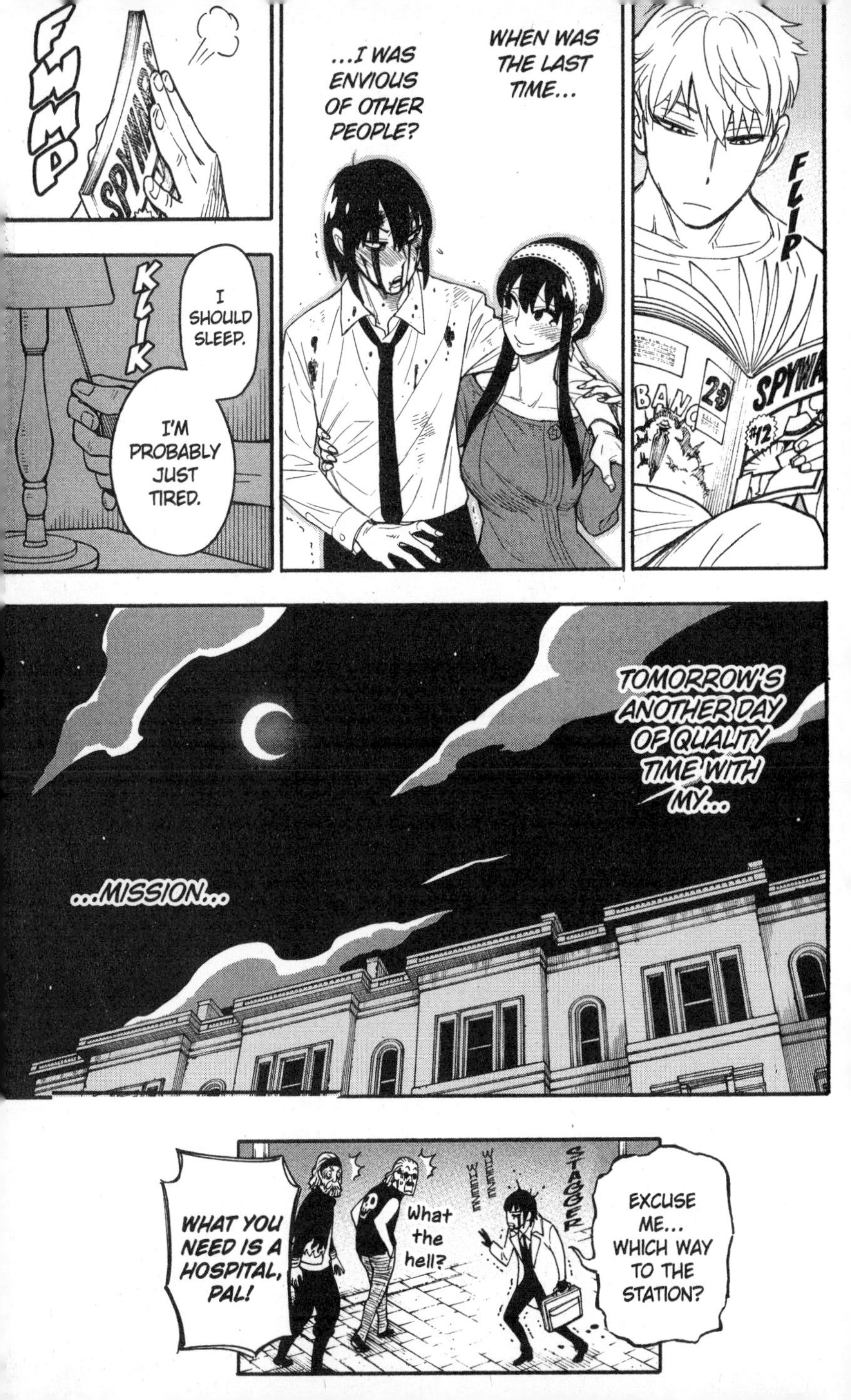
FLIP
SPYWA
#12
BANG
29
WHEN WAS THE LAST TIME...
...I WAS ENVIOUS OF OTHER PEOPLE?
FWMP
SPYWA
KLIK
I SHOULD SLEEP.
I'M PROBABLY JUST TIRED.
TOMORROW'S ANOTHER DAY OF QUALITY TIME WITH MY...
...MISSION...
EXCUSE ME... WHICH WAY TO THE STATION?
STAGGER
WHEEZE
WHEEZE
What the hell?
WHAT YOU NEED IS A HOSPITAL, PAL!

SPY×FAMILY

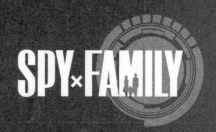

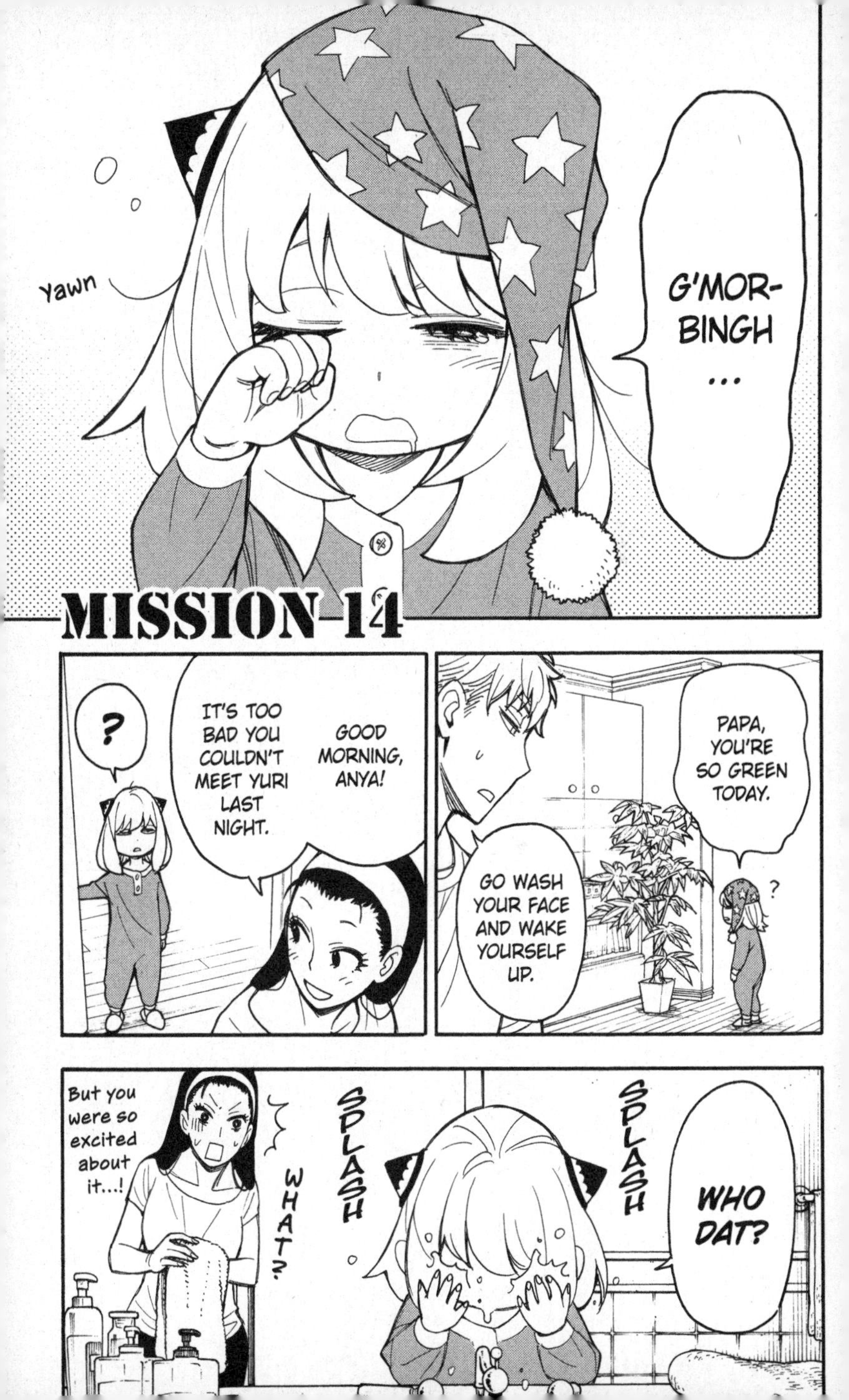
G'MOR-BINGH...
Yawn
MISSION 14
PAPA, YOU'RE SO GREEN TODAY.
?
GO WASH YOUR FACE AND WAKE YOURSELF UP.
GOOD MORNING, ANYA!
IT'S TOO BAD YOU COULDN'T MEET YURI LAST NIGHT.
?
WHO DAT?
SPLASH
SPLASH
WHAT?
But you were so excited about it...!

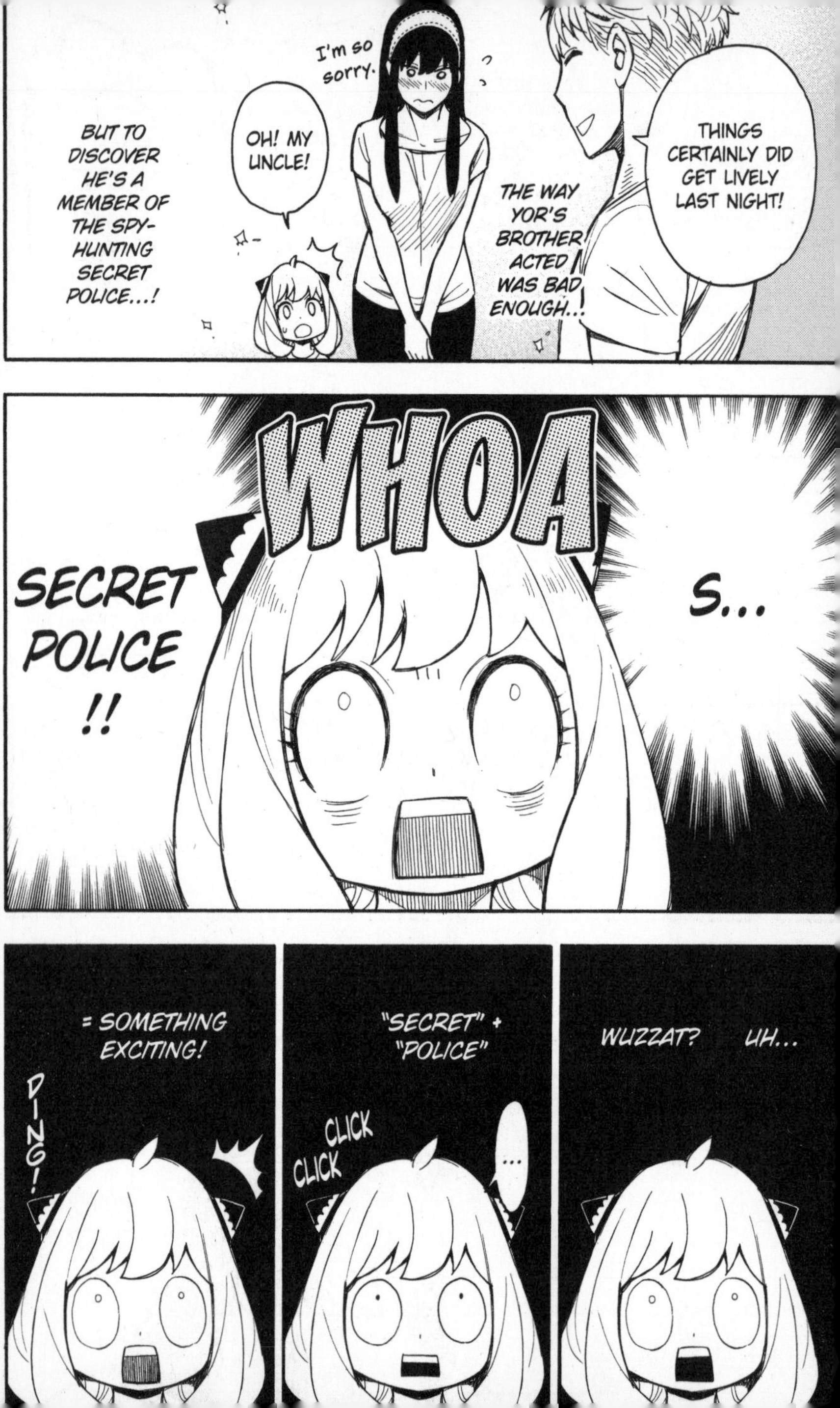
THINGS CERTAINLY DID GET LIVELY LAST NIGHT!
THE WAY YOR'S BROTHER ACTED WAS BAD ENOUGH...
I'm so sorry.
OH! MY UNCLE!
BUT TO DISCOVER HE'S A MEMBER OF THE SPY-HUNTING SECRET POLICE...!
S...
WHOA
SECRET POLICE !!
UH...
WUZZAT?
...
"SECRET" + "POLICE"
CLICK
CLICK
= SOMETHING EXCITING!
DING!

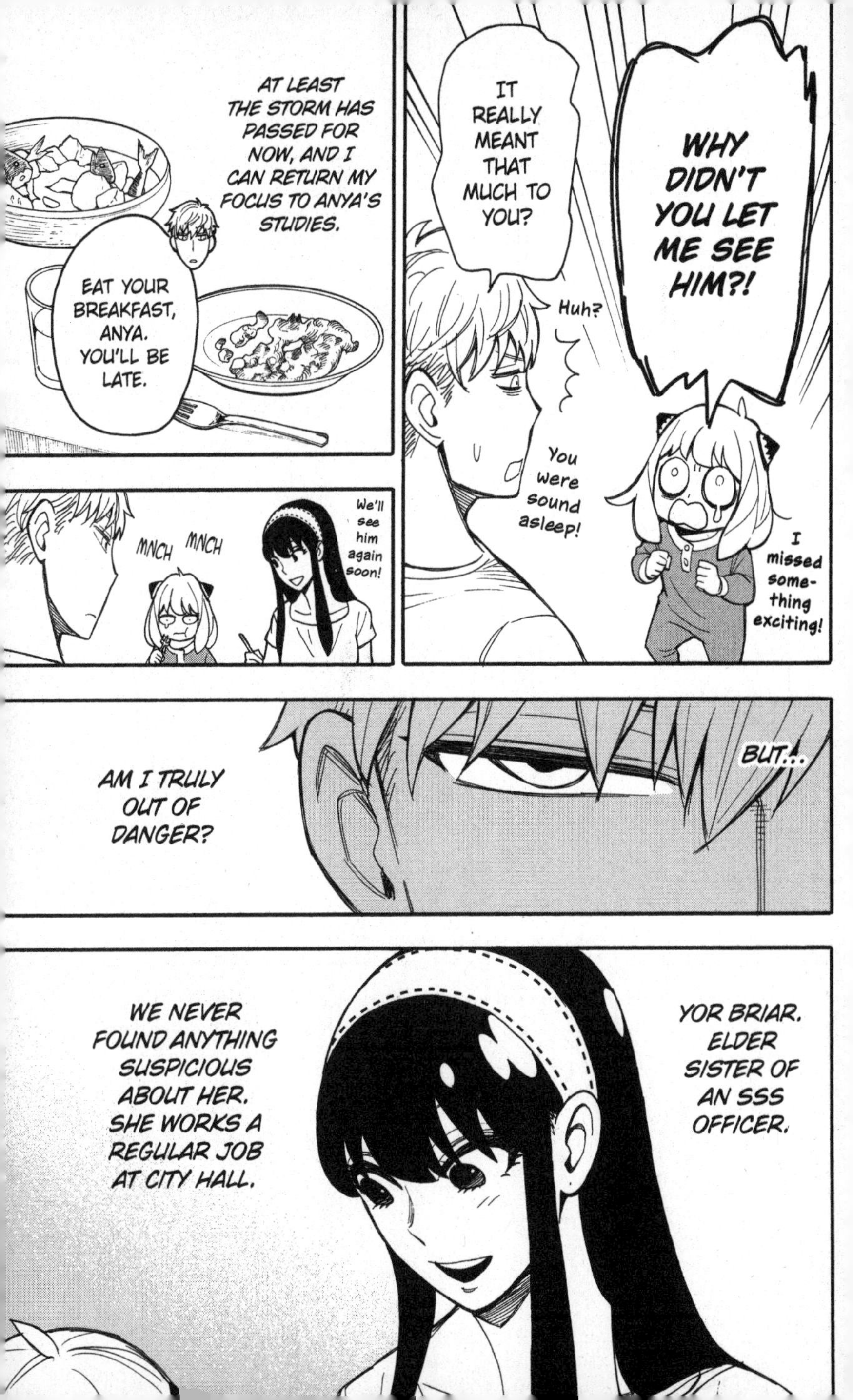
WHY DIDN'T YOU LET ME SEE HIM?!
Huh?
IT REALLY MEANT THAT MUCH TO YOU?
I missed something exciting!
You were sound asleep!
AT LEAST THE STORM HAS PASSED FOR NOW, AND I CAN RETURN MY FOCUS TO ANYA'S STUDIES.
EAT YOUR BREAKFAST, ANYA. YOU'LL BE LATE.
We'll see him again soon!
MNCH MNCH
BUT...
AM I TRULY OUT OF DANGER?
YOR BRIAR. ELDER SISTER OF AN SSS OFFICER.
WE NEVER FOUND ANYTHING SUSPICIOUS ABOUT HER. SHE WORKS A REGULAR JOB AT CITY HALL.

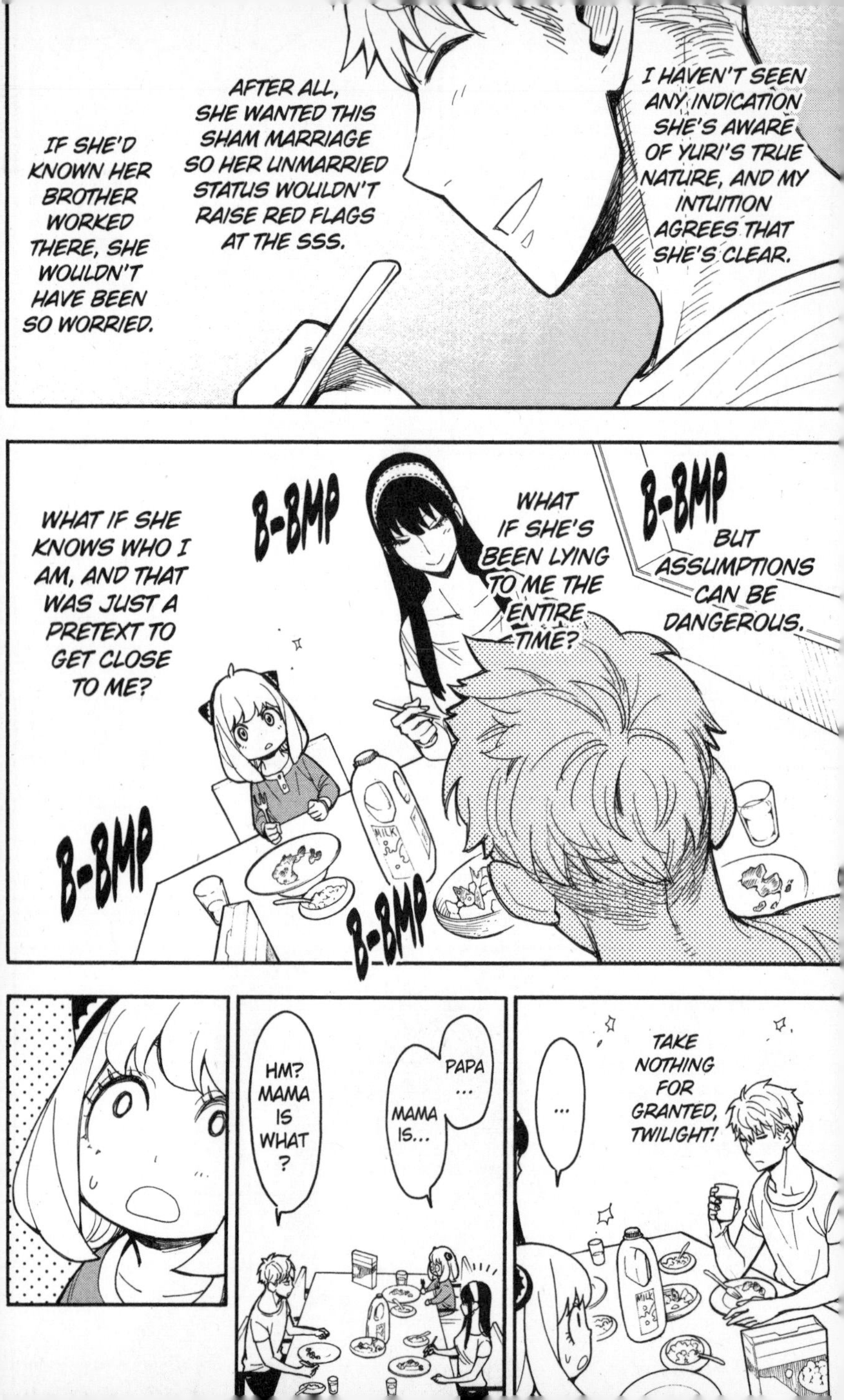
I HAVEN'T SEEN ANY INDICATION SHE'S AWARE OF YURI'S TRUE NATURE, AND MY INTUITION AGREES THAT SHE'S CLEAR.
AFTER ALL, SHE WANTED THIS SHAM MARRIAGE SO HER UNMARRIED STATUS WOULDN'T RAISE RED FLAGS AT THE SSS.
IF SHE'D KNOWN HER BROTHER WORKED THERE, SHE WOULDN'T HAVE BEEN SO WORRIED.
BUT ASSUMPTIONS CAN BE DANGEROUS.
B-BMP
WHAT IF SHE'S BEEN LYING TO ME THE ENTIRE TIME?
B-BMP
WHAT IF SHE KNOWS WHO I AM, AND THAT WAS JUST A PRETEXT TO GET CLOSE TO ME?
B-BMP
B-BMP
TAKE NOTHING FOR GRANTED, TWILIGHT!
...
PAPA ...
MAMA IS...
HM? MAMA IS WHAT ?

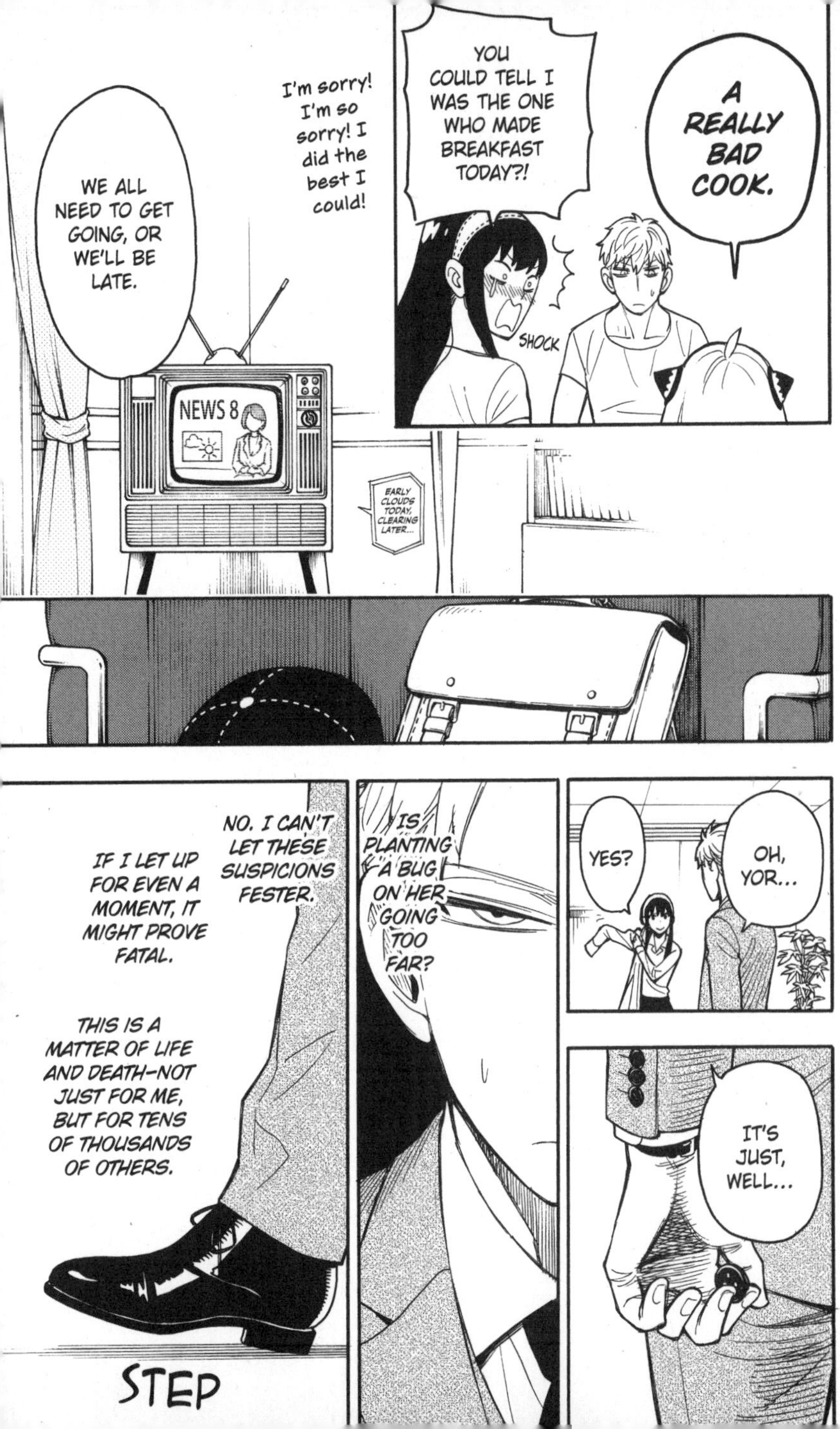
A REALLY BAD COOK.
YOU COULD TELL I WAS THE ONE WHO MADE BREAKFAST TODAY?!
SHOCK
I'm sorry! I'm so sorry! I did the best I could!
WE ALL NEED TO GET GOING, OR WE'LL BE LATE.
NEWS 8
EARLY CLOUDS TODAY, CLEARING LATER...
OH, YOR...
YES?
IT'S JUST, WELL...
IS PLANTING A BUG ON HER GOING TOO FAR?
NO. I CAN'T LET THESE SUSPICIONS FESTER.
IF I LET UP FOR EVEN A MOMENT, IT MIGHT PROVE FATAL.
THIS IS A MATTER OF LIFE AND DEATH—NOT JUST FOR ME, BUT FOR TENS OF THOUSANDS OF OTHERS.
STEP

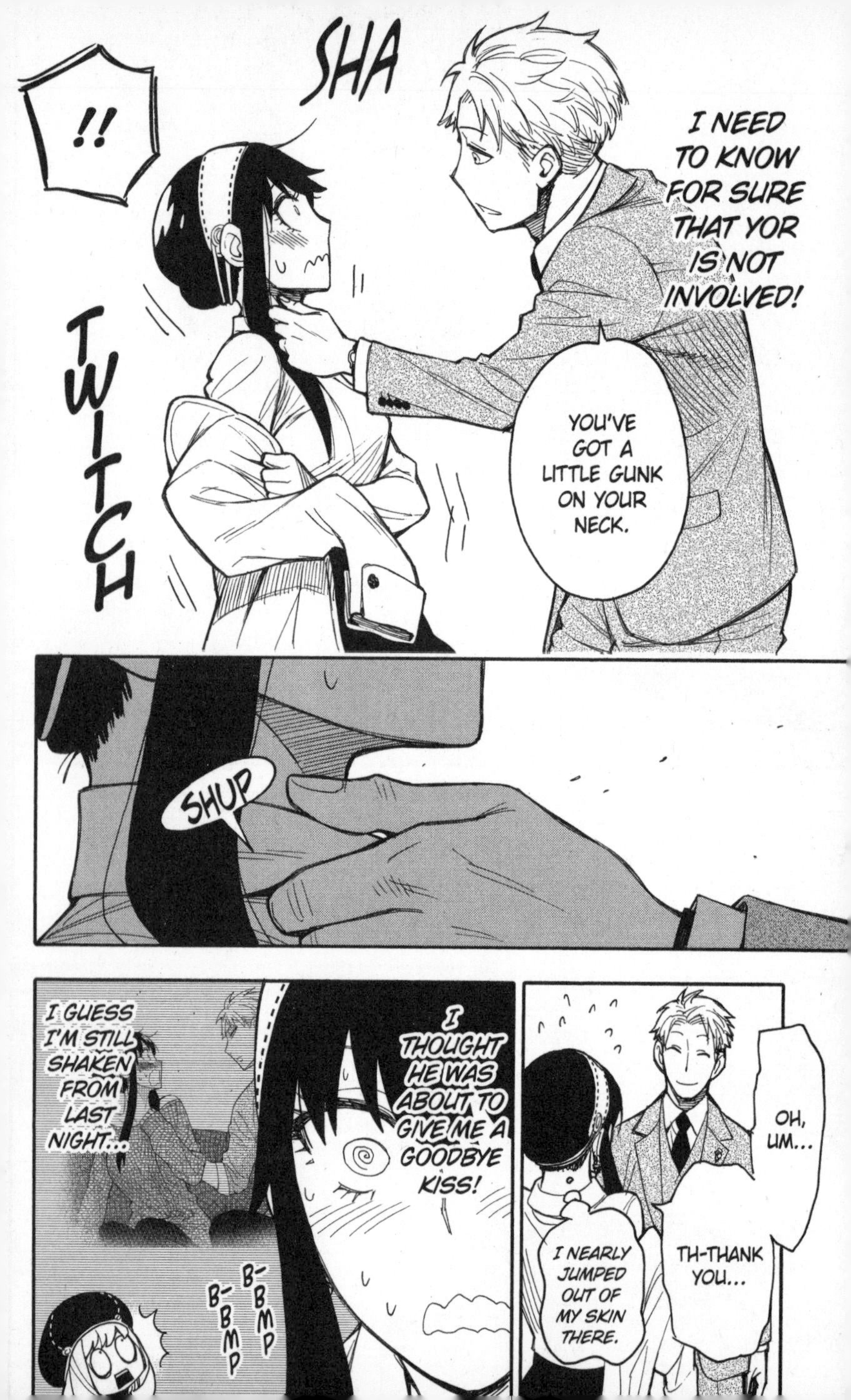
I NEED TO KNOW FOR SURE THAT YOR IS NOT INVOLVED!
SHA
!!
YOU'VE GOT A LITTLE GUNK ON YOUR NECK.
TWITCH
SHUP
OH, UM...
TH-THANK YOU...
I NEARLY JUMPED OUT OF MY SKIN THERE.
I THOUGHT HE WAS ABOUT TO GIVE ME A GOODBYE KISS!
I GUESS I'M STILL SHAKEN FROM LAST NIGHT...
B-BMP
B-BMP

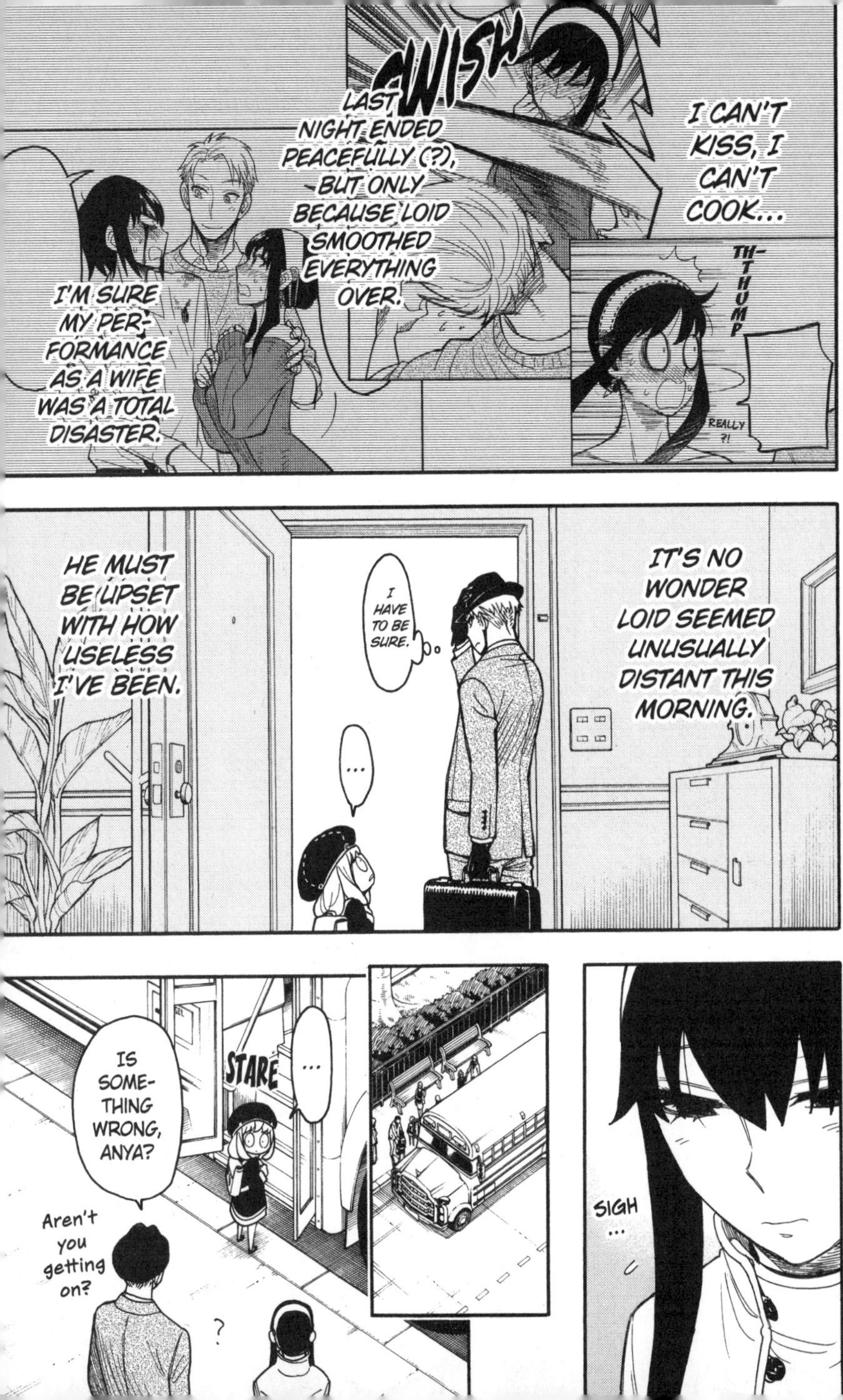
SWISH
I CAN'T KISS, I CAN'T COOK...
LAST NIGHT ENDED PEACEFULLY (?), BUT ONLY BECAUSE LOID SMOOTHED EVERYTHING OVER.
TH-THUMP
REALLY ?!
I'M SURE MY PER-FORMANCE AS A WIFE WAS A TOTAL DISASTER.
IT'S NO WONDER LOID SEEMED UNUSUALLY DISTANT THIS MORNING.
I HAVE TO BE SURE.
...
HE MUST BE UPSET WITH HOW USELESS I'VE BEEN.
SIGH...
...
STARE
IS SOME-THING WRONG, ANYA?
Aren't you getting on?
?

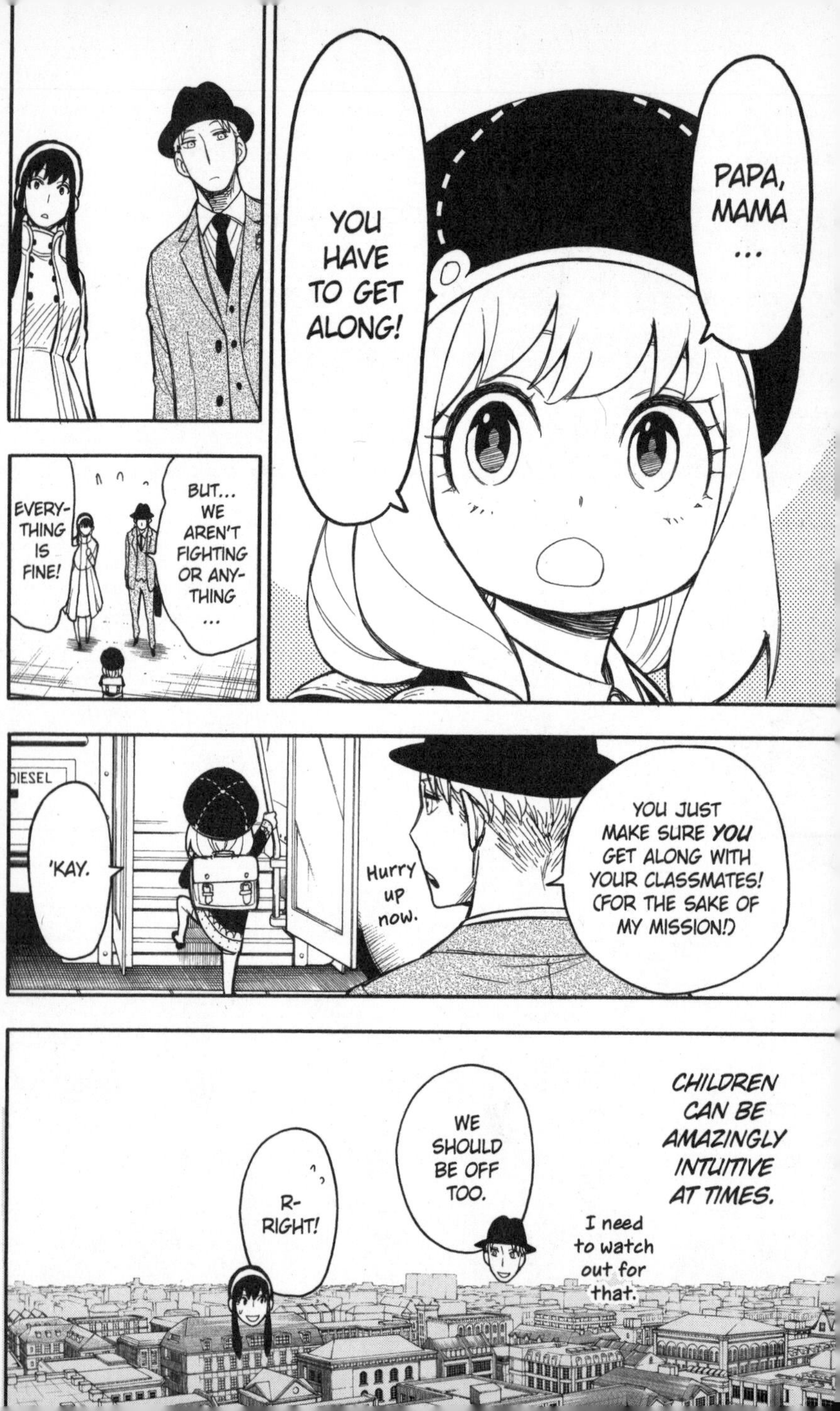
PAPA, MAMA ...
YOU HAVE TO GET ALONG!
BUT... WE AREN'T FIGHTING OR ANYTHING ...
EVERYTHING IS FINE!
YOU JUST MAKE SURE YOU GET ALONG WITH YOUR CLASSMATES! (FOR THE SAKE OF MY MISSION!)
Hurry up now.
'KAY.
DIESEL
CHILDREN CAN BE AMAZINGLY INTUITIVE AT TIMES.
I need to watch out for that.
WE SHOULD BE OFF TOO.
R-RIGHT!

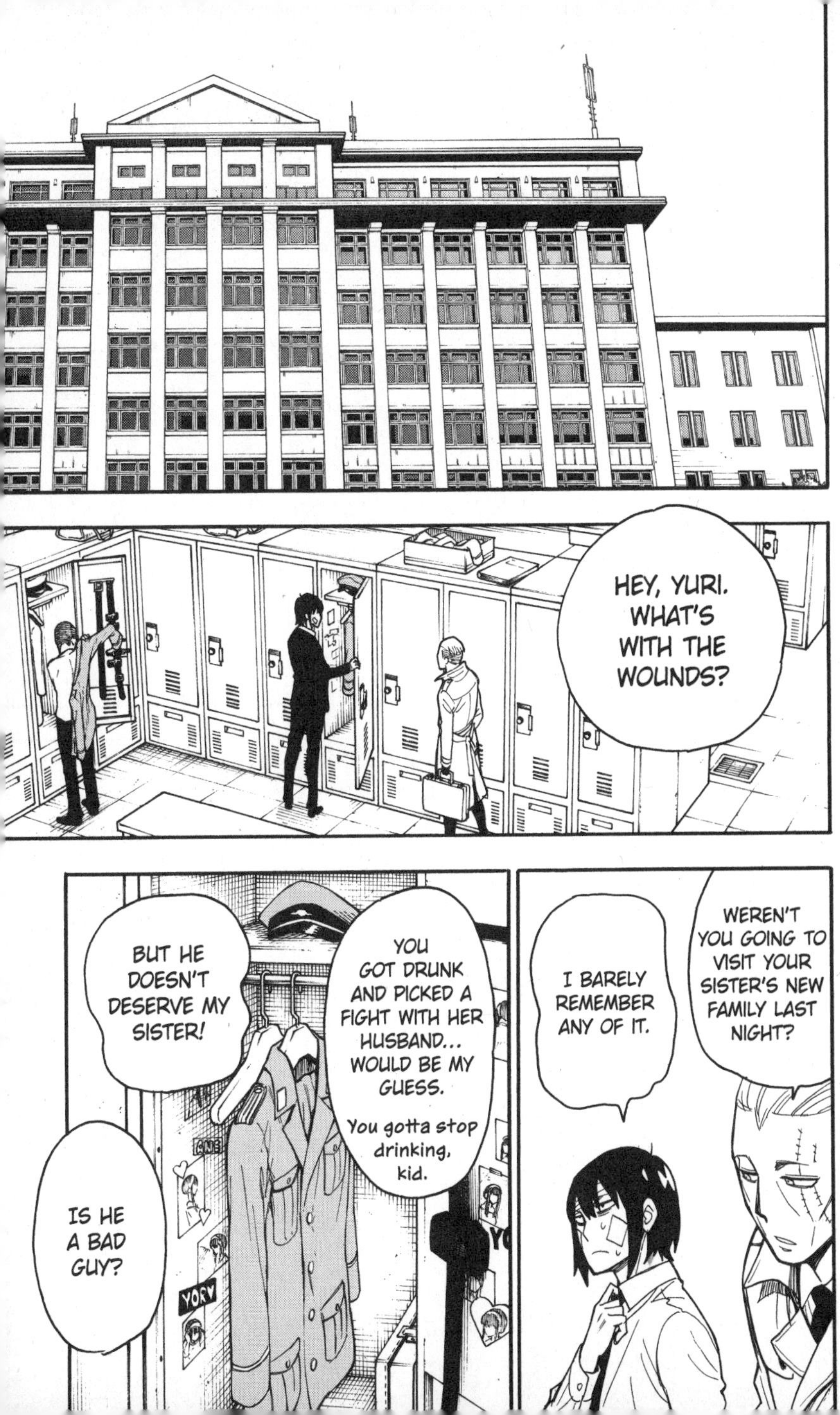
HEY, YURI. WHAT'S WITH THE WOUNDS?
WEREN'T YOU GOING TO VISIT YOUR SISTER'S NEW FAMILY LAST NIGHT?
I BARELY REMEMBER ANY OF IT.
YOU GOT DRUNK AND PICKED A FIGHT WITH HER HUSBAND... WOULD BE MY GUESS.
You gotta stop drinking, kid.
BUT HE DOESN'T DESERVE MY SISTER!
IS HE A BAD GUY?

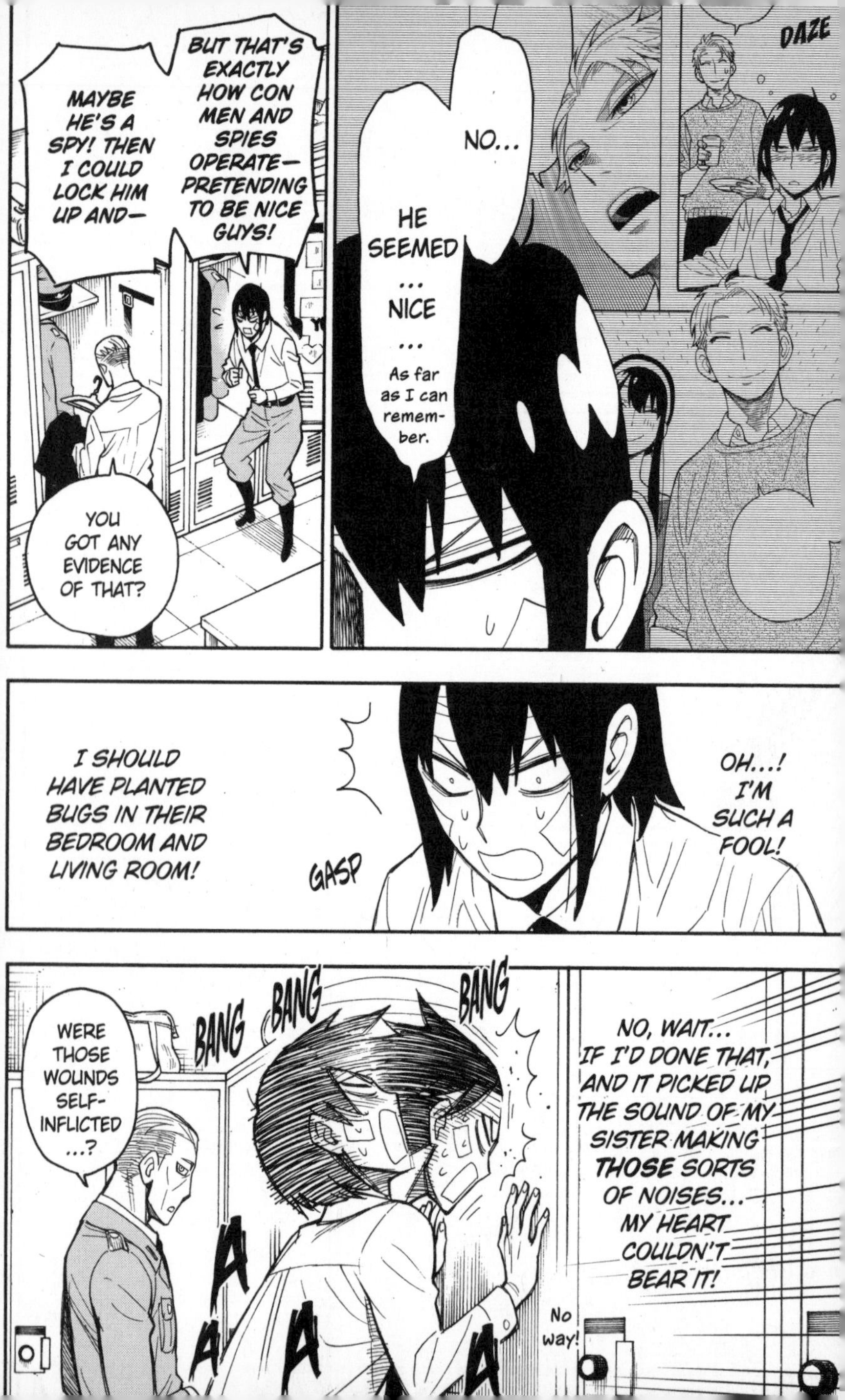
DAZE
NO...
HE SEEMED ... NICE ...
As far as I can remember.
BUT THAT'S EXACTLY HOW CON MEN AND SPIES OPERATE—PRETENDING TO BE NICE GUYS!
MAYBE HE'S A SPY! THEN I COULD LOCK HIM UP AND—
YOU GOT ANY EVIDENCE OF THAT?
OH...! I'M SUCH A FOOL!
GASP
I SHOULD HAVE PLANTED BUGS IN THEIR BEDROOM AND LIVING ROOM!
NO, WAIT... IF I'D DONE THAT, AND IT PICKED UP THE SOUND OF MY SISTER MAKING THOSE SORTS OF NOISES... MY HEART COULDN'T BEAR IT!
No way!
BANG
BANG
BANG
WERE THOSE WOUNDS SELF-INFLICTED ...?
A
A
A
A
A

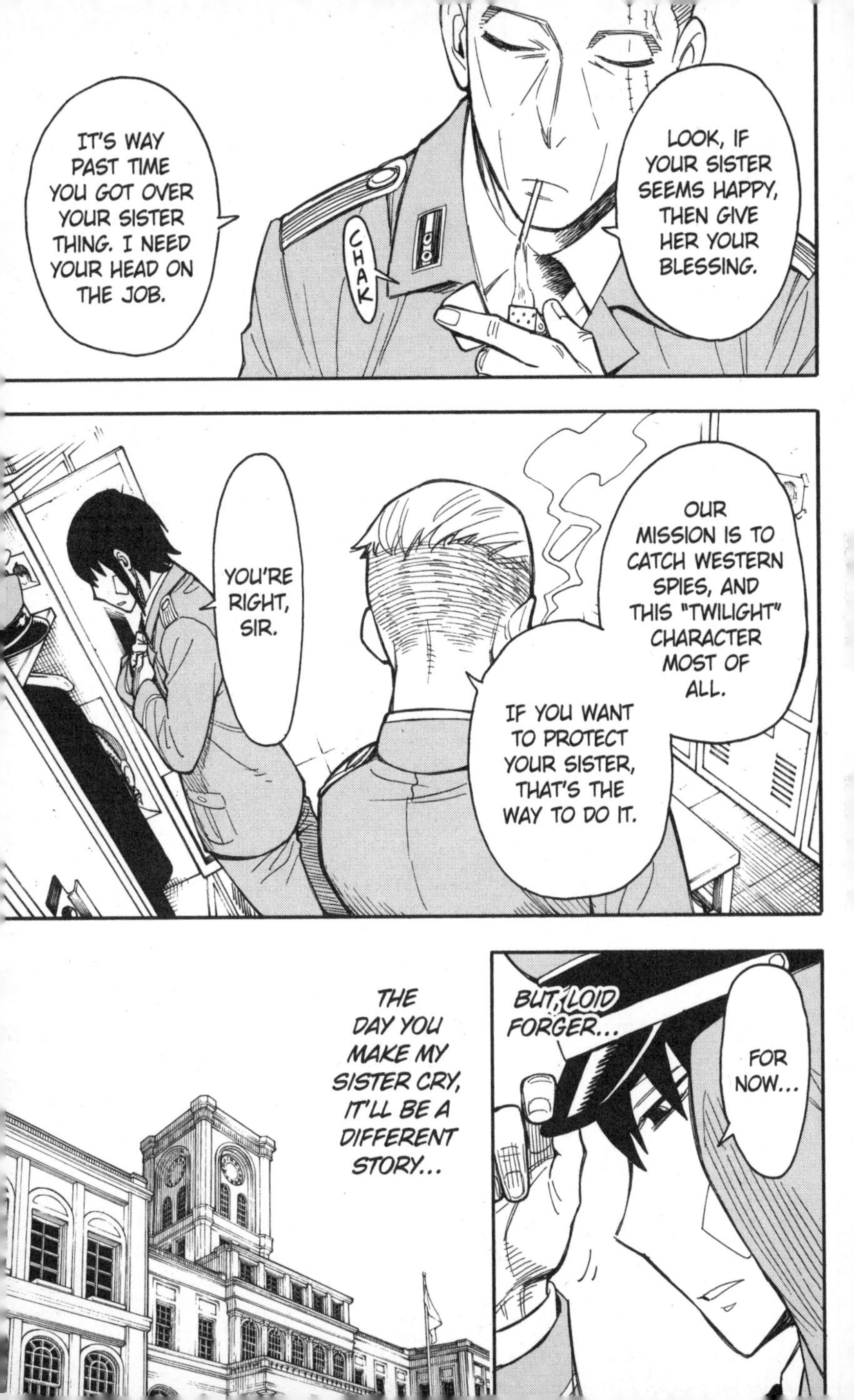
LOOK, IF YOUR SISTER SEEMS HAPPY, THEN GIVE HER YOUR BLESSING.
CHAK
IT'S WAY PAST TIME YOU GOT OVER YOUR SISTER THING. I NEED YOUR HEAD ON THE JOB.
OUR MISSION IS TO CATCH WESTERN SPIES, AND THIS "TWILIGHT" CHARACTER MOST OF ALL.
IF YOU WANT TO PROTECT YOUR SISTER, THAT'S THE WAY TO DO IT.
YOU'RE RIGHT, SIR.
FOR NOW...
BUT, LOID FORGER...
THE DAY YOU MAKE MY SISTER CRY, IT'LL BE A DIFFERENT STORY...

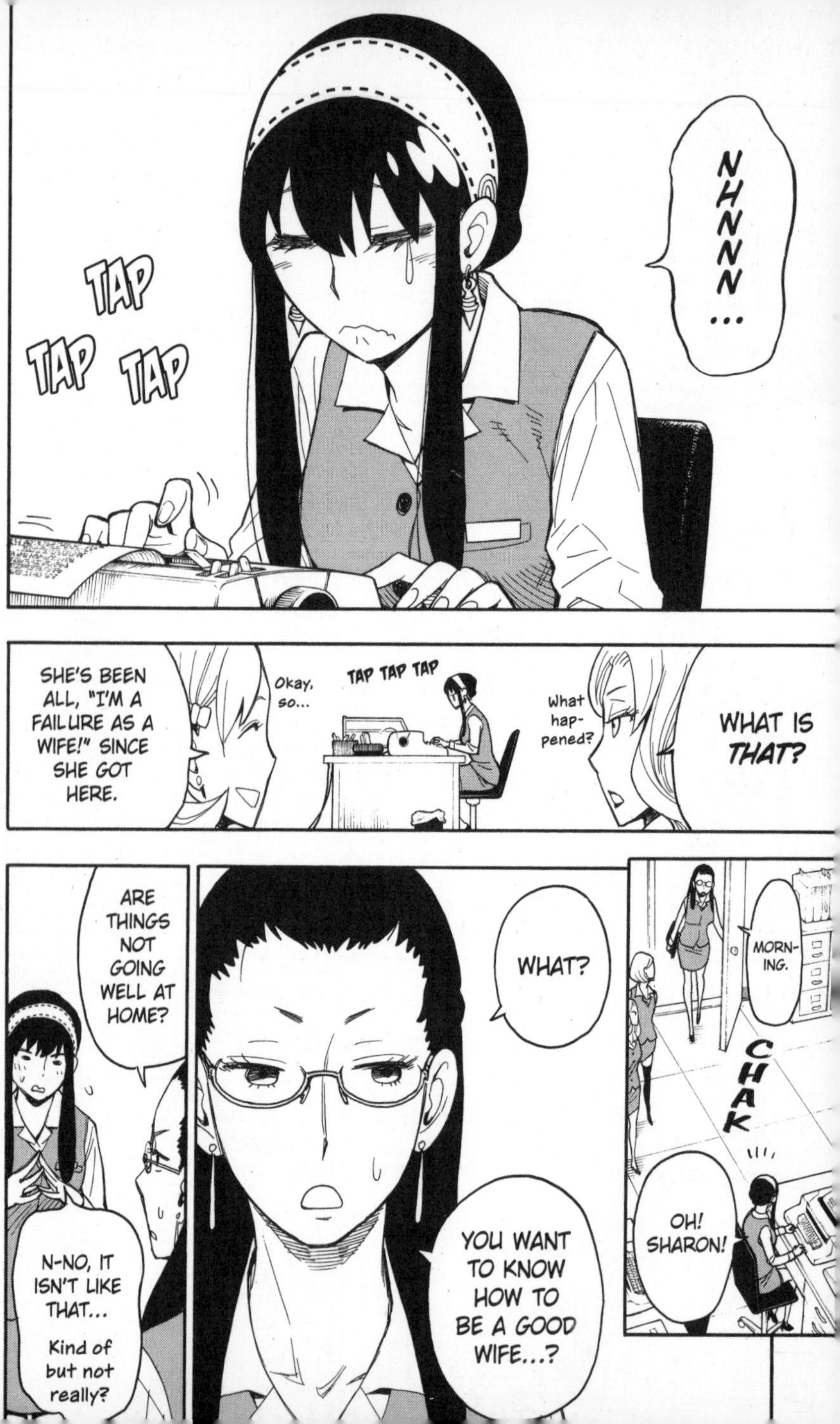
NHNNN...
TAP
TAP TAP
WHAT IS THAT?
What happened?
TAP TAP TAP
Okay, so...
SHE'S BEEN ALL, "I'M A FAILURE AS A WIFE!" SINCE SHE GOT HERE.
MORNING.
CHAK
OH! SHARON!
WHAT?
YOU WANT TO KNOW HOW TO BE A GOOD WIFE...?
ARE THINGS NOT GOING WELL AT HOME?
N-NO, IT ISN'T LIKE THAT...
Kind of but not really?

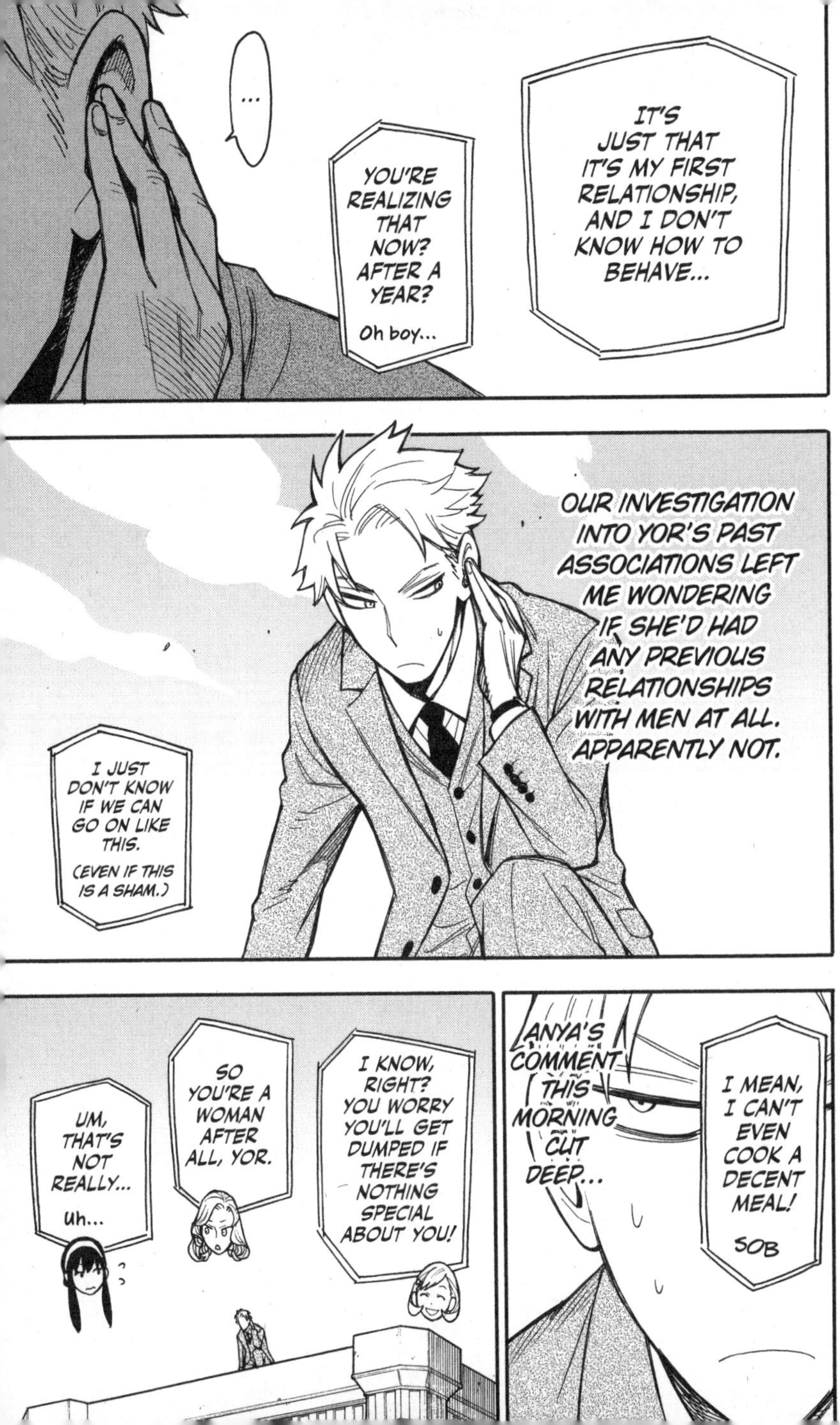
IT'S JUST THAT IT'S MY FIRST RELATIONSHIP, AND I DON'T KNOW HOW TO BEHAVE...
YOU'RE REALIZING THAT NOW? AFTER A YEAR?
Oh boy...
...
OUR INVESTIGATION INTO YOR'S PAST ASSOCIATIONS LEFT ME WONDERING IF SHE'D HAD ANY PREVIOUS RELATIONSHIPS WITH MEN AT ALL. APPARENTLY NOT.
I JUST DON'T KNOW IF WE CAN GO ON LIKE THIS.
(EVEN IF THIS IS A SHAM.)
I MEAN, I CAN'T EVEN COOK A DECENT MEAL!
SOB
ANYA'S COMMENT THIS MORNING CUT DEEP...
I KNOW, RIGHT? YOU WORRY YOU'LL GET DUMPED IF THERE'S NOTHING SPECIAL ABOUT YOU!
SO YOU'RE A WOMAN AFTER ALL, YOR.
UM, THAT'S NOT REALLY...
uh...

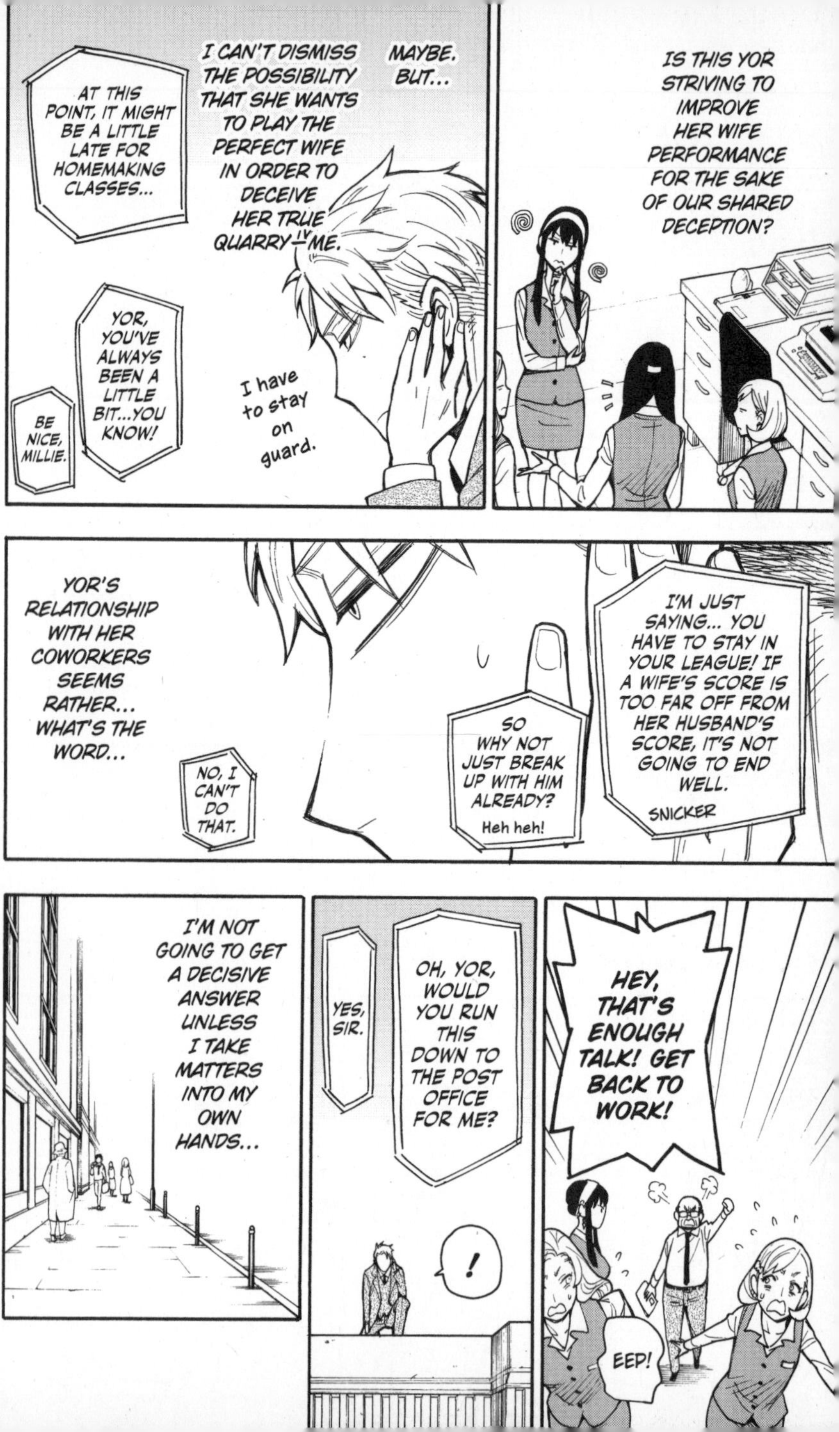
IS THIS YOR STRIVING TO IMPROVE HER WIFE PERFORMANCE FOR THE SAKE OF OUR SHARED DECEPTION?
MAYBE. BUT...
I CAN'T DISMISS THE POSSIBILITY THAT SHE WANTS TO PLAY THE PERFECT WIFE IN ORDER TO DECEIVE HER TRUE QUARRY—ME.
AT THIS POINT, IT MIGHT BE A LITTLE LATE FOR HOMEMAKING CLASSES...
YOR, YOU'VE ALWAYS BEEN A LITTLE BIT...YOU KNOW!
I have to stay on guard.
BE NICE, MILLIE.
I'M JUST SAYING... YOU HAVE TO STAY IN YOUR LEAGUE! IF A WIFE'S SCORE IS TOO FAR OFF FROM HER HUSBAND'S SCORE, IT'S NOT GOING TO END WELL.
SNICKER
SO WHY NOT JUST BREAK UP WITH HIM ALREADY?
Heh heh!
NO, I CAN'T DO THAT.
YOR'S RELATIONSHIP WITH HER COWORKERS SEEMS RATHER... WHAT'S THE WORD...
HEY, THAT'S ENOUGH TALK! GET BACK TO WORK!
EEP!
OH, YOR, WOULD YOU RUN THIS DOWN TO THE POST OFFICE FOR ME?
YES, SIR.
!
I'M NOT GOING TO GET A DECISIVE ANSWER UNLESS I TAKE MATTERS INTO MY OWN HANDS...

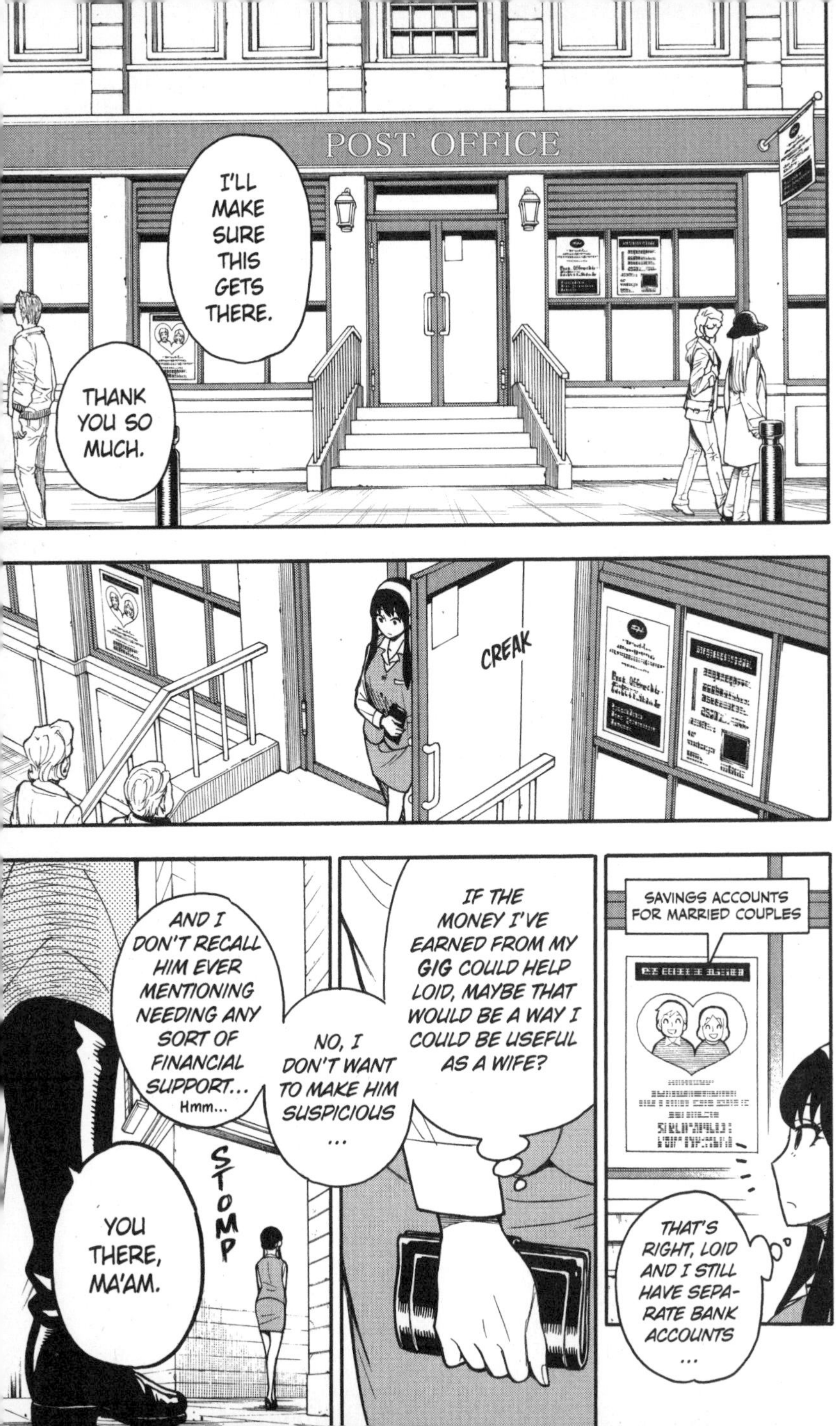
POST OFFICE
I'LL MAKE SURE THIS GETS THERE.
THANK YOU SO MUCH.
CREAK
SAVINGS ACCOUNTS FOR MARRIED COUPLES
THAT'S RIGHT, LOID AND I STILL HAVE SEPA-RATE BANK ACCOUNTS ...
IF THE MONEY I'VE EARNED FROM MY GIG COULD HELP LOID, MAYBE THAT WOULD BE A WAY I COULD BE USEFUL AS A WIFE?
NO, I DON'T WANT TO MAKE HIM SUSPICIOUS ...
AND I DON'T RECALL HIM EVER MENTIONING NEEDING ANY SORT OF FINANCIAL SUPPORT...
Hmm...
STOMP
YOU THERE, MA'AM.

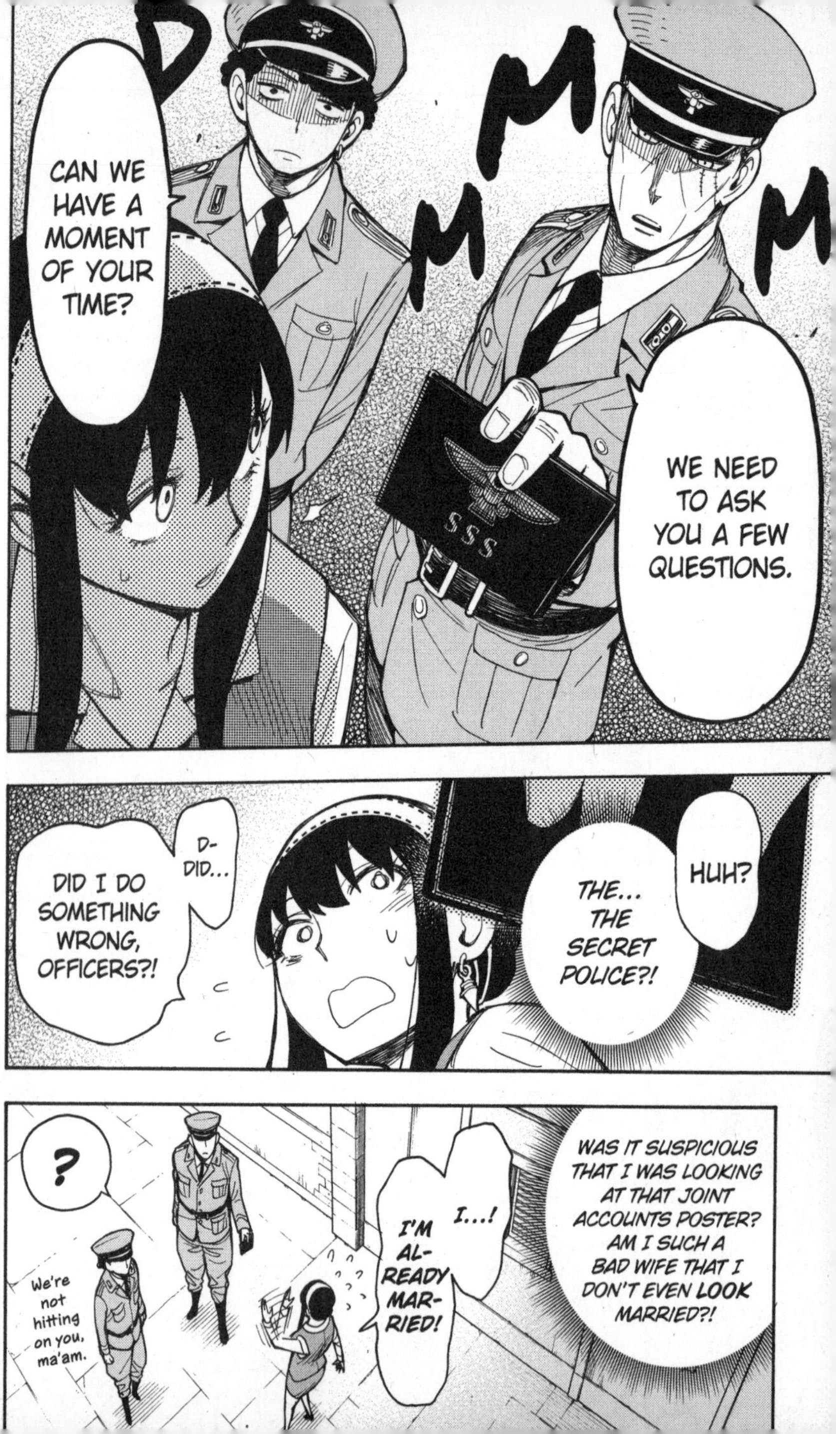
DMMMM
CAN WE HAVE A MOMENT OF YOUR TIME?
WE NEED TO ASK YOU A FEW QUESTIONS.
HUH?
THE... THE SECRET POLICE?!
D- DID...
DID I DO SOMETHING WRONG, OFFICERS?!
WAS IT SUSPICIOUS THAT I WAS LOOKING AT THAT JOINT ACCOUNTS POSTER? AM I SUCH A BAD WIFE THAT I DON'T EVEN LOOK MARRIED?!
I...!
I'M AL-READY MAR-RIED!
?
We're not hitting on you, ma'am.

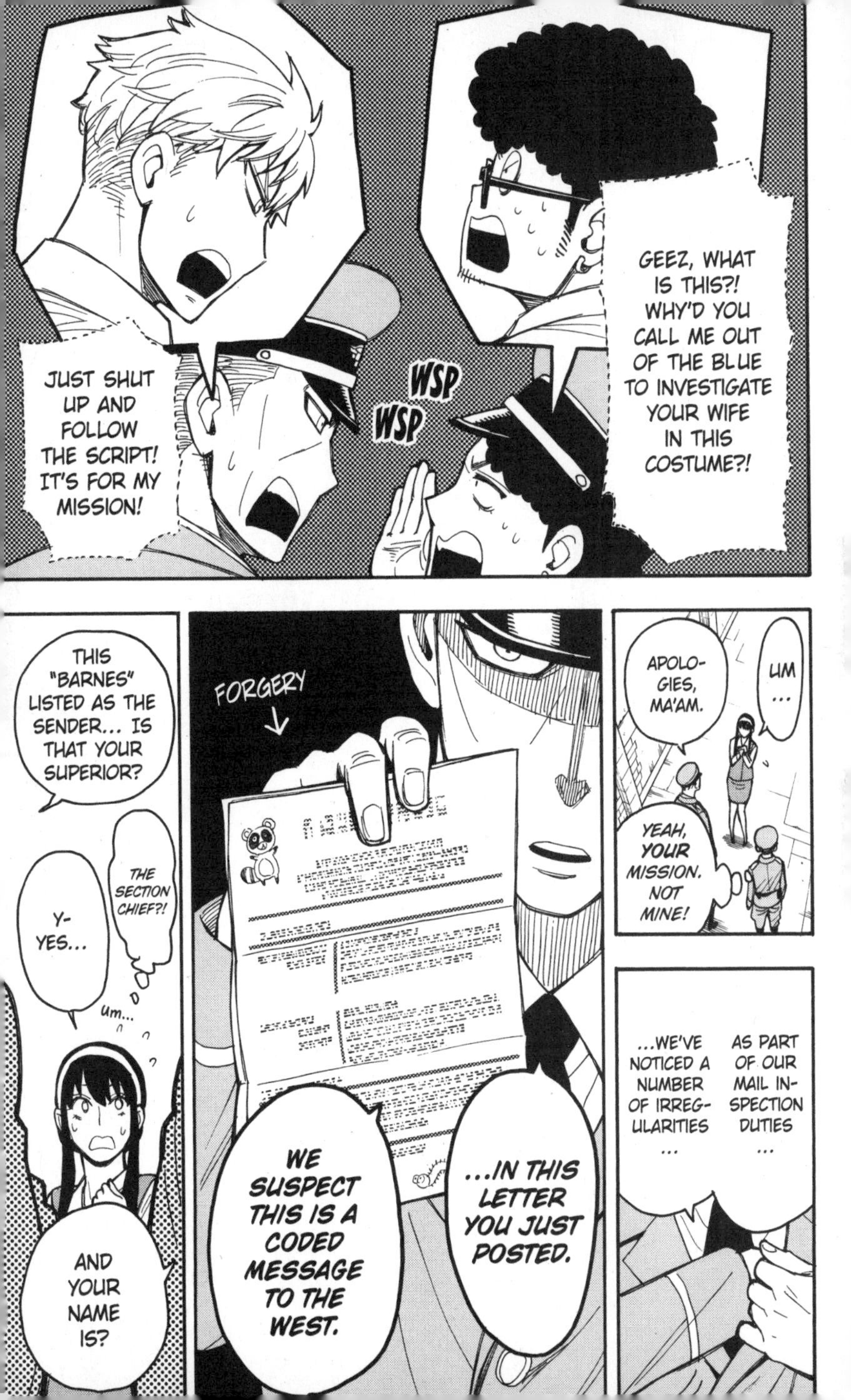
GEEZ, WHAT IS THIS?! WHY'D YOU CALL ME OUT OF THE BLUE TO INVESTIGATE YOUR WIFE IN THIS COSTUME?!
WSP
WSP
JUST SHUT UP AND FOLLOW THE SCRIPT! IT'S FOR MY MISSION!
UM...
APOLO-GIES, MA'AM.
YEAH, YOUR MISSION. NOT MINE!
AS PART OF OUR MAIL IN-SPECTION DUTIES...
...WE'VE NOTICED A NUMBER OF IRREG-ULARITIES...
FORGERY
...IN THIS LETTER YOU JUST POSTED.
WE SUSPECT THIS IS A CODED MESSAGE TO THE WEST.
THIS "BARNES" LISTED AS THE SENDER... IS THAT YOUR SUPERIOR?
THE SECTION CHIEF?!
Y-YES...
um...
AND YOUR NAME IS?

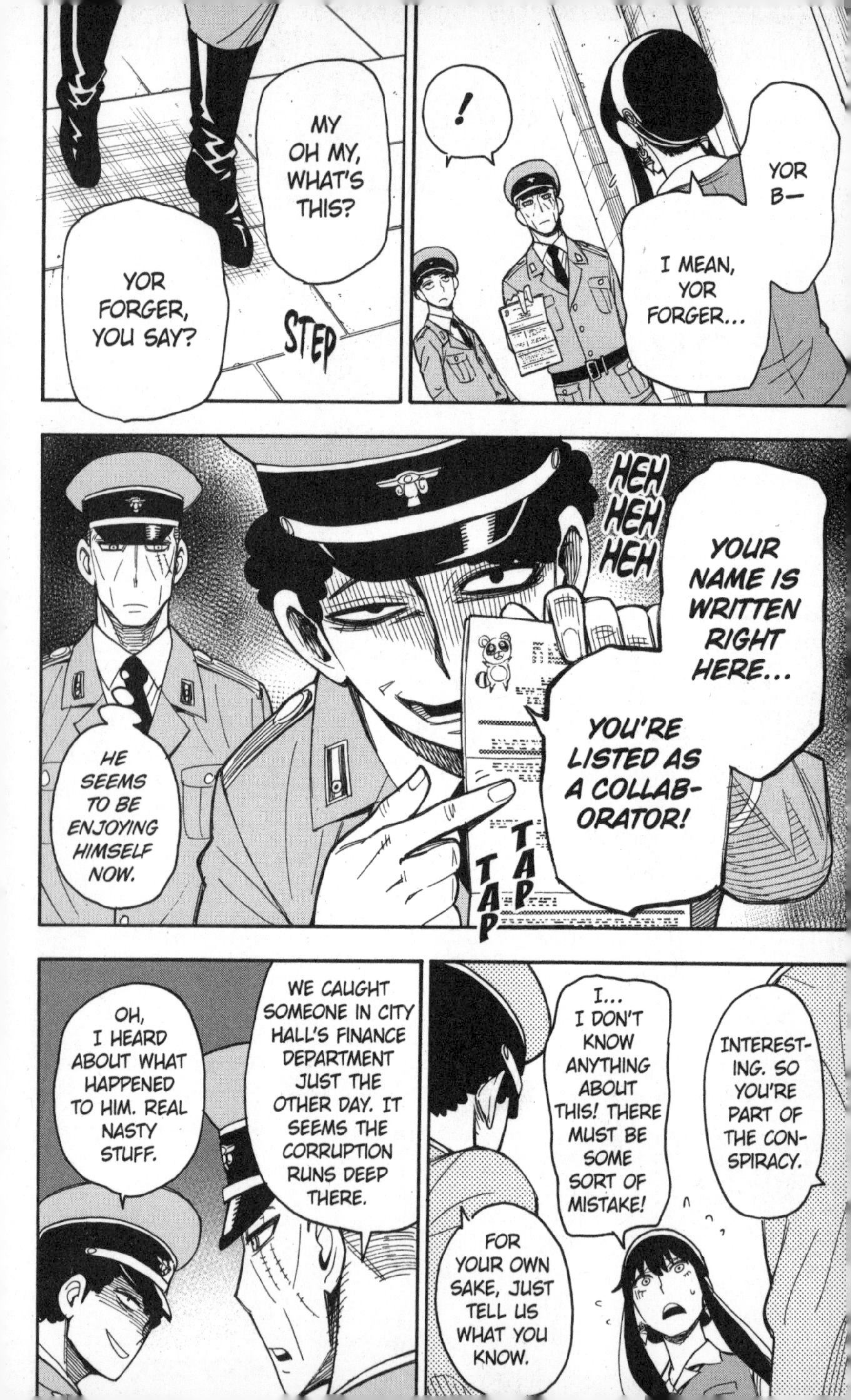
YOR B—
I MEAN, YOR FORGER...
!
MY OH MY, WHAT'S THIS?
YOR FORGER, YOU SAY?
STEP
HEH HEH HEH
YOUR NAME IS WRITTEN RIGHT HERE...
YOU'RE LISTED AS A COLLAB-ORATOR!
TAP TAP
HE SEEMS TO BE ENJOYING HIMSELF NOW.
INTEREST-ING. SO YOU'RE PART OF THE CON-SPIRACY.
I... I DON'T KNOW ANYTHING ABOUT THIS! THERE MUST BE SOME SORT OF MISTAKE!
FOR YOUR OWN SAKE, JUST TELL US WHAT YOU KNOW.
WE CAUGHT SOMEONE IN CITY HALL'S FINANCE DEPARTMENT JUST THE OTHER DAY. IT SEEMS THE CORRUPTION RUNS DEEP THERE.
OH, I HEARD ABOUT WHAT HAPPENED TO HIM. REAL NASTY STUFF.

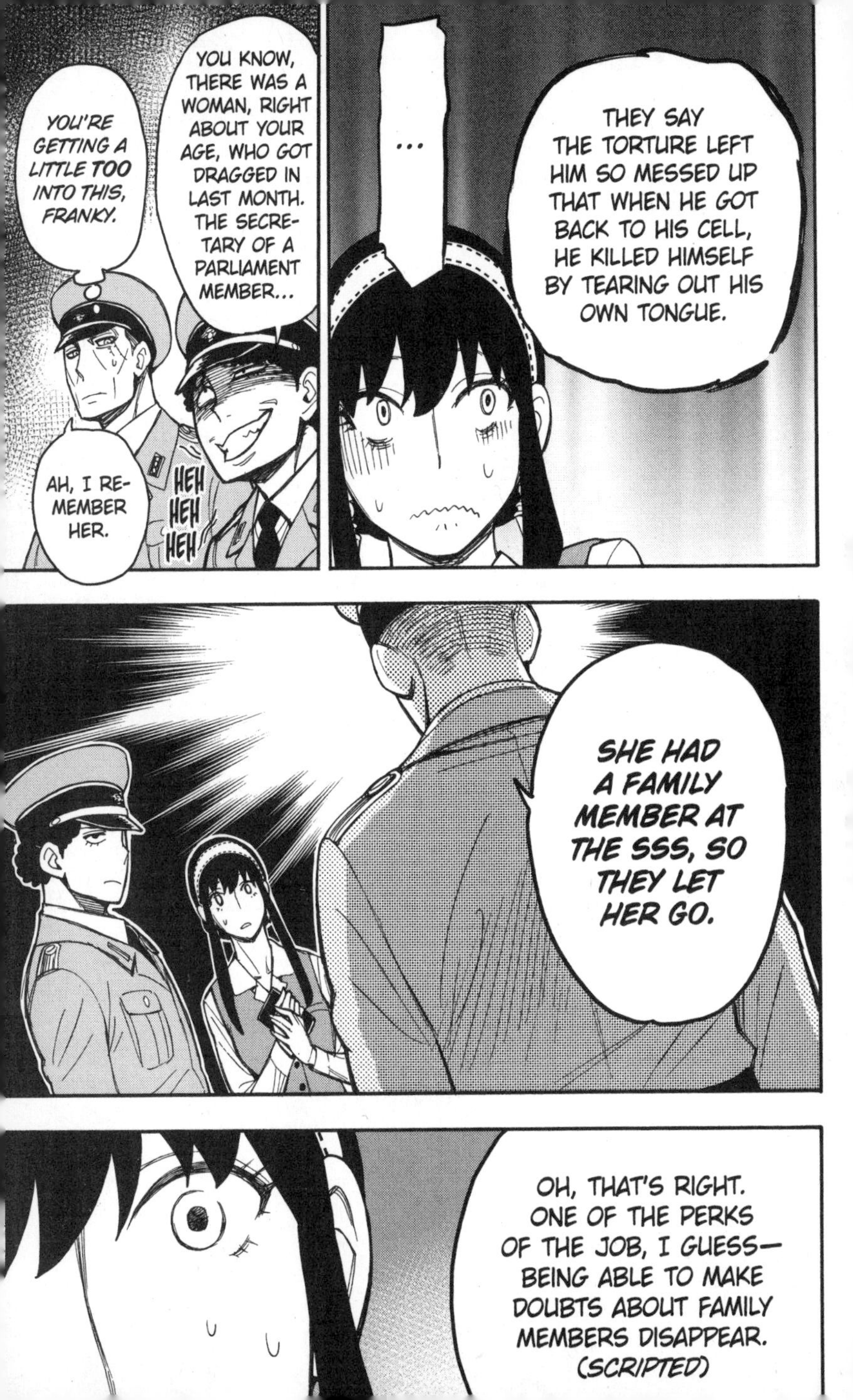
THEY SAY THE TORTURE LEFT HIM SO MESSED UP THAT WHEN HE GOT BACK TO HIS CELL, HE KILLED HIMSELF BY TEARING OUT HIS OWN TONGUE.
...
YOU KNOW, THERE WAS A WOMAN, RIGHT ABOUT YOUR AGE, WHO GOT DRAGGED IN LAST MONTH. THE SECRETARY OF A PARLIAMENT MEMBER...
YOU'RE GETTING A LITTLE TOO INTO THIS, FRANKY.
HEH HEH HEH
AH, I REMEMBER HER.
SHE HAD A FAMILY MEMBER AT THE SSS, SO THEY LET HER GO.
OH, THAT'S RIGHT. ONE OF THE PERKS OF THE JOB, I GUESS— BEING ABLE TO MAKE DOUBTS ABOUT FAMILY MEMBERS DISAPPEAR.
(SCRIPTED)

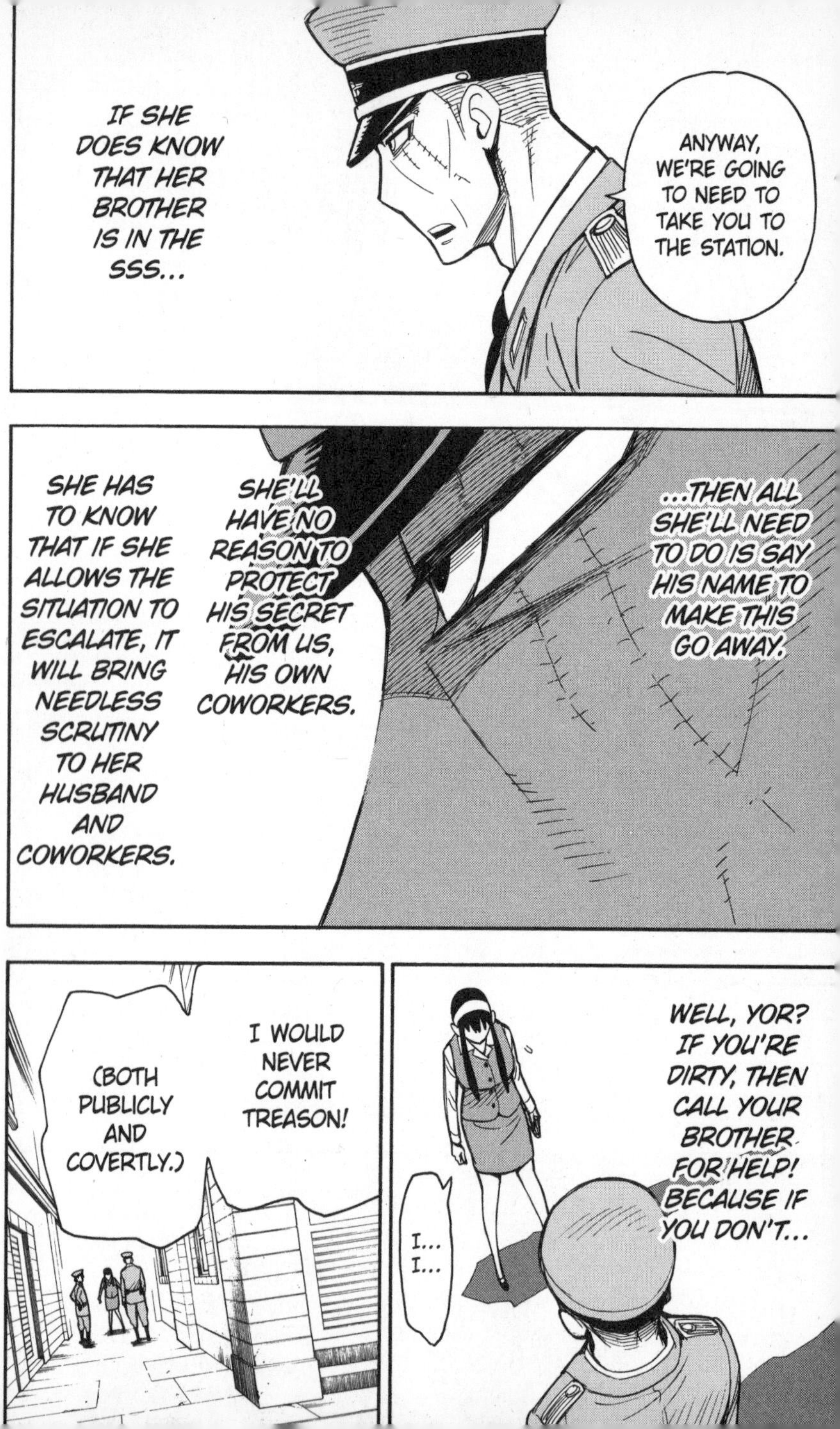
ANYWAY, WE'RE GOING TO NEED TO TAKE YOU TO THE STATION.
IF SHE DOES KNOW THAT HER BROTHER IS IN THE SSS...
...THEN ALL SHE'LL NEED TO DO IS SAY HIS NAME TO MAKE THIS GO AWAY.
SHE'LL HAVE NO REASON TO PROTECT HIS SECRET FROM US, HIS OWN COWORKERS.
SHE HAS TO KNOW THAT IF SHE ALLOWS THE SITUATION TO ESCALATE, IT WILL BRING NEEDLESS SCRUTINY TO HER HUSBAND AND COWORKERS.
WELL, YOR? IF YOU'RE DIRTY, THEN CALL YOUR BROTHER FOR HELP! BECAUSE IF YOU DON'T...
I... I...
I WOULD NEVER COMMIT TREASON!
(BOTH PUBLICLY AND COVERTLY.)

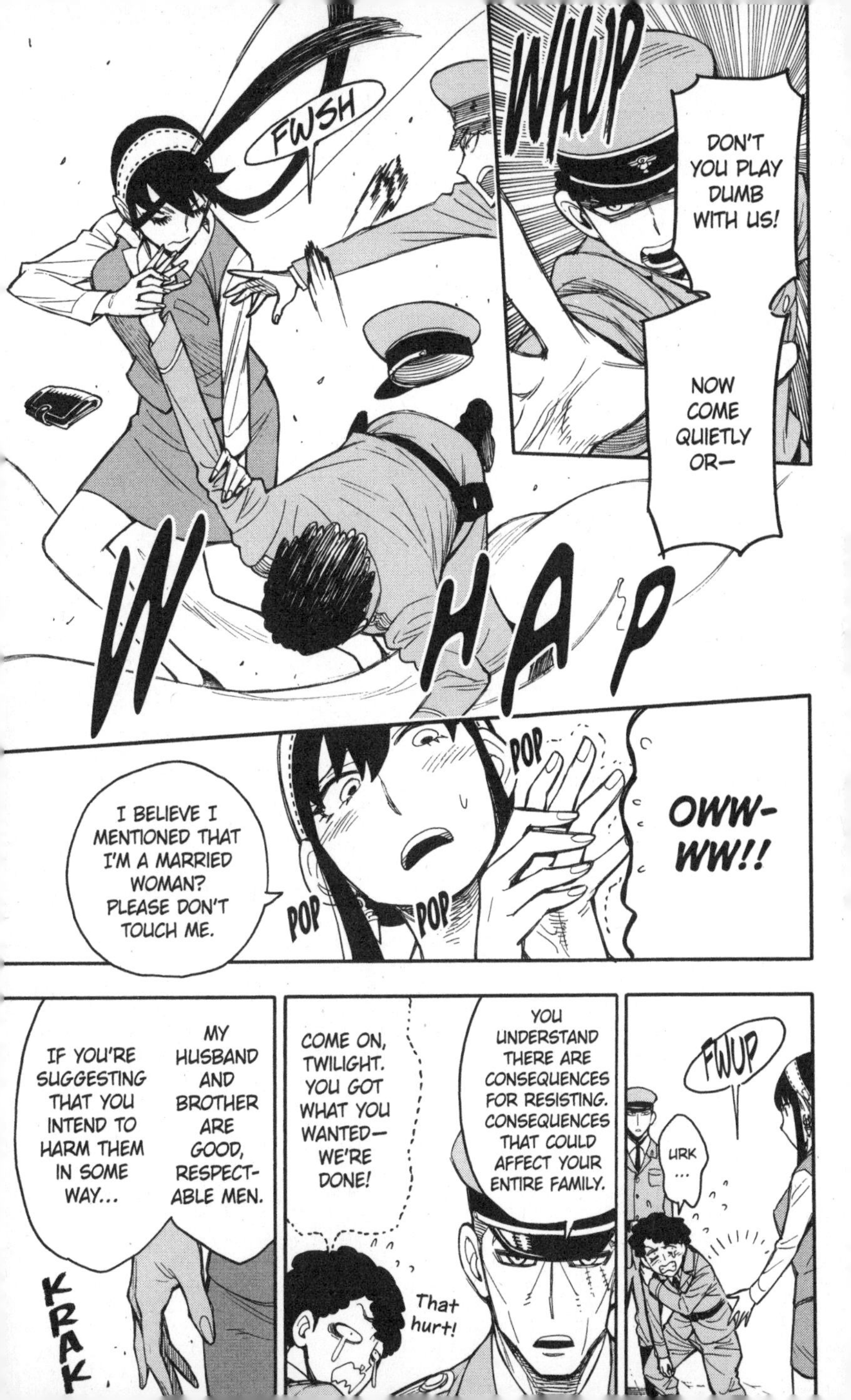
WHUP
DON'T YOU PLAY DUMB WITH US!
NOW COME QUIETLY OR—
FWSH
WHAP
OWW-WW!!
POP
POP
POP
I BELIEVE I MENTIONED THAT I'M A MARRIED WOMAN? PLEASE DON'T TOUCH ME.
FWUP
URK...
YOU UNDERSTAND THERE ARE CONSEQUENCES FOR RESISTING. CONSEQUENCES THAT COULD AFFECT YOUR ENTIRE FAMILY.
COME ON, TWILIGHT. YOU GOT WHAT YOU WANTED— WE'RE DONE!
That hurt!
MY HUSBAND AND BROTHER ARE GOOD, RESPECT-ABLE MEN.
IF YOU'RE SUGGESTING THAT YOU INTEND TO HARM THEM IN SOME WAY...
KRAK

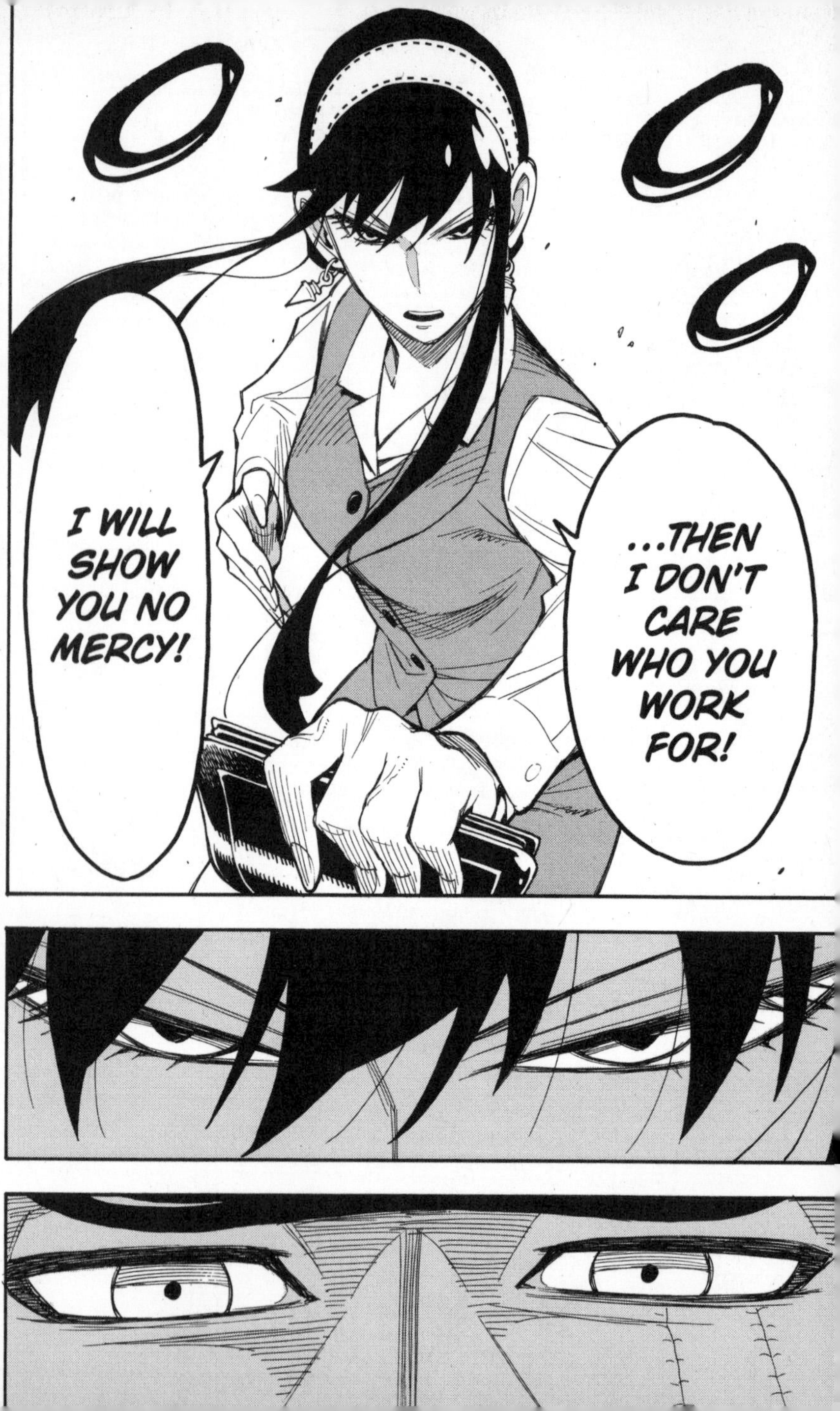
...THEN I DON'T CARE WHO YOU WORK FOR!
I WILL SHOW YOU NO MERCY!

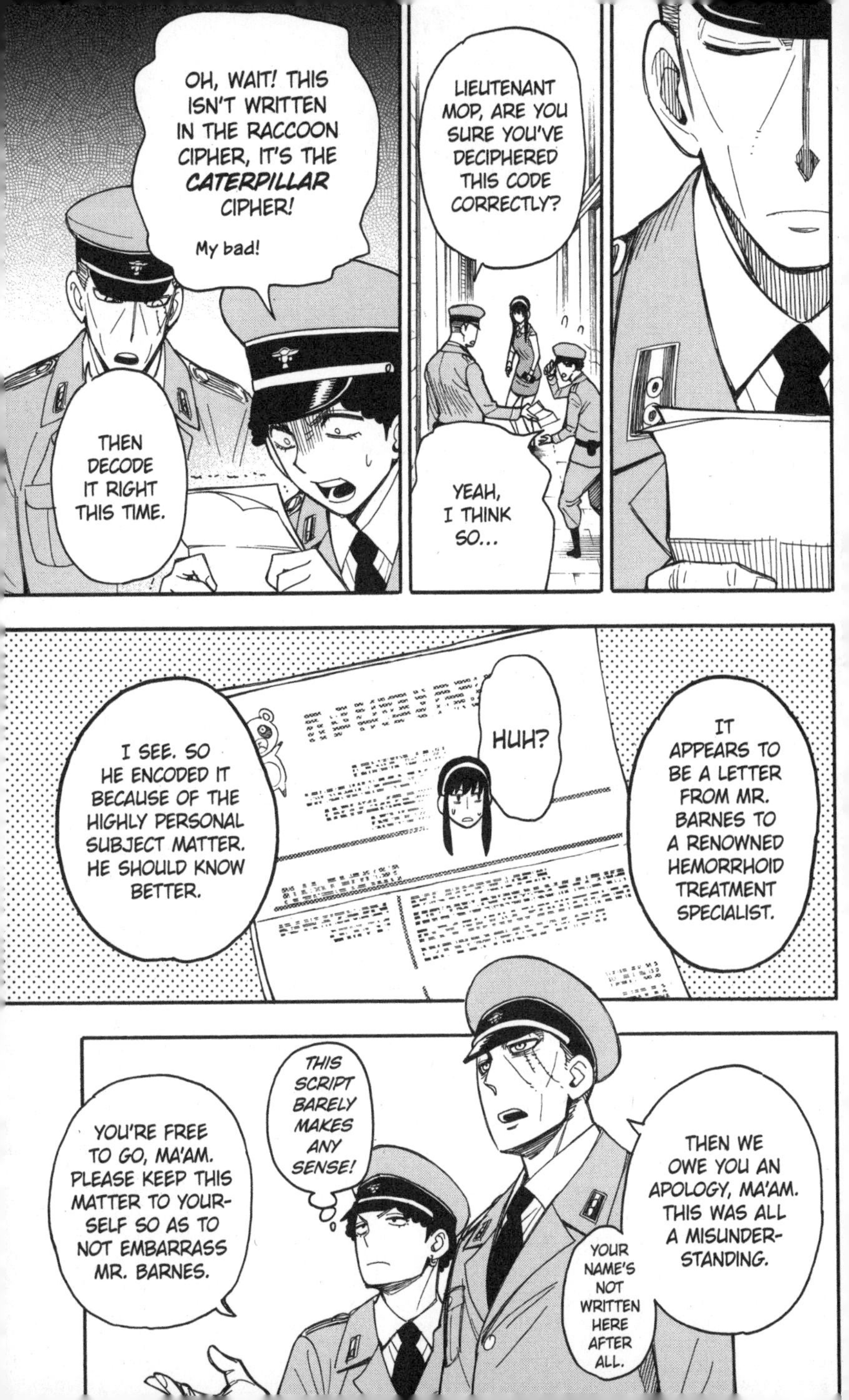
LIEUTENANT MOP, ARE YOU SURE YOU'VE DECIPHERED THIS CODE CORRECTLY?
YEAH, I THINK SO...
OH, WAIT! THIS ISN'T WRITTEN IN THE RACCOON CIPHER, IT'S THE CATERPILLAR CIPHER!
My bad!
THEN DECODE IT RIGHT THIS TIME.
IT APPEARS TO BE A LETTER FROM MR. BARNES TO A RENOWNED HEMORRHOID TREATMENT SPECIALIST.
HUH?
I SEE. SO HE ENCODED IT BECAUSE OF THE HIGHLY PERSONAL SUBJECT MATTER. HE SHOULD KNOW BETTER.
THEN WE OWE YOU AN APOLOGY, MA'AM. THIS WAS ALL A MISUNDER-STANDING.
YOUR NAME'S NOT WRITTEN HERE AFTER ALL.
THIS SCRIPT BARELY MAKES ANY SENSE!
YOU'RE FREE TO GO, MA'AM. PLEASE KEEP THIS MATTER TO YOUR-SELF SO AS TO NOT EMBARRASS MR. BARNES.

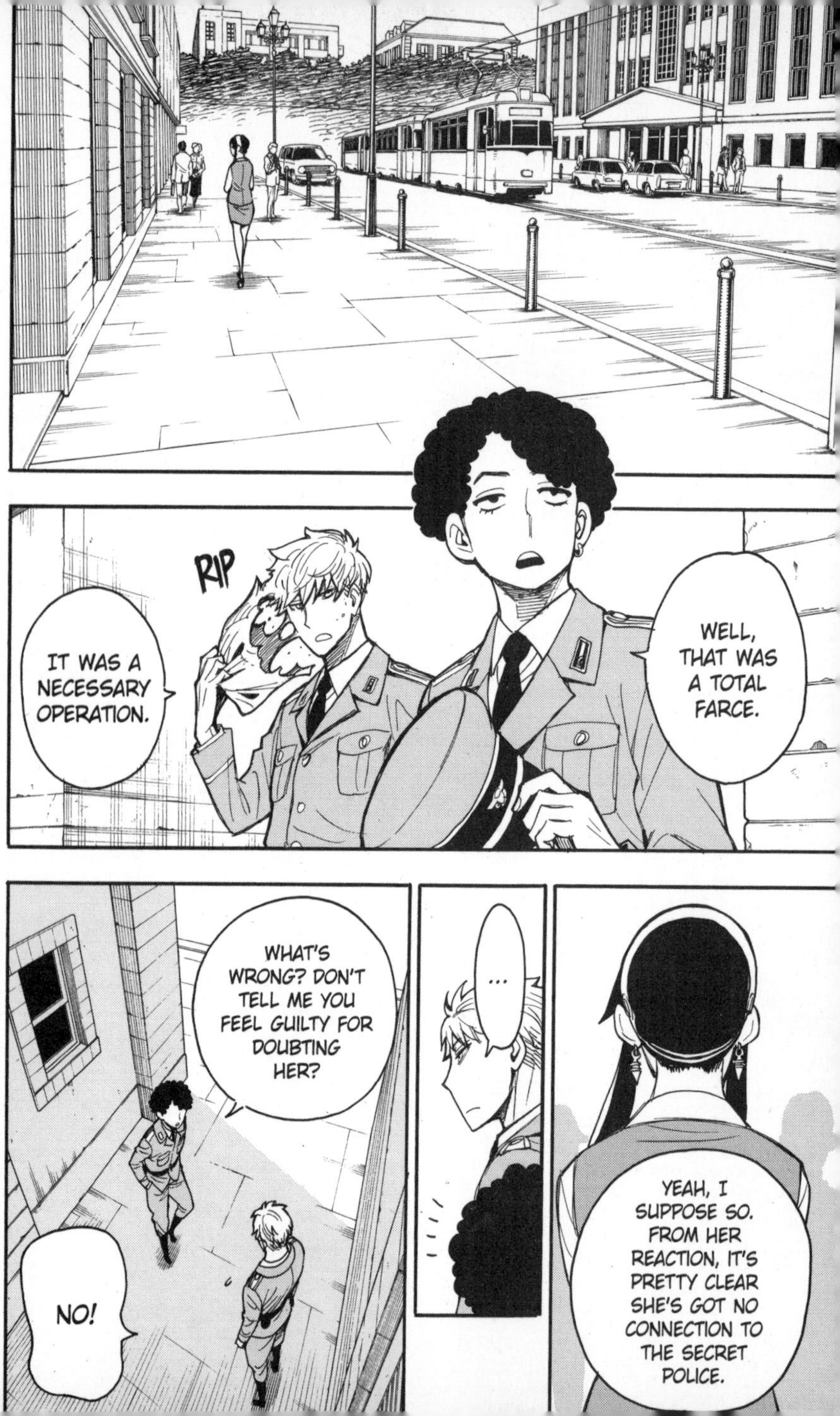
WELL, THAT WAS A TOTAL FARCE.
RIP
IT WAS A NECESSARY OPERATION.
YEAH, I SUPPOSE SO. FROM HER REACTION, IT'S PRETTY CLEAR SHE'S GOT NO CONNECTION TO THE SECRET POLICE.
...
WHAT'S WRONG? DON'T TELL ME YOU FEEL GUILTY FOR DOUBTING HER?
NO!

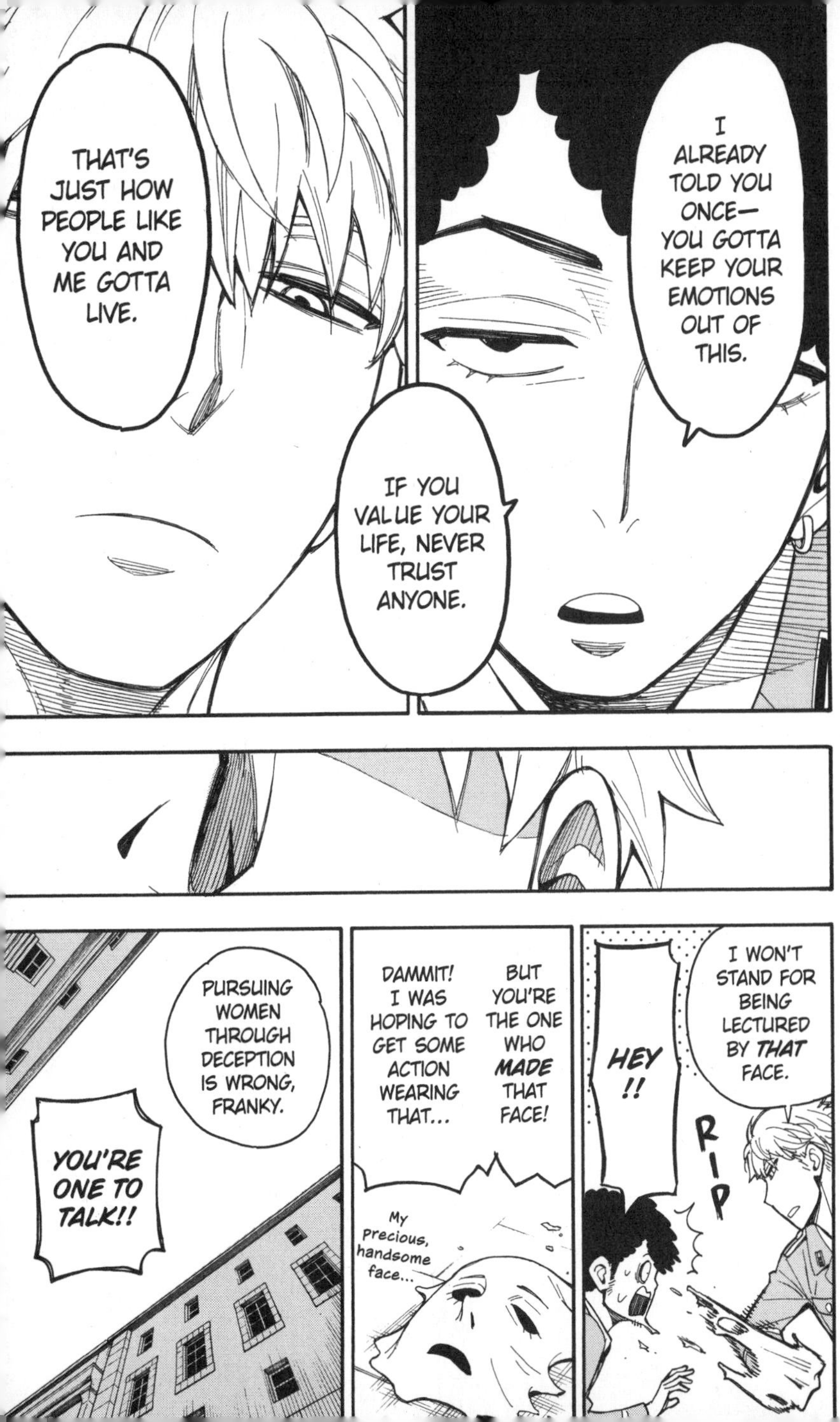
I ALREADY TOLD YOU ONCE—YOU GOTTA KEEP YOUR EMOTIONS OUT OF THIS.
IF YOU VALUE YOUR LIFE, NEVER TRUST ANYONE.
THAT'S JUST HOW PEOPLE LIKE YOU AND ME GOTTA LIVE.
I WON'T STAND FOR BEING LECTURED BY *THAT* FACE.
HEY!!
RIP
BUT YOU'RE THE ONE WHO *MADE* THAT FACE!
DAMMIT! I WAS HOPING TO GET SOME ACTION WEARING THAT...
My precious, handsome face...
PURSUING WOMEN THROUGH DECEPTION IS WRONG, FRANKY.
YOU'RE ONE TO TALK!!

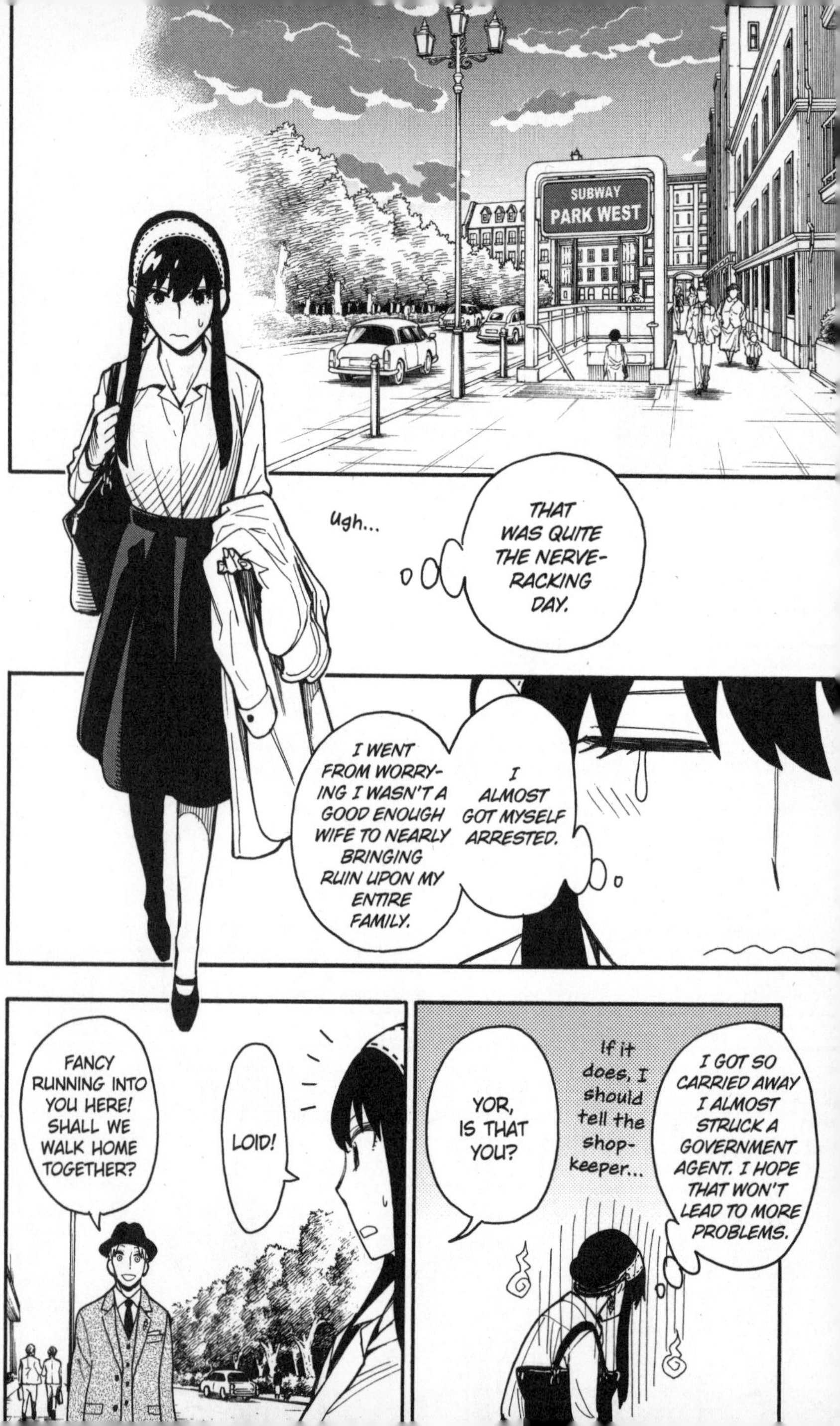
SUBWAY
PARK WEST
THAT WAS QUITE THE NERVE-RACKING DAY.
Ugh...
I ALMOST GOT MYSELF ARRESTED.
I WENT FROM WORRYING I WASN'T A GOOD ENOUGH WIFE TO NEARLY BRINGING RUIN UPON MY ENTIRE FAMILY.
I GOT SO CARRIED AWAY I ALMOST STRUCK A GOVERNMENT AGENT. I HOPE THAT WON'T LEAD TO MORE PROBLEMS.
If it does, I should tell the shop-keeper...
YOR, IS THAT YOU?
LOID!
FANCY RUNNING INTO YOU HERE! SHALL WE WALK HOME TOGETHER?

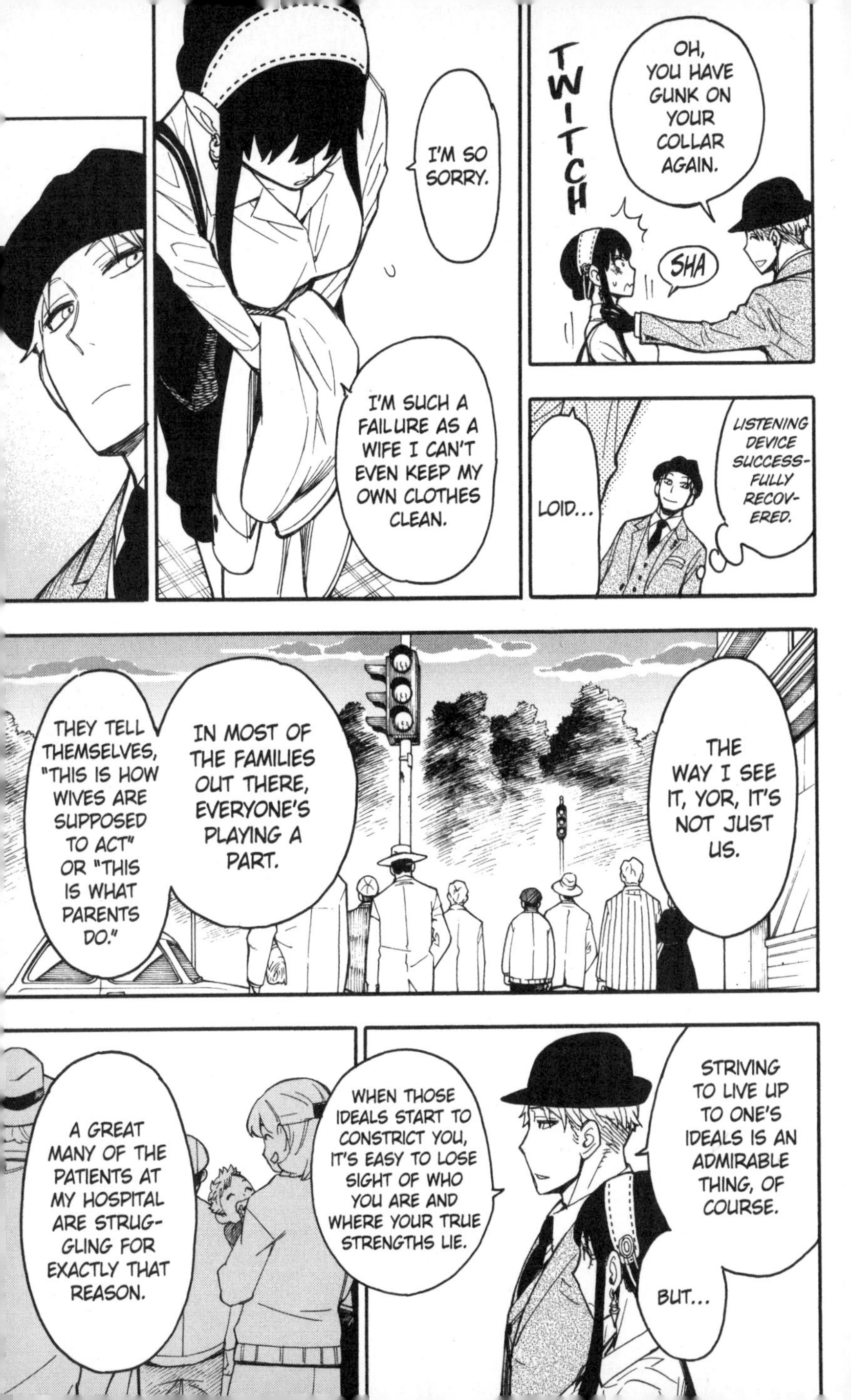
OH, YOU HAVE GUNK ON YOUR COLLAR AGAIN.
TWITCH
SHA
LISTENING DEVICE SUCCESSFULLY RECOVERED.
LOID...
I'M SO SORRY.
I'M SUCH A FAILURE AS A WIFE I CAN'T EVEN KEEP MY OWN CLOTHES CLEAN.
THE WAY I SEE IT, YOR, IT'S NOT JUST US.
IN MOST OF THE FAMILIES OUT THERE, EVERYONE'S PLAYING A PART.
THEY TELL THEMSELVES, "THIS IS HOW WIVES ARE SUPPOSED TO ACT" OR "THIS IS WHAT PARENTS DO."
STRIVING TO LIVE UP TO ONE'S IDEALS IS AN ADMIRABLE THING, OF COURSE.
BUT...
WHEN THOSE IDEALS START TO CONSTRICT YOU, IT'S EASY TO LOSE SIGHT OF WHO YOU ARE AND WHERE YOUR TRUE STRENGTHS LIE.
A GREAT MANY OF THE PATIENTS AT MY HOSPITAL ARE STRUGGLING FOR EXACTLY THAT REASON.

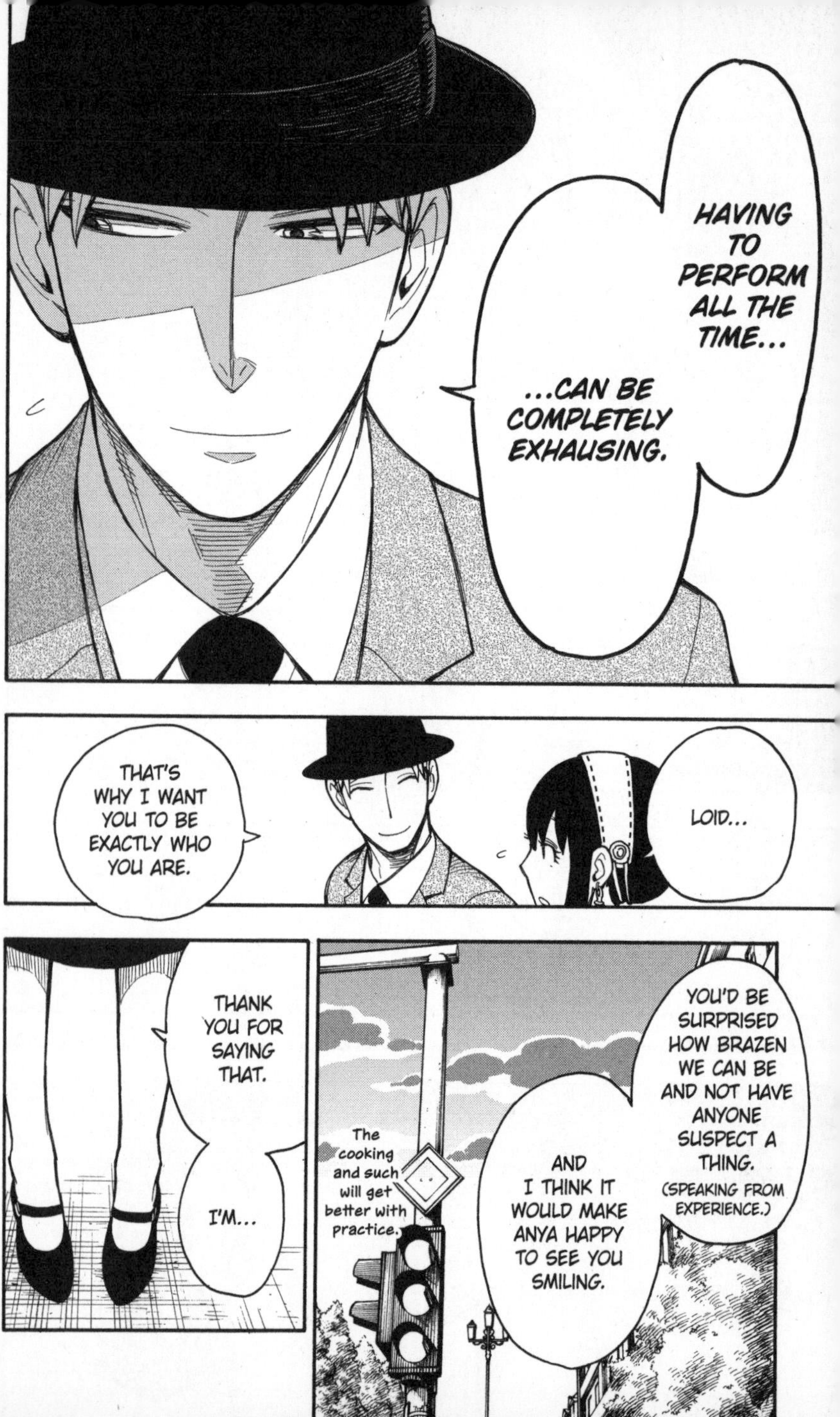
HAVING TO PERFORM ALL THE TIME...
...CAN BE COMPLETELY EXHAUSING.
LOID...
THAT'S WHY I WANT YOU TO BE EXACTLY WHO YOU ARE.
YOU'D BE SURPRISED HOW BRAZEN WE CAN BE AND NOT HAVE ANYONE SUSPECT A THING.
(SPEAKING FROM EXPERIENCE.)
AND I THINK IT WOULD MAKE ANYA HAPPY TO SEE YOU SMILING.
The cooking and such will get better with practice.
THANK YOU FOR SAYING THAT.
I'M...

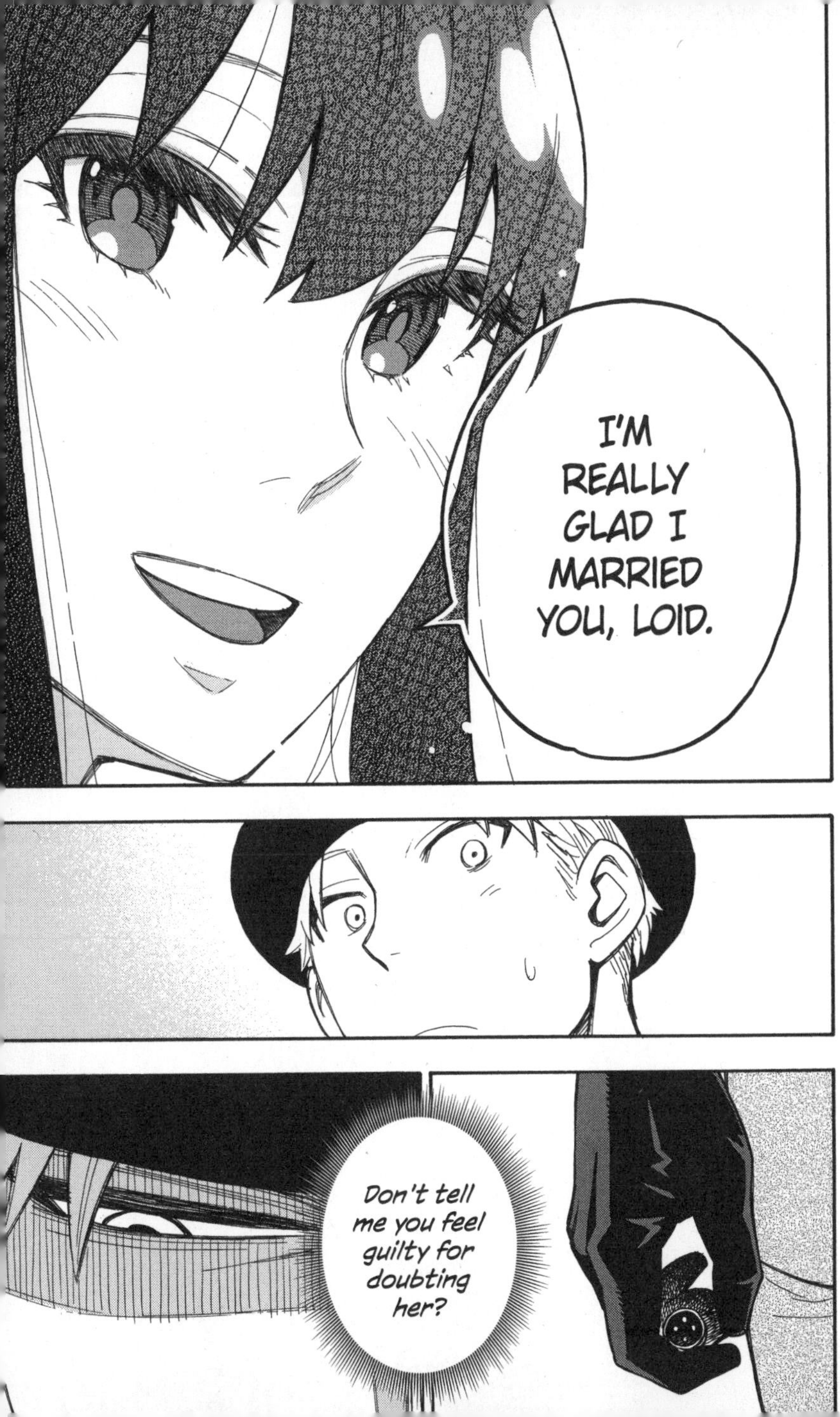
I'M REALLY GLAD I MARRIED YOU, LOID.
Don't tell me you feel guilty for doubting her?

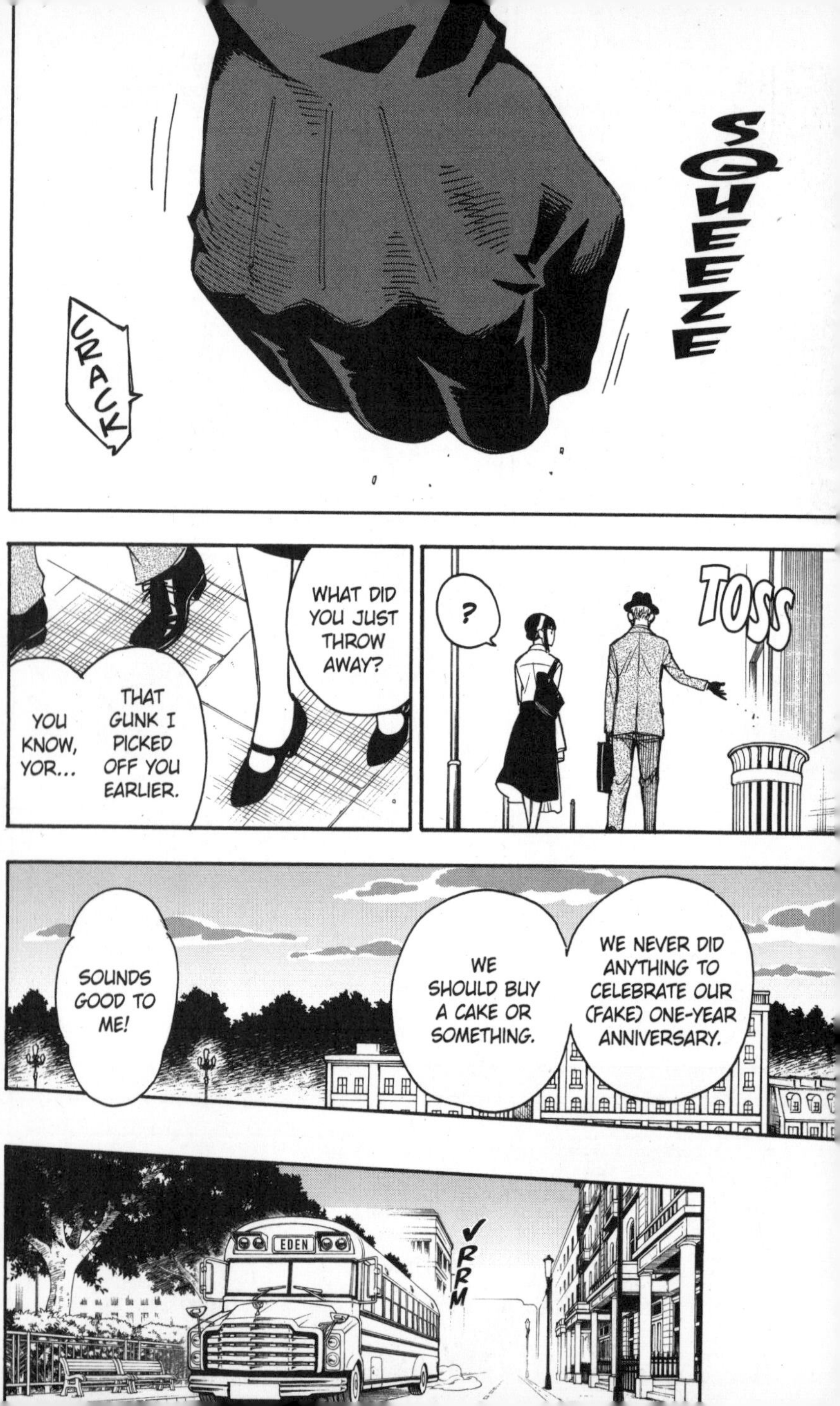
SQUEEZE
CRACK
TOSS
?
WHAT DID YOU JUST THROW AWAY?
THAT GUNK I PICKED OFF YOU EARLIER.
YOU KNOW, YOR...
WE NEVER DID ANYTHING TO CELEBRATE OUR (FAKE) ONE-YEAR ANNIVERSARY.
WE SHOULD BUY A CAKE OR SOMETHING.
SOUNDS GOOD TO ME!
EDEN
VRRM

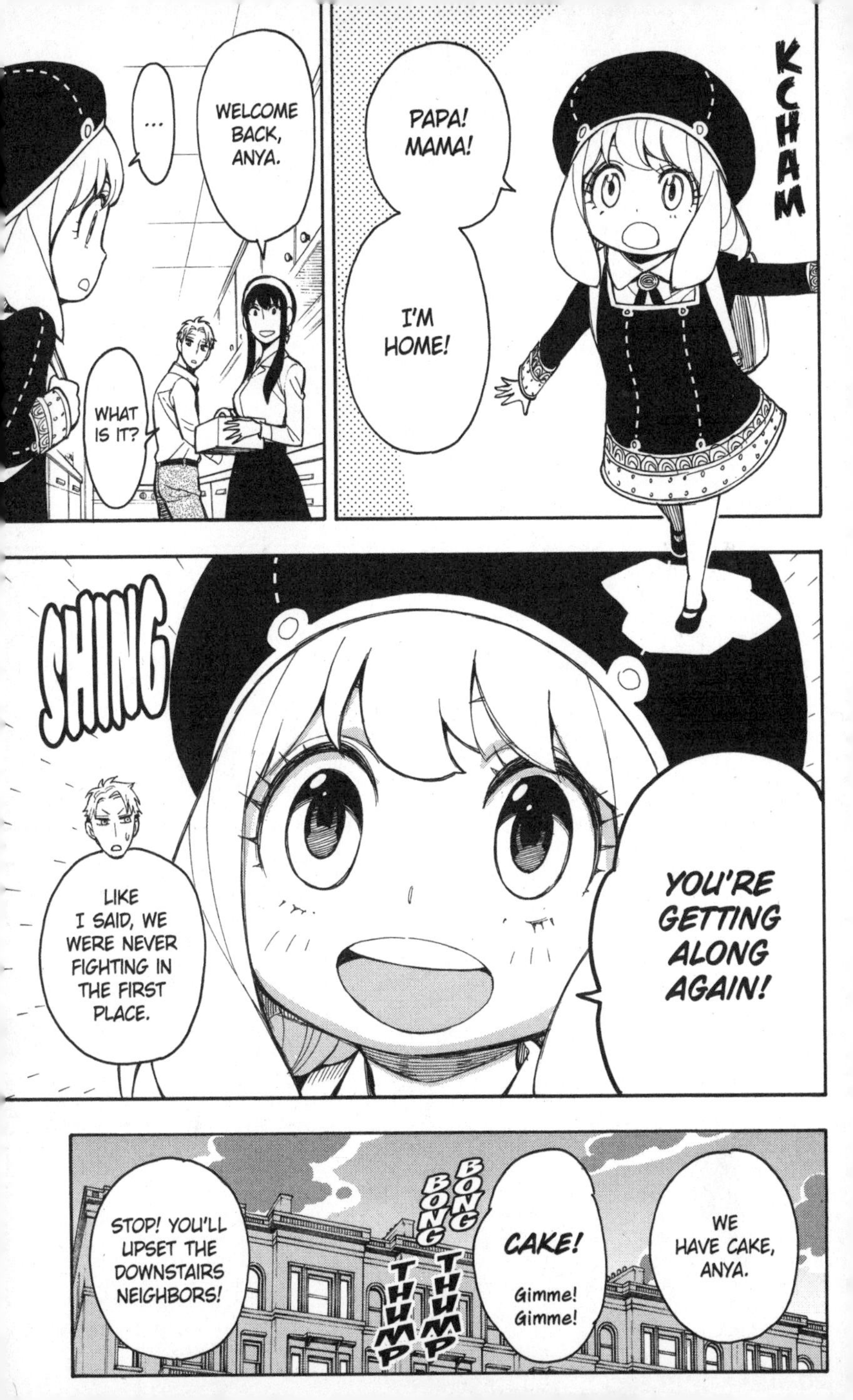
KCHAM
PAPA! MAMA!
I'M HOME!
WELCOME BACK, ANYA.
...
WHAT IS IT?
SHING
YOU'RE GETTING ALONG AGAIN!
LIKE I SAID, WE WERE NEVER FIGHTING IN THE FIRST PLACE.
WE HAVE CAKE, ANYA.
CAKE!
Gimme! Gimme!
BONG BONG
THUMP THUMP
BONG
THUMP
STOP! YOU'LL UPSET THE DOWNSTAIRS NEIGHBORS!

SPY×FAMILY

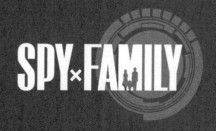

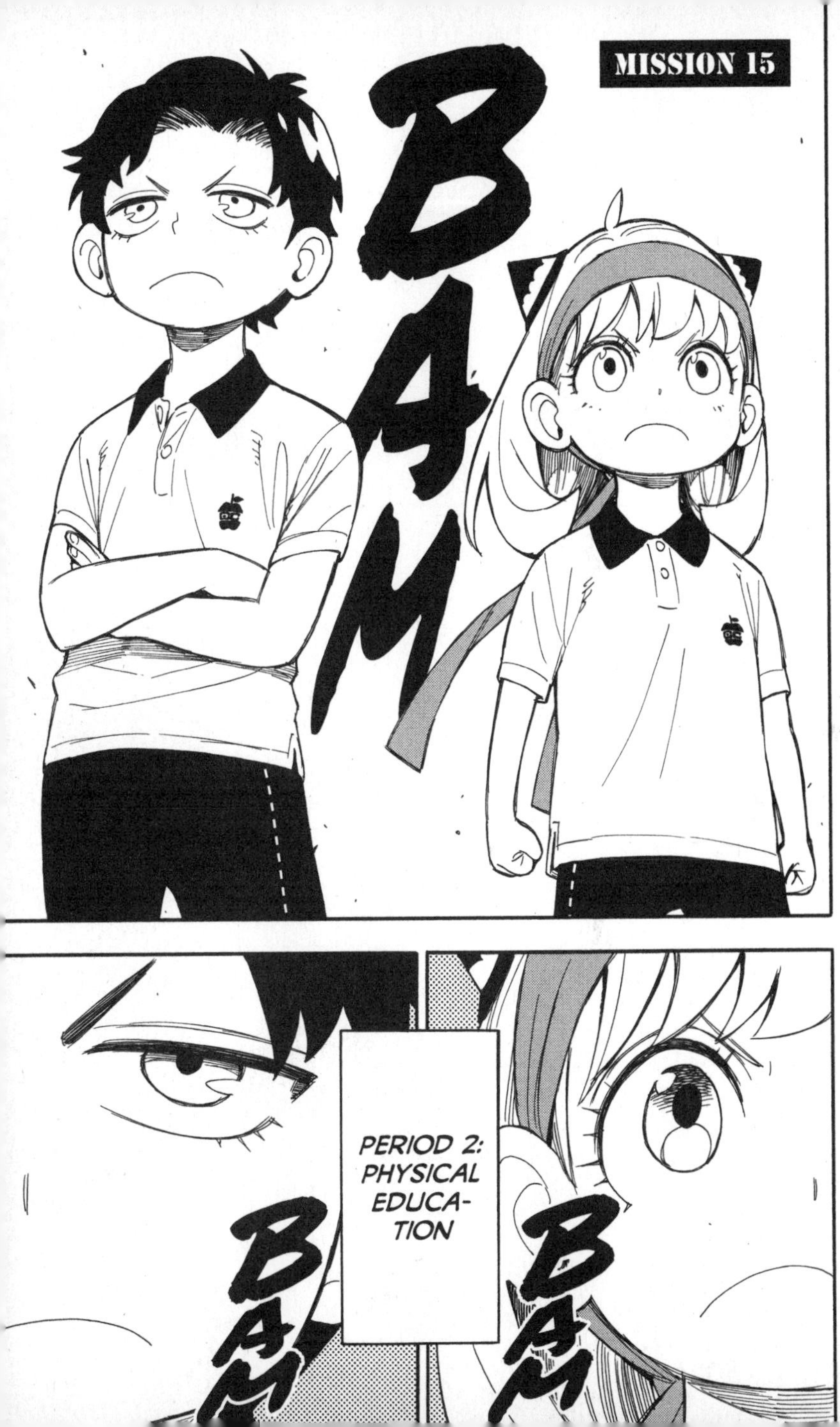
MISSION 15
BAM
BAM
PERIOD 2: PHYSICAL EDUCA- TION
BAM

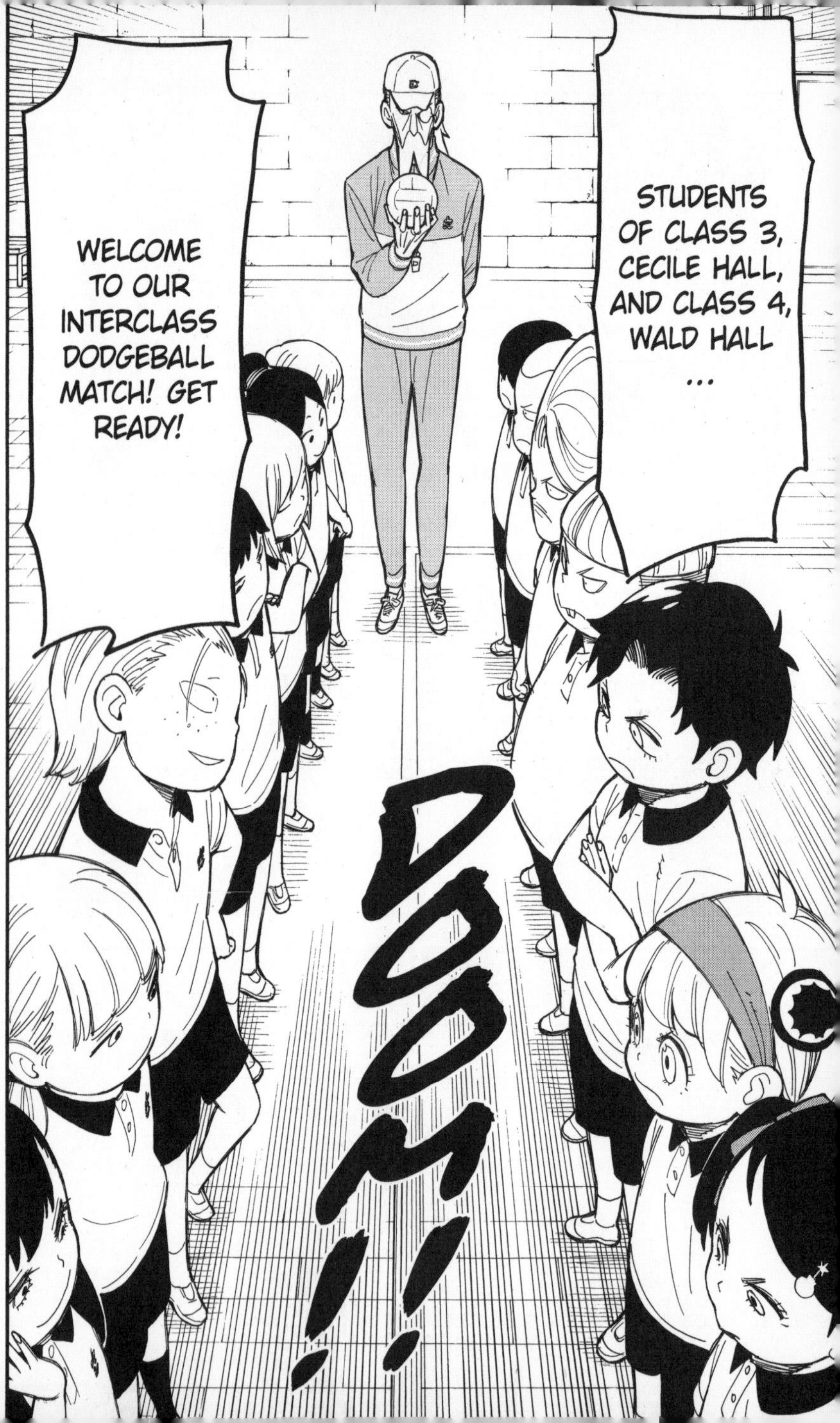
STUDENTS OF CLASS 3, CECILE HALL, AND CLASS 4, WALD HALL ...
WELCOME TO OUR INTERCLASS DODGEBALL MATCH! GET READY!
DOOM!!

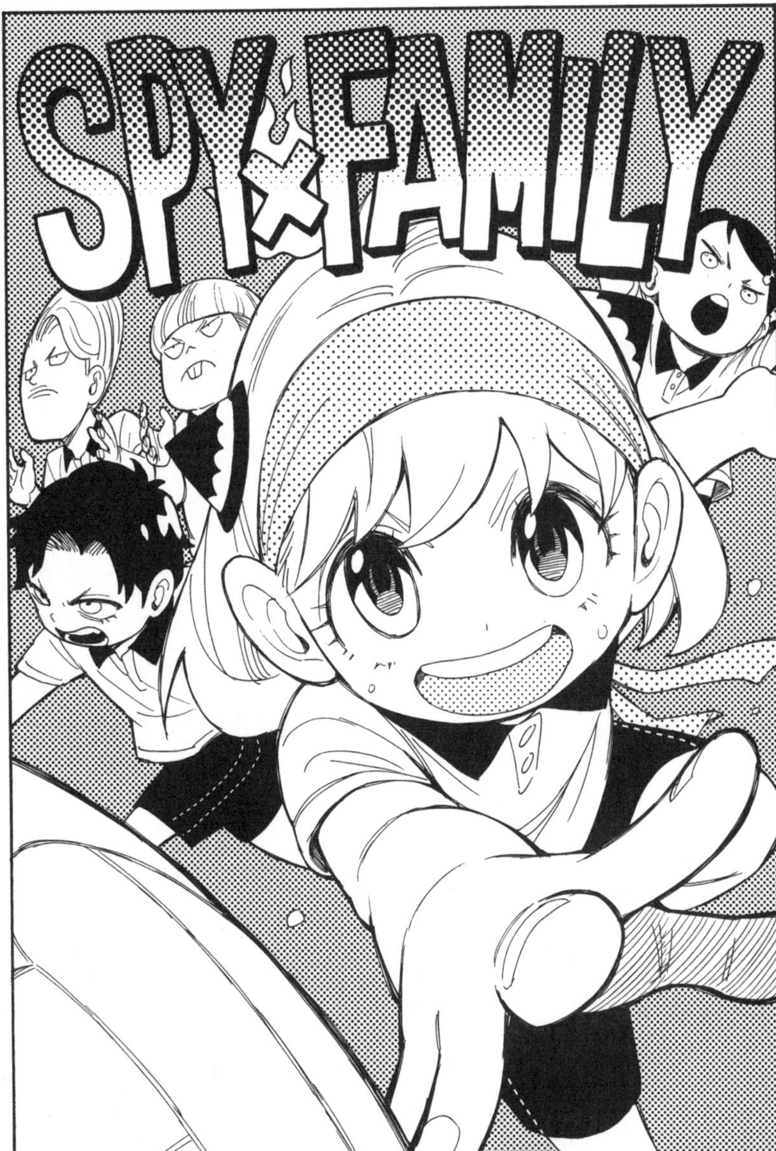
SPY×FAMILY

MISSION 15

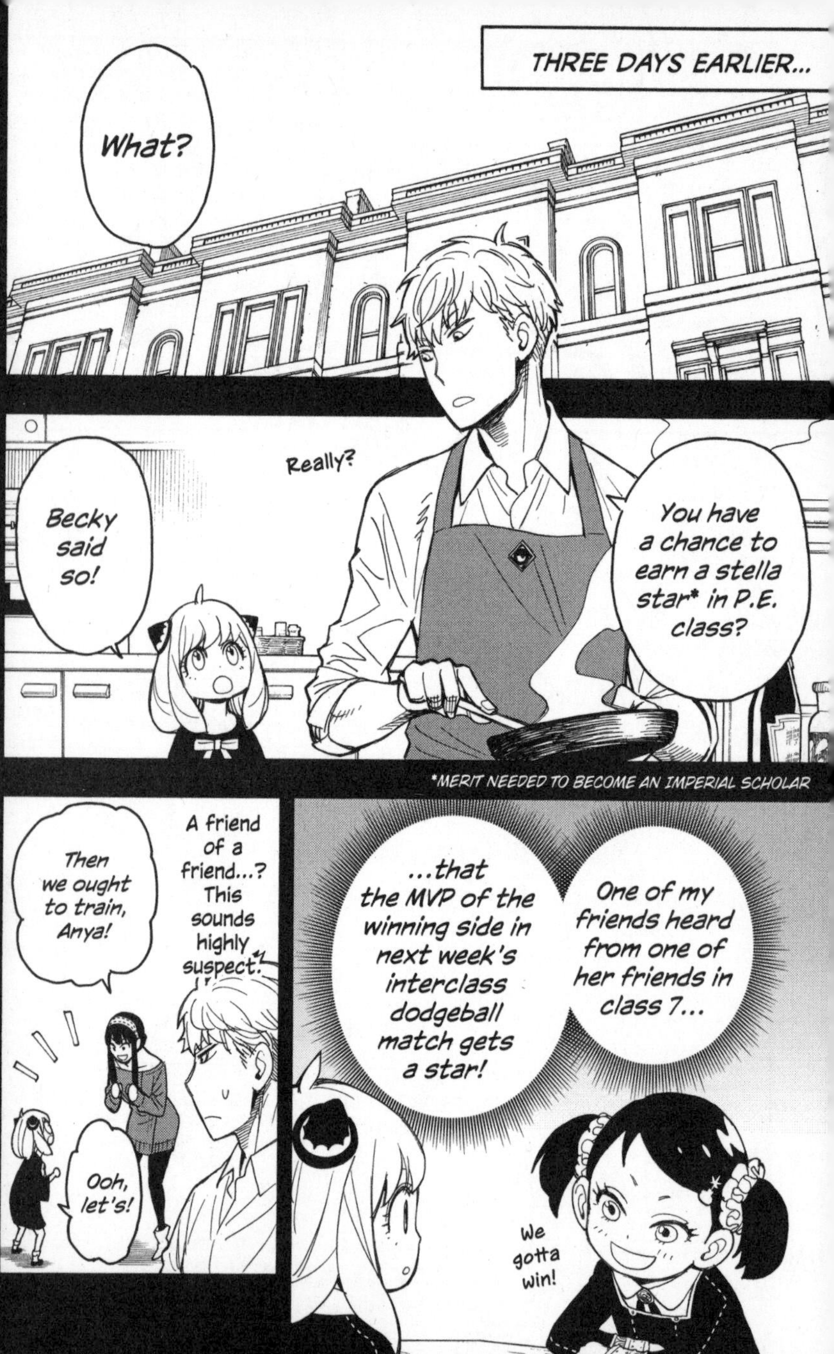
THREE DAYS EARLIER...
What?
You have a chance to earn a stella star* in P.E. class?
Really?
Becky said so!
*MERIT NEEDED TO BECOME AN IMPERIAL SCHOLAR
One of my friends heard from one of her friends in class 7...
...that the MVP of the winning side in next week's interclass dodgeball match gets a star!
We gotta win!
A friend of a friend...? This sounds highly suspect.
Then we ought to train, Anya!
Ooh, let's!

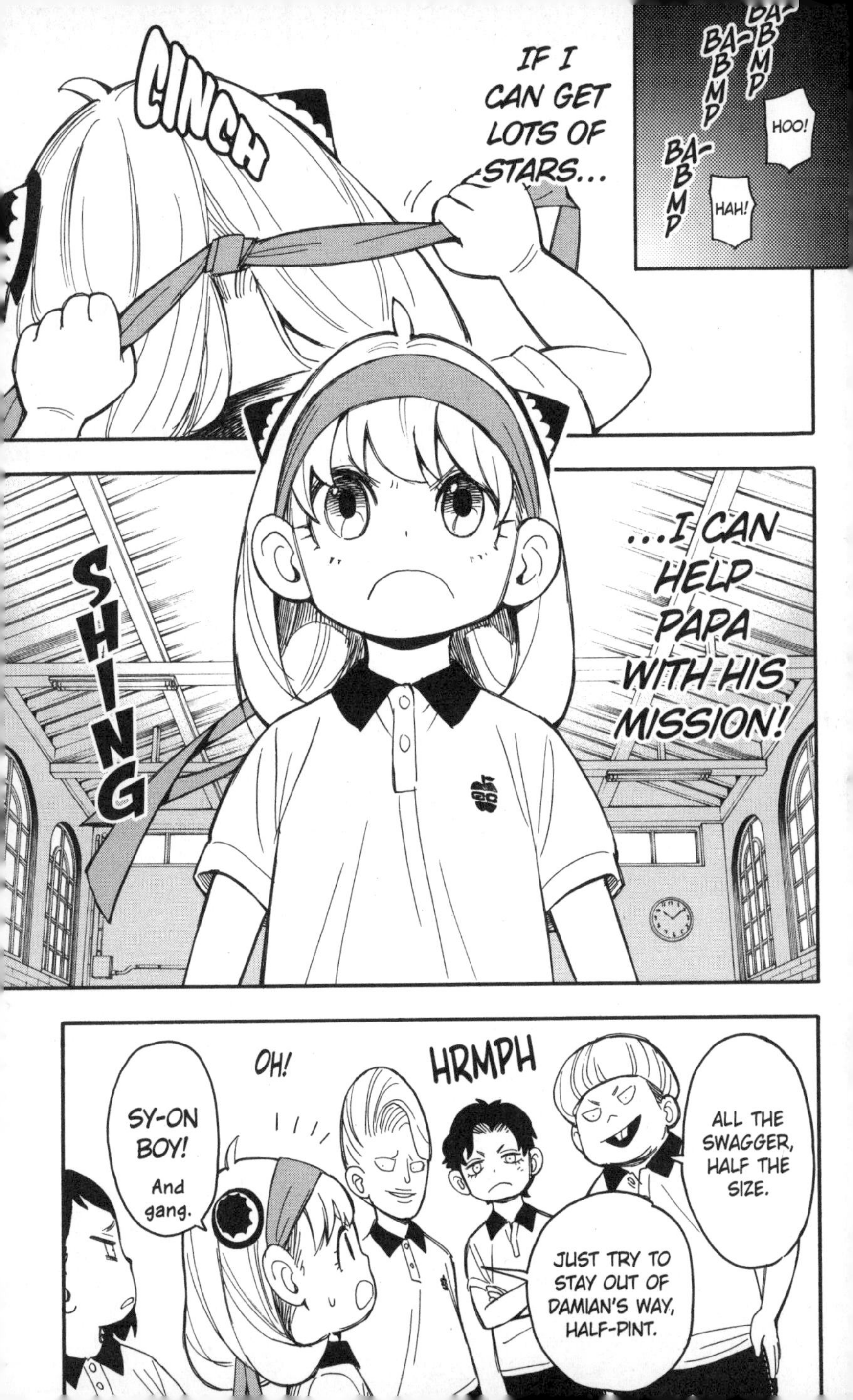
BA-BUMP
BA-BUMP
BA-BUMP
HOO!
HAH!
CINCH
IF I CAN GET LOTS OF STARS...
...I CAN HELP PAPA WITH HIS MISSION!
SHING
ALL THE SWAGGER, HALF THE SIZE.
JUST TRY TO STAY OUT OF DAMIAN'S WAY, HALF-PINT.
HRMPH
OH!
SY-ON BOY!
And gang.

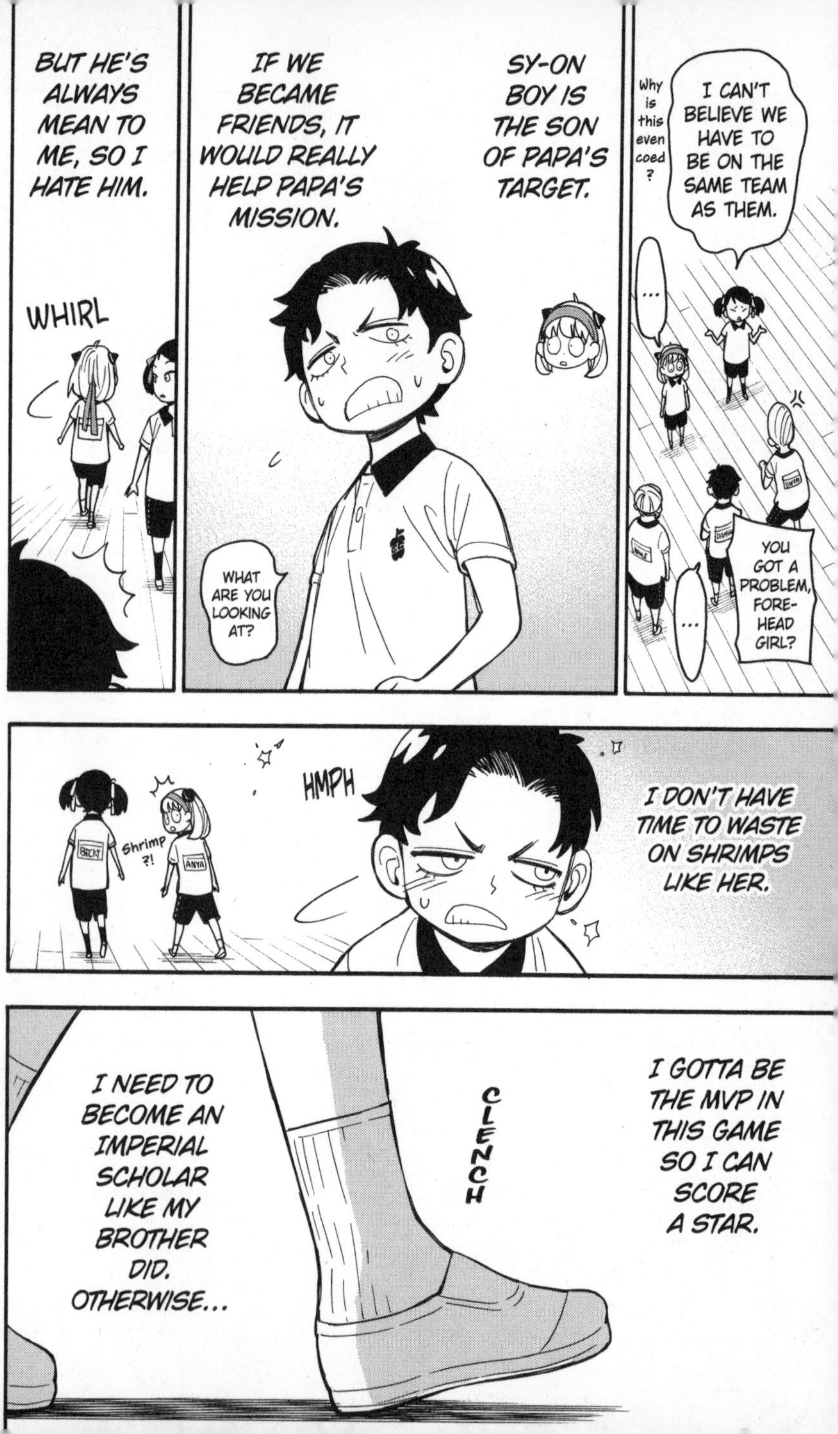
I CAN'T BELIEVE WE HAVE TO BE ON THE SAME TEAM AS THEM.
Why is this even coed?
...
YOU GOT A PROBLEM, FORE-HEAD GIRL?
...
SY-ON BOY IS THE SON OF PAPA'S TARGET.
IF WE BECAME FRIENDS, IT WOULD REALLY HELP PAPA'S MISSION.
WHAT ARE YOU LOOKING AT?
BUT HE'S ALWAYS MEAN TO ME, SO I HATE HIM.
WHIRL
I DON'T HAVE TIME TO WASTE ON SHRIMPS LIKE HER.
HMPH
Shrimp?!
BECKY
ANYA
I GOTTA BE THE MVP IN THIS GAME SO I CAN SCORE A STAR.
CLENCH
I NEED TO BECOME AN IMPERIAL SCHOLAR LIKE MY BROTHER DID. OTHERWISE...

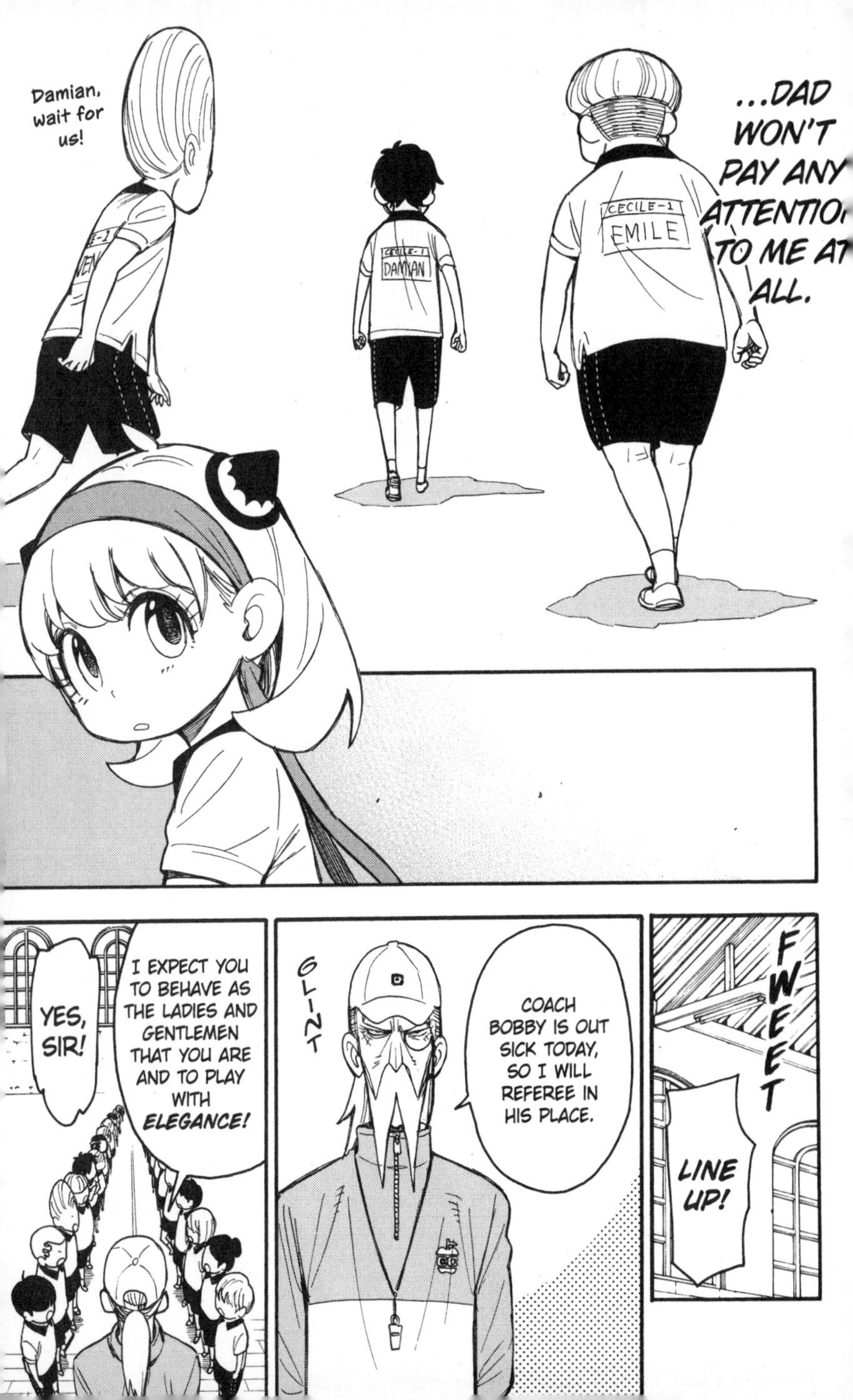
...DAD WON'T PAY ANY ATTENTIO TO ME AT ALL.
CECILE-1 EMILE
CECILE-1 DAMIAN
Damian, wait for us!
FWEET
LINE UP!
GLINT
COACH BOBBY IS OUT SICK TODAY, SO I WILL REFEREE IN HIS PLACE.
I EXPECT YOU TO BEHAVE AS THE LADIES AND GENTLEMEN THAT YOU ARE AND TO PLAY WITH *ELEGANCE!*
YES, SIR!

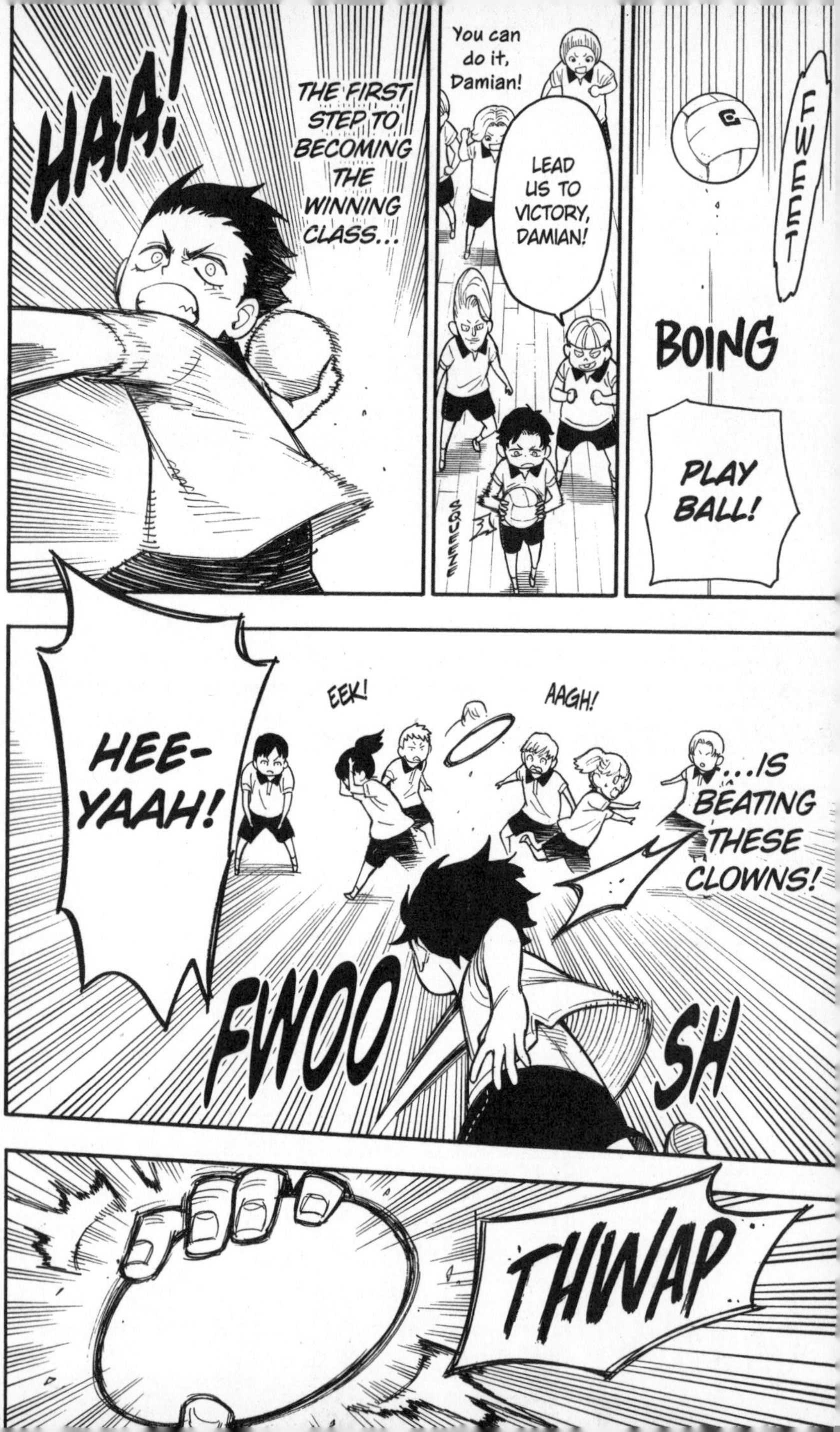
FWEET
BOING
PLAY BALL!
You can do it, Damian!
LEAD US TO VICTORY, DAMIAN!
SQUEEZE
THE FIRST STEP TO BECOMING THE WINNING CLASS...
HAA!
...IS BEATING THESE CLOWNS!
AAGH!
EEK!
HEE-YAAH!
FWOOSH
THWAP

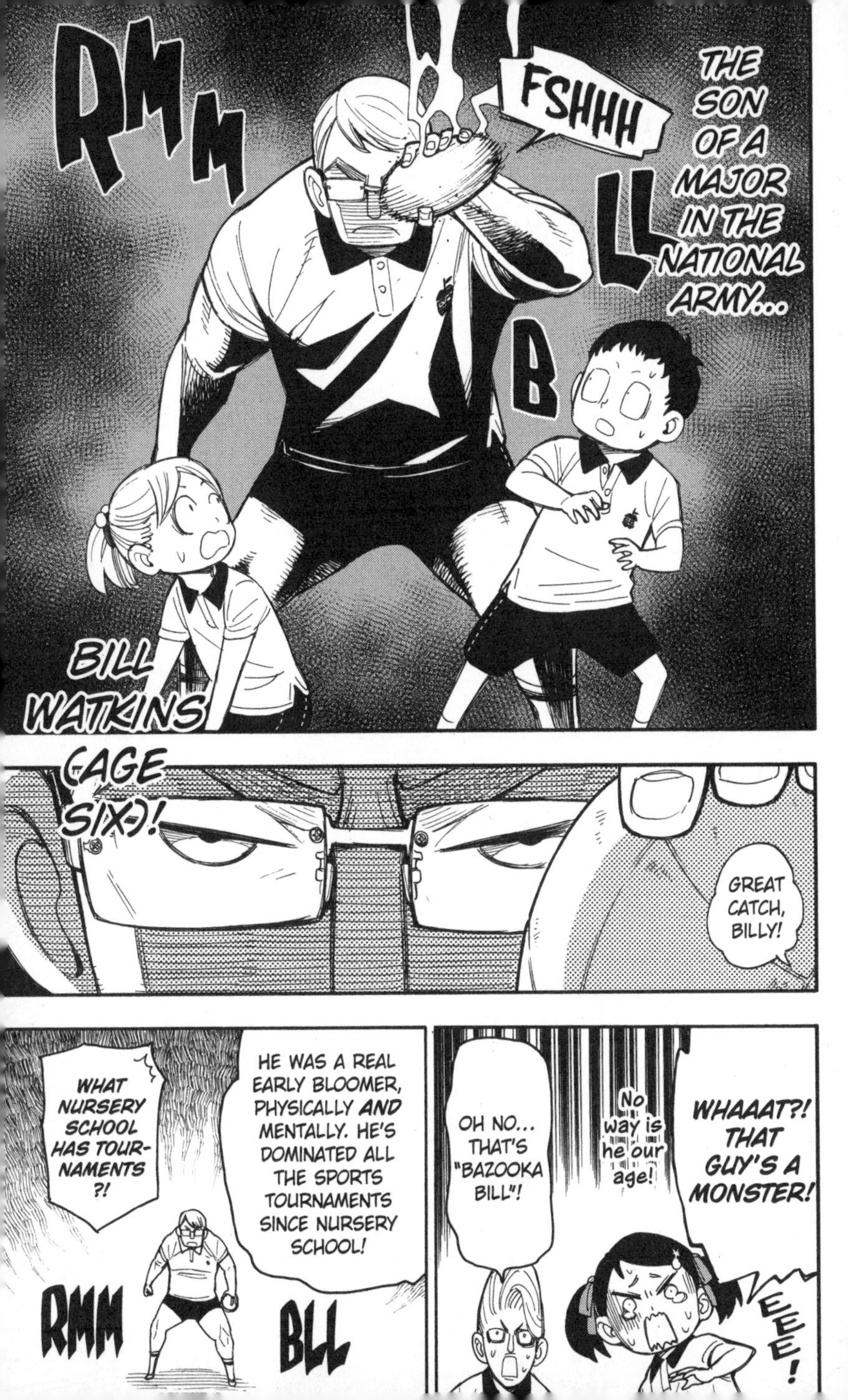
FSHHH
THE SON OF A MAJOR IN THE NATIONAL ARMY...
RMMBLL
BILL WATKINS (AGE SIX)!
GREAT CATCH, BILLY!
WHAAAT?! THAT GUY'S A MONSTER!
EEEE!
No way is he our age!
OH NO... THAT'S "BAZOOKA BILL"!
HE WAS A REAL EARLY BLOOMER, PHYSICALLY AND MENTALLY. HE'S DOMINATED ALL THE SPORTS TOURNAMENTS SINCE NURSERY SCHOOL!
WHAT NURSERY SCHOOL HAS TOURNAMENTS?!
RMM
BLL

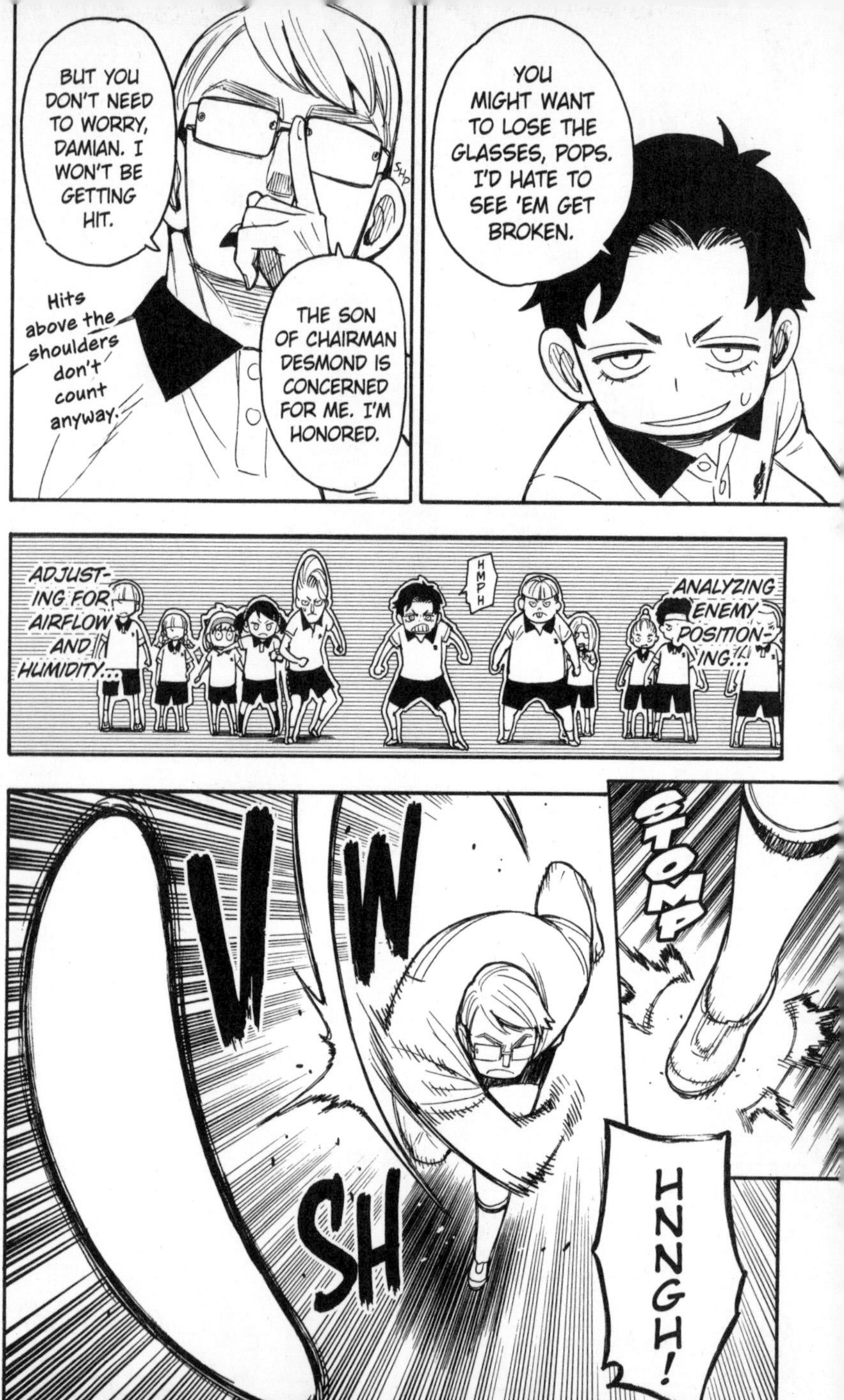
YOU MIGHT WANT TO LOSE THE GLASSES, POPS. I'D HATE TO SEE 'EM GET BROKEN.
THE SON OF CHAIRMAN DESMOND IS CONCERNED FOR ME. I'M HONORED.
SHP
BUT YOU DON'T NEED TO WORRY, DAMIAN. I WON'T BE GETTING HIT.
Hits above the shoulders don't count anyway.
ANALYZING ENEMY POSITIONING...
HMPH
ADJUSTING FOR AIRFLOW AND HUMIDITY...
STOMP
HNNGH!
VWSH

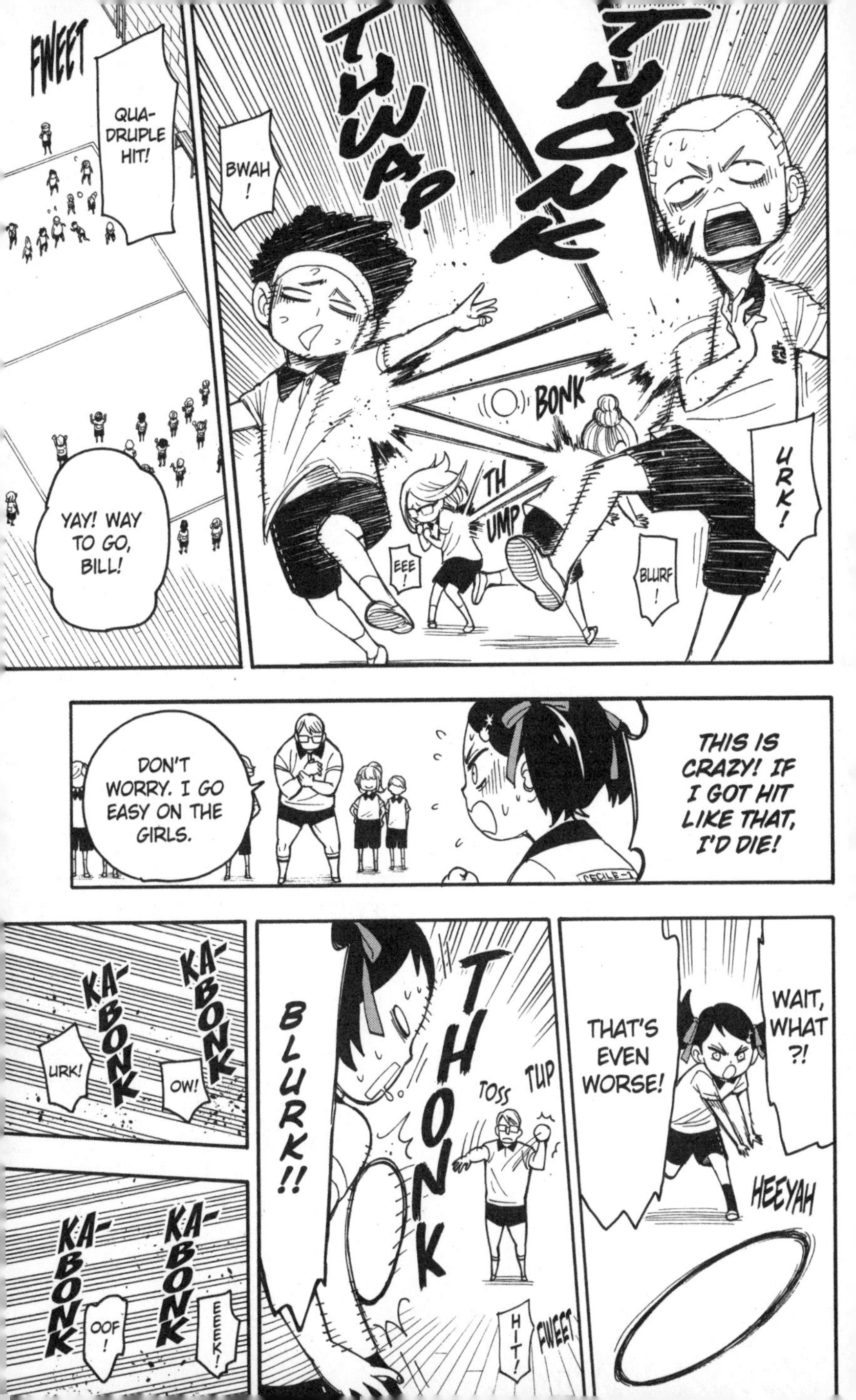
THONK
THWAP
BWAH!
URK!
BONK
THUMP
BLURF!
EEE!
FWEET
QUADRUPLE HIT!
YAY! WAY TO GO, BILL!
THIS IS CRAZY! IF I GOT HIT LIKE THAT, I'D DIE!
DON'T WORRY. I GO EASY ON THE GIRLS.
CECILE-1
WAIT, WHAT?!
THAT'S EVEN WORSE!
HEEYAH
TUP
TOSS
THONK
BLURK!!
HIT!
FWEET
KA-BONK
OW!
KA-BONK
URK!
KA-BONK
EEEK!
KA-BONK
OOF!

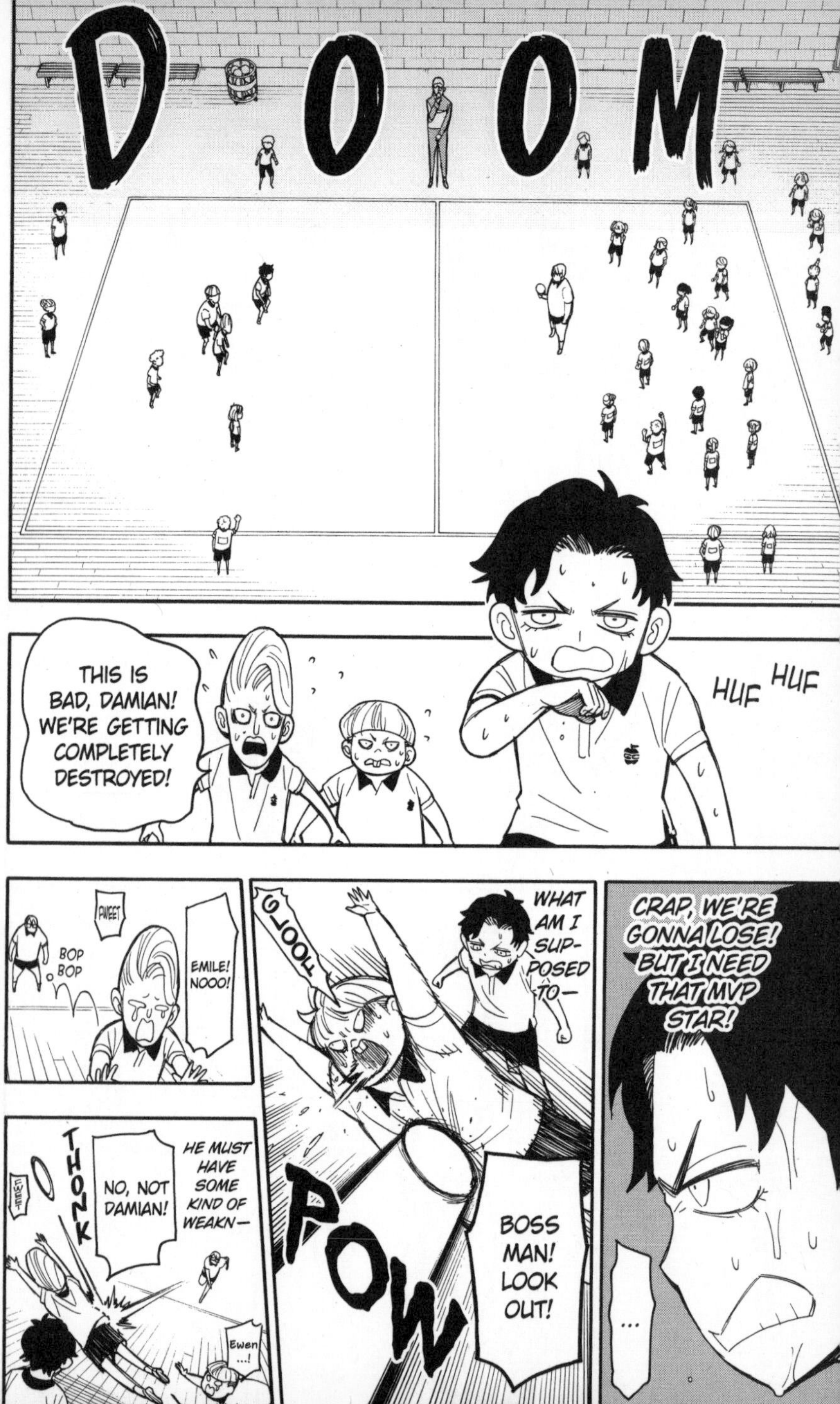
DOOM
HUF HUF
THIS IS BAD, DAMIAN! WE'RE GETTING COMPLETELY DESTROYED!
CRAP, WE'RE GONNA LOSE! BUT I NEED THAT MVP STAR!
...
WHAT AM I SUP-POSED TO—
POW
BOSS MAN! LOOK OUT!
EMILE! NOOO!
FWEET
BOP BOP
HE MUST HAVE SOME KIND OF WEAKN—
NO, NOT DAMIAN!
THONK
FWEET
Ewen ...!

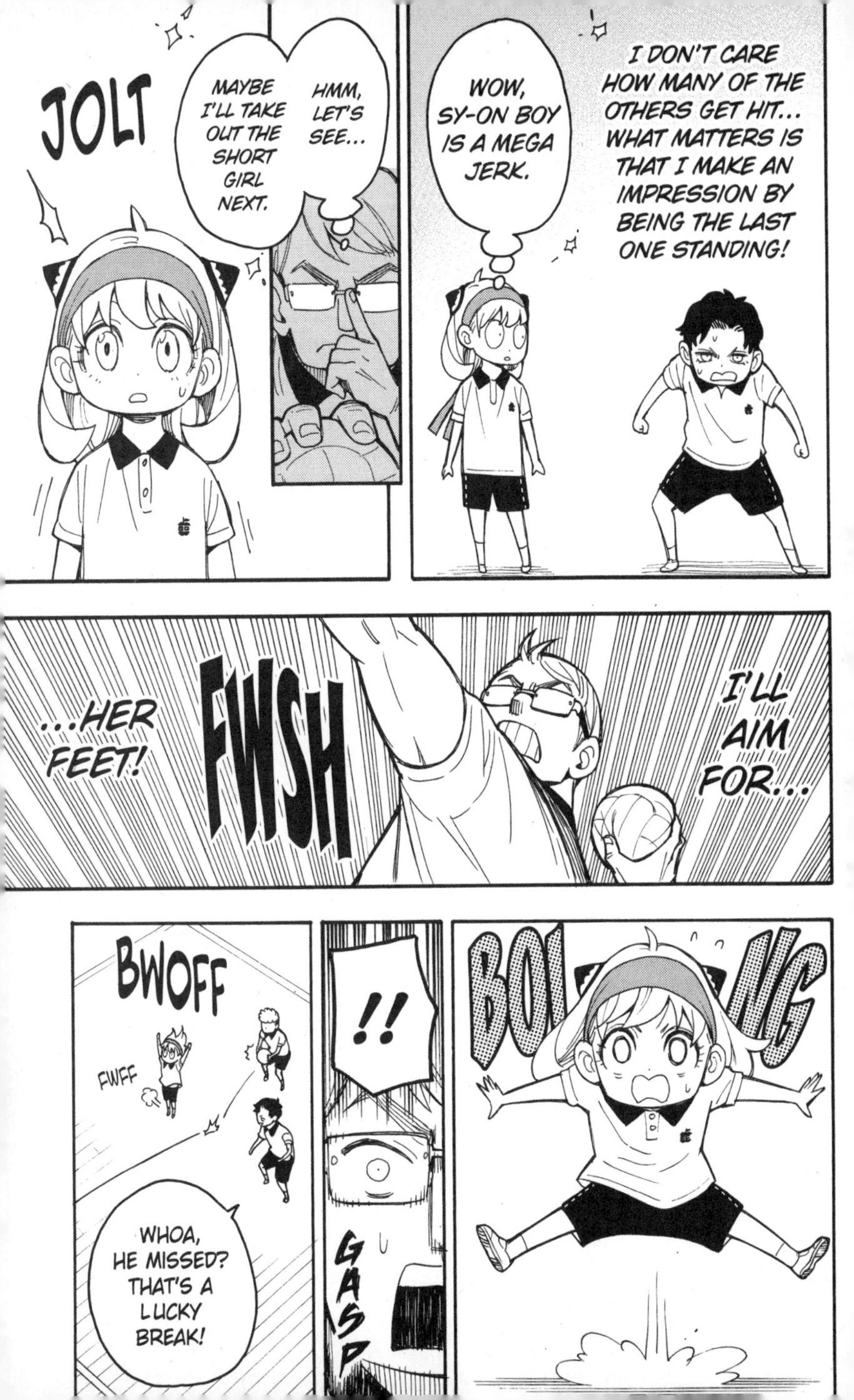
I DON'T CARE HOW MANY OF THE OTHERS GET HIT... WHAT MATTERS IS THAT I MAKE AN IMPRESSION BY BEING THE LAST ONE STANDING!
WOW, SY-ON BOY IS A MEGA JERK.
HMM, LET'S SEE...
MAYBE I'LL TAKE OUT THE SHORT GIRL NEXT.
JOLT
I'LL AIM FOR...
FWSH
...HER FEET!
BOING
!!
GASP
BWOFF
FWFF
WHOA, HE MISSED? THAT'S A LUCKY BREAK!

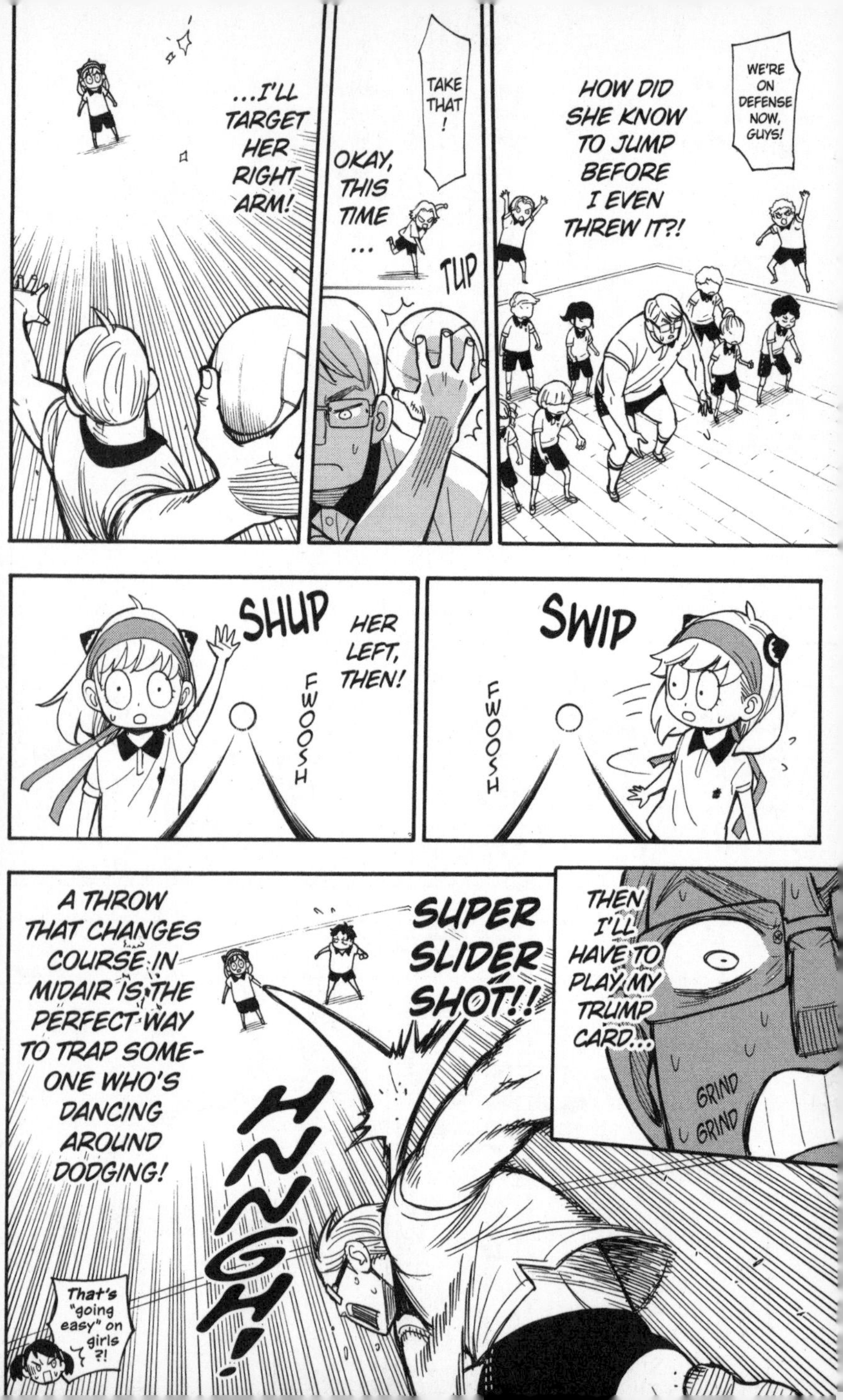
WE'RE ON DEFENSE NOW, GUYS!
HOW DID SHE KNOW TO JUMP BEFORE I EVEN THREW IT?!
TAKE THAT!
OKAY, THIS TIME...
TUP
...I'LL TARGET HER RIGHT ARM!
SWIP
FWOOSH
SHUP
HER LEFT, THEN!
FWOOSH
THEN I'LL HAVE TO PLAY MY TRUMP CARD...
GRIND GRIND
SUPER SLIDER SHOT!!
A THROW THAT CHANGES COURSE IN MIDAIR IS THE PERFECT WAY TO TRAP SOME-ONE WHO'S DANCING AROUND DODGING!
HNNGH!
That's "going easy" on girls?!

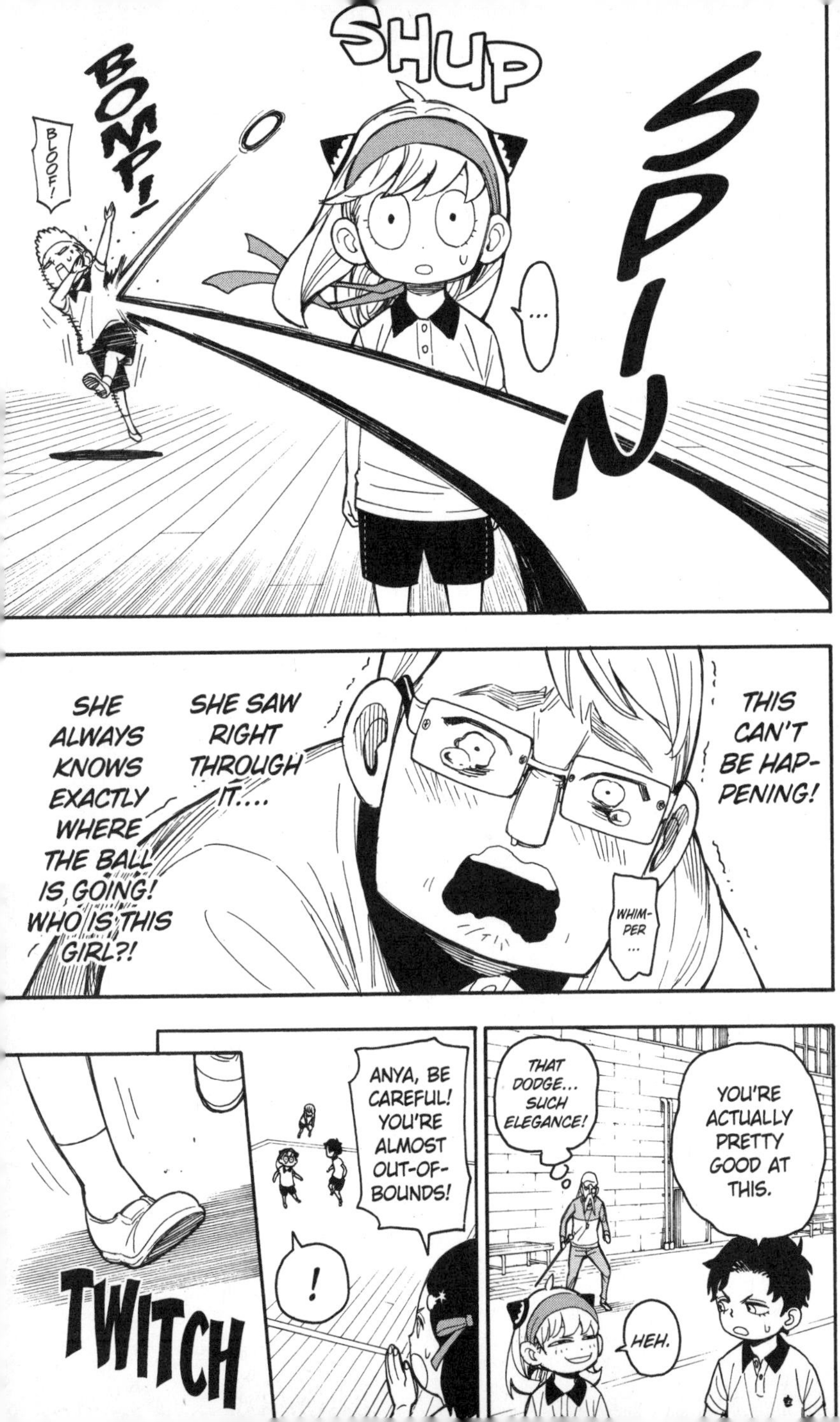
SHUP
SPIN
...
BOMP!
BLOOF!
THIS CAN'T BE HAP-PENING!
WHIMPER...
SHE SAW RIGHT THROUGH IT....
SHE ALWAYS KNOWS EXACTLY WHERE THE BALL IS GOING! WHO IS THIS GIRL?!
YOU'RE ACTUALLY PRETTY GOOD AT THIS.
THAT DODGE... SUCH ELEGANCE!
HEH.
ANYA, BE CAREFUL! YOU'RE ALMOST OUT-OF-BOUNDS!
!
TWITCH

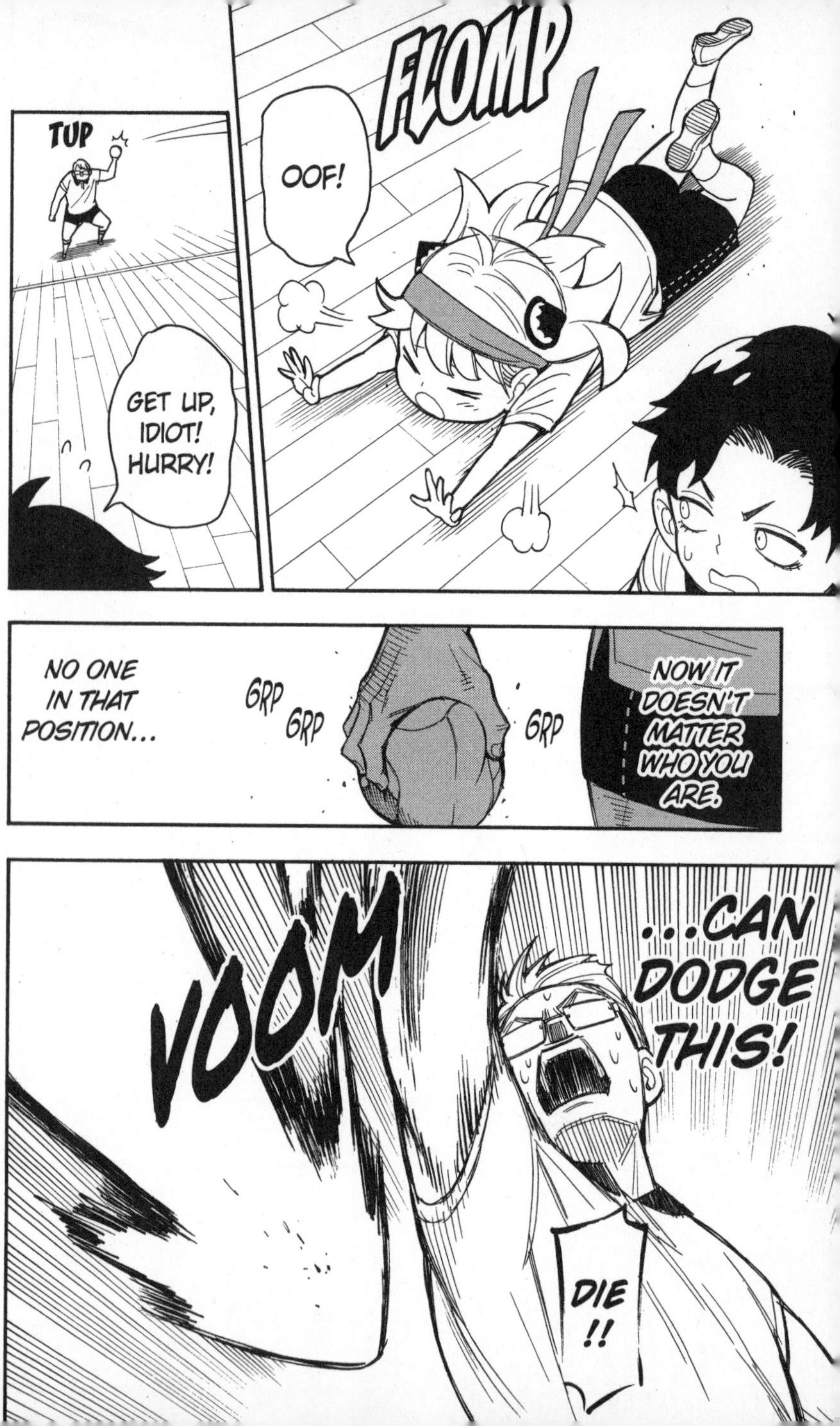
FLOMP
OOF!
TUP
GET UP, IDIOT! HURRY!
NOW IT DOESN'T MATTER WHO YOU ARE.
GRP
GRP
GRP
NO ONE IN THAT POSITION...
...CAN DODGE THIS!
VOOM
DIE !!

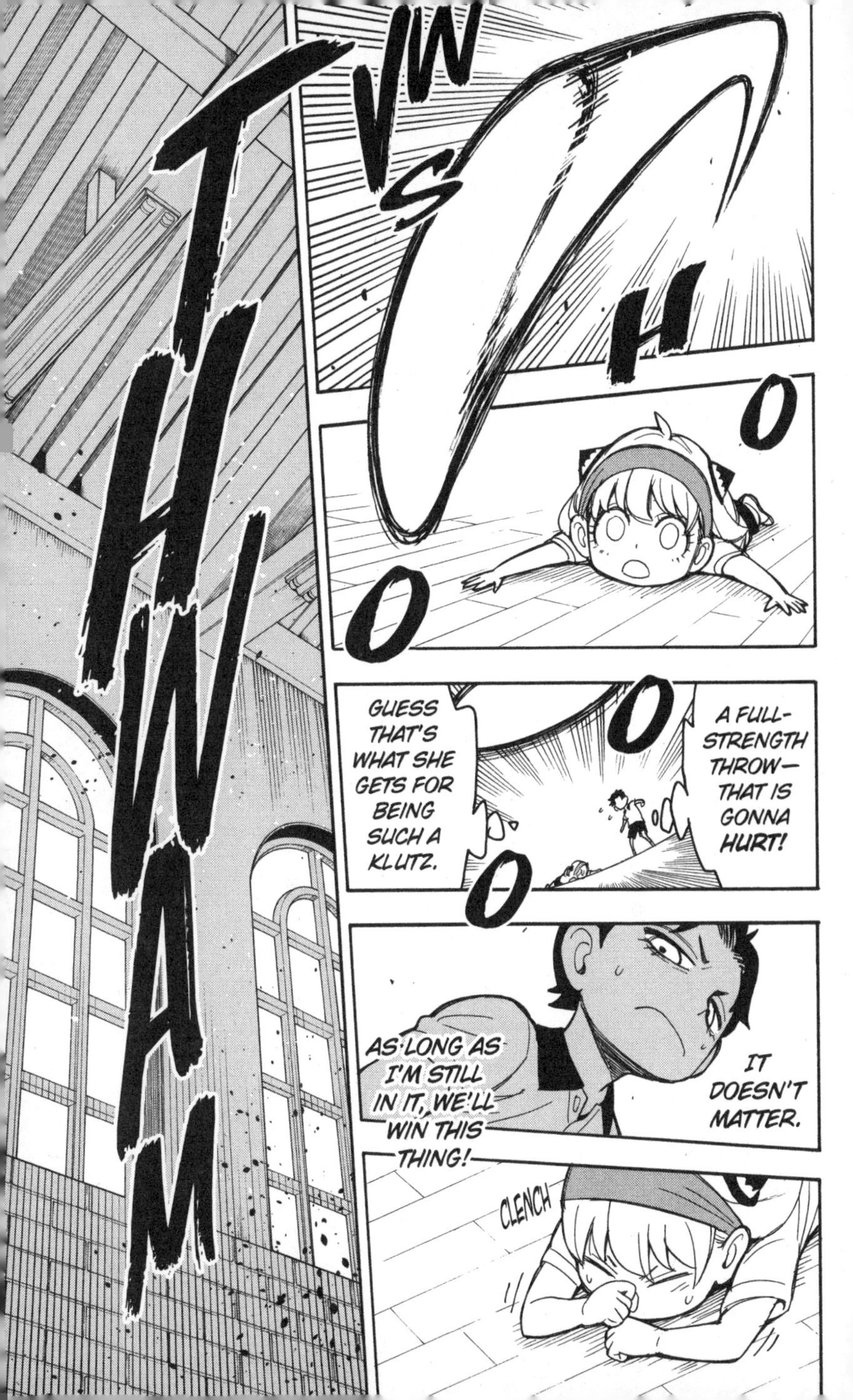
VWSHOOOO
A FULL-STRENGTH THROW—THAT IS GONNA HURT!
GUESS THAT'S WHAT SHE GETS FOR BEING SUCH A KLUTZ.
IT DOESN'T MATTER.
AS LONG AS I'M STILL IN IT, WE'LL WIN THIS THING!
CLENCH
THWAM

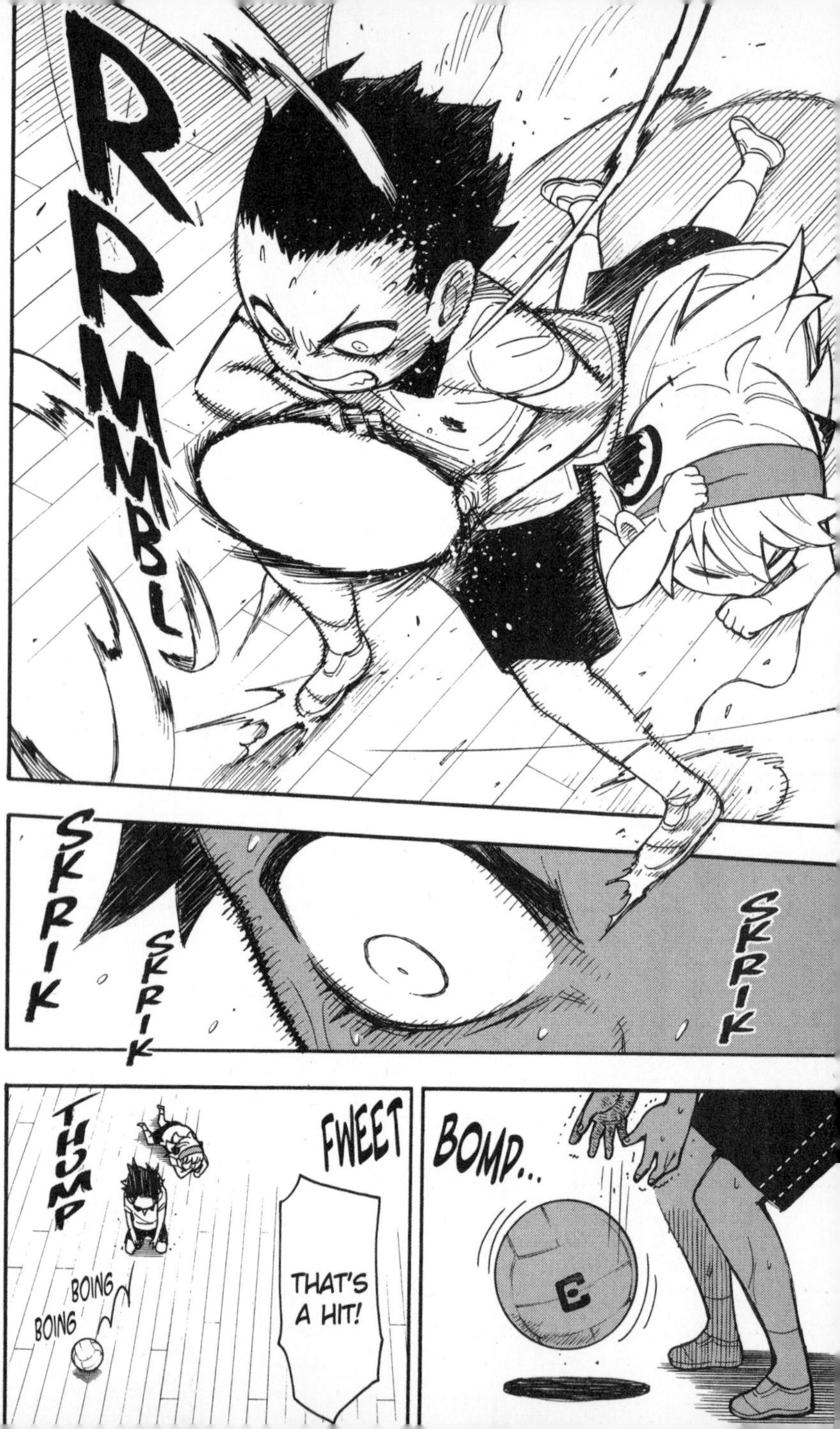
RRMMBL
SKRIK
SKRIK
SKRIK
BOMP...
FWEET
THAT'S A HIT!
THUMP
BOING
BOING

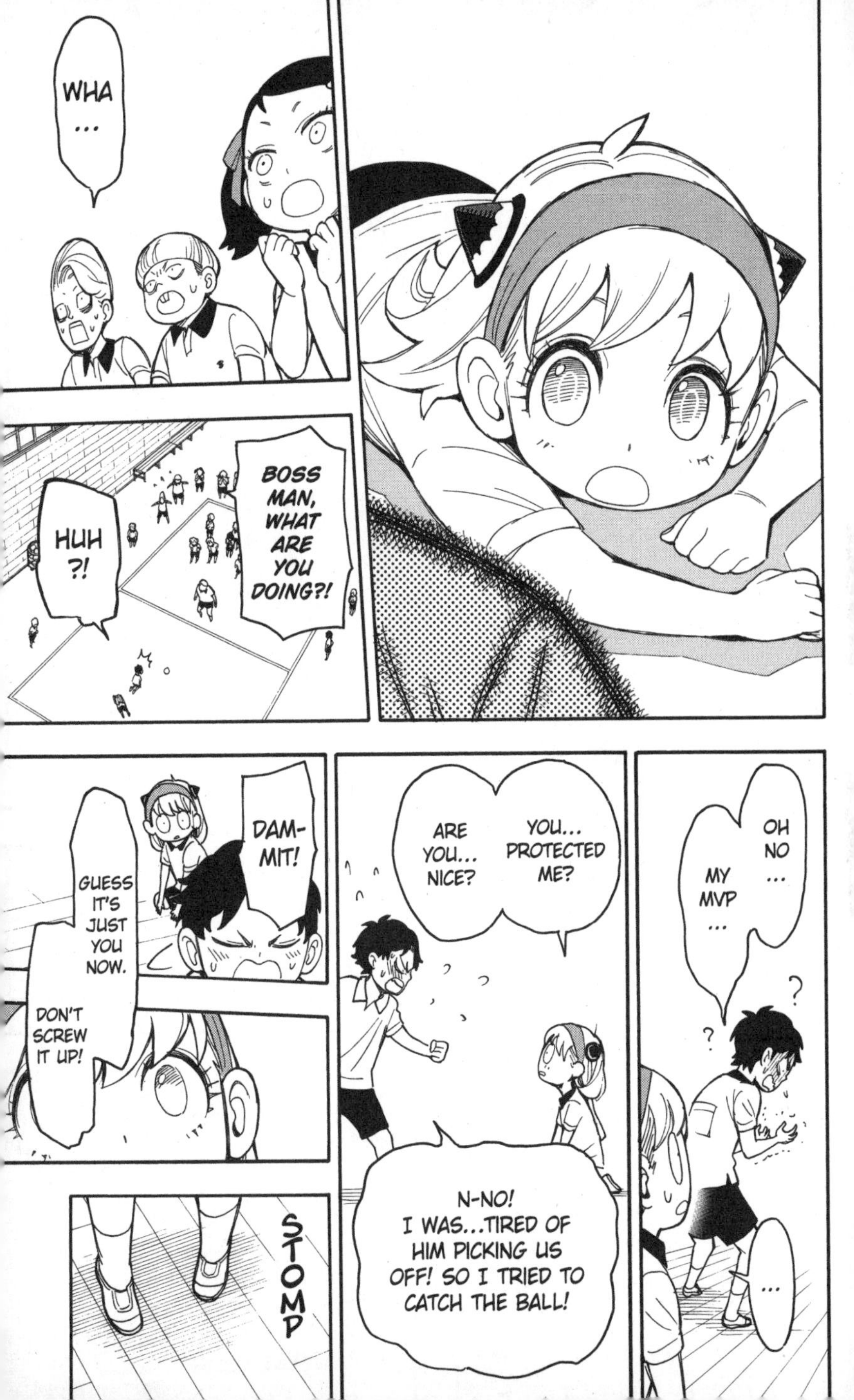
WHA...
BOSS MAN, WHAT ARE YOU DOING?!
HUH?!
OH NO... MY MVP...
...
YOU... PROTECTED ME?
ARE YOU... NICE?
N-NO! I WAS...TIRED OF HIM PICKING US OFF! SO I TRIED TO CATCH THE BALL!
DAM-MIT!
GUESS IT'S JUST YOU NOW. DON'T SCREW IT UP!
STOMP

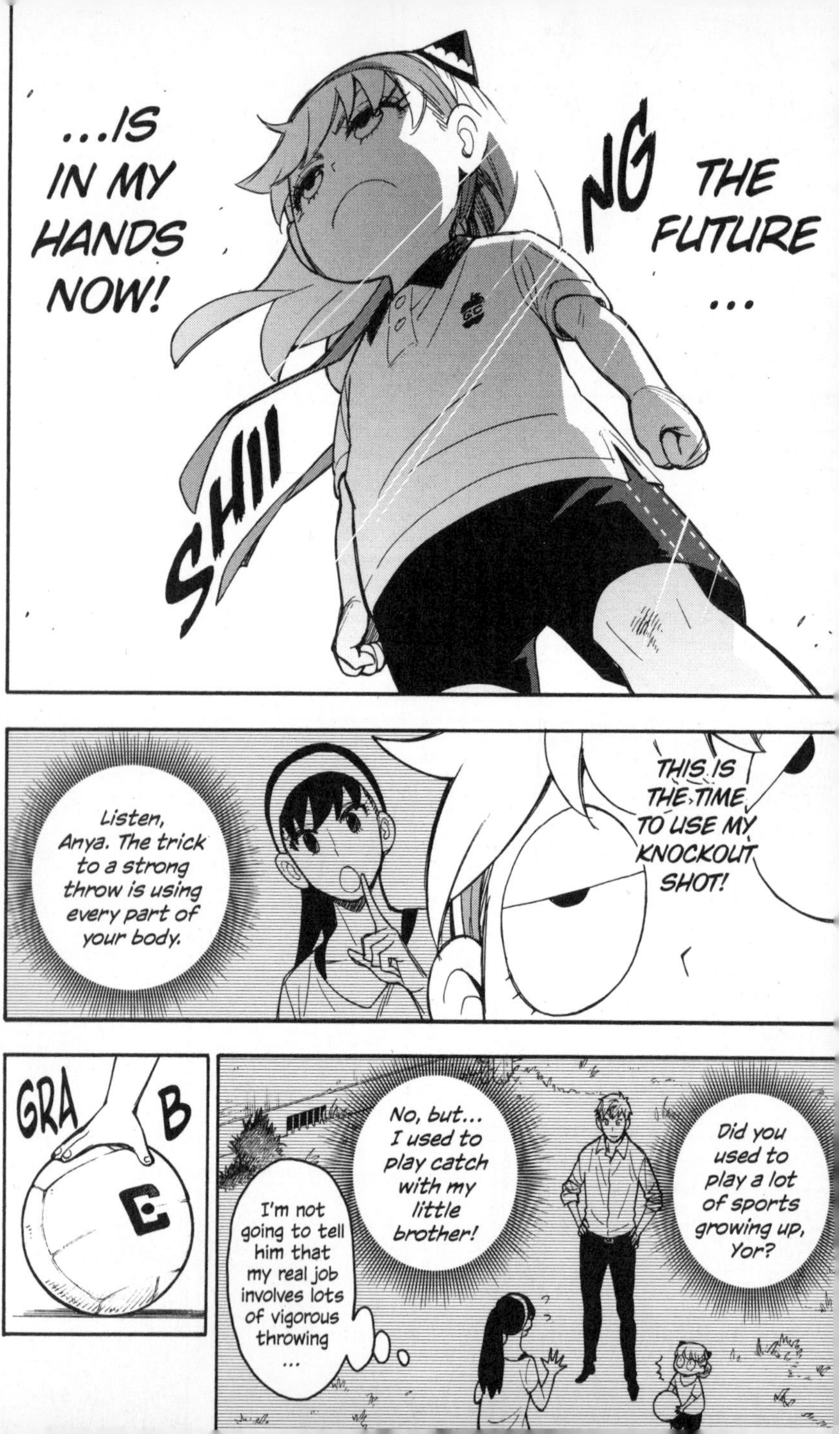
THE FUTURE ...
...IS IN MY HANDS NOW!
SHIII
NG
THIS IS THE TIME TO USE MY KNOCKOUT SHOT!
Listen, Anya. The trick to a strong throw is using every part of your body.
Did you used to play a lot of sports growing up, Yor?
No, but... I used to play catch with my little brother!
I'm not going to tell him that my real job involves lots of vigorous throwing ...
GRA
B

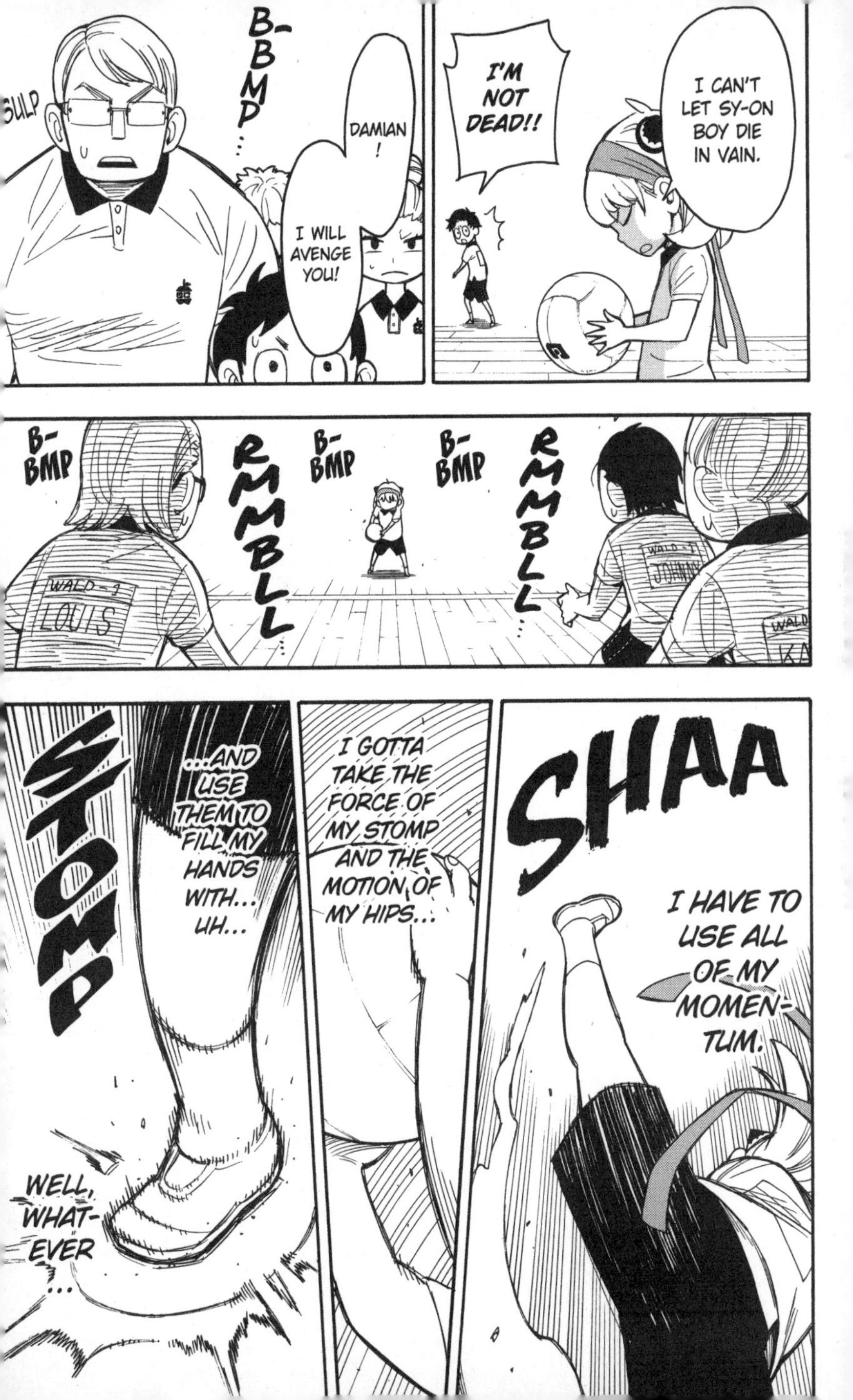
I CAN'T LET SY-ON BOY DIE IN VAIN.
I'M NOT DEAD!!
DAMIAN!
I WILL AVENGE YOU!
B-BMP...
GULP
RMMBLL...
WALD-1 JOHNNY
B-BMP
B-BMP
RMMBLL...
B-BMP
WALD-1 LOUIS
SHAA
I HAVE TO USE ALL OF MY MOMEN-TUM.
I GOTTA TAKE THE FORCE OF MY STOMP AND THE MOTION OF MY HIPS...
STOMP
...AND USE THEM TO FILL MY HANDS WITH... UH...
WELL, WHAT-EVER...

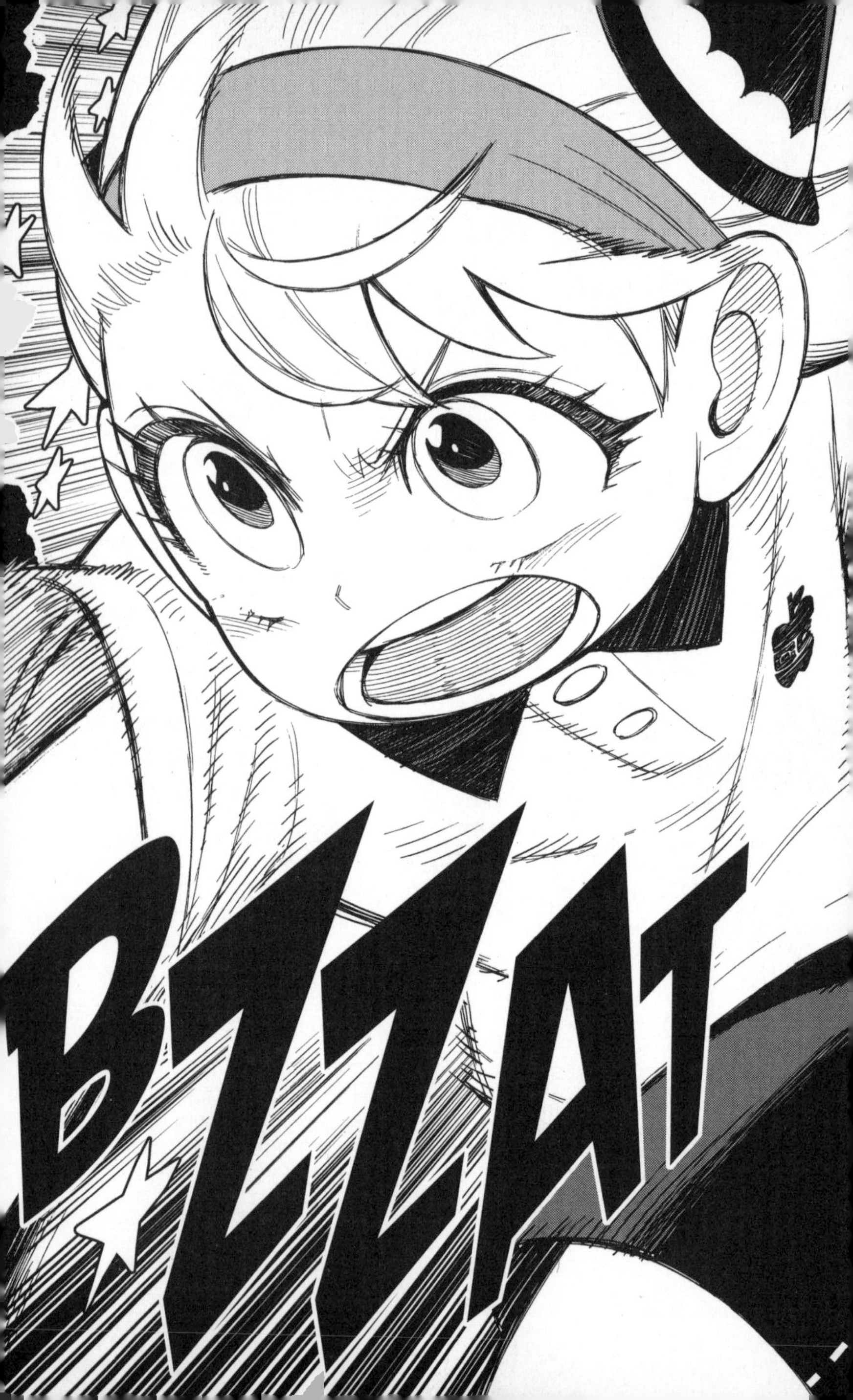
BZZAT

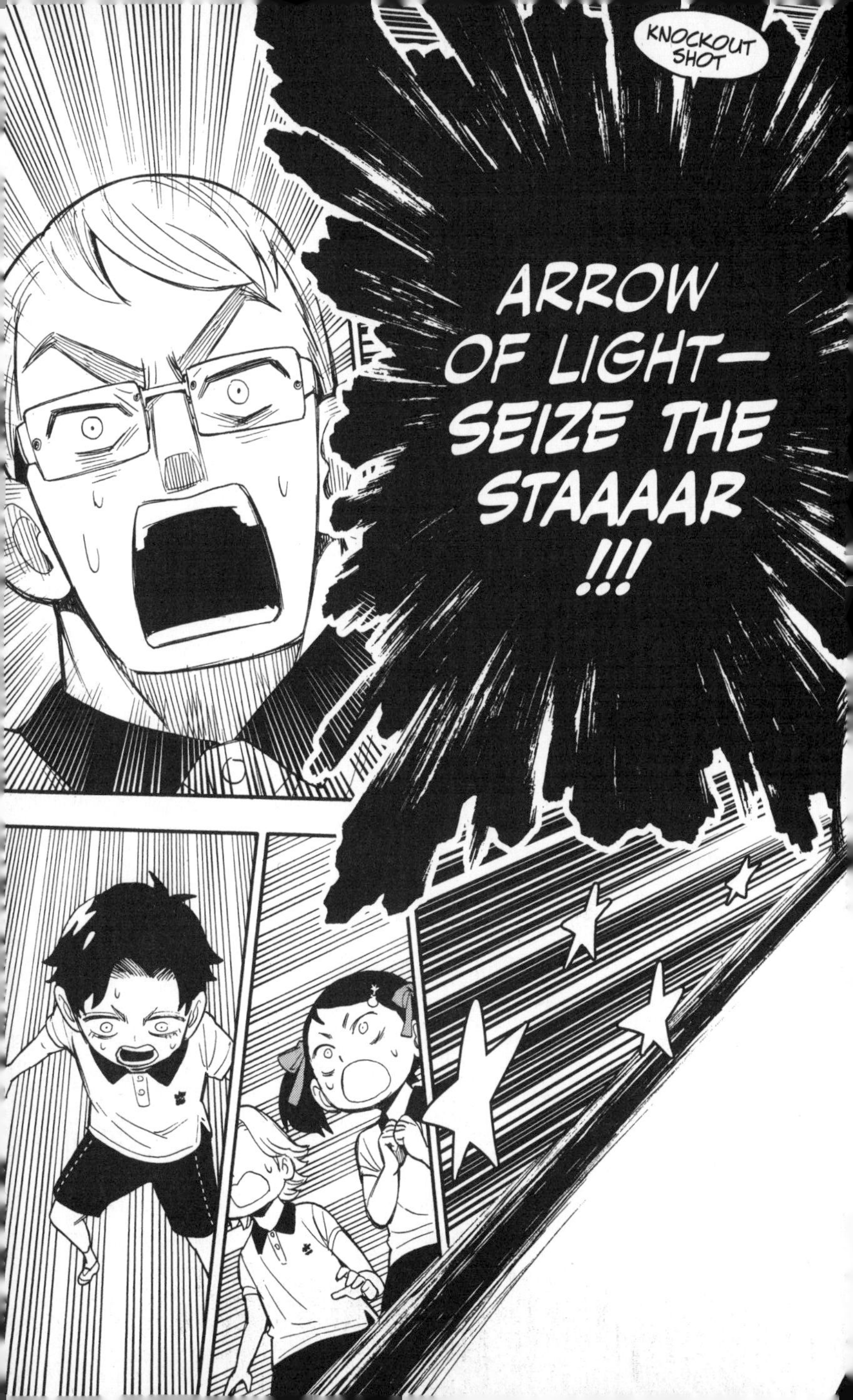
KNOCKOUT SHOT
ARROW OF LIGHT— SEIZE THE STAAAAR !!!

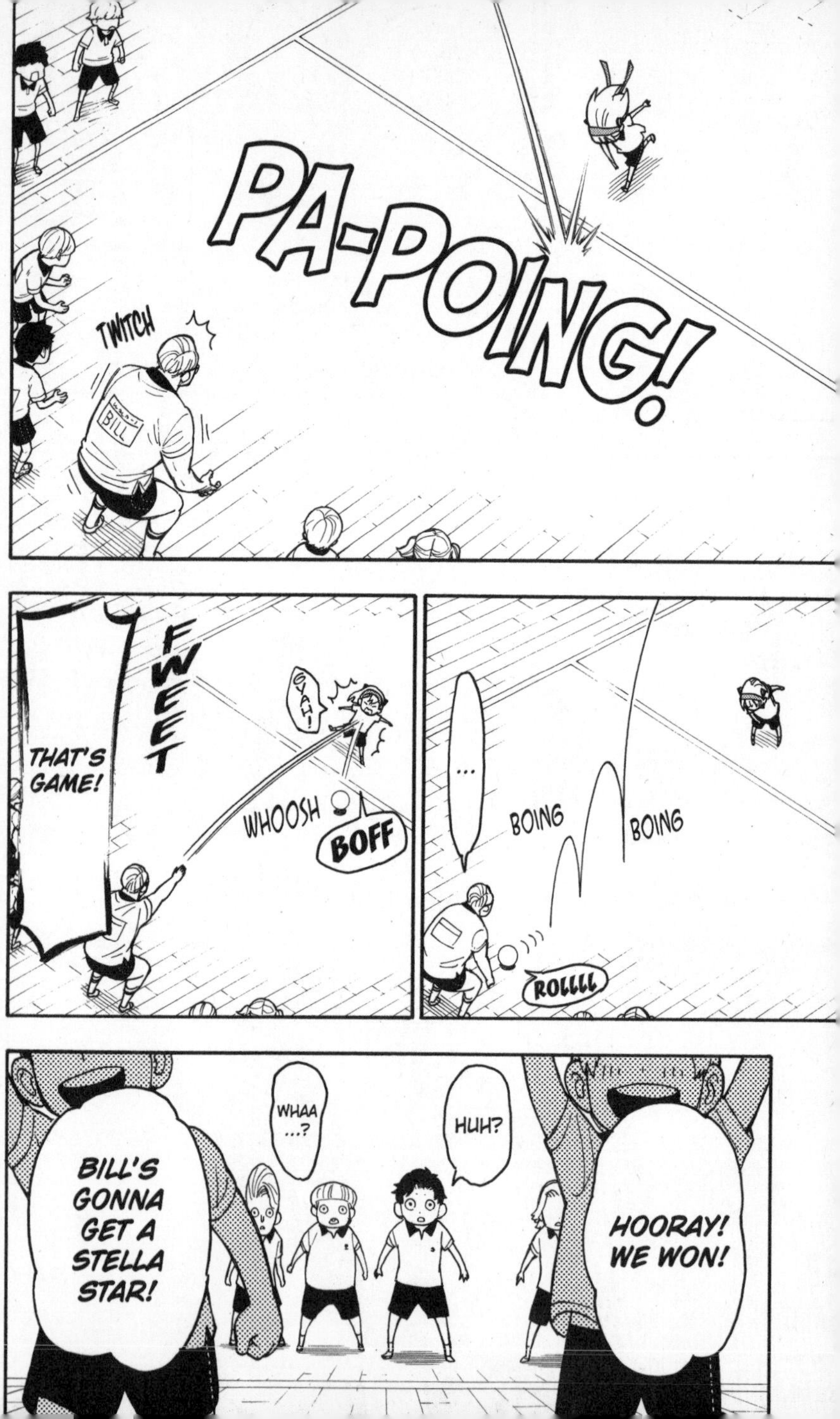
PA-POING!
TWITCH
BILL
...
BOING
BOING
ROLLLL
FWEET
THAT'S GAME!
GYAH!
WHOOSH
BOFF
HOORAY! WE WON!
HUH?
WHAA ...?
BILL'S GONNA GET A STELLA STAR!

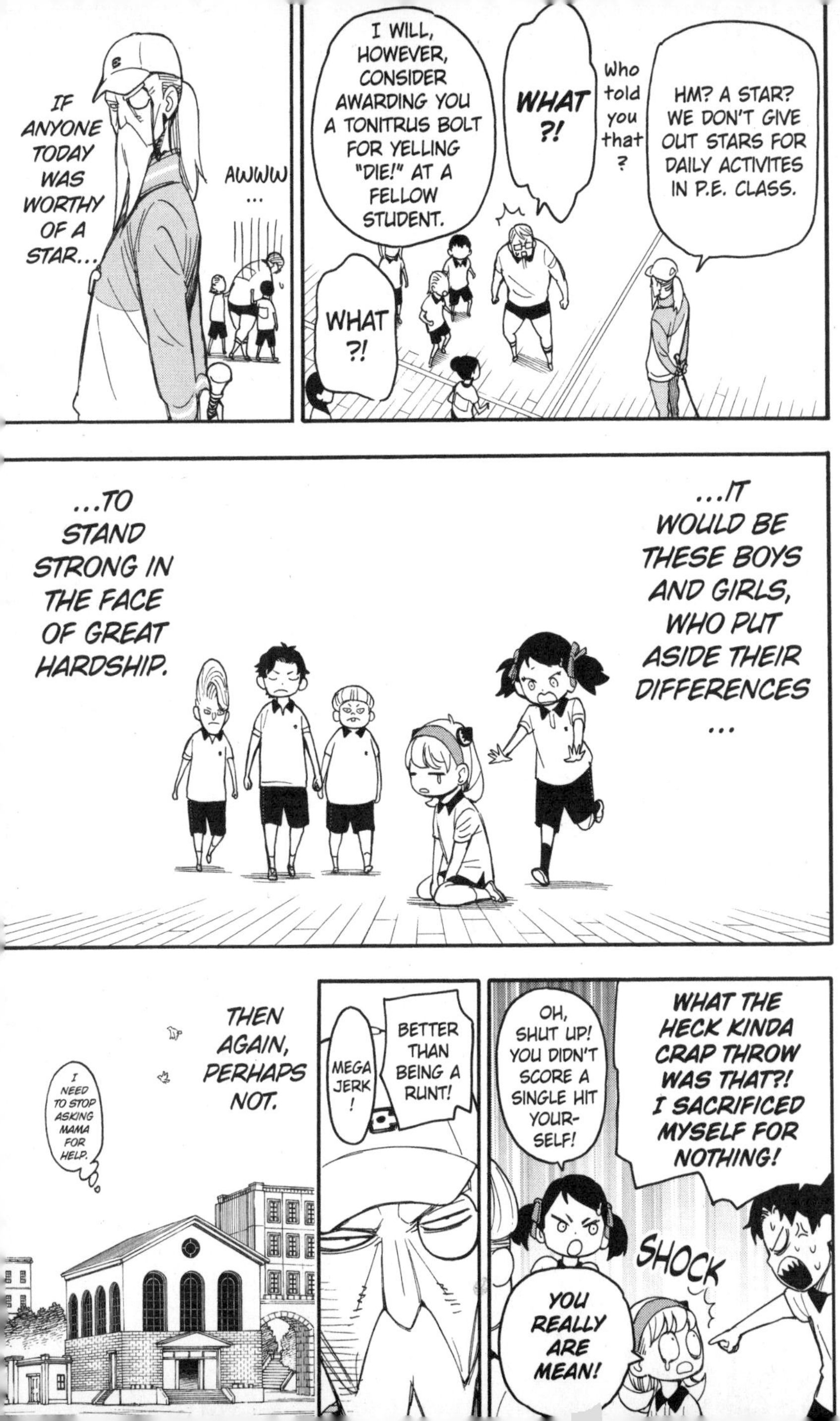
HM? A STAR? WE DON'T GIVE OUT STARS FOR DAILY ACTIVITES IN P.E. CLASS.
Who told you that?
WHAT?!
I WILL, HOWEVER, CONSIDER AWARDING YOU A TONITRUS BOLT FOR YELLING "DIE!" AT A FELLOW STUDENT.
WHAT?!
AWWW...
IF ANYONE TODAY WAS WORTHY OF A STAR...
...IT WOULD BE THESE BOYS AND GIRLS, WHO PUT ASIDE THEIR DIFFERENCES...
...TO STAND STRONG IN THE FACE OF GREAT HARDSHIP.
WHAT THE HECK KINDA CRAP THROW WAS THAT?! I SACRIFICED MYSELF FOR NOTHING!
OH, SHUT UP! YOU DIDN'T SCORE A SINGLE HIT YOURSELF!
SHOCK
YOU REALLY ARE MEAN!
BETTER THAN BEING A RUNT!
MEGA JERK!
THEN AGAIN, PERHAPS NOT.
I NEED TO STOP ASKING MAMA FOR HELP.

SPY×FAMILY

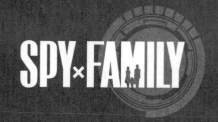

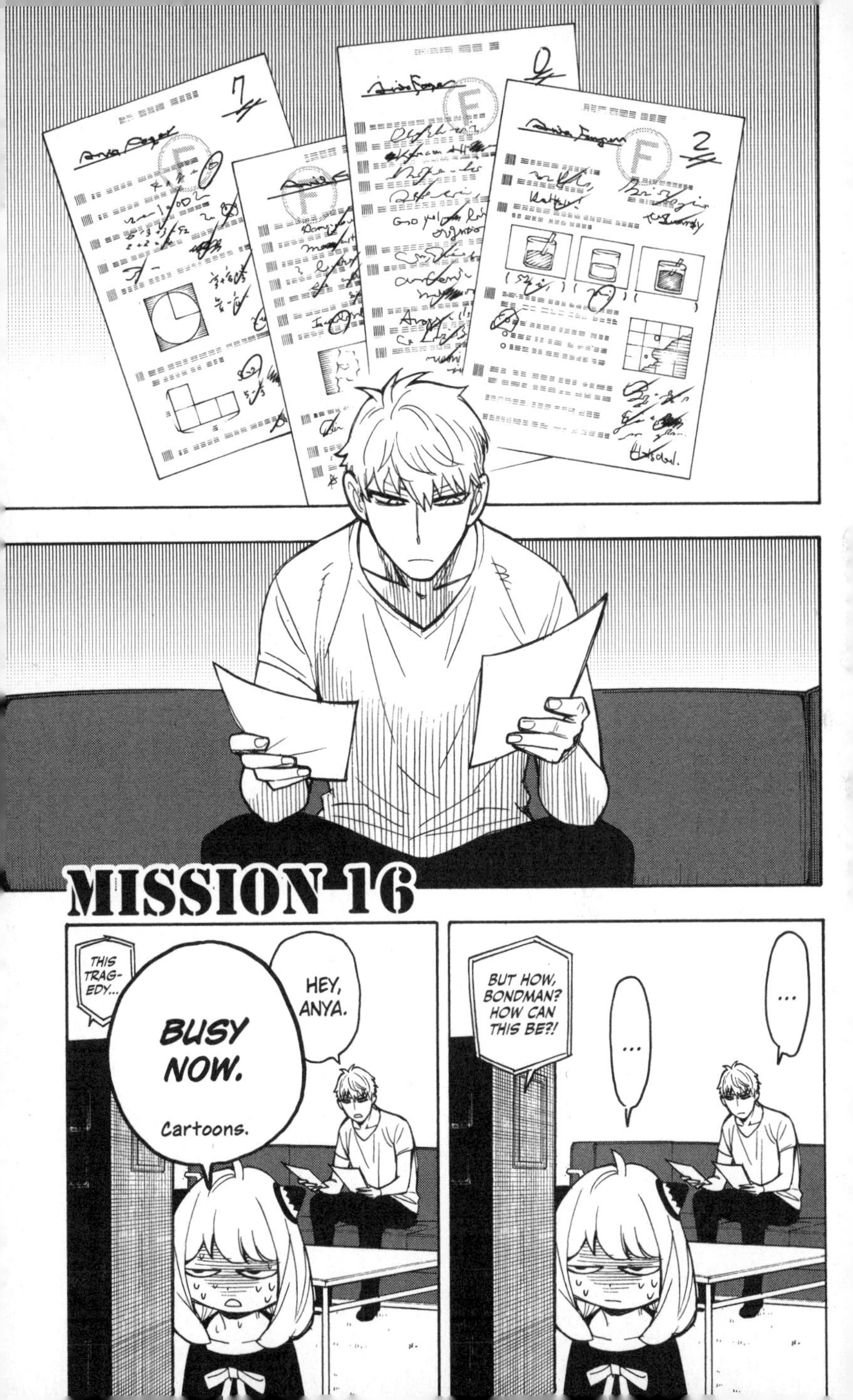
MISSION 16
...
...
BUT HOW, BONDMAN? HOW CAN THIS BE?!
HEY, ANYA.
BUSY NOW.
Cartoons.
THIS TRAG-EDY...

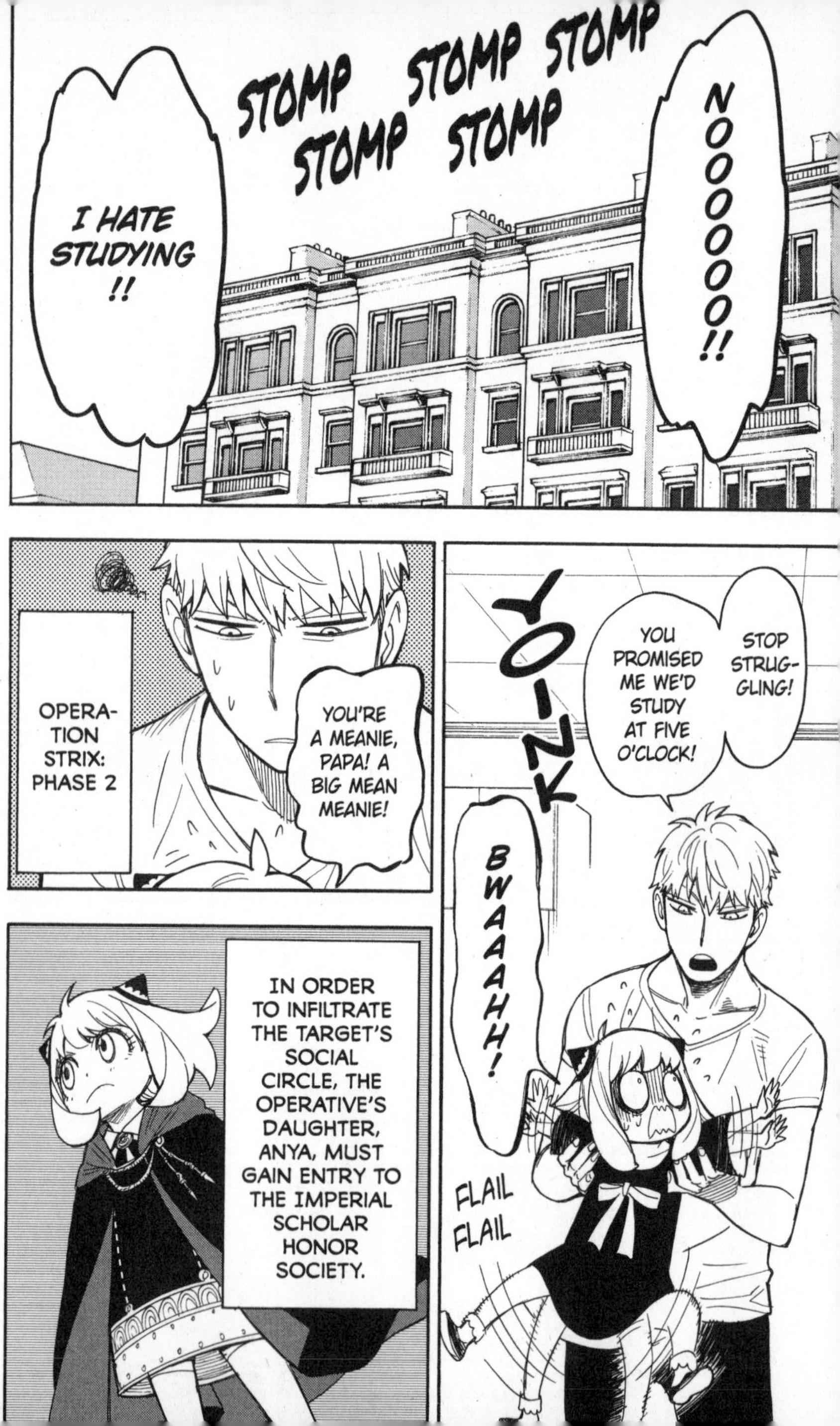
NOOOOOOOO!!
STOMP STOMP STOMP
STOMP STOMP
I HATE STUDYING !!
STOP STRUG-GLING!
YOU PROMISED ME WE'D STUDY AT FIVE O'CLOCK!
YO-INK
BWAAAAHH!
FLAIL FLAIL
YOU'RE A MEANIE, PAPA! A BIG MEAN MEANIE!
OPERA-TION STRIX: PHASE 2
IN ORDER TO INFILTRATE THE TARGET'S SOCIAL CIRCLE, THE OPERATIVE'S DAUGHTER, ANYA, MUST GAIN ENTRY TO THE IMPERIAL SCHOLAR HONOR SOCIETY.

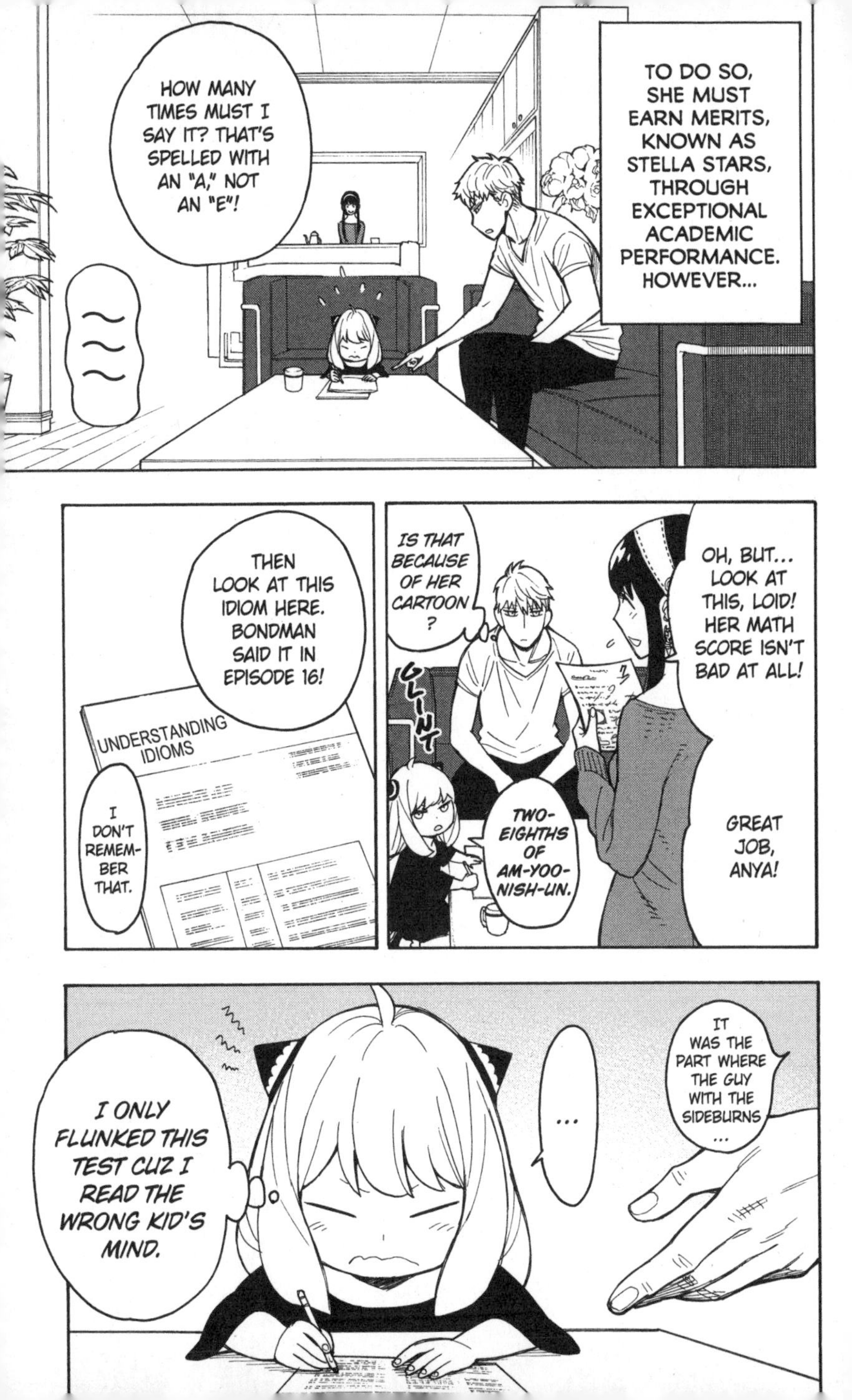
TO DO SO, SHE MUST EARN MERITS, KNOWN AS STELLA STARS, THROUGH EXCEPTIONAL ACADEMIC PERFORMANCE. HOWEVER...
HOW MANY TIMES MUST I SAY IT? THAT'S SPELLED WITH AN "A," NOT AN "E"!
OH, BUT... LOOK AT THIS, LOID! HER MATH SCORE ISN'T BAD AT ALL!
IS THAT BECAUSE OF HER CARTOON?
GLINT
GREAT JOB, ANYA!
TWO-EIGHTHS OF AM-YOO-NISH-UN.
THEN LOOK AT THIS IDIOM HERE. BONDMAN SAID IT IN EPISODE 16!
UNDERSTANDING IDIOMS
I DON'T REMEM-BER THAT.
IT WAS THE PART WHERE THE GUY WITH THE SIDEBURNS ...
...
I ONLY FLUNKED THIS TEST CUZ I READ THE WRONG KID'S MIND.

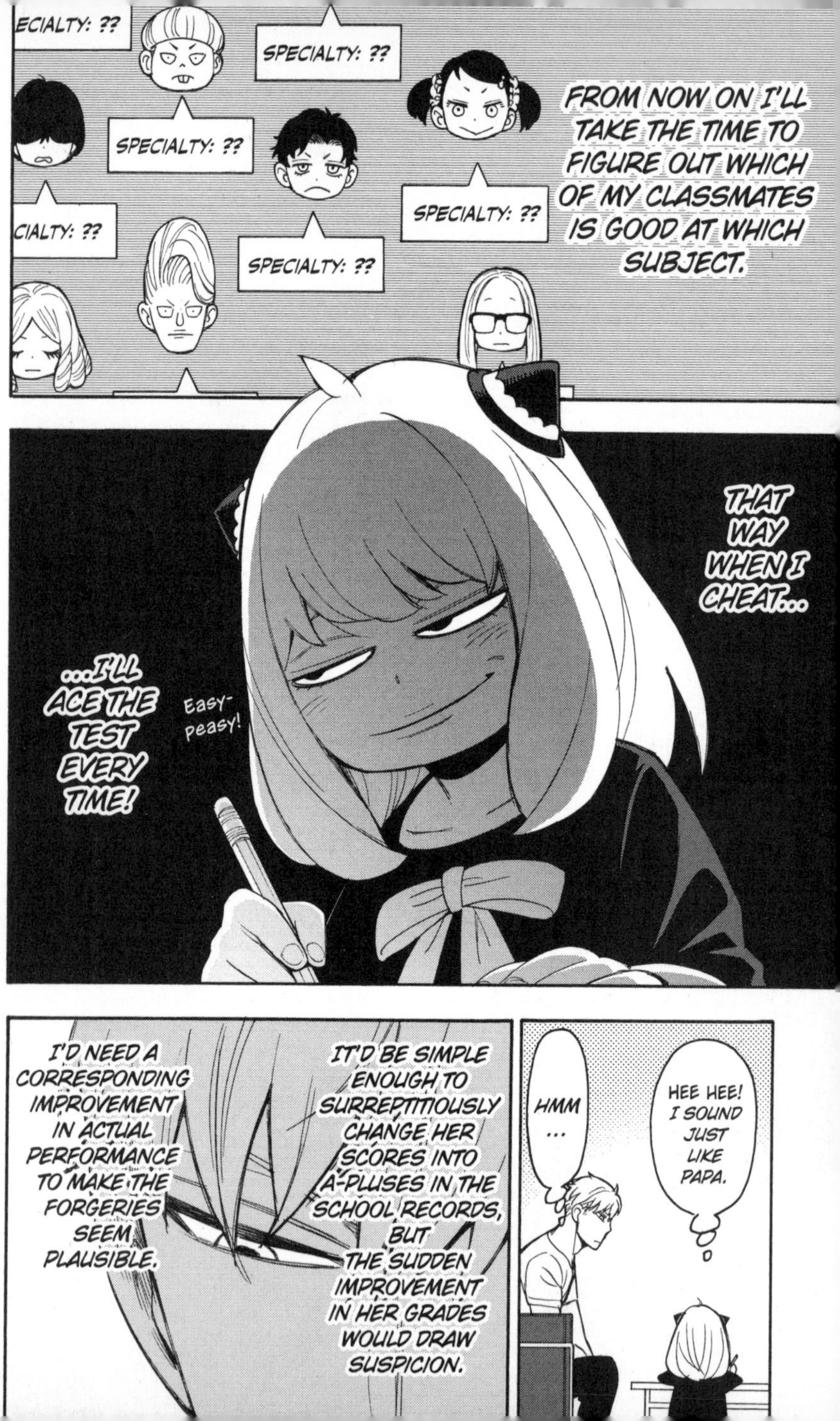
FROM NOW ON I'LL TAKE THE TIME TO FIGURE OUT WHICH OF MY CLASSMATES IS GOOD AT WHICH SUBJECT.
SPECIALTY: ??
SPECIALTY: ??
SPECIALTY: ??
SPECIALTY: ??
SPECIALTY: ??
ECIALTY: ??
CIALTY: ??
THAT WAY WHEN I CHEAT...
...I'LL ACE THE TEST EVERY TIME!
Easy-peasy!
HEE HEE! I SOUND JUST LIKE PAPA.
HMM ...
IT'D BE SIMPLE ENOUGH TO SURREPTITIOUSLY CHANGE HER SCORES INTO A-PLUSES IN THE SCHOOL RECORDS, BUT THE SUDDEN IMPROVEMENT IN HER GRADES WOULD DRAW SUSPICION.
I'D NEED A CORRESPONDING IMPROVEMENT IN ACTUAL PERFORMANCE TO MAKE THE FORGERIES SEEM PLAUSIBLE.

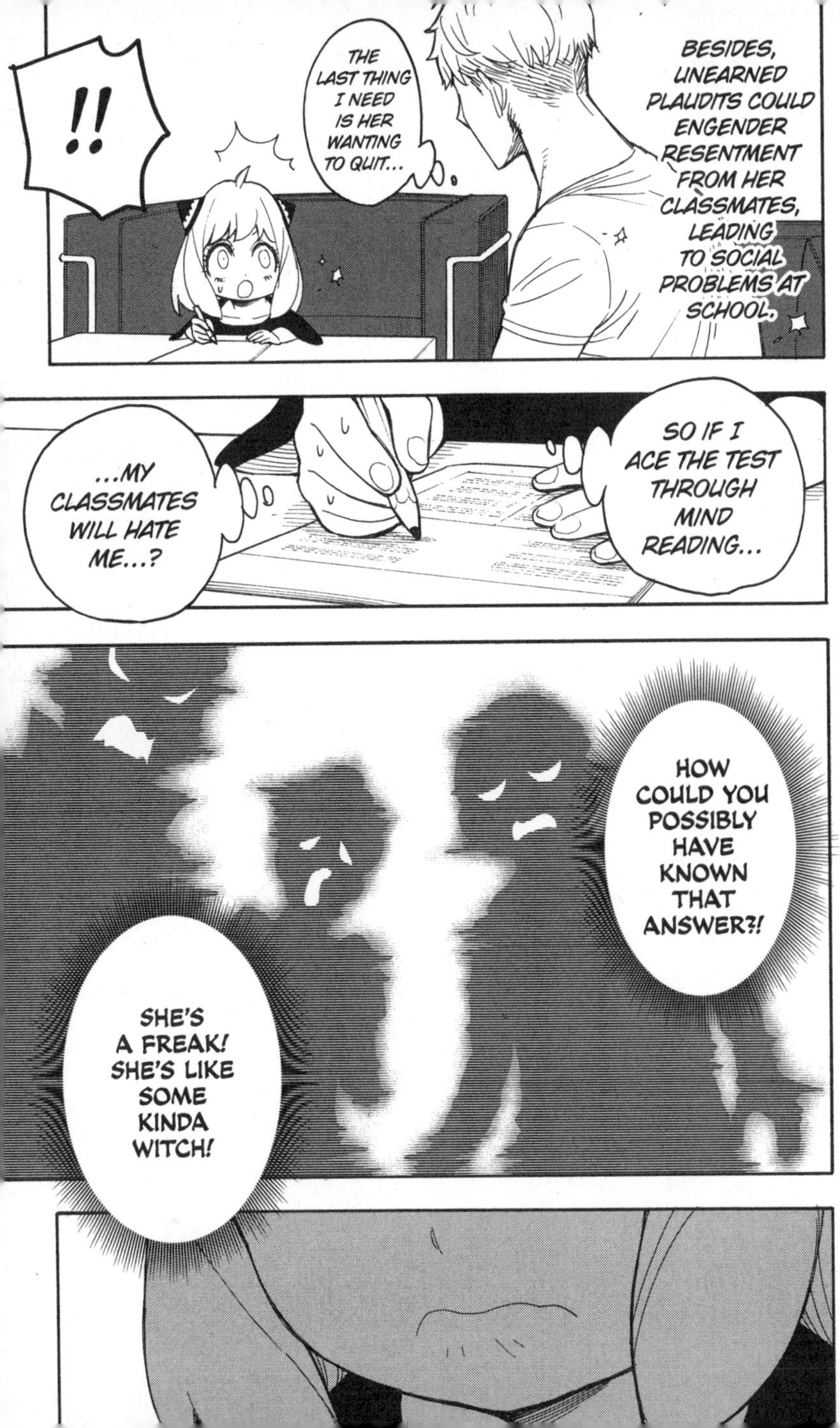
BESIDES, UNEARNED PLAUDITS COULD ENGENDER RESENTMENT FROM HER CLASSMATES, LEADING TO SOCIAL PROBLEMS AT SCHOOL.
THE LAST THING I NEED IS HER WANTING TO QUIT...
!!
SO IF I ACE THE TEST THROUGH MIND READING...
...MY CLASSMATES WILL HATE ME...?
HOW COULD YOU POSSIBLY HAVE KNOWN THAT ANSWER?!
SHE'S A FREAK! SHE'S LIKE SOME KINDA WITCH!

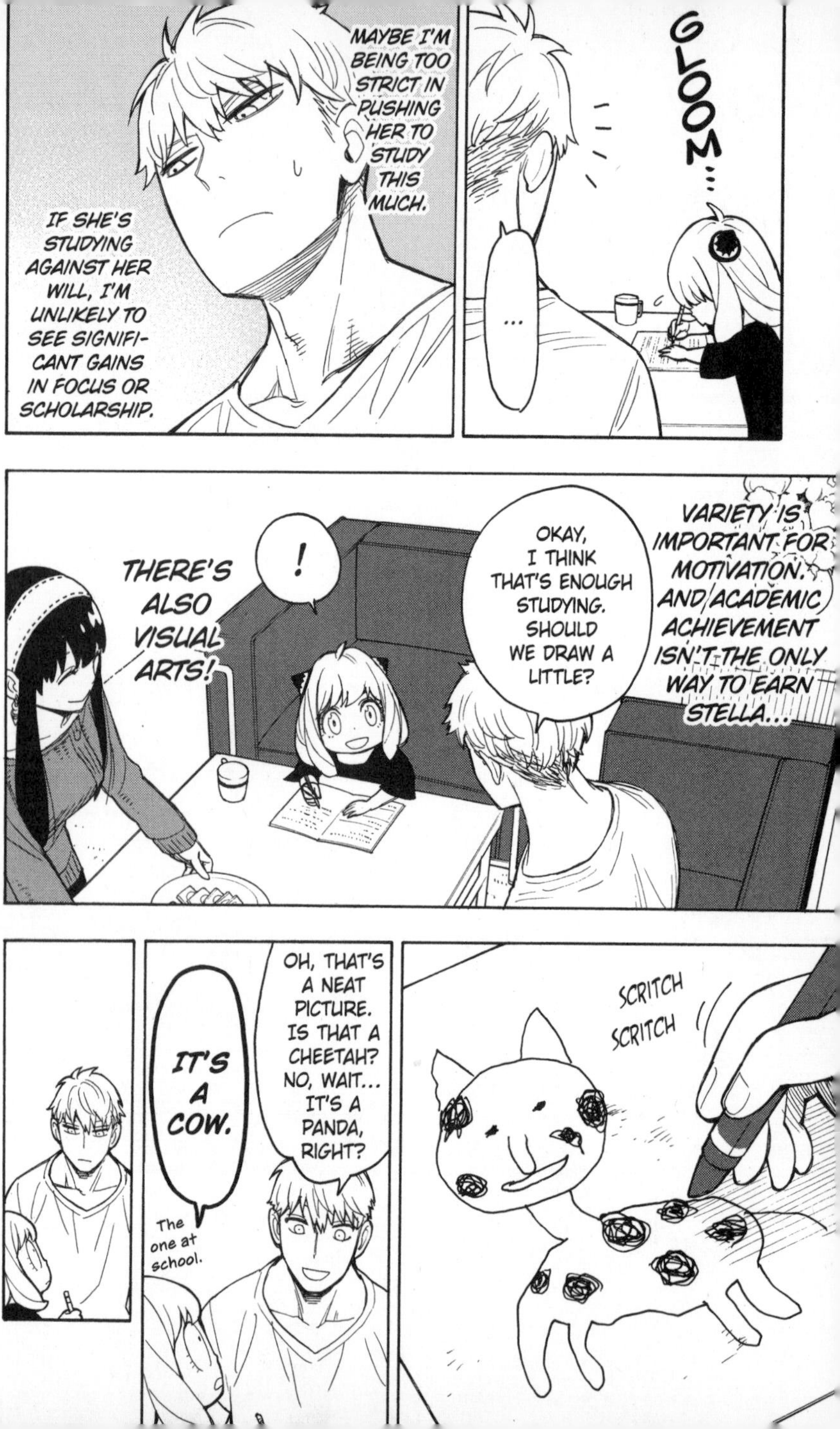
GLOOM...
...
MAYBE I'M BEING TOO STRICT IN PUSHING HER TO STUDY THIS MUCH.
IF SHE'S STUDYING AGAINST HER WILL, I'M UNLIKELY TO SEE SIGNIFICANT GAINS IN FOCUS OR SCHOLARSHIP.
VARIETY IS IMPORTANT FOR MOTIVATION. AND ACADEMIC ACHIEVEMENT ISN'T THE ONLY WAY TO EARN STELLA...
OKAY, I THINK THAT'S ENOUGH STUDYING. SHOULD WE DRAW A LITTLE?
!
THERE'S ALSO VISUAL ARTS!
SCRITCH SCRITCH
OH, THAT'S A NEAT PICTURE. IS THAT A CHEETAH? NO, WAIT... IT'S A PANDA, RIGHT?
IT'S A COW.
The one at school.

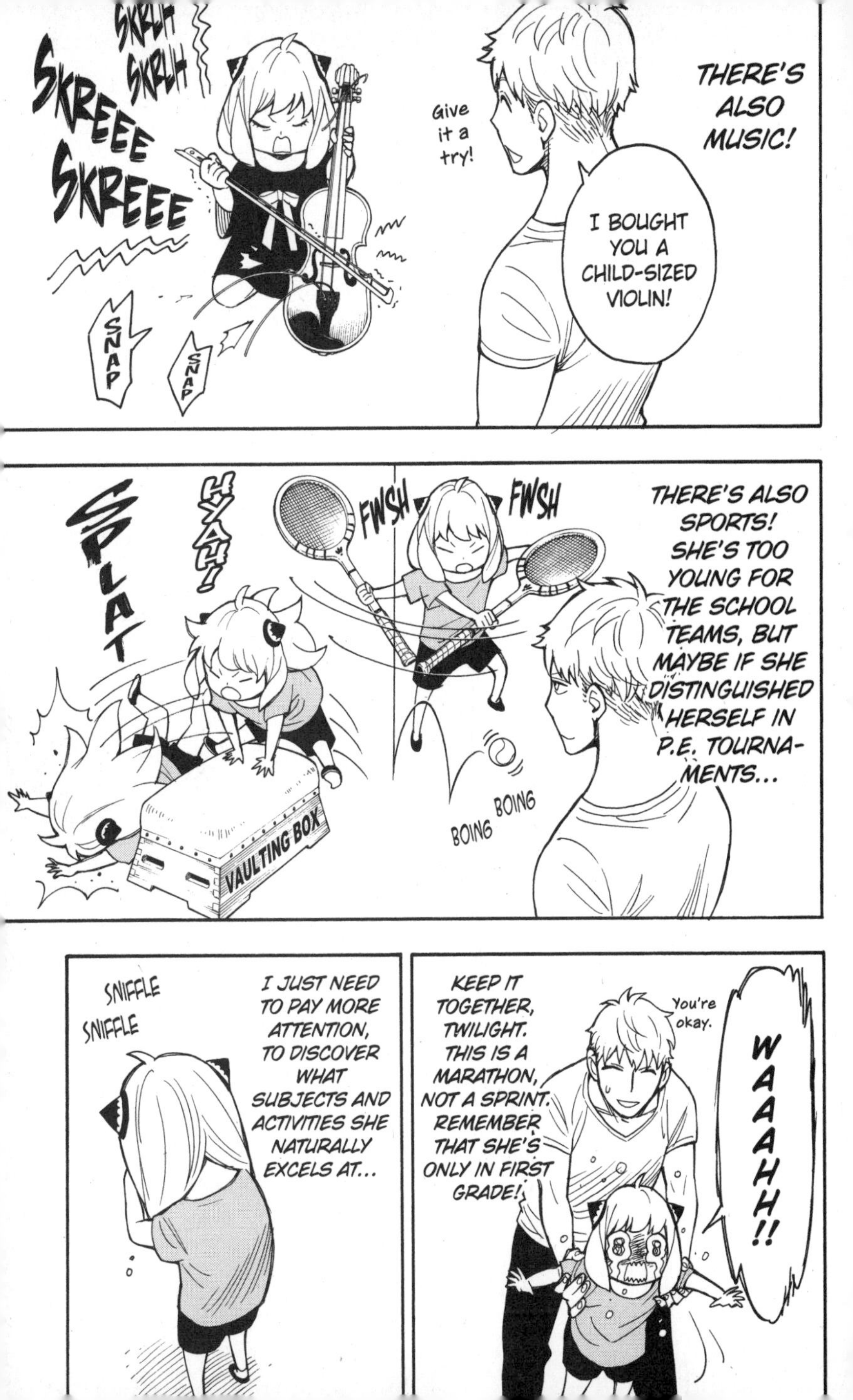
THERE'S ALSO MUSIC!
I BOUGHT YOU A CHILD-SIZED VIOLIN!
Give it a try!
SKRUH SKRUH
SKREEE SKREEE
SNAP
SNAP
THERE'S ALSO SPORTS! SHE'S TOO YOUNG FOR THE SCHOOL TEAMS, BUT MAYBE IF SHE DISTINGUISHED HERSELF IN P.E. TOURNAMENTS...
FWSH
FWSH
BOING BOING
HYAH!
SPLAT
VAULTING BOX
WAAAAHH!!
You're okay.
KEEP IT TOGETHER, TWILIGHT. THIS IS A MARATHON, NOT A SPRINT. REMEMBER THAT SHE'S ONLY IN FIRST GRADE!
I JUST NEED TO PAY MORE ATTENTION, TO DISCOVER WHAT SUBJECTS AND ACTIVITIES SHE NATURALLY EXCELS AT...
SNIFFLE
SNIFFLE

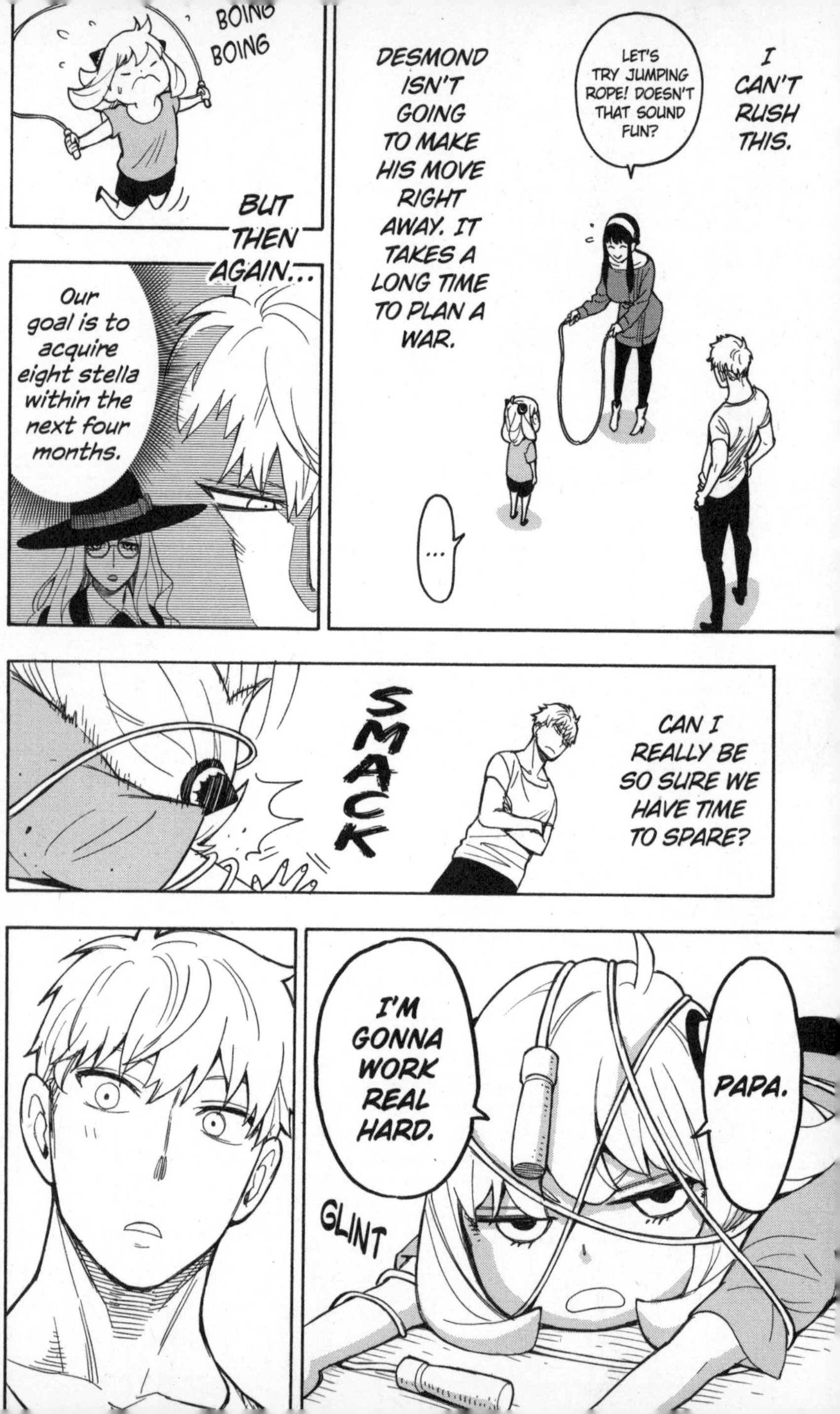
I CAN'T RUSH THIS.
LET'S TRY JUMPING ROPE! DOESN'T THAT SOUND FUN?
DESMOND ISN'T GOING TO MAKE HIS MOVE RIGHT AWAY. IT TAKES A LONG TIME TO PLAN A WAR.
...
BOING BOING
BUT THEN AGAIN...
Our goal is to acquire eight stella within the next four months.
CAN I REALLY BE SO SURE WE HAVE TIME TO SPARE?
SMACK
PAPA.
I'M GONNA WORK REAL HARD.
GLINT

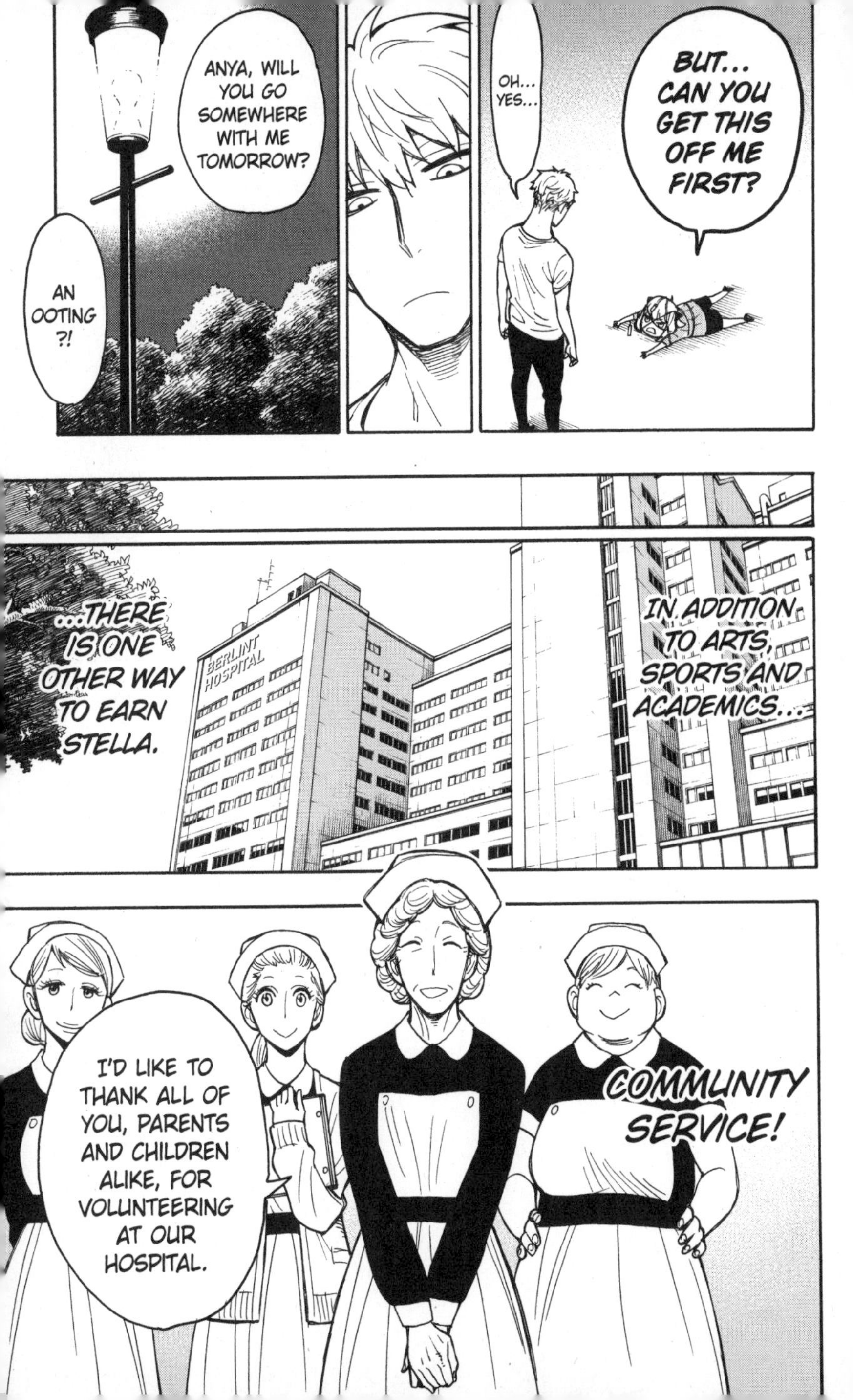
BUT... CAN YOU GET THIS OFF ME FIRST?
OH... YES...
ANYA, WILL YOU GO SOMEWHERE WITH ME TOMORROW?
AN OOTING?!
IN ADDITION TO ARTS, SPORTS AND ACADEMICS...
BERLINT HOSPITAL
...THERE IS ONE OTHER WAY TO EARN STELLA.
COMMUNITY SERVICE!
I'D LIKE TO THANK ALL OF YOU, PARENTS AND CHILDREN ALIKE, FOR VOLUNTEERING AT OUR HOSPITAL.

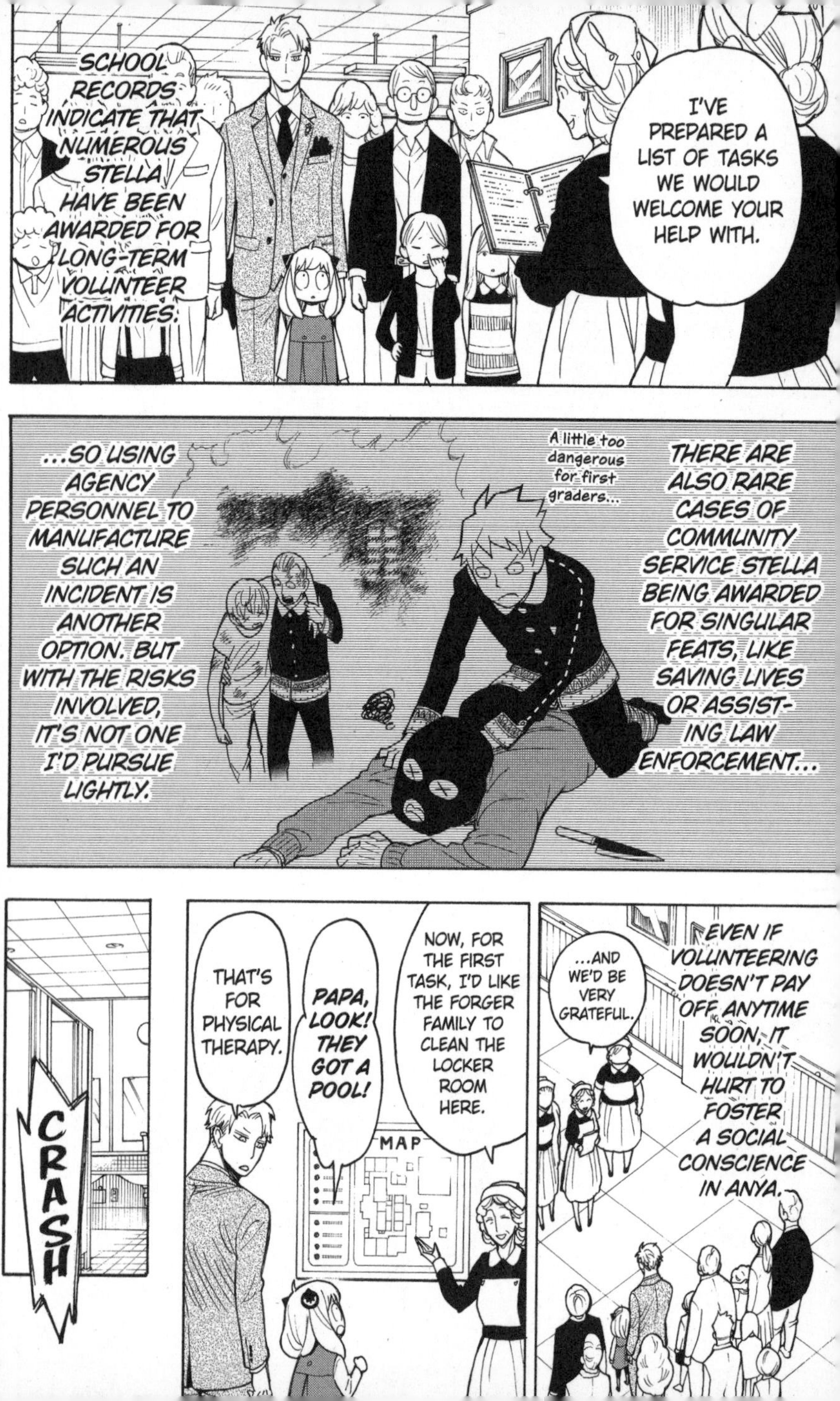
I'VE PREPARED A LIST OF TASKS WE WOULD WELCOME YOUR HELP WITH.
SCHOOL RECORDS INDICATE THAT NUMEROUS STELLA HAVE BEEN AWARDED FOR LONG-TERM VOLUNTEER ACTIVITIES.
THERE ARE ALSO RARE CASES OF COMMUNITY SERVICE STELLA BEING AWARDED FOR SINGULAR FEATS, LIKE SAVING LIVES OR ASSIST-ING LAW ENFORCEMENT...
A little too dangerous for first graders...
...SO USING AGENCY PERSONNEL TO MANUFACTURE SUCH AN INCIDENT IS ANOTHER OPTION. BUT WITH THE RISKS INVOLVED, IT'S NOT ONE I'D PURSUE LIGHTLY.
EVEN IF VOLUNTEERING DOESN'T PAY OFF ANYTIME SOON, IT WOULDN'T HURT TO FOSTER A SOCIAL CONSCIENCE IN ANYA.
...AND WE'D BE VERY GRATEFUL.
NOW, FOR THE FIRST TASK, I'D LIKE THE FORGER FAMILY TO CLEAN THE LOCKER ROOM HERE.
MAP
PAPA, LOOK! THEY GOT A POOL!
THAT'S FOR PHYSICAL THERAPY.
CRASH

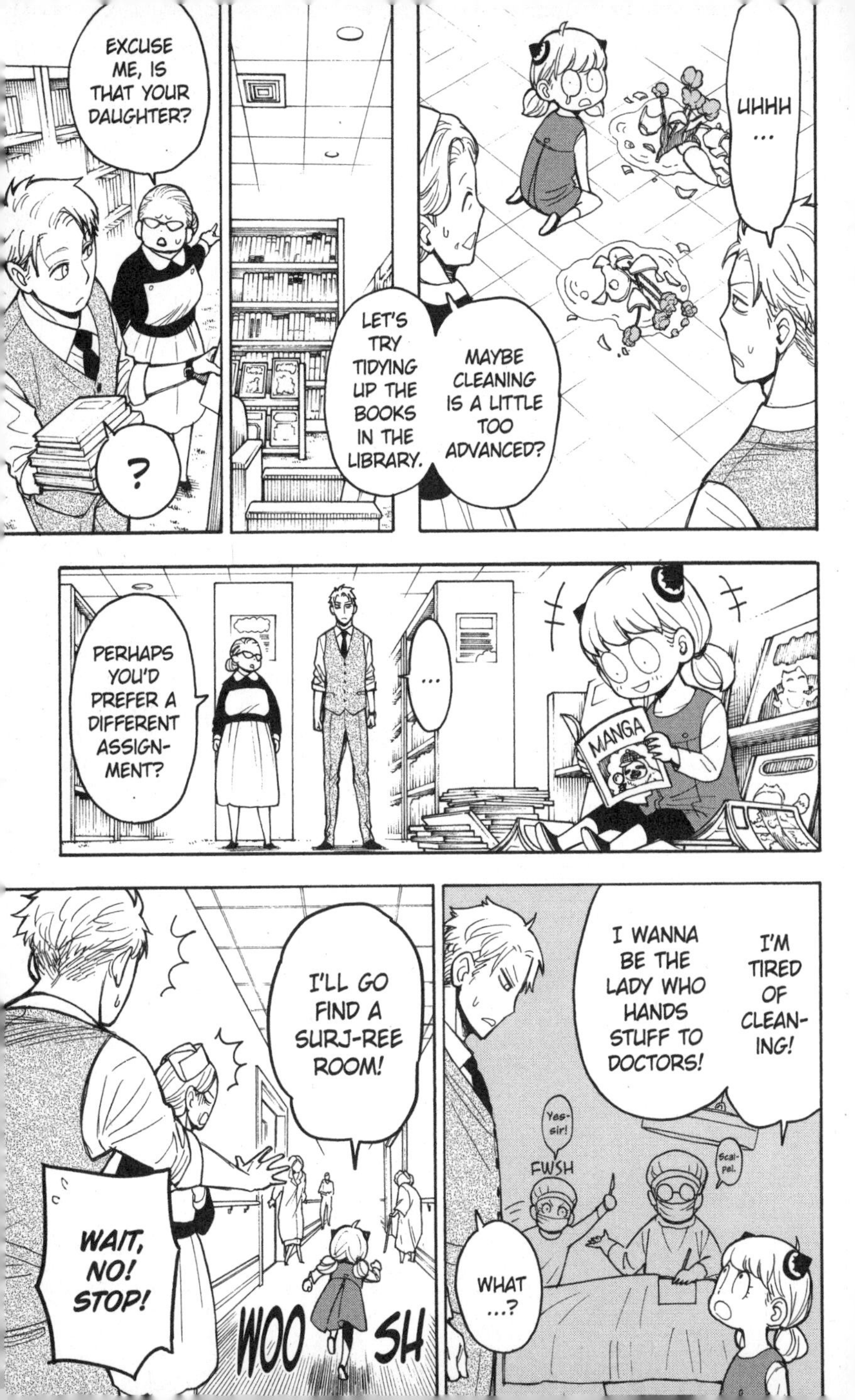
UHHH ...
MAYBE CLEANING IS A LITTLE TOO ADVANCED?
LET'S TRY TIDYING UP THE BOOKS IN THE LIBRARY.
EXCUSE ME, IS THAT YOUR DAUGHTER?
?
...
PERHAPS YOU'D PREFER A DIFFERENT ASSIGN-MENT?
MANGA
I'M TIRED OF CLEAN-ING!
I WANNA BE THE LADY WHO HANDS STUFF TO DOCTORS!
Yes-sir!
FWSH
Scal-pel.
WHAT ...?
I'LL GO FIND A SURJ-REE ROOM!
WAIT, NO! STOP!
WOO SH

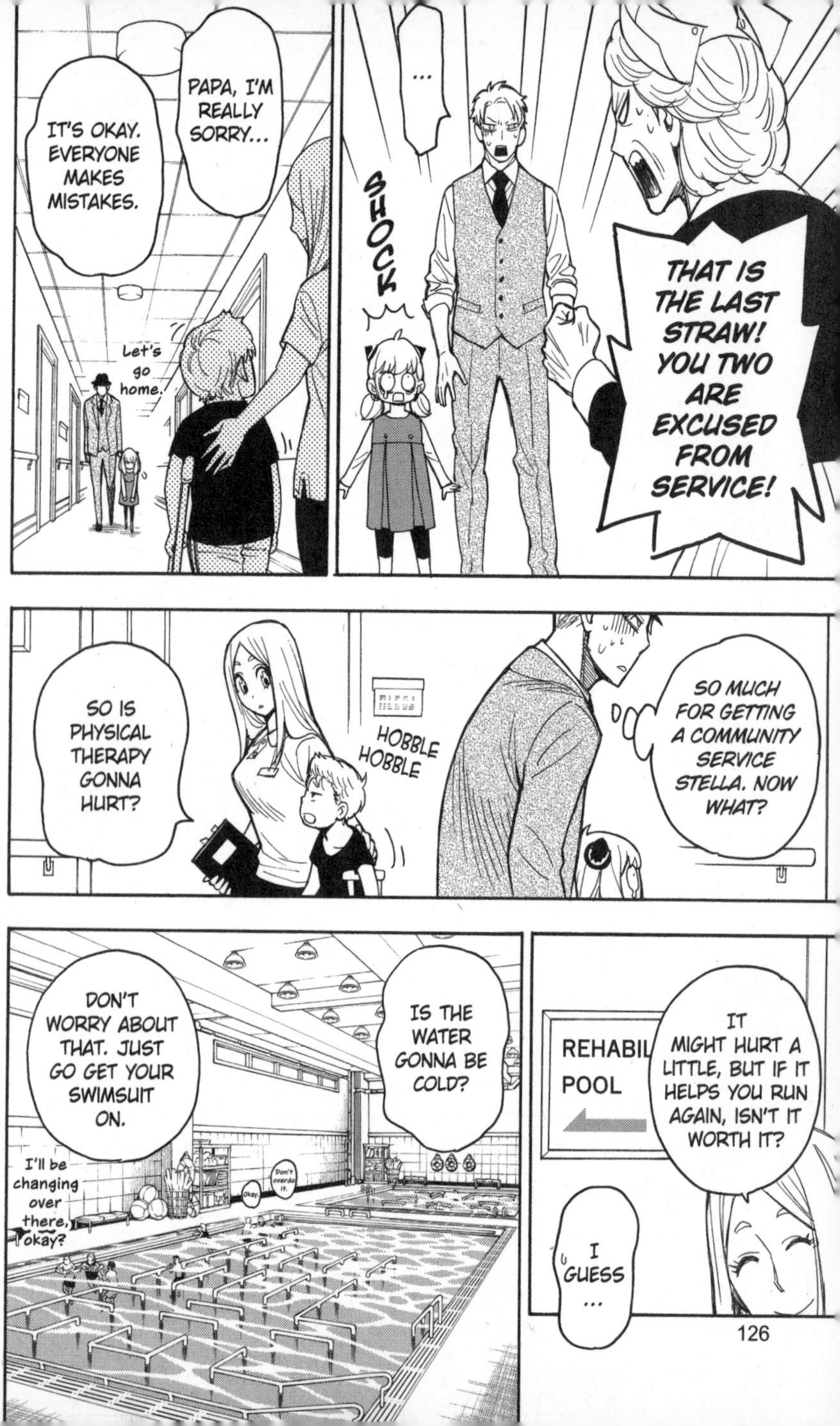
THAT IS THE LAST STRAW! YOU TWO ARE EXCUSED FROM SERVICE!
...
SHOCK
PAPA, I'M REALLY SORRY...
IT'S OKAY. EVERYONE MAKES MISTAKES.
Let's go home.
SO MUCH FOR GETTING A COMMUNITY SERVICE STELLA. NOW WHAT?
HOBBLE HOBBLE
SO IS PHYSICAL THERAPY GONNA HURT?
IT MIGHT HURT A LITTLE, BUT IF IT HELPS YOU RUN AGAIN, ISN'T IT WORTH IT?
REHABIL
POOL
I GUESS...
IS THE WATER GONNA BE COLD?
DON'T WORRY ABOUT THAT. JUST GO GET YOUR SWIMSUIT ON.
Don't overdo it.
Okay.
I'll be changing over there, okay?

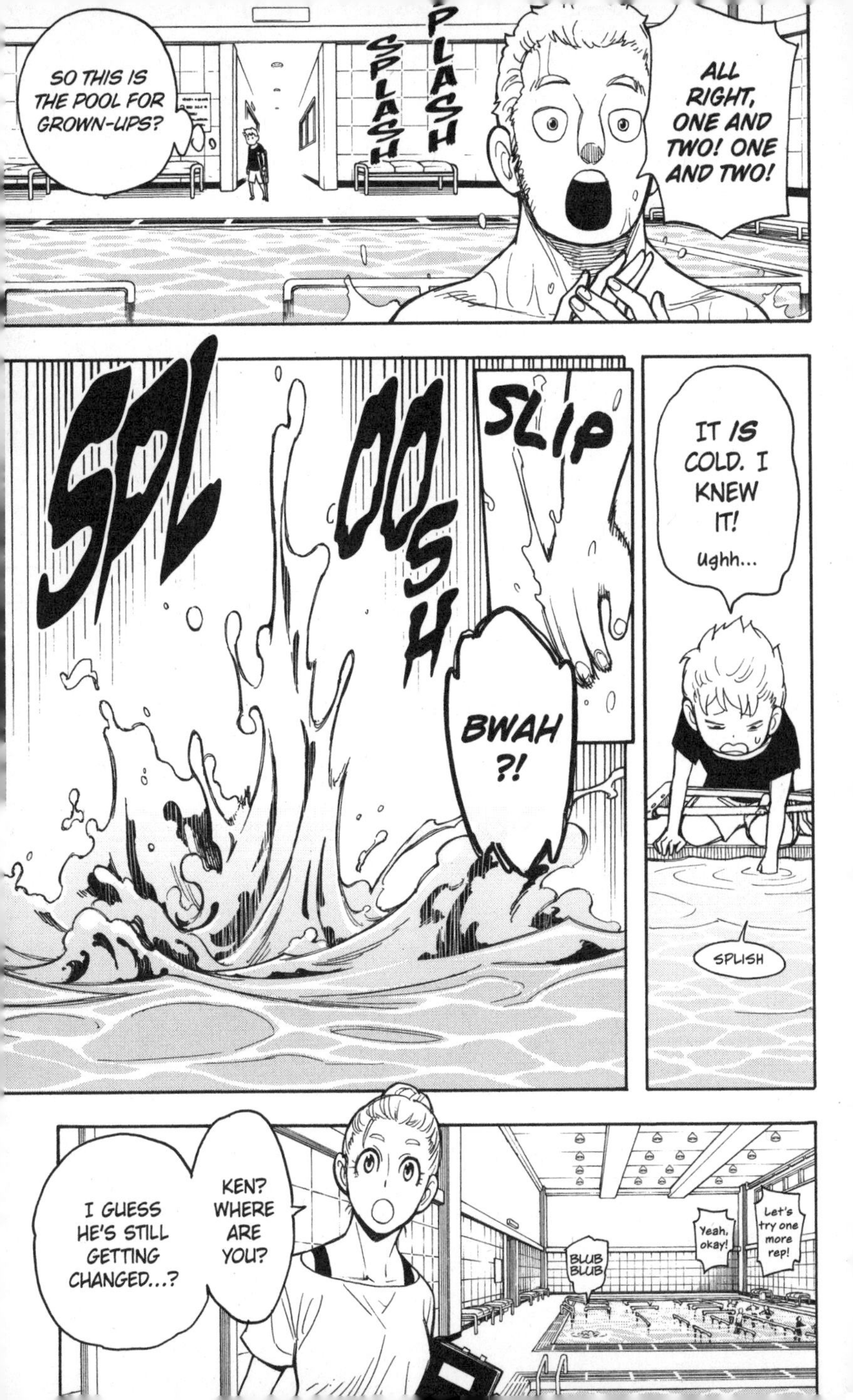
ALL RIGHT, ONE AND TWO! ONE AND TWO!
SPLASH SPLASH
SO THIS IS THE POOL FOR GROWN-UPS?
IT IS COLD. I KNEW IT!
ughh...
SPLISH
SLIP
BWAH ?!
SPLOOSH
Let's try one more rep!
Yeah, okay!
BLUB BLUB
KEN? WHERE ARE YOU?
I GUESS HE'S STILL GETTING CHANGED...?

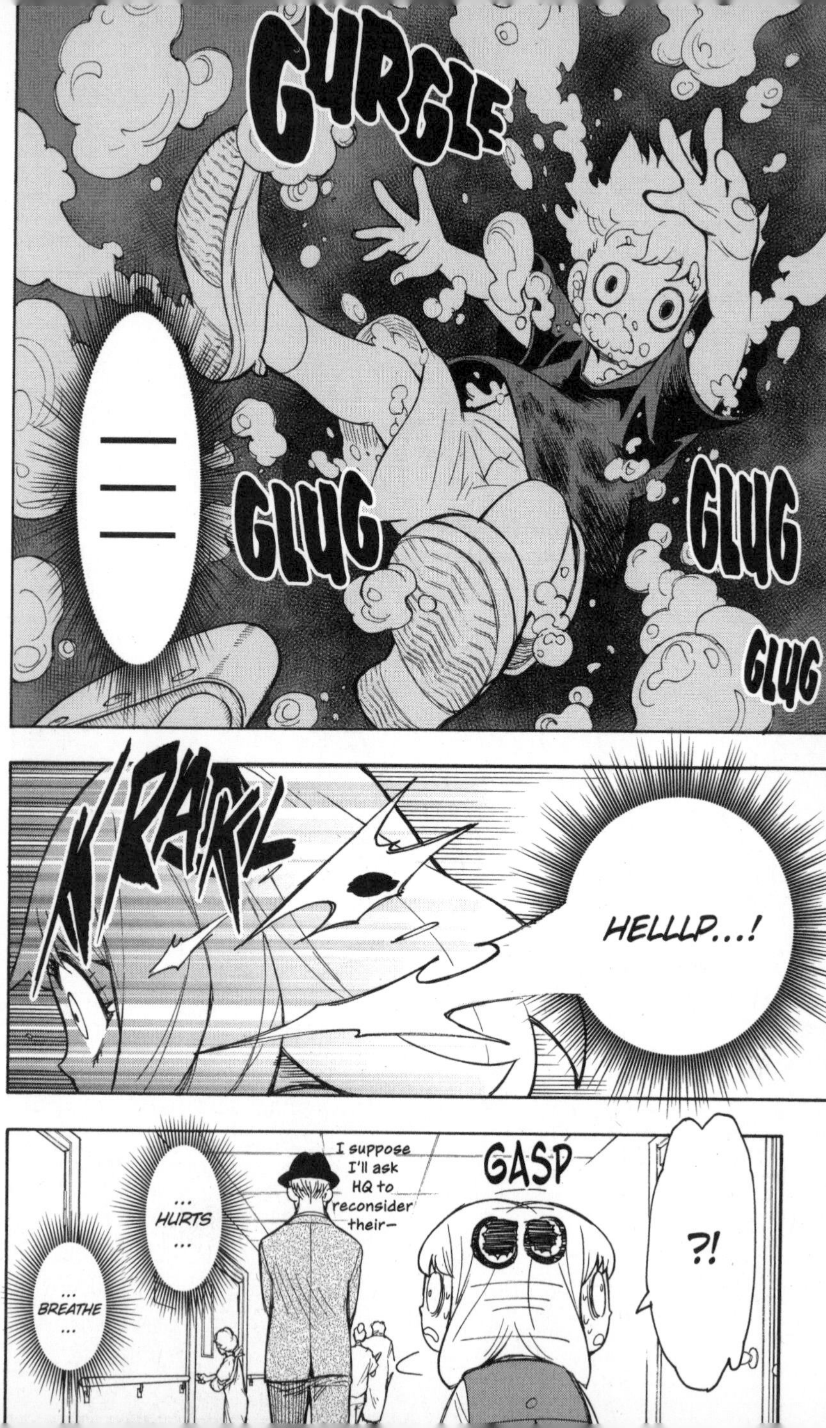
GURGLE
GLUG
GLUG
GLUG
HELLLP...!
?!
GASP
I suppose I'll ask HQ to reconsider their—
... HURTS ...
... BREATHE ...

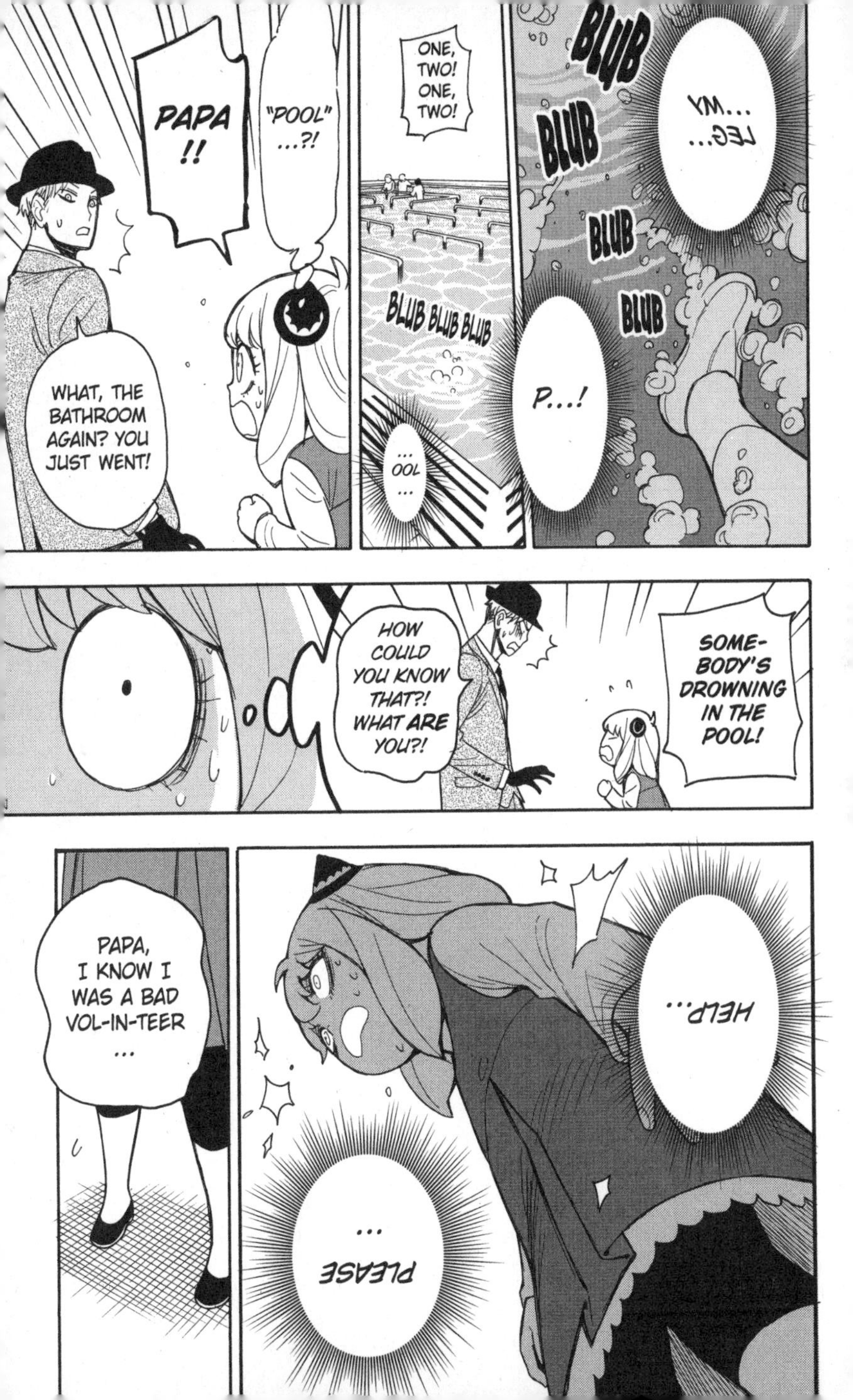
...MY LEG...
BLUB
BLUB
BLUB
BLUB
P...!
ONE, TWO! ONE, TWO!
BLUB BLUB BLUB
...OOL...
"POOL" ...?!
PAPA!!
WHAT, THE BATHROOM AGAIN? YOU JUST WENT!
SOME-BODY'S DROWNING IN THE POOL!
HOW COULD YOU KNOW THAT?! WHAT ARE YOU?!
HELP...
PLEASE...
PAPA, I KNOW I WAS A BAD VOL-IN-TEER ...

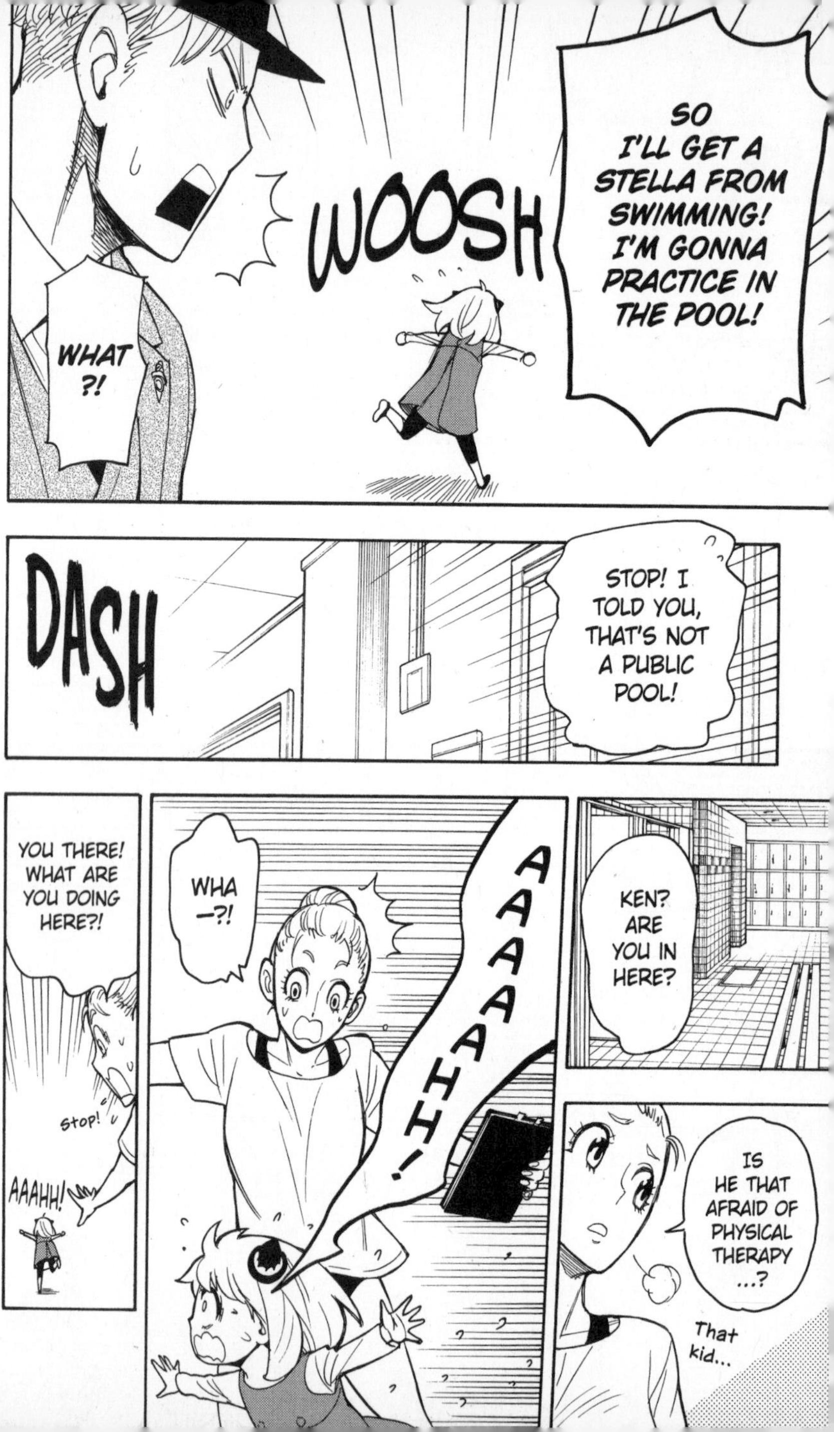
SO I'LL GET A STELLA FROM SWIMMING! I'M GONNA PRACTICE IN THE POOL!
WOOSH
WHAT ?!
STOP! I TOLD YOU, THAT'S NOT A PUBLIC POOL!
DASH
KEN? ARE YOU IN HERE?
IS HE THAT AFRAID OF PHYSICAL THERAPY ...?
That kid...
WHA —?!
AAAAAAHH!
YOU THERE! WHAT ARE YOU DOING HERE?!
Stop!
AAAHH!

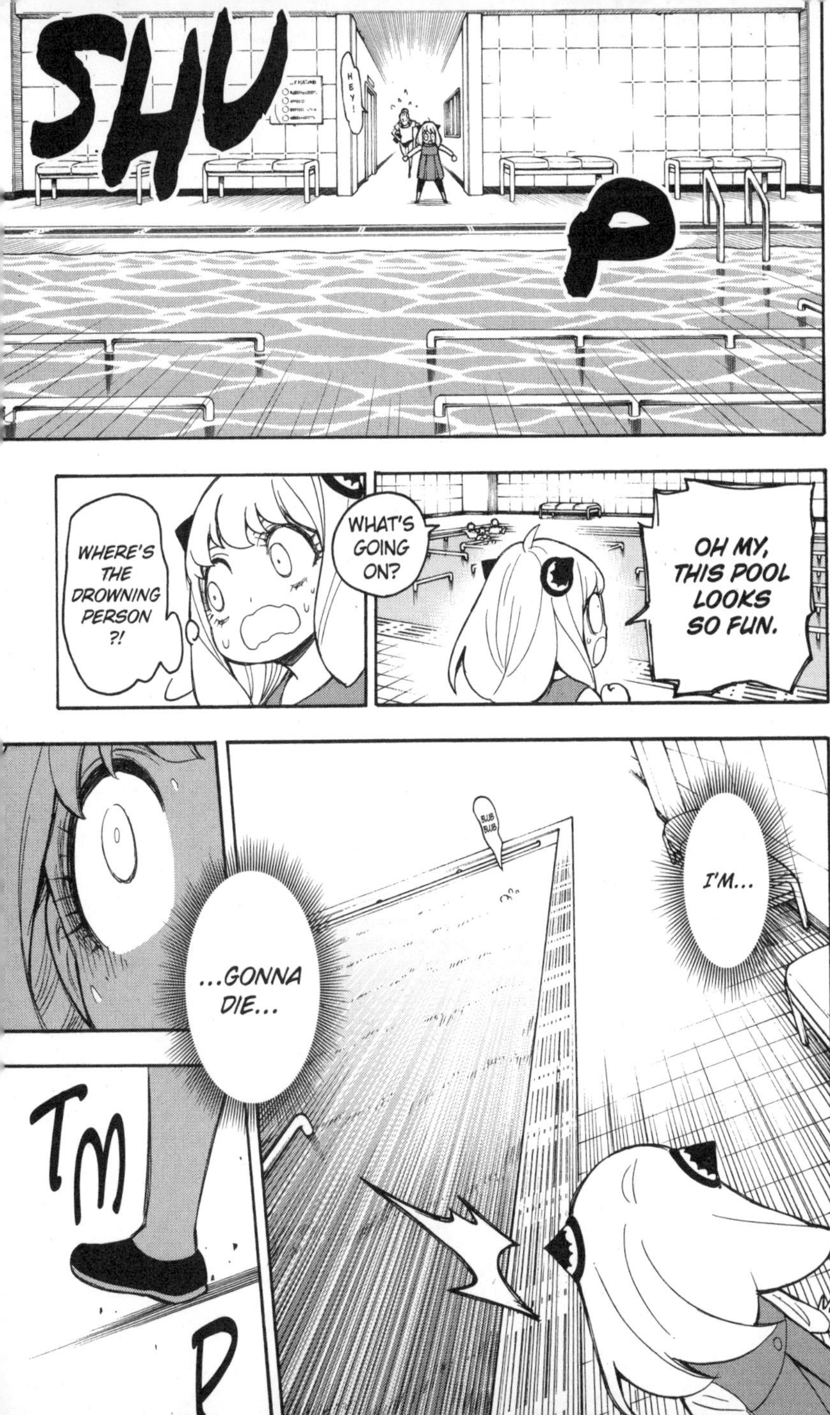
SHU
P
HEY!
OH MY, THIS POOL LOOKS SO FUN.
WHAT'S GOING ON?
WHERE'S THE DROWNING PERSON ?!
I'M...
BLUB BLUB
...GONNA DIE...
TM
P

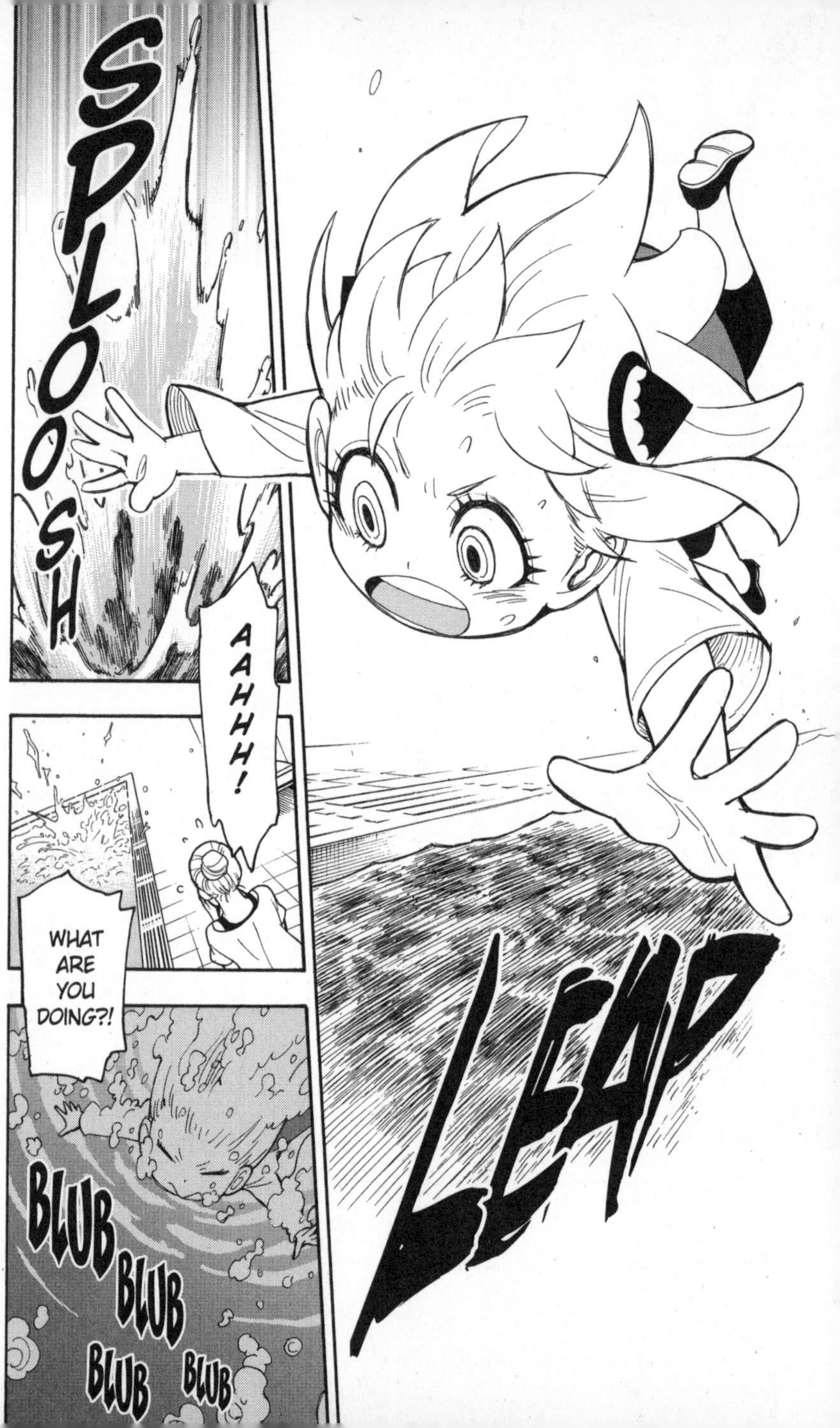

LEAP
SPLOOOSH
AAHHHH!
WHAT ARE YOU DOING?!
BLUB BLUB
BLUB BLUB

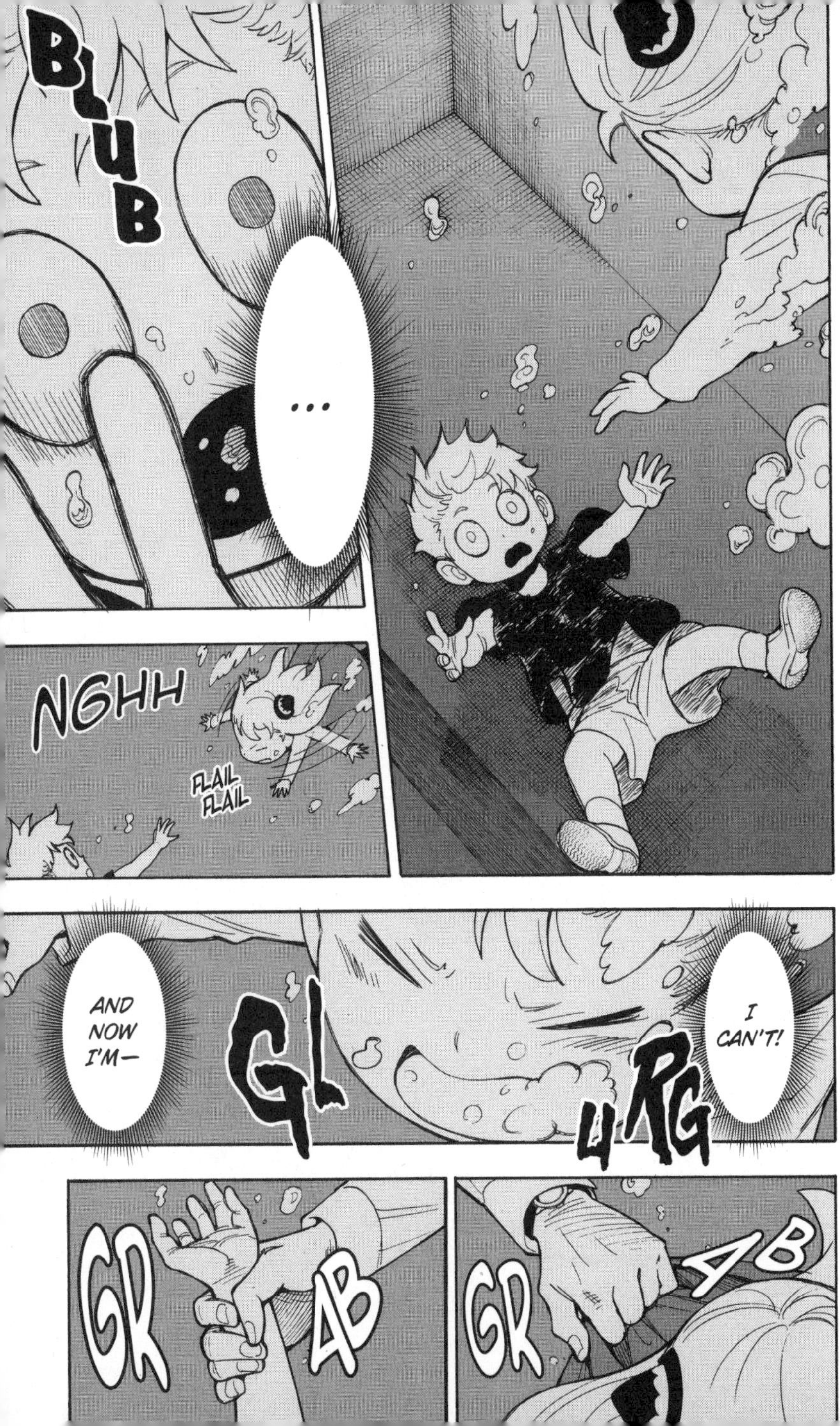
BLUB
...
NGHH
FLAIL FLAIL
I CAN'T!
URG
GL
AND NOW I'M—
GRAB
GRAB

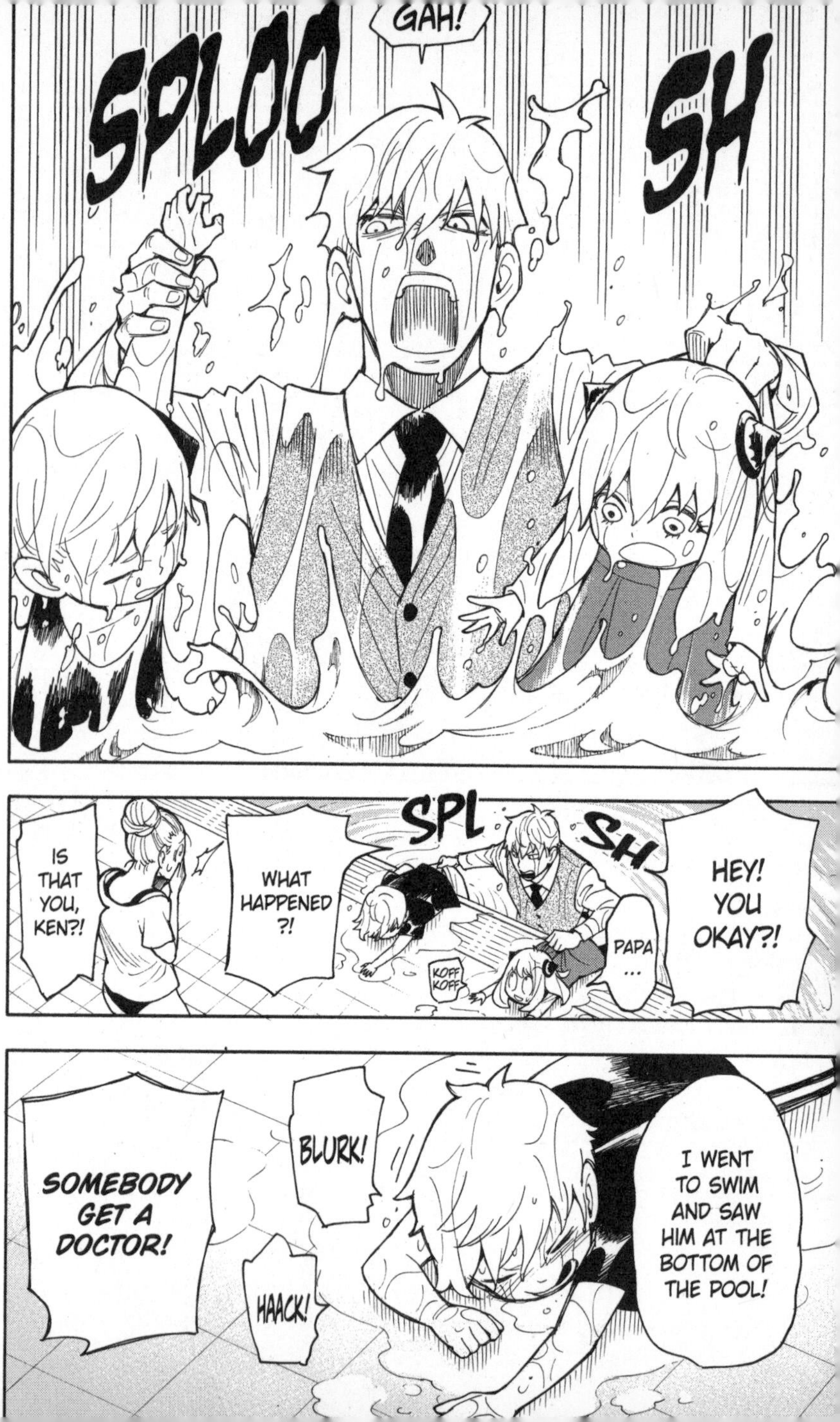
GAH!
SPLOOSH
HEY! YOU OKAY?!
PAPA...
SPLSH
KOFF KOFF
WHAT HAPPENED?!
IS THAT YOU, KEN?!
I WENT TO SWIM AND SAW HIM AT THE BOTTOM OF THE POOL!
BLURK!
HAACK!
SOMEBODY GET A DOCTOR!

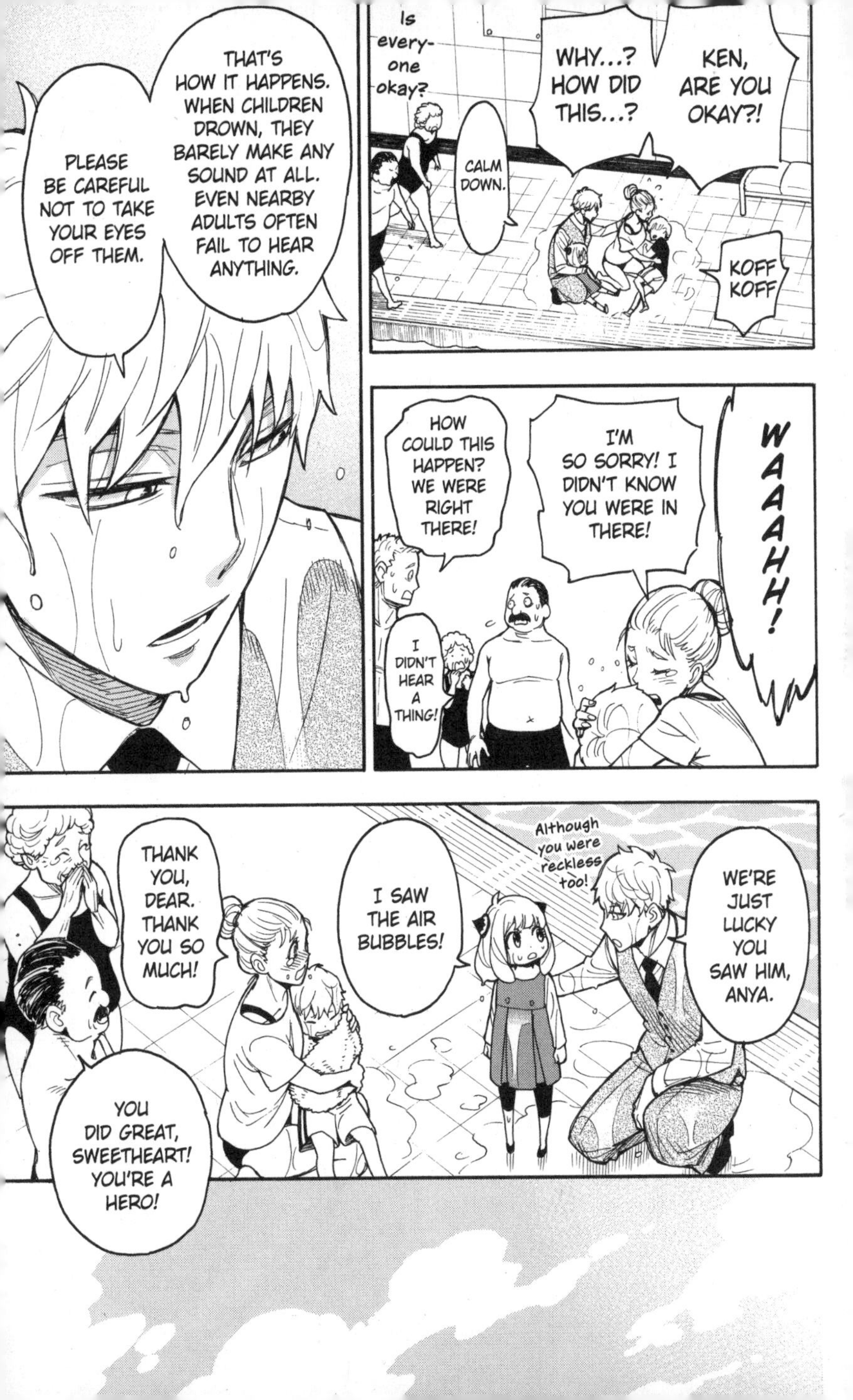
KEN, ARE YOU OKAY?!
WHY...? HOW DID THIS...?
Is everyone okay?
CALM DOWN.
KOFF KOFF
WAAAHH!
I'M SO SORRY! I DIDN'T KNOW YOU WERE IN THERE!
HOW COULD THIS HAPPEN? WE WERE RIGHT THERE!
I DIDN'T HEAR A THING!
THAT'S HOW IT HAPPENS. WHEN CHILDREN DROWN, THEY BARELY MAKE ANY SOUND AT ALL. EVEN NEARBY ADULTS OFTEN FAIL TO HEAR ANYTHING.
PLEASE BE CAREFUL NOT TO TAKE YOUR EYES OFF THEM.
WE'RE JUST LUCKY YOU SAW HIM, ANYA.
Although you were reckless too!
I SAW THE AIR BUBBLES!
THANK YOU, DEAR. THANK YOU SO MUCH!
YOU DID GREAT, SWEETHEART! YOU'RE A HERO!

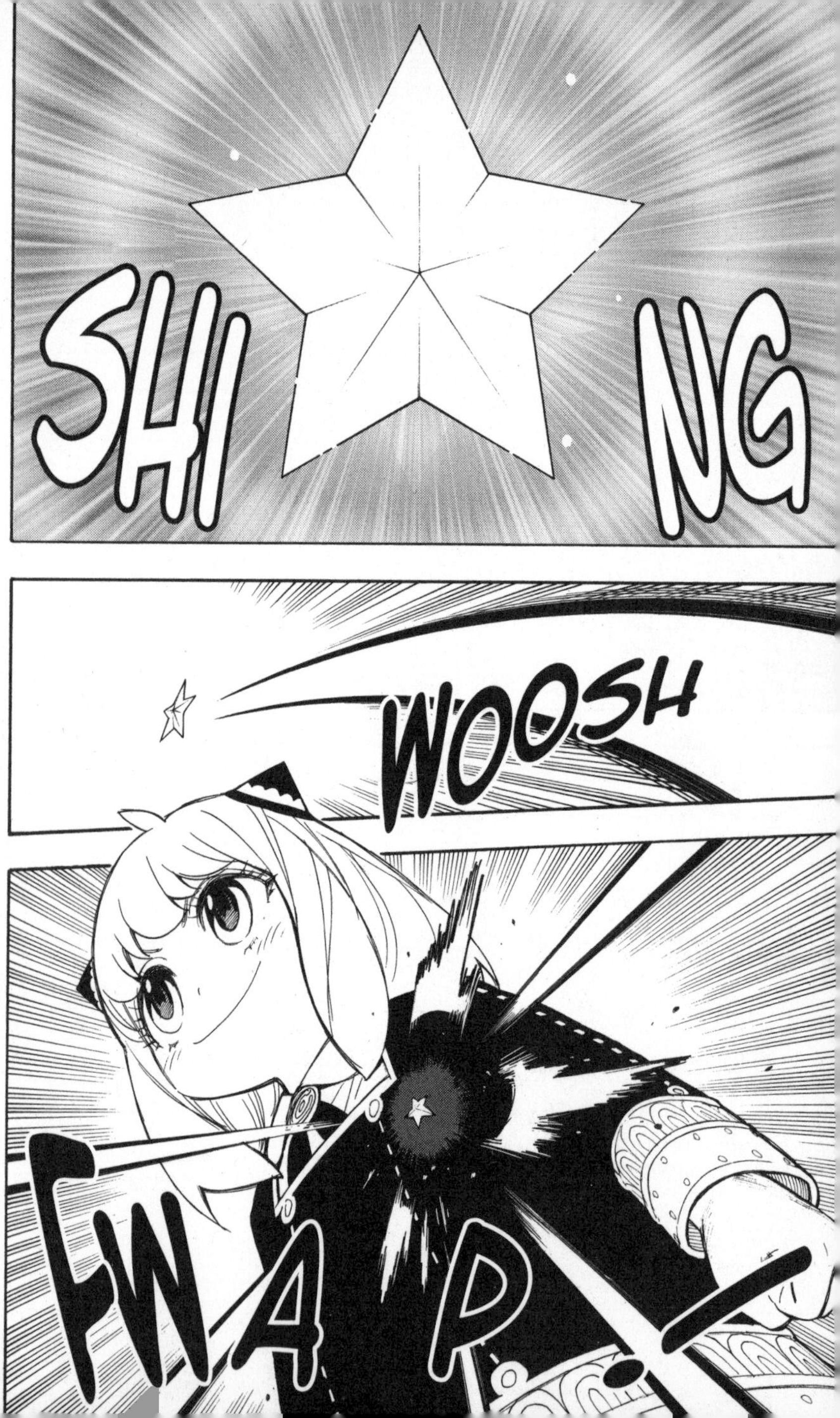
SHI NG
WOOSH
FWAP!

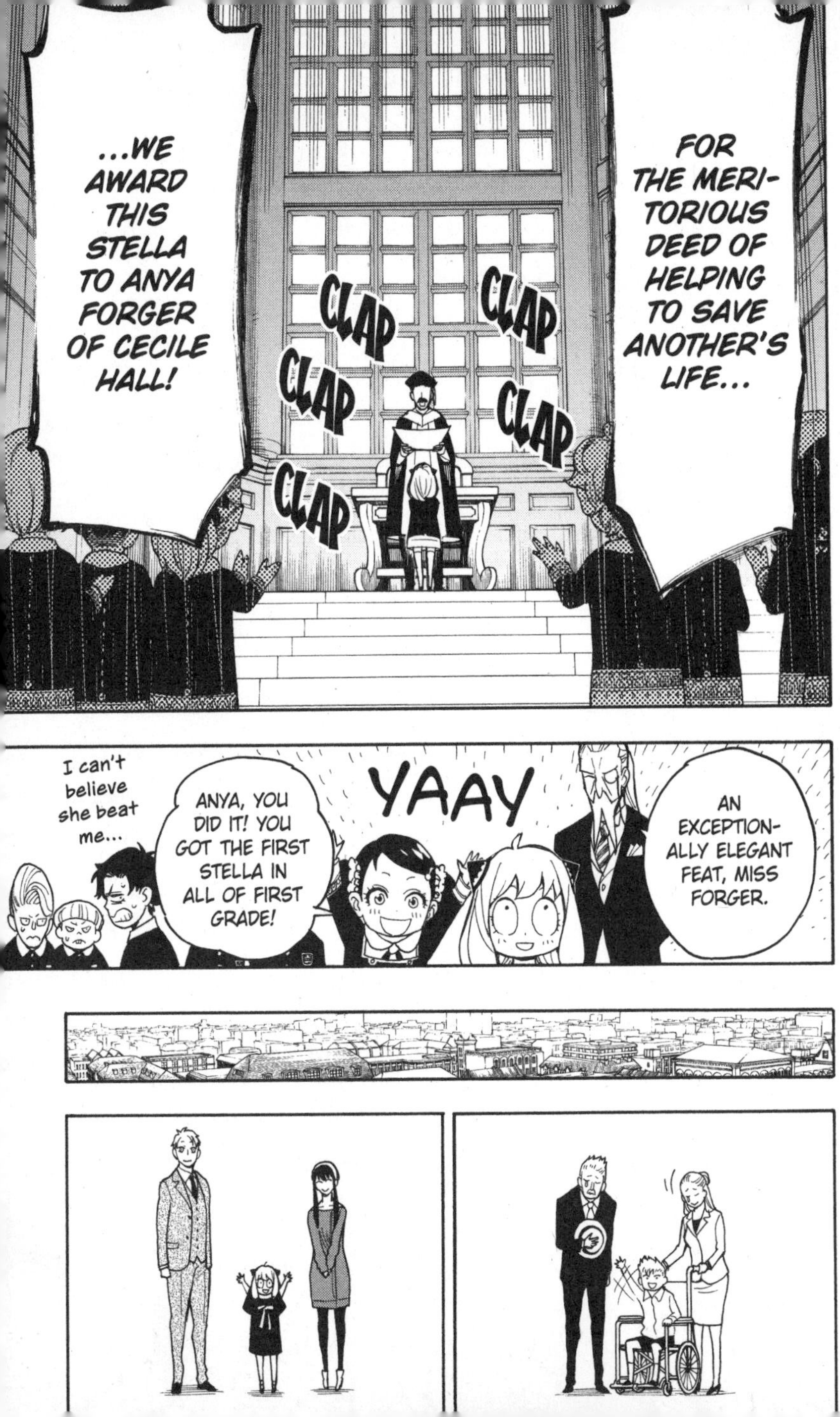
FOR THE MERITORIOUS DEED OF HELPING TO SAVE ANOTHER'S LIFE...
CLAP CLAP
CLAP CLAP CLAP
...WE AWARD THIS STELLA TO ANYA FORGER OF CECILE HALL!
AN EXCEPTIONALLY ELEGANT FEAT, MISS FORGER.
YAAY
ANYA, YOU DID IT! YOU GOT THE FIRST STELLA IN ALL OF FIRST GRADE!
I can't believe she beat me...

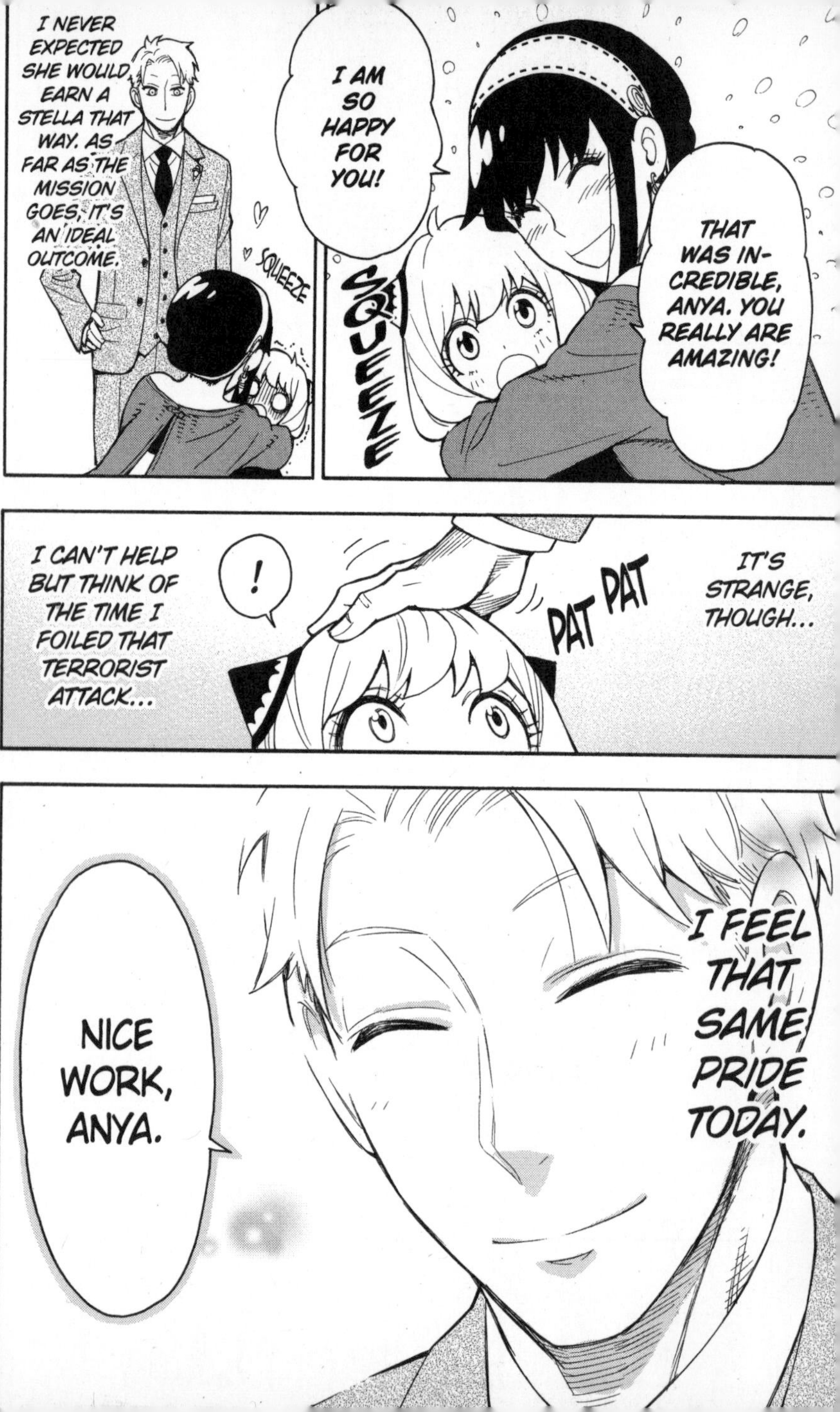
THAT WAS INCREDIBLE, ANYA. YOU REALLY ARE AMAZING!
I AM SO HAPPY FOR YOU!
SQUEEZE
I NEVER EXPECTED SHE WOULD EARN A STELLA THAT WAY. AS FAR AS THE MISSION GOES, IT'S AN IDEAL OUTCOME.
SQUEEZE
IT'S STRANGE, THOUGH...
PAT PAT
!
I CAN'T HELP BUT THINK OF THE TIME I FOILED THAT TERRORIST ATTACK...
I FEEL THAT SAME PRIDE TODAY.
NICE WORK, ANYA.

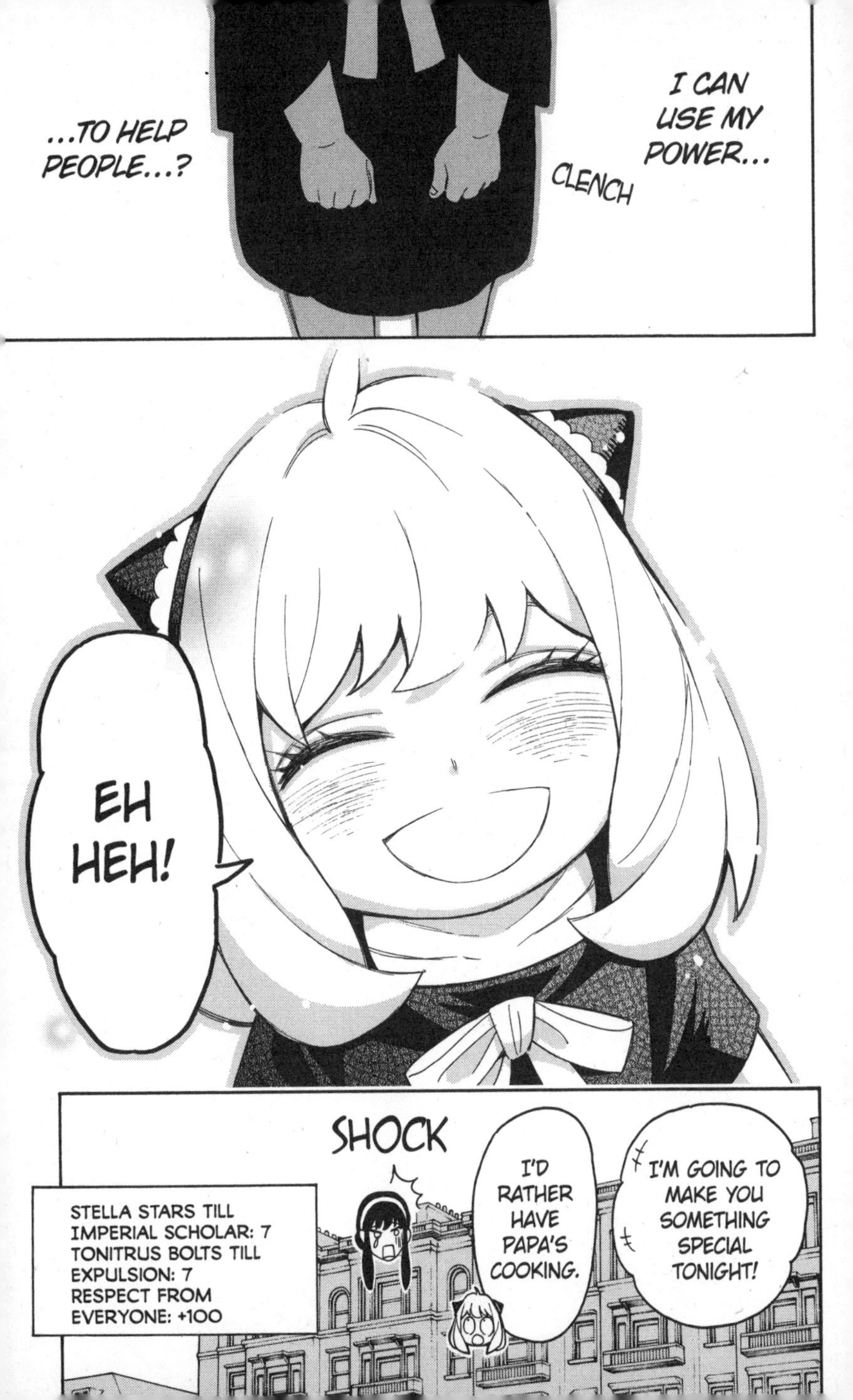
I CAN USE MY POWER...
CLENCH
...TO HELP PEOPLE...?
EH HEH!
I'M GOING TO MAKE YOU SOMETHING SPECIAL TONIGHT!
I'D RATHER HAVE PAPA'S COOKING.
SHOCK
STELLA STARS TILL IMPERIAL SCHOLAR: 7
TONITRUS BOLTS TILL EXPULSION: 7
RESPECT FROM EVERYONE: +100

SPY×FAMILY

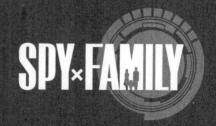

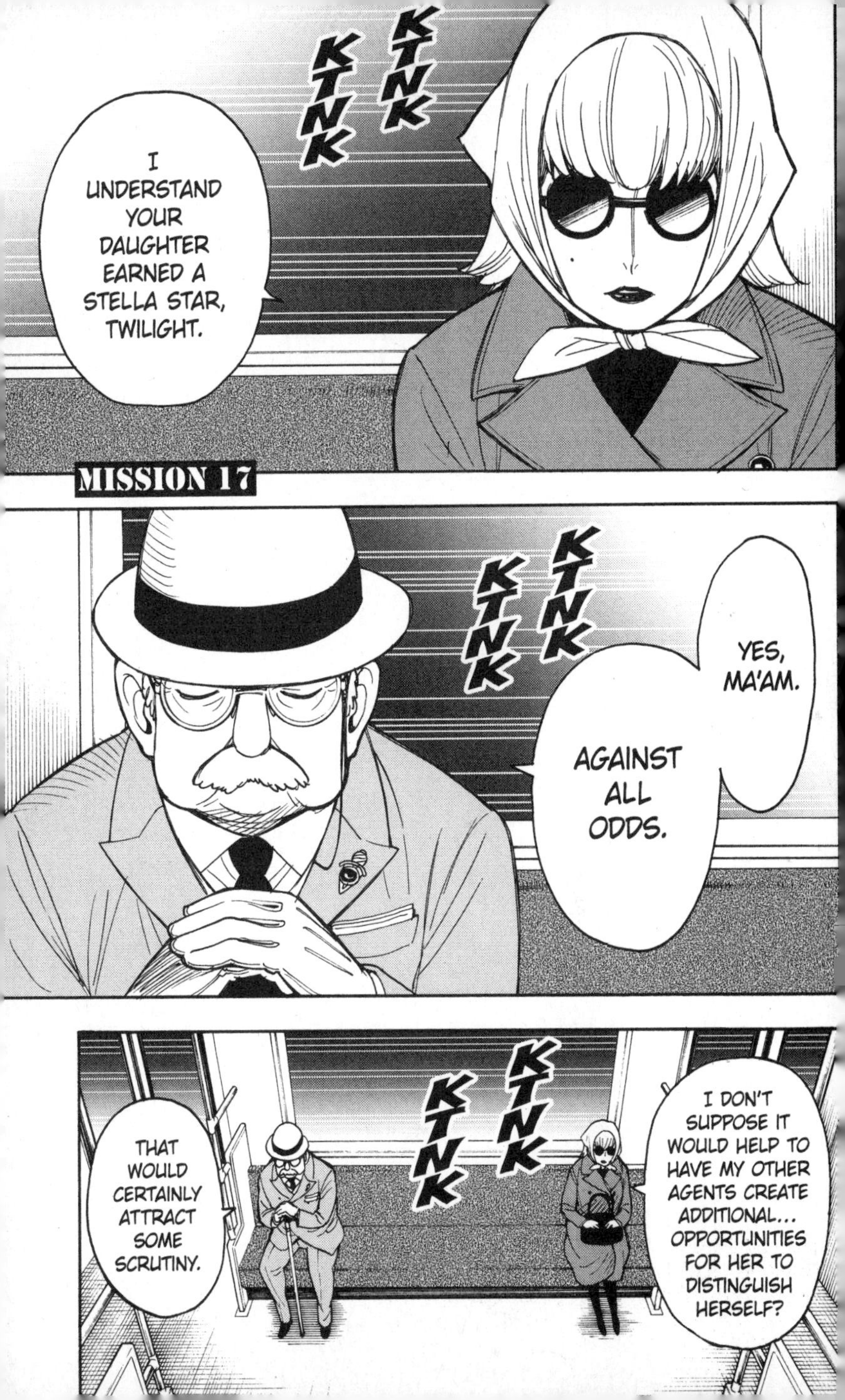
KTNK KTNK
I UNDERSTAND YOUR DAUGHTER EARNED A STELLA STAR, TWILIGHT.
MISSION 17
YES, MA'AM.
AGAINST ALL ODDS.
KTNK KTNK
I DON'T SUPPOSE IT WOULD HELP TO HAVE MY OTHER AGENTS CREATE ADDITIONAL... OPPORTUNITIES FOR HER TO DISTINGUISH HERSELF?
KTNK KTNK
THAT WOULD CERTAINLY ATTRACT SOME SCRUTINY.

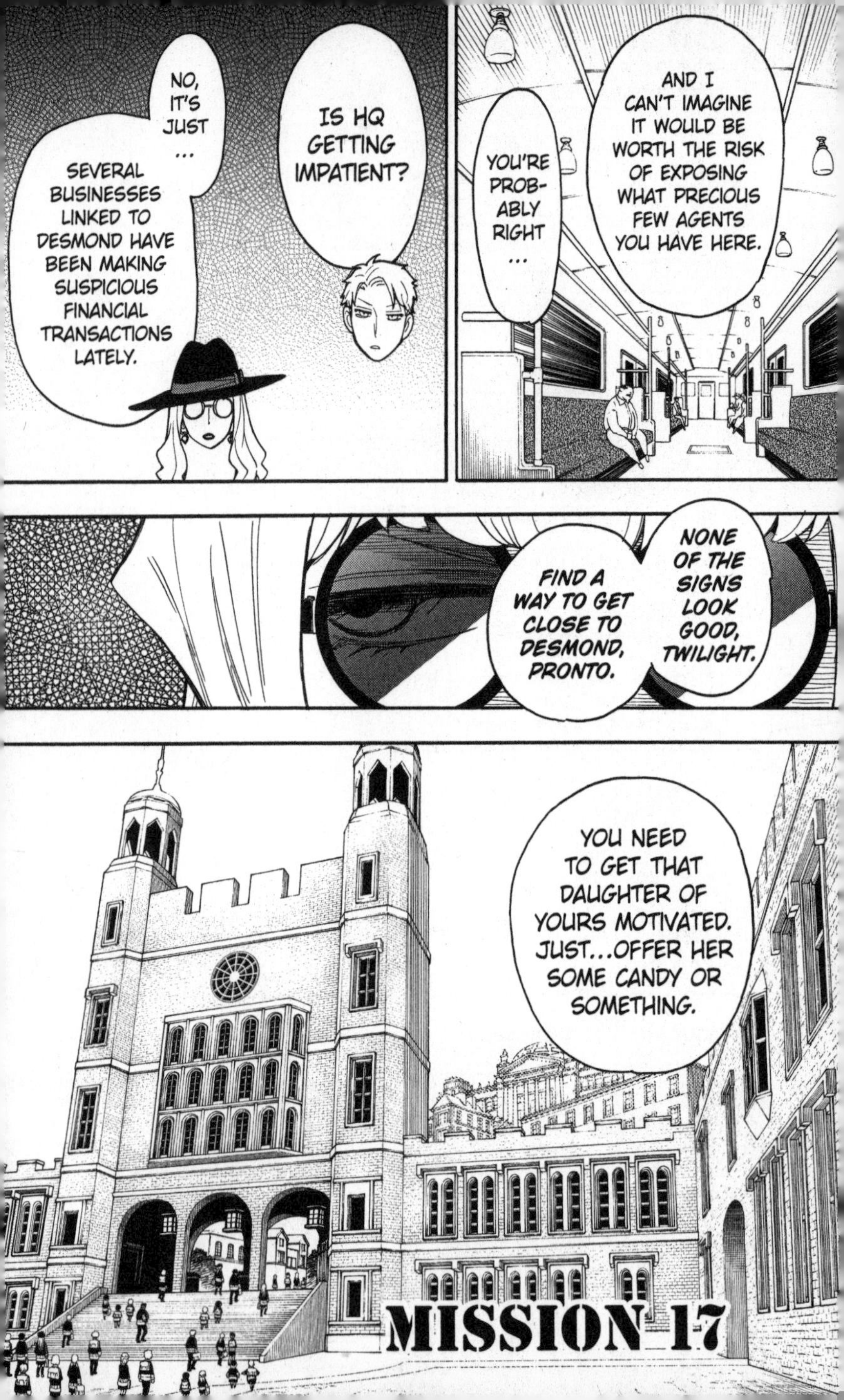
AND I CAN'T IMAGINE IT WOULD BE WORTH THE RISK OF EXPOSING WHAT PRECIOUS FEW AGENTS YOU HAVE HERE.
YOU'RE PROB-ABLY RIGHT ...
IS HQ GETTING IMPATIENT?
NO, IT'S JUST ... SEVERAL BUSINESSES LINKED TO DESMOND HAVE BEEN MAKING SUSPICIOUS FINANCIAL TRANSACTIONS LATELY.
NONE OF THE SIGNS LOOK GOOD, TWILIGHT.
FIND A WAY TO GET CLOSE TO DESMOND, PRONTO.
YOU NEED TO GET THAT DAUGHTER OF YOURS MOTIVATED. JUST...OFFER HER SOME CANDY OR SOMETHING.
MISSION 17

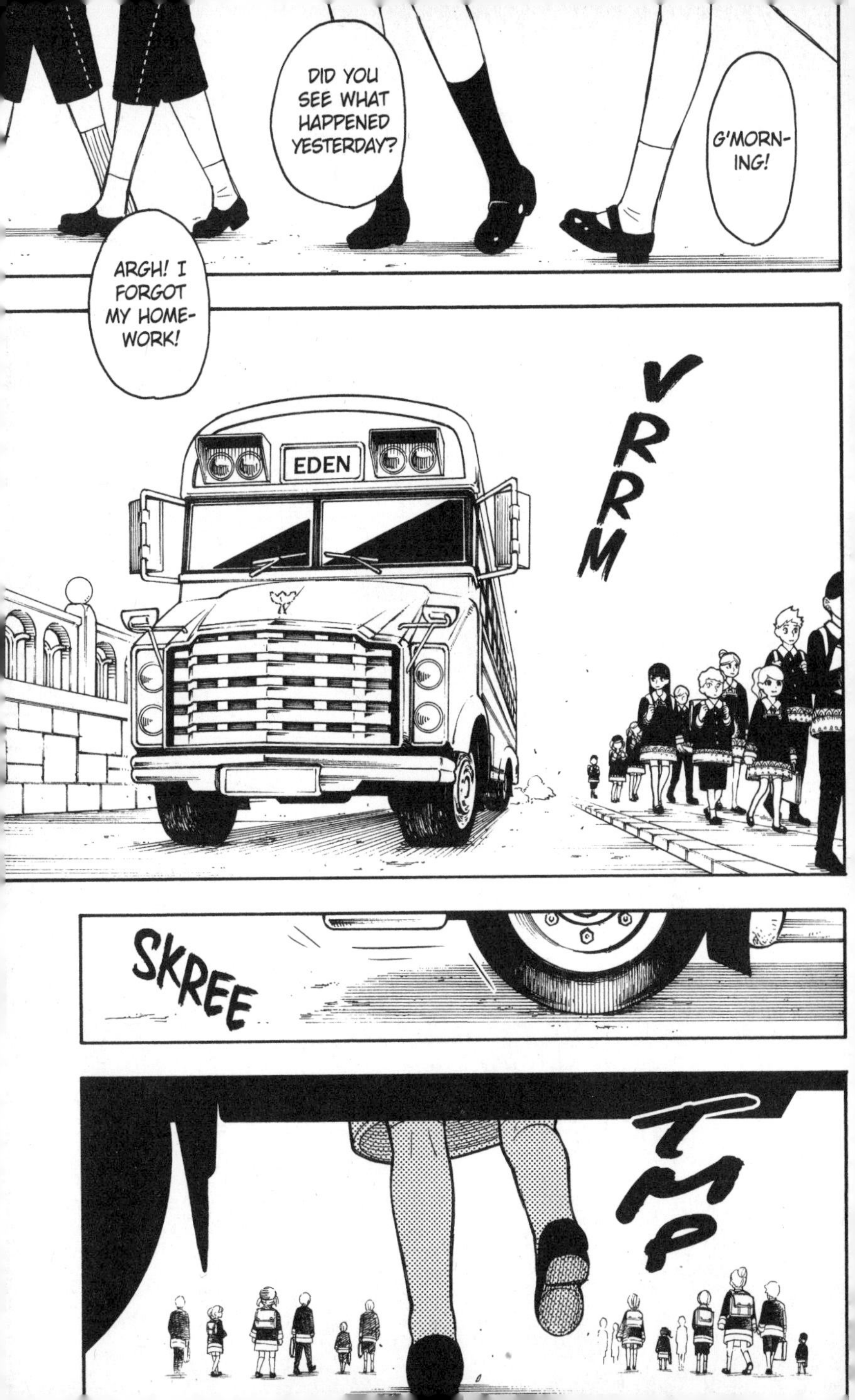
G'MORNING!
DID YOU SEE WHAT HAPPENED YESTERDAY?
ARGH! I FORGOT MY HOMEWORK!
EDEN
VRRM
SKREE
TMP

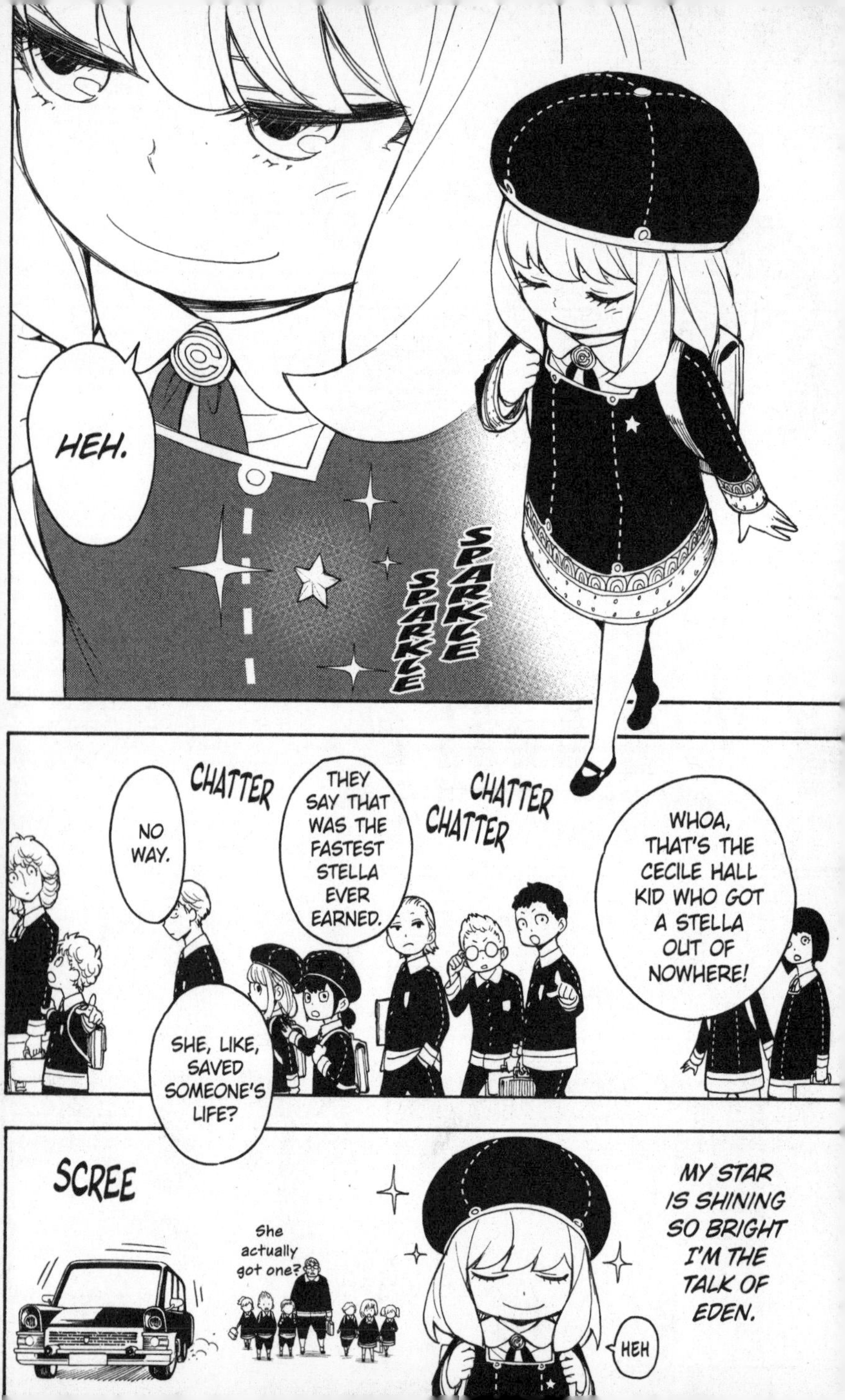

SPARKLE
SPARKLE
HEH.
WHOA, THAT'S THE CECILE HALL KID WHO GOT A STELLA OUT OF NOWHERE!
CHATTER
CHATTER
THEY SAY THAT WAS THE FASTEST STELLA EVER EARNED.
CHATTER
NO WAY.
SHE, LIKE, SAVED SOMEONE'S LIFE?
MY STAR IS SHINING SO BRIGHT I'M THE TALK OF EDEN.
HEH
She actually got one?
SCREE

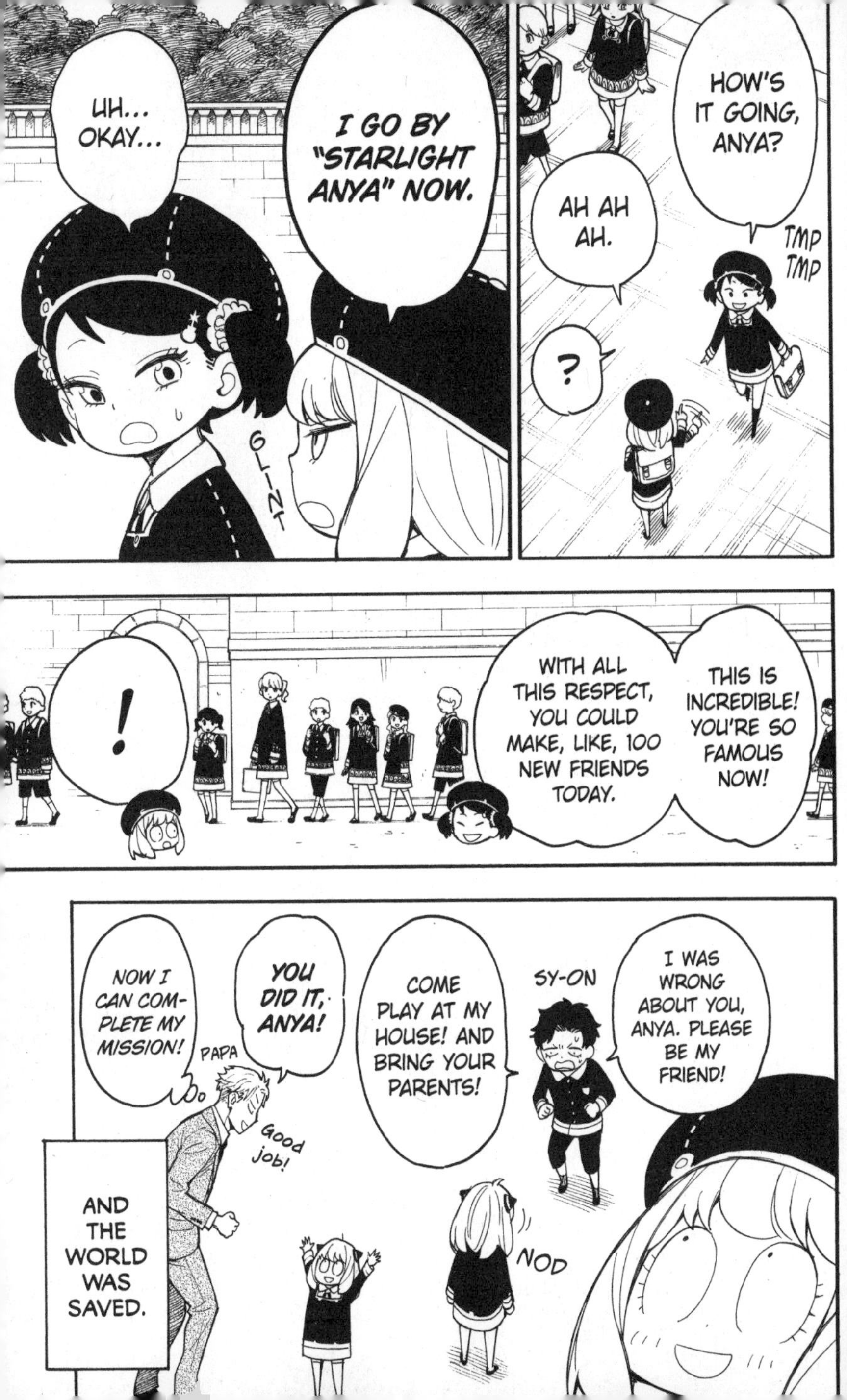
HOW'S IT GOING, ANYA?
TMP TMP
AH AH AH.
?
I GO BY "STARLIGHT ANYA" NOW.
GLINT
UH... OKAY...
THIS IS INCREDIBLE! YOU'RE SO FAMOUS NOW!
WITH ALL THIS RESPECT, YOU COULD MAKE, LIKE, 100 NEW FRIENDS TODAY.
!
I WAS WRONG ABOUT YOU, ANYA. PLEASE BE MY FRIEND!
SY-ON
COME PLAY AT MY HOUSE! AND BRING YOUR PARENTS!
YOU DID IT, ANYA!
PAPA
NOW I CAN COM-PLETE MY MISSION!
Good job!
NOD
AND THE WORLD WAS SAVED.

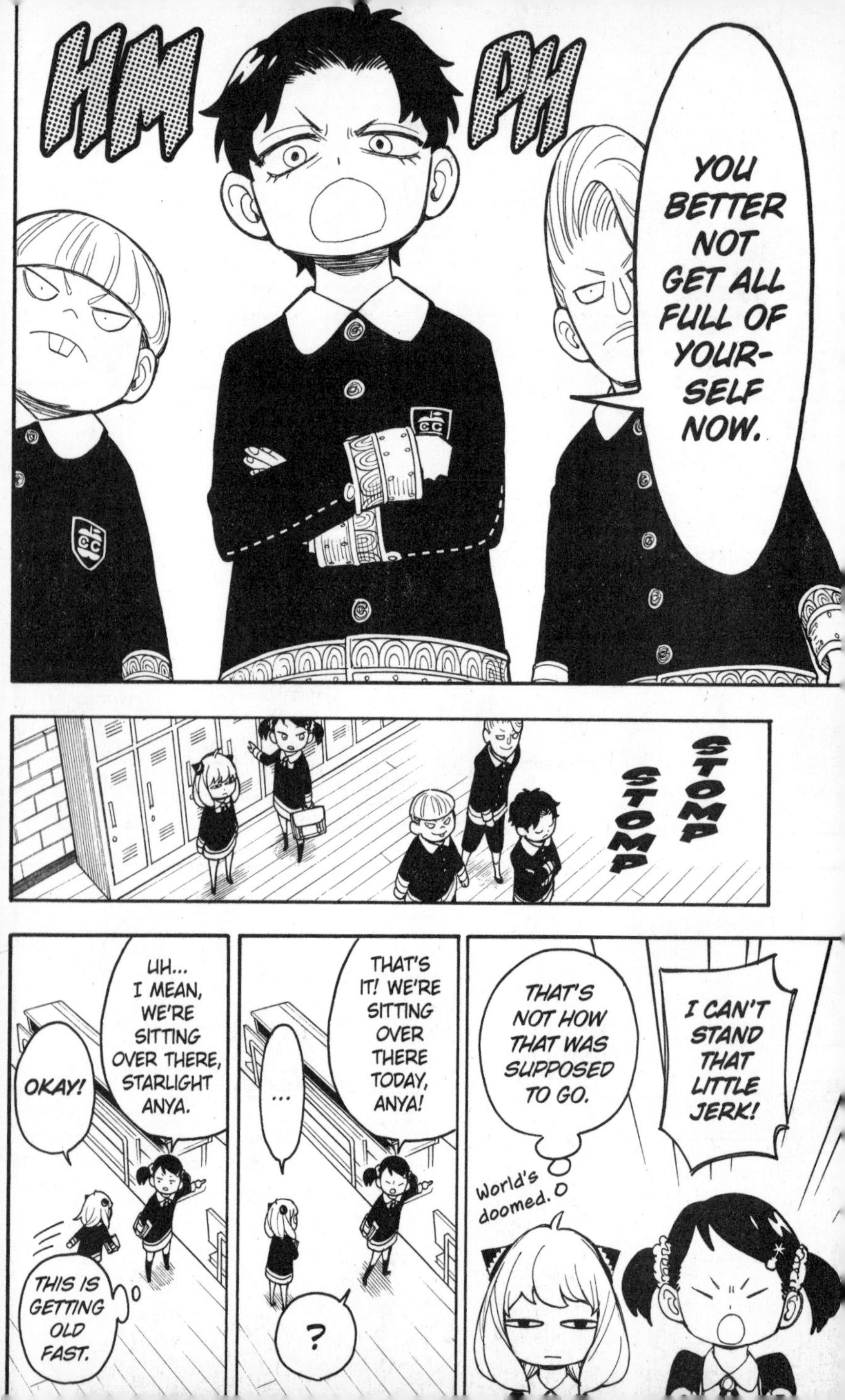
YOU BETTER NOT GET ALL FULL OF YOURSELF NOW.
HMPH
STOMP STOMP
I CAN'T STAND THAT LITTLE JERK!
THAT'S NOT HOW THAT WAS SUPPOSED TO GO.
World's doomed.
THAT'S IT! WE'RE SITTING OVER THERE TODAY, ANYA!
...
?
UH... I MEAN, WE'RE SITTING OVER THERE, STARLIGHT ANYA.
OKAY!
THIS IS GETTING OLD FAST.

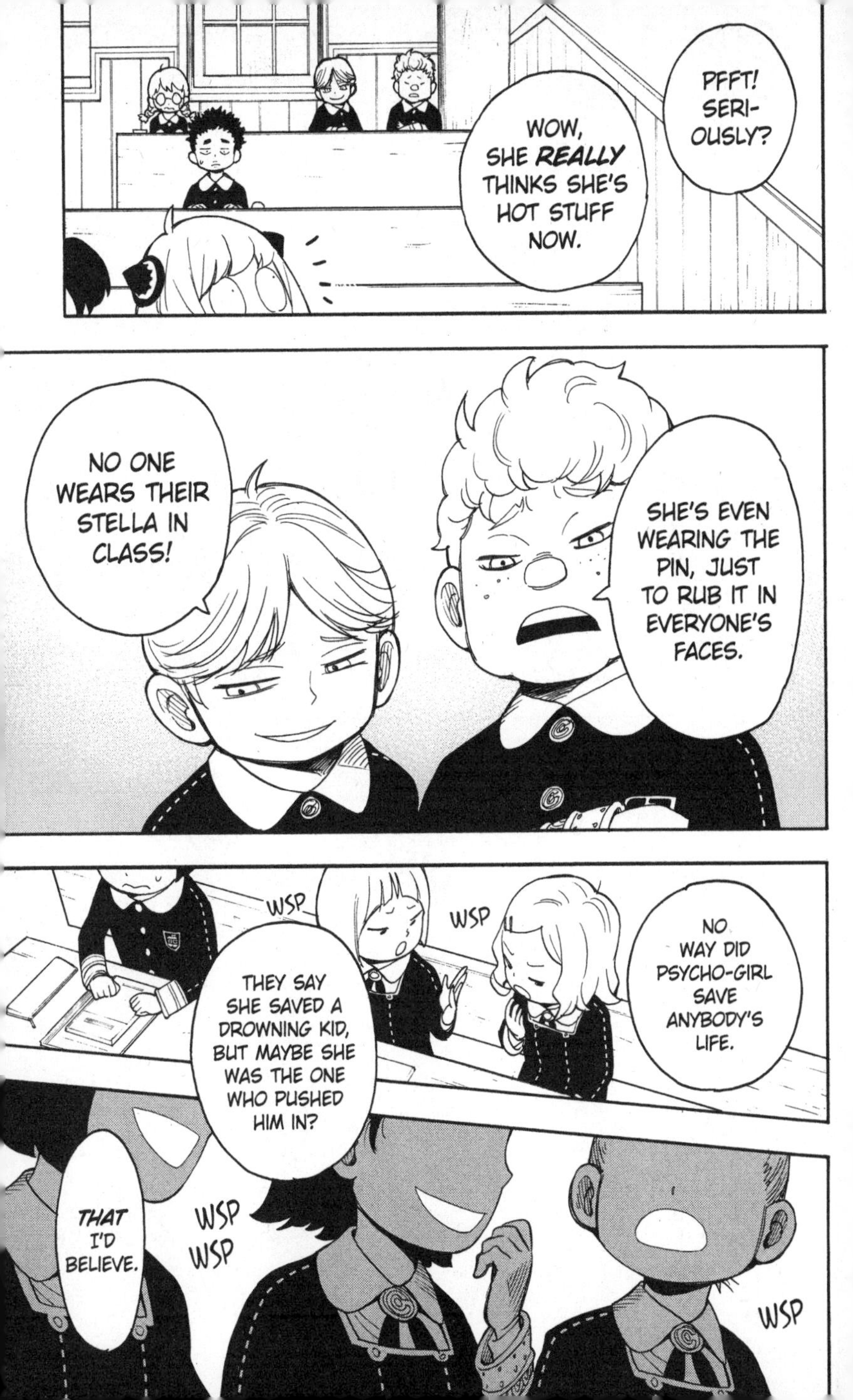
PFFT! SERI-OUSLY?
WOW, SHE REALLY THINKS SHE'S HOT STUFF NOW.
SHE'S EVEN WEARING THE PIN, JUST TO RUB IT IN EVERYONE'S FACES.
NO ONE WEARS THEIR STELLA IN CLASS!
NO WAY DID PSYCHO-GIRL SAVE ANYBODY'S LIFE.
WSP
THEY SAY SHE SAVED A DROWNING KID, BUT MAYBE SHE WAS THE ONE WHO PUSHED HIM IN?
WSP
WSP
WSP WSP
THAT I'D BELIEVE.

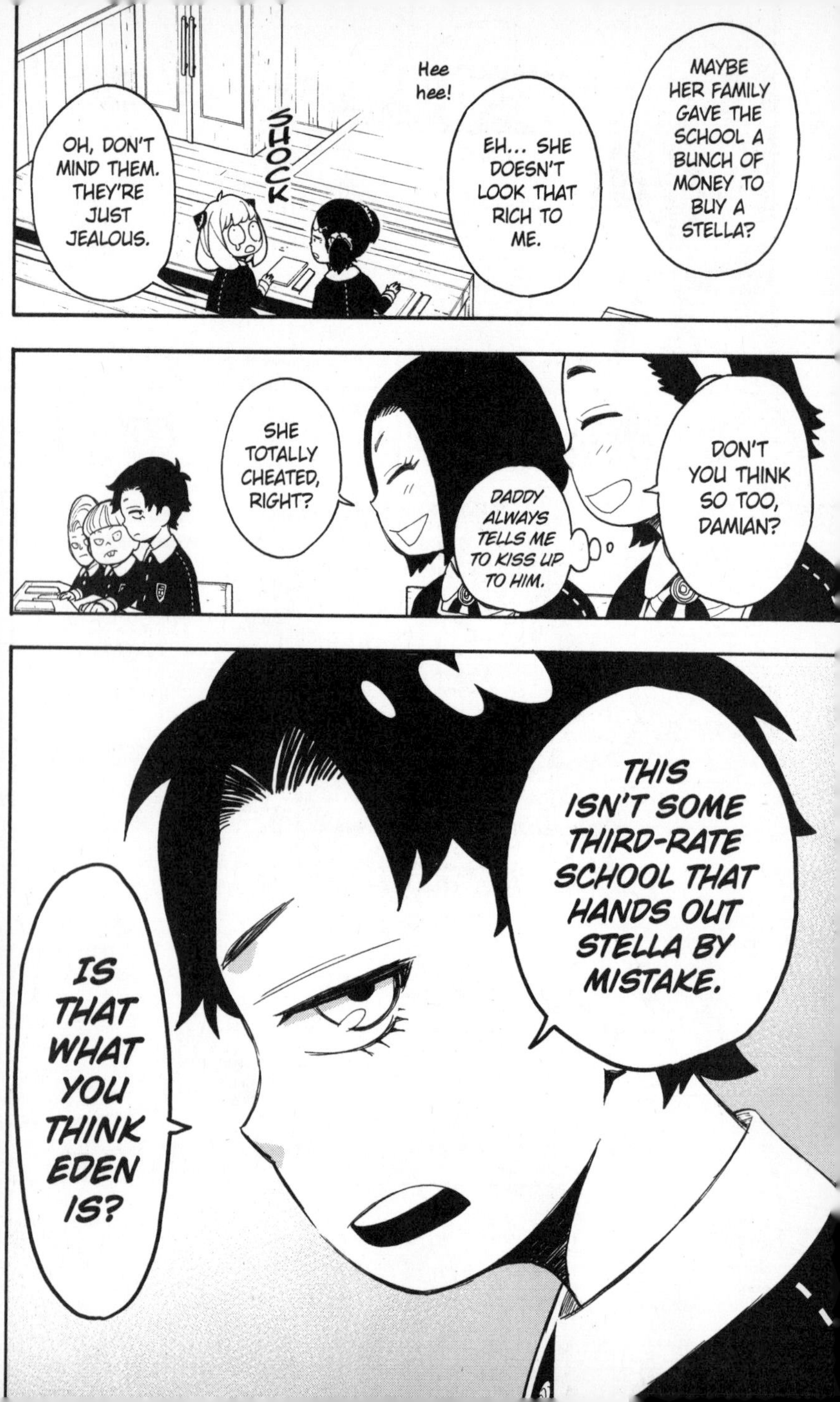
MAYBE HER FAMILY GAVE THE SCHOOL A BUNCH OF MONEY TO BUY A STELLA?
Hee hee!
EH... SHE DOESN'T LOOK THAT RICH TO ME.
SHOCK
OH, DON'T MIND THEM. THEY'RE JUST JEALOUS.
DON'T YOU THINK SO TOO, DAMIAN?
DADDY ALWAYS TELLS ME TO KISS UP TO HIM.
SHE TOTALLY CHEATED, RIGHT?
THIS ISN'T SOME THIRD-RATE SCHOOL THAT HANDS OUT STELLA BY MISTAKE.
IS THAT WHAT YOU THINK EDEN IS?

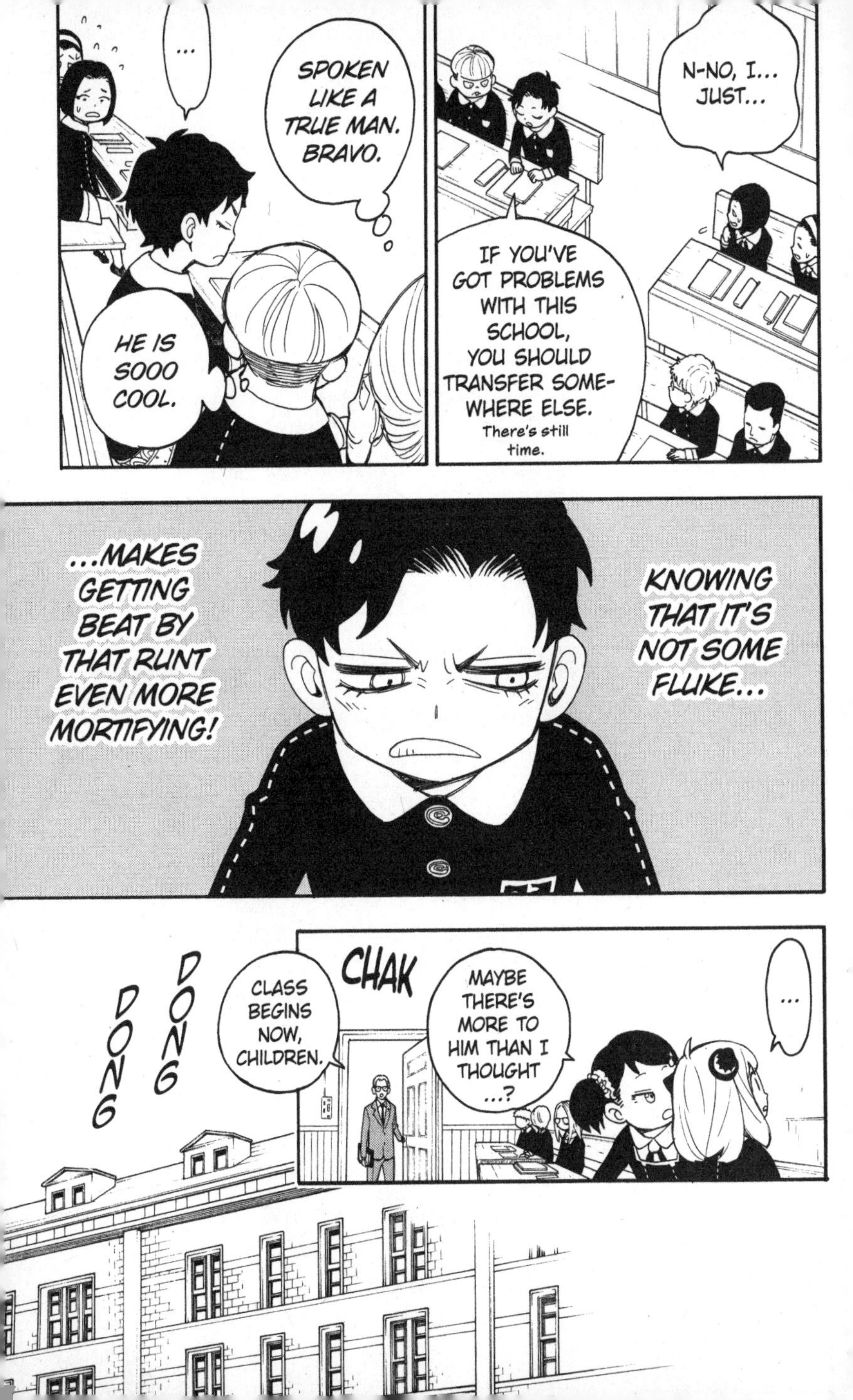
N-NO, I... JUST...
IF YOU'VE GOT PROBLEMS WITH THIS SCHOOL, YOU SHOULD TRANSFER SOMEWHERE ELSE. There's still time.
SPOKEN LIKE A TRUE MAN. BRAVO.
...
HE IS SOOO COOL.
KNOWING THAT IT'S NOT SOME FLUKE...
...MAKES GETTING BEAT BY THAT RUNT EVEN MORE MORTIFYING!
...
MAYBE THERE'S MORE TO HIM THAN I THOUGHT ...?
CHAK
CLASS BEGINS NOW, CHILDREN.
DONG
DONG

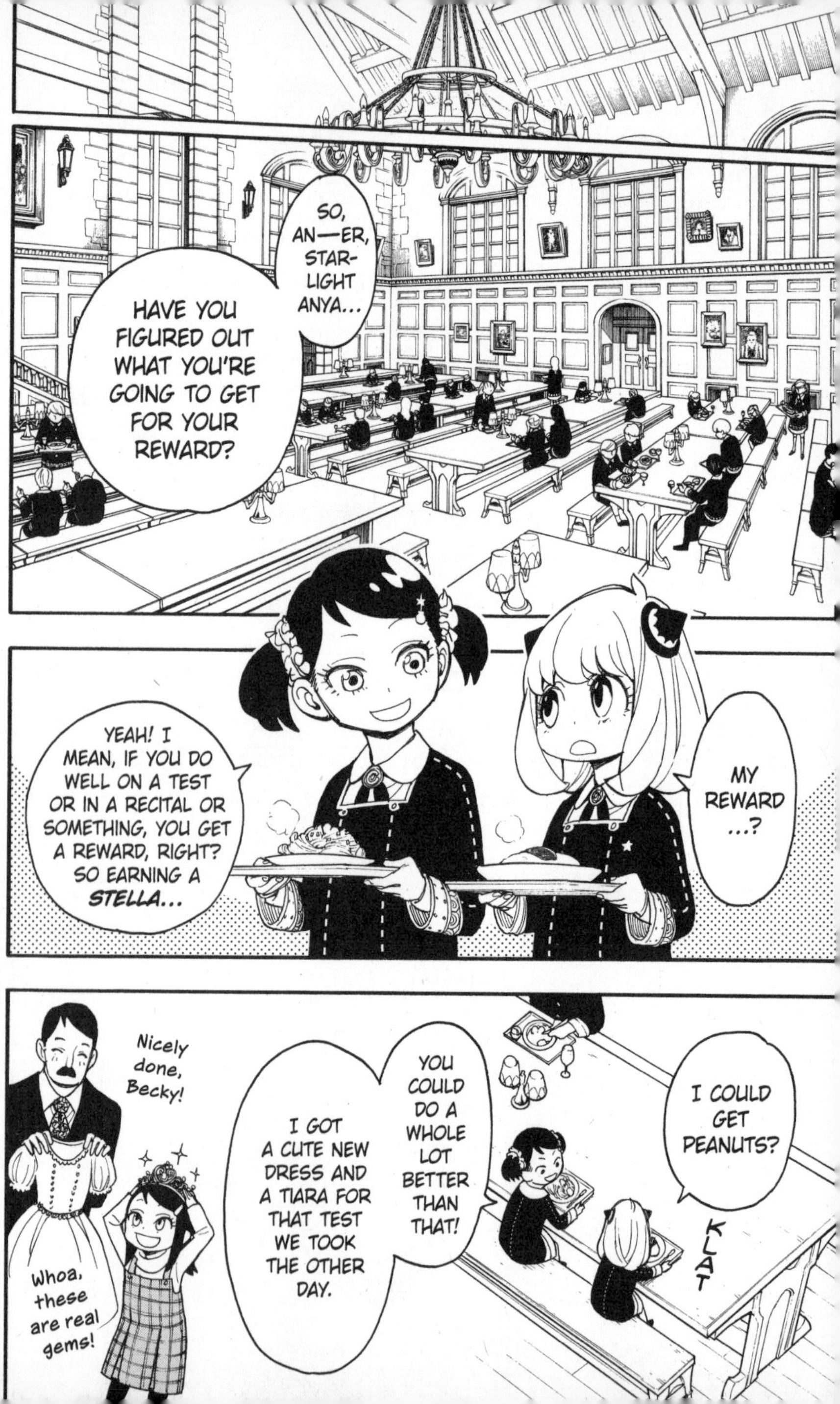
SO, AN—ER, STAR-LIGHT ANYA...
HAVE YOU FIGURED OUT WHAT YOU'RE GOING TO GET FOR YOUR REWARD?
MY REWARD ...?
YEAH! I MEAN, IF YOU DO WELL ON A TEST OR IN A RECITAL OR SOMETHING, YOU GET A REWARD, RIGHT? SO EARNING A *STELLA*...
I COULD GET PEANUTS?
KLAT
YOU COULD DO A WHOLE LOT BETTER THAN THAT!
I GOT A CUTE NEW DRESS AND A TIARA FOR THAT TEST WE TOOK THE OTHER DAY.
Nicely done, Becky!
Whoa, these are real gems!

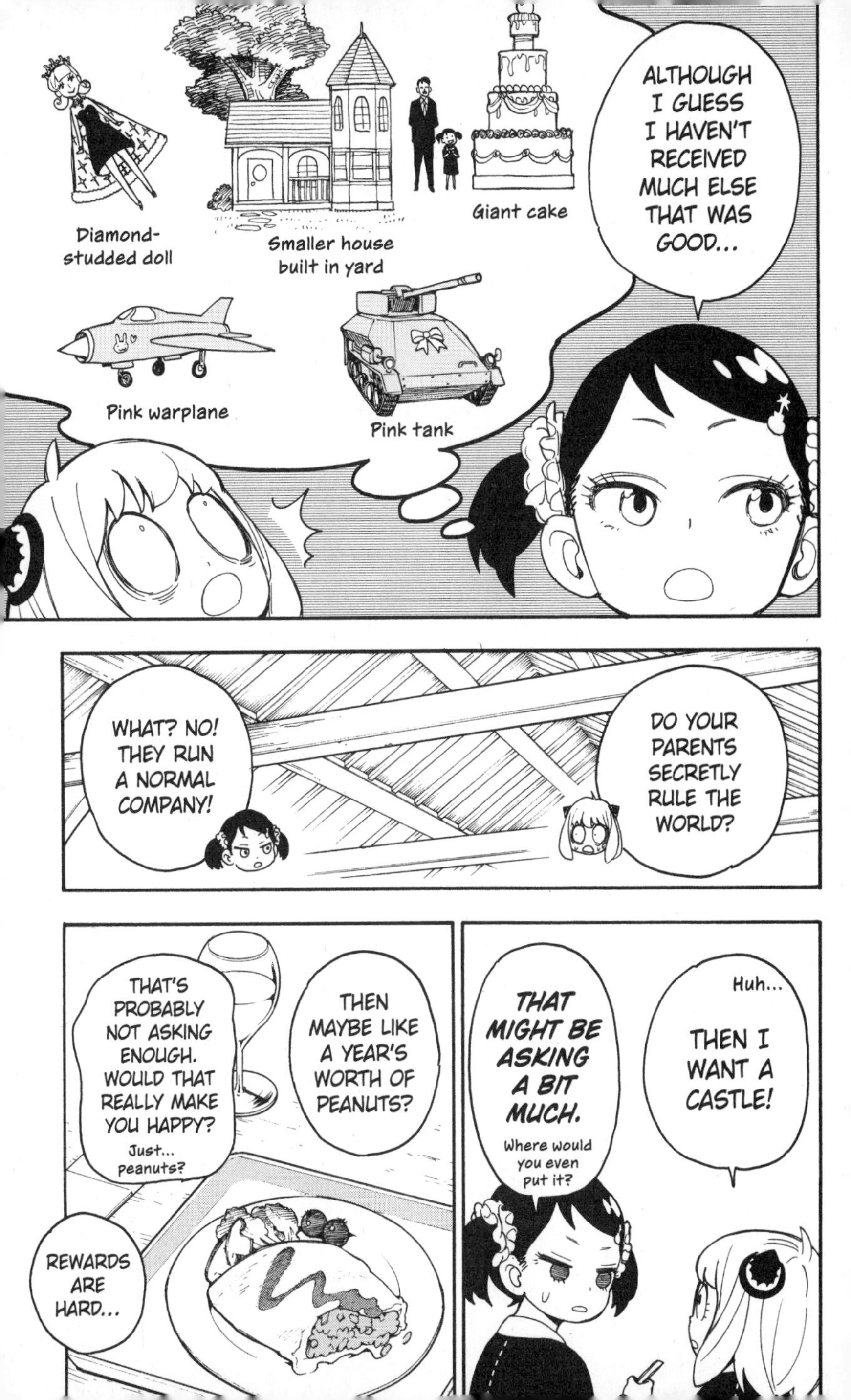
ALTHOUGH I GUESS I HAVEN'T RECEIVED MUCH ELSE THAT WAS GOOD...
Giant cake
Smaller house built in yard
Diamond-studded doll
Pink tank
Pink warplane
DO YOUR PARENTS SECRETLY RULE THE WORLD?
WHAT? NO! THEY RUN A NORMAL COMPANY!
Huh...
THEN I WANT A CASTLE!
THAT MIGHT BE ASKING A BIT MUCH.
Where would you even put it?
THEN MAYBE LIKE A YEAR'S WORTH OF PEANUTS?
THAT'S PROBABLY NOT ASKING ENOUGH. WOULD THAT REALLY MAKE YOU HAPPY?
Just... peanuts?
REWARDS ARE HARD...

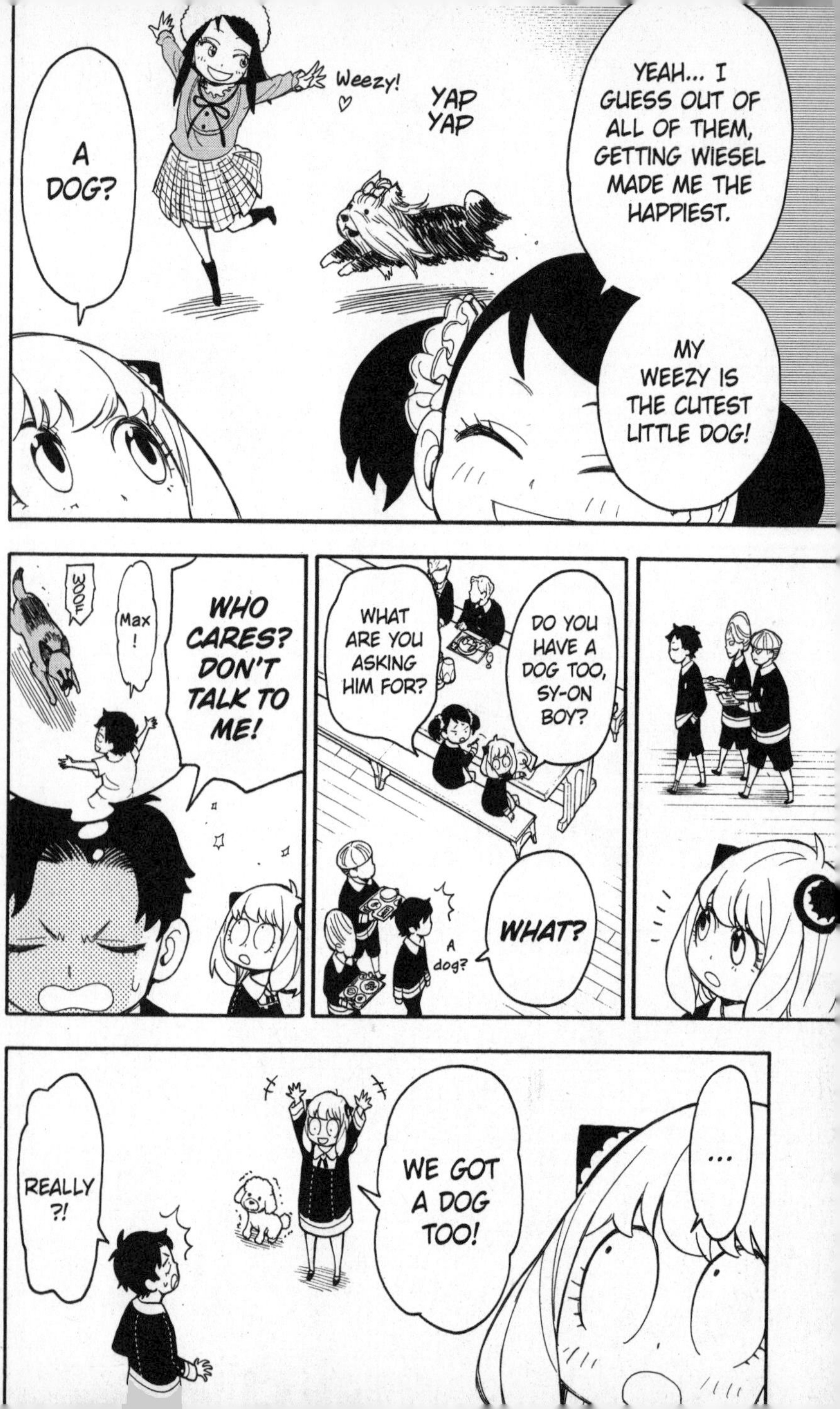
YEAH... I GUESS OUT OF ALL OF THEM, GETTING WIESEL MADE ME THE HAPPIEST.
MY WEEZY IS THE CUTEST LITTLE DOG!
Weezy! ♡
YAP YAP
A DOG?
DO YOU HAVE A DOG TOO, SY-ON BOY?
WHAT ARE YOU ASKING HIM FOR?
WHAT?
A dog?
WHO CARES? DON'T TALK TO ME!
Max!
WOOF
...
WE GOT A DOG TOO!
REALLY?!

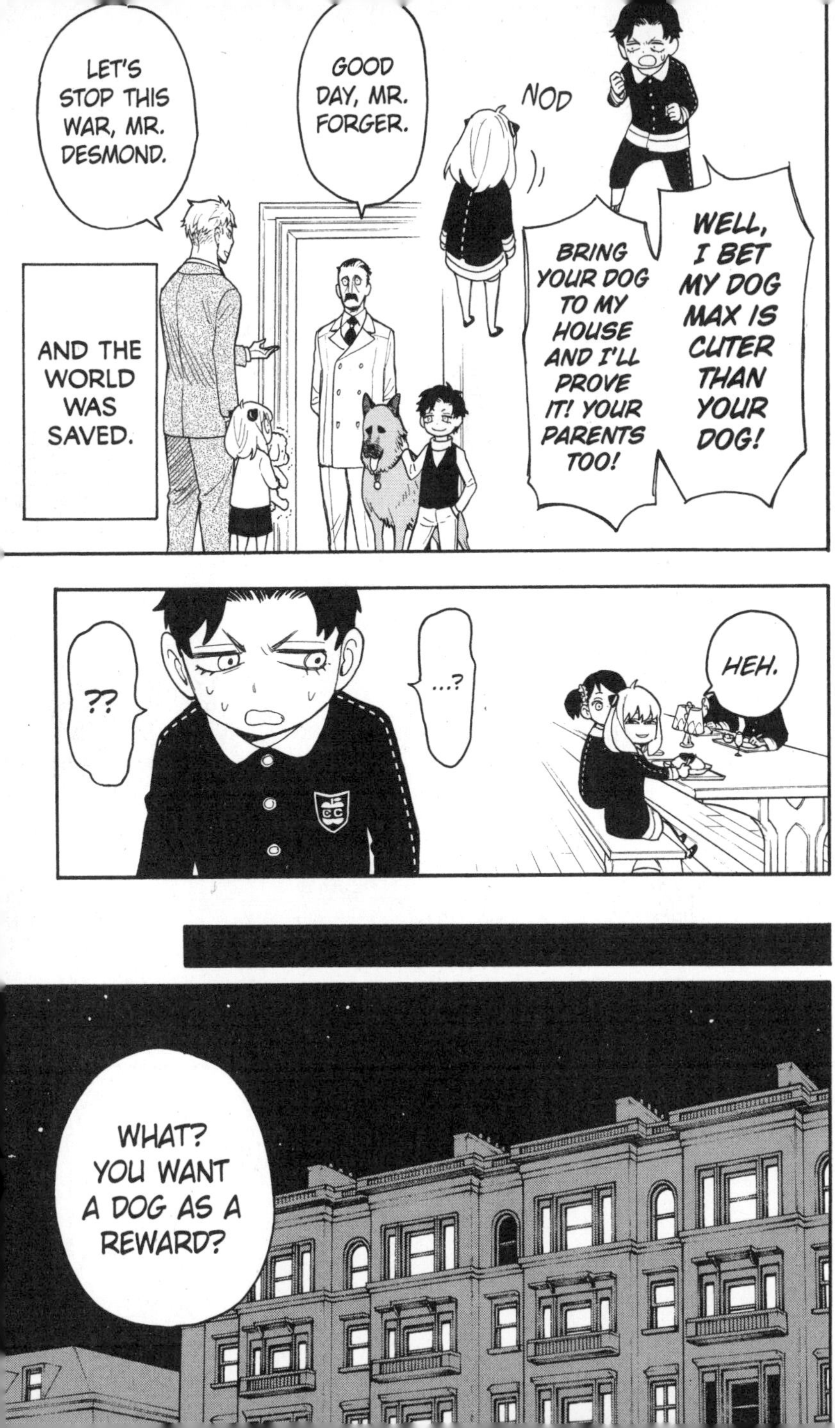
WELL, I BET MY DOG MAX IS CUTER THAN YOUR DOG!
BRING YOUR DOG TO MY HOUSE AND I'LL PROVE IT! YOUR PARENTS TOO!
NOD
GOOD DAY, MR. FORGER.
LET'S STOP THIS WAR, MR. DESMOND.
AND THE WORLD WAS SAVED.
HEH.
...?
??
WHAT? YOU WANT A DOG AS A REWARD?

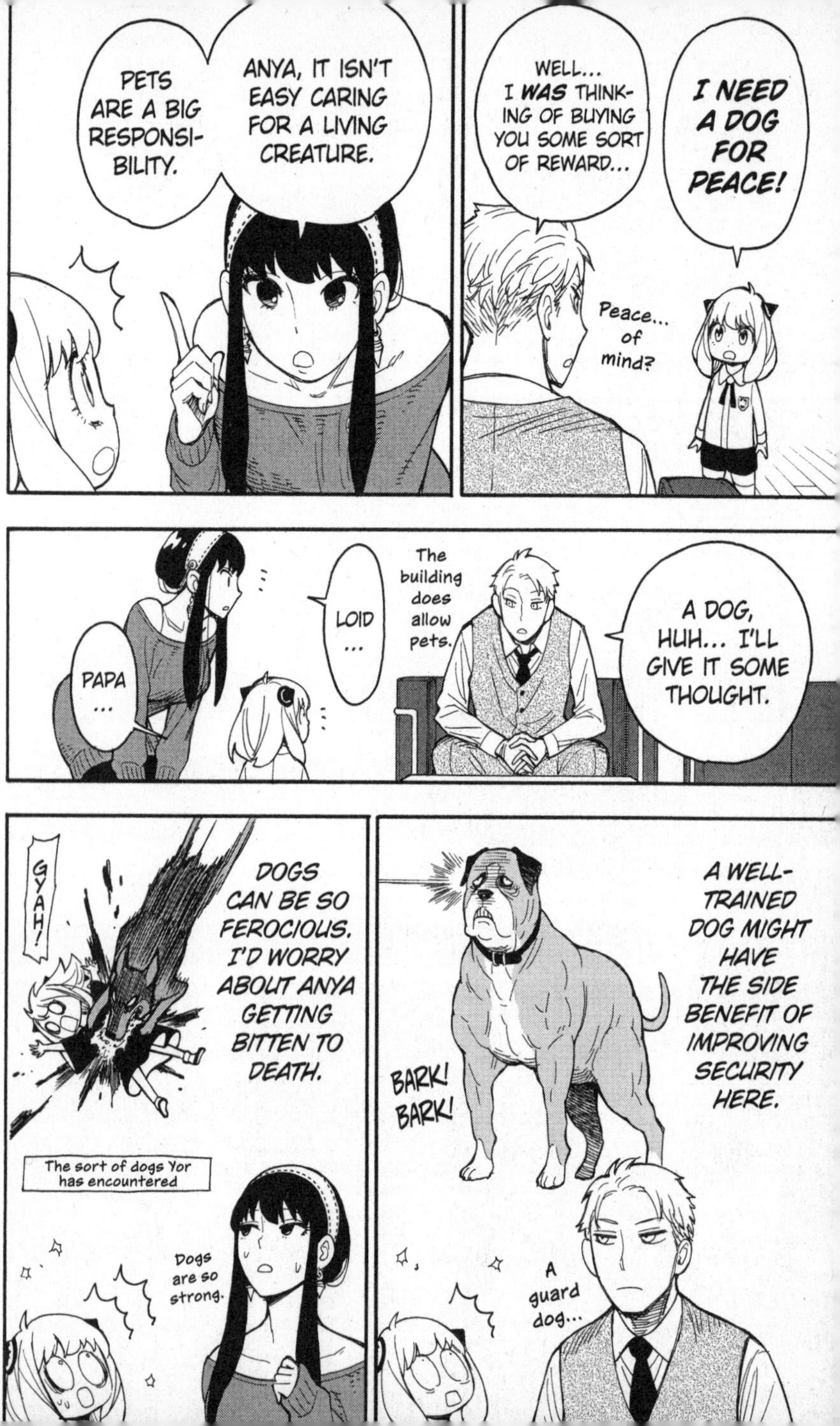
I NEED A DOG FOR PEACE!
WELL... I WAS THINKING OF BUYING YOU SOME SORT OF REWARD...
Peace... of mind?
ANYA, IT ISN'T EASY CARING FOR A LIVING CREATURE.
PETS ARE A BIG RESPONSIBILITY.
A DOG, HUH... I'LL GIVE IT SOME THOUGHT.
The building does allow pets.
LOID...
PAPA...
A WELL-TRAINED DOG MIGHT HAVE THE SIDE BENEFIT OF IMPROVING SECURITY HERE.
BARK! BARK!
A guard dog...
DOGS CAN BE SO FEROCIOUS. I'D WORRY ABOUT ANYA GETTING BITTEN TO DEATH.
GYAH!
The sort of dogs Yor has encountered
Dogs are so strong.

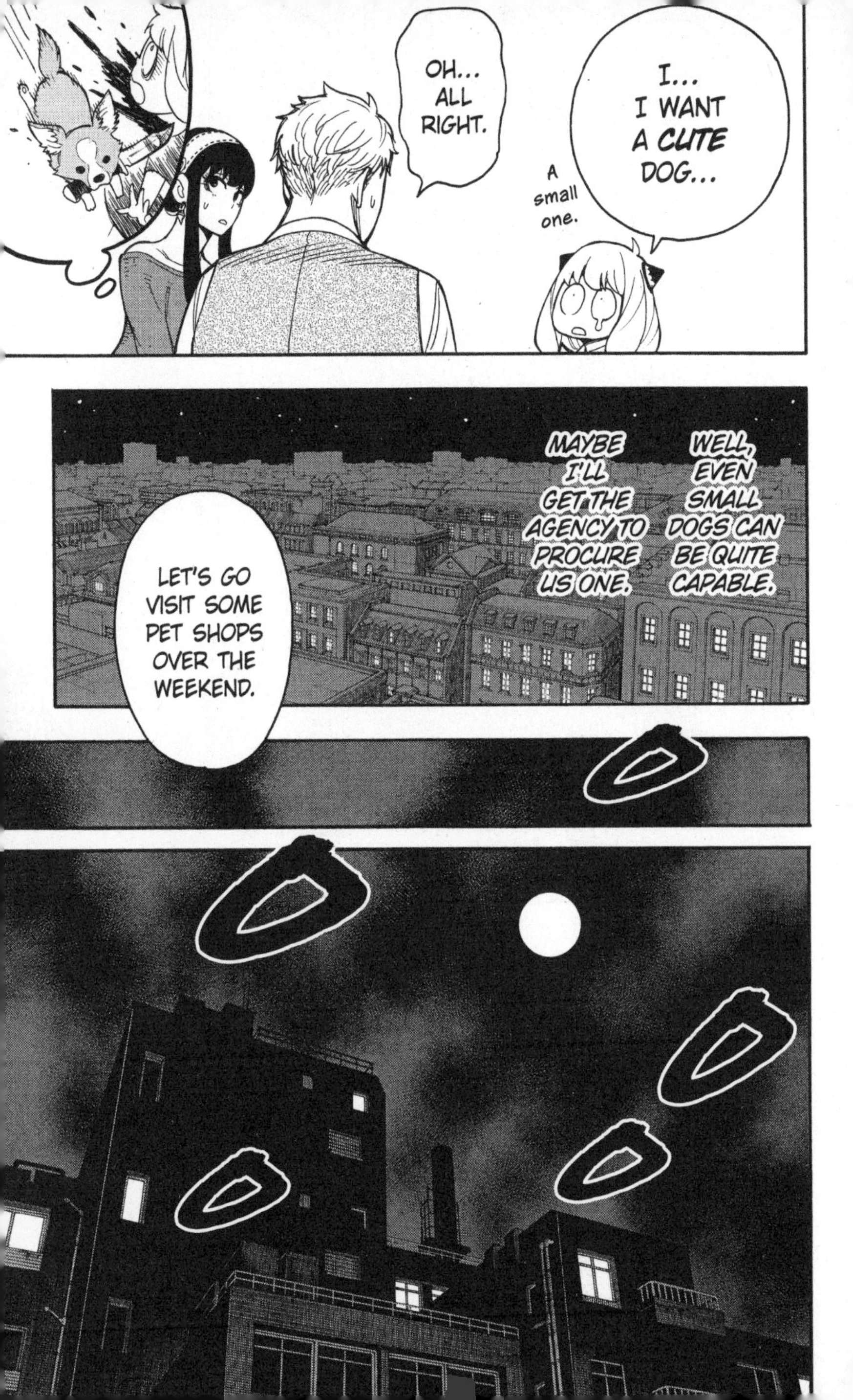
I... I WANT A CUTE DOG...
A small one.
OH... ALL RIGHT.
WELL, EVEN SMALL DOGS CAN BE QUITE CAPABLE.
MAYBE I'LL GET THE AGENCY TO PROCURE US ONE.
LET'S GO VISIT SOME PET SHOPS OVER THE WEEKEND.

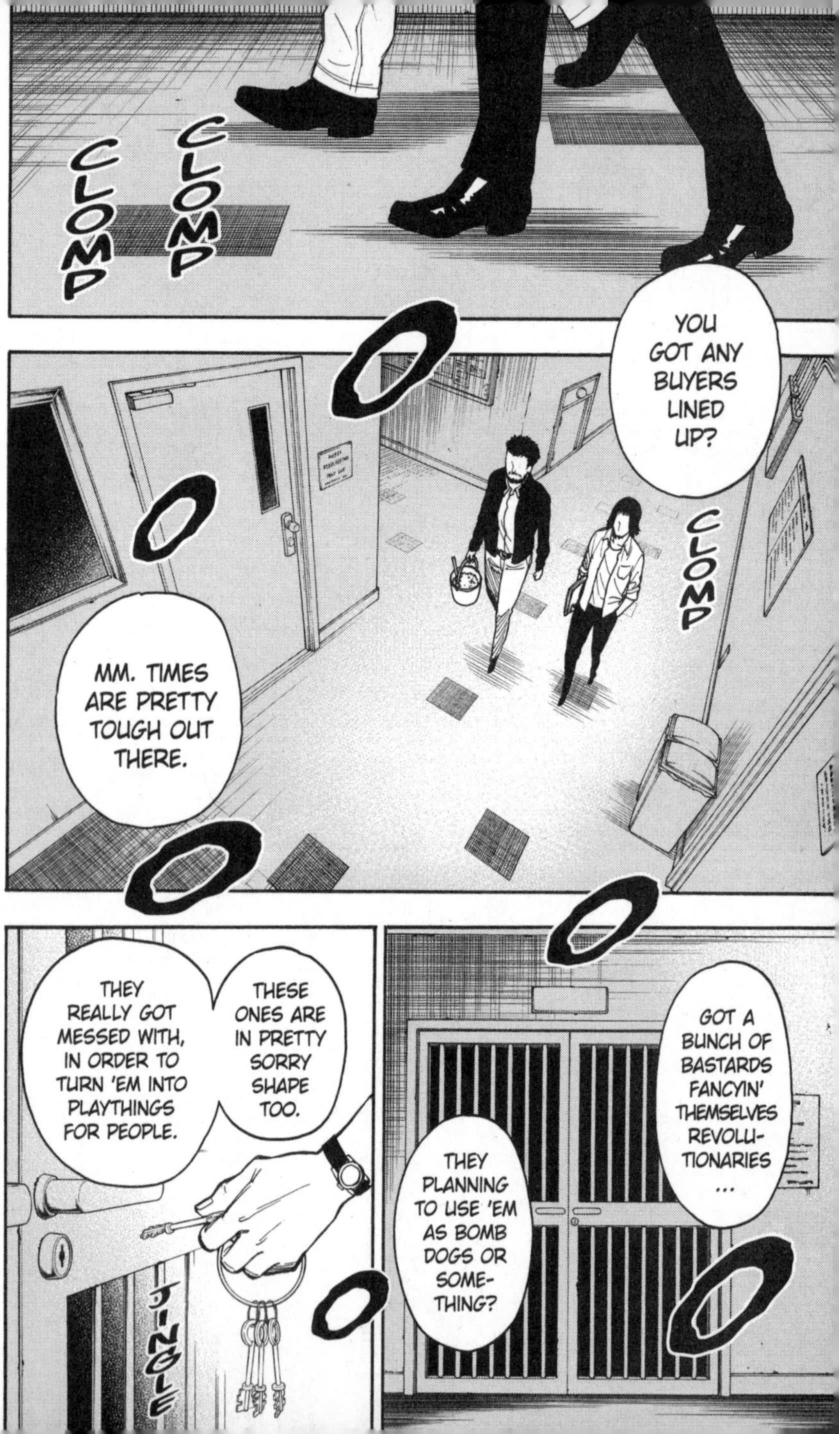
CLOMP
CLOMP
YOU GOT ANY BUYERS LINED UP?
CLOMP
MM. TIMES ARE PRETTY TOUGH OUT THERE.
GOT A BUNCH OF BASTARDS FANCYIN' THEMSELVES REVOLUTIONARIES ...
THEY PLANNING TO USE 'EM AS BOMB DOGS OR SOME-THING?
THESE ONES ARE IN PRETTY SORRY SHAPE TOO.
THEY REALLY GOT MESSED WITH, IN ORDER TO TURN 'EM INTO PLAYTHINGS FOR PEOPLE.
JINGLE

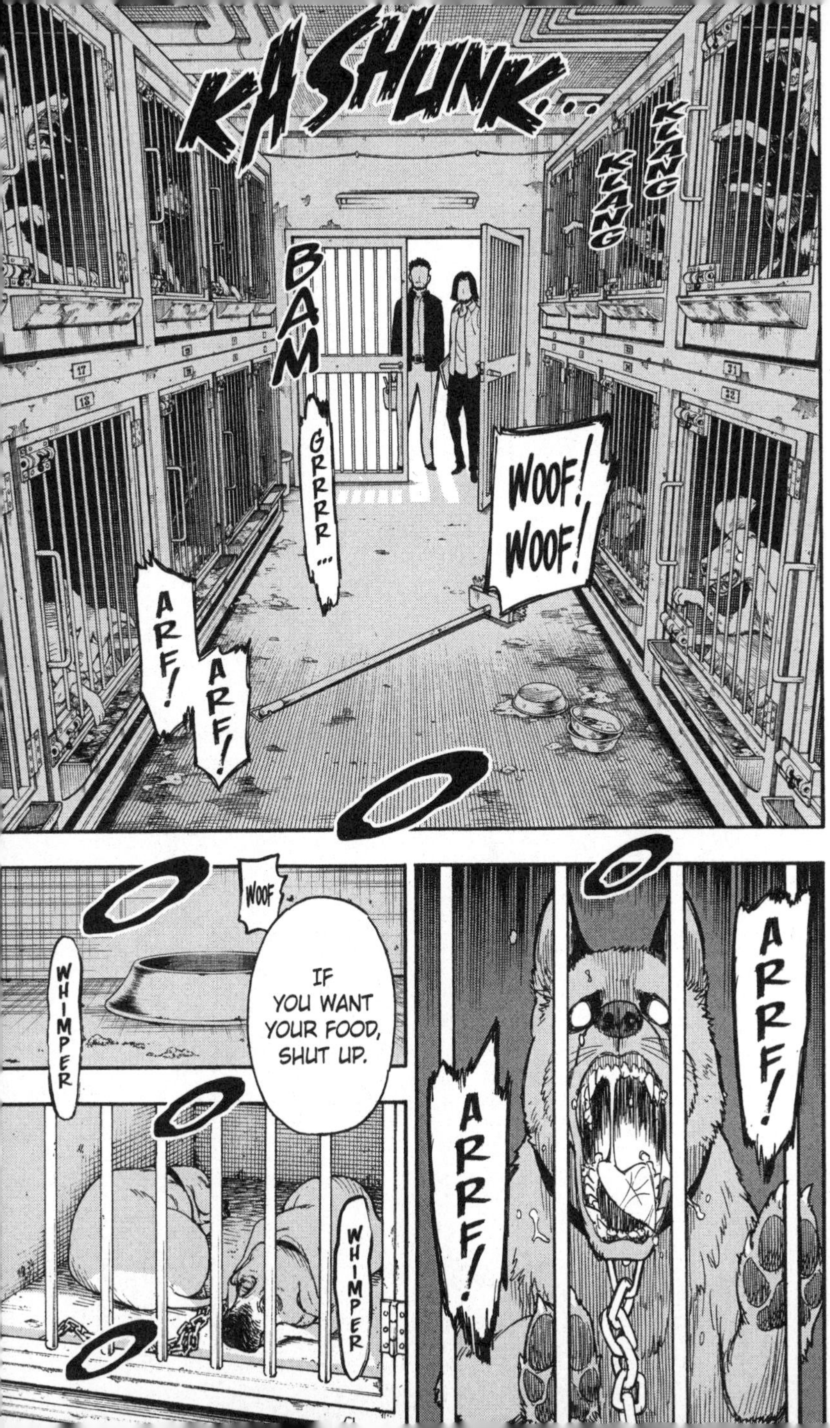
KASHUNK...
KLANG
KLANG
BAM
WOOF! WOOF!
GRRRR...
ARF!
ARF!
ARRRF!
ARRRF!
WOOF
IF YOU WANT YOUR FOOD, SHUT UP.
WHIMPER
WHIMPER

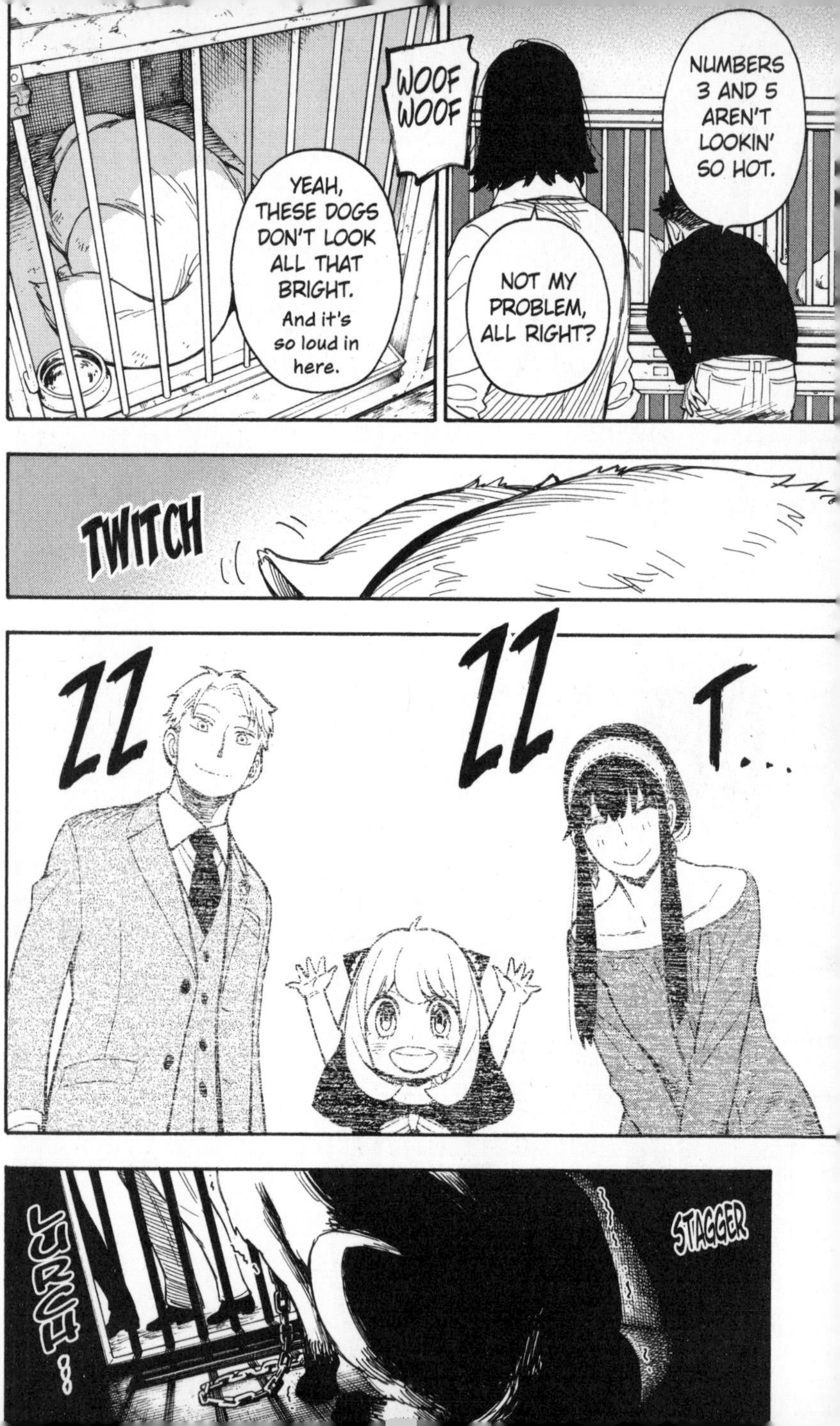
NUMBERS 3 AND 5 AREN'T LOOKIN' SO HOT.
NOT MY PROBLEM, ALL RIGHT?
WOOF WOOF
YEAH, THESE DOGS DON'T LOOK ALL THAT BRIGHT.
And it's so loud in here.
TWITCH
ZZ
ZZ
T...
STAGGER
LURCH...

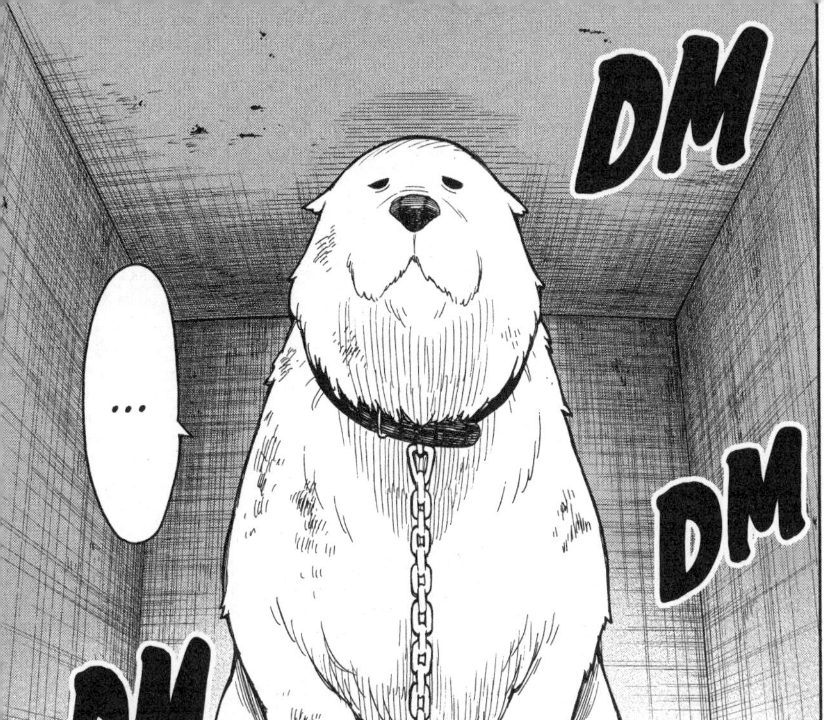
DM
DM
...
DM
DM

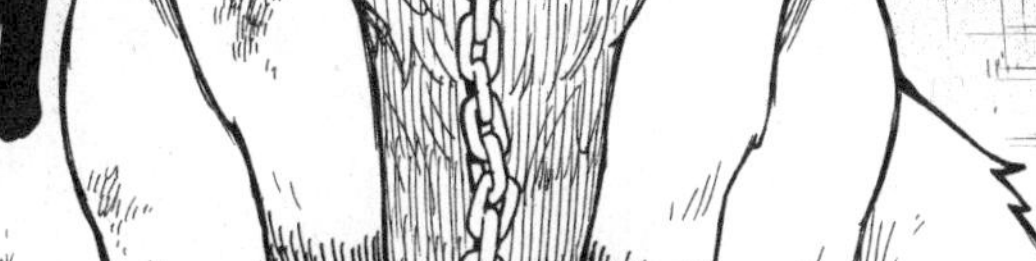
And that one, and that one...
I'm glad they look weak!

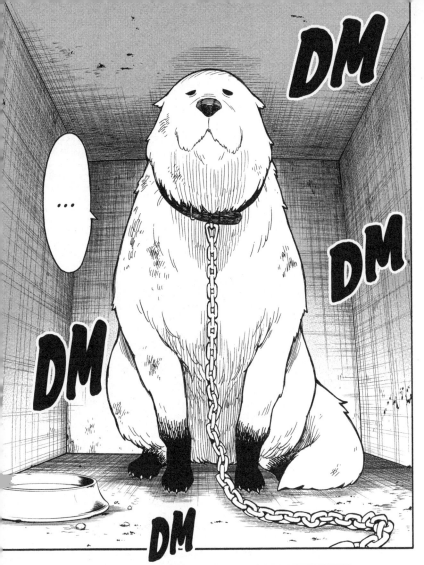

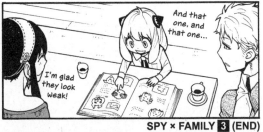

SPYxFAMILY VOL. 3

SPECIAL THANKS LIST

·CLASSIFIED·

ART ASSISTANCE

AMASHIMA	MAEHATA
SATOSHI KIMURA	YUICHI OZAKI
MIO AYATSUKA	MAFUYU KONISHI
KAZUKI NONAKA	KEISUKE HOSHINOYA

GRAPHIC NOVEL DESIGN

HIDEAKI SHIMADA	ERI ARAKAWA

GRAPHIC NOVEL EDITOR

KANAKO YANAGIDA

MANAGING EDITOR

SHIHEI LIN

NOW THAT THE MANGA IS BEING SERIALIZED, I'M STUCK AT HOME ALL DAY AND GETTING SICK OF IT. I WANT TO GO SOMEWHERE. I WANT TO EXPLORE THE GREAT OUTDOORS. I WANT TO BE REBORN ON ANOTHER WORLD. ANYWAY, I HOPE YOU'LL BUY VOLUME 4.

—TATSUYA ENDO

EYES ONLY READ & ~~DESTROY~~ EYES ONLY

← THIS IS THE SECOND EXTRA MISSION CREATED FOR PUBLICATION IN *WEEKLY SHONEN JUMP*. WE PUT A LOT OF EFFORT INTO IT, SO I ASKED TO HAVE IT INCLUDED HERE. OUR GOAL WAS TO DO SOMETHING A LITTLE DIFFERENT FROM THE PREVIOUS ONE AND TO MAKE IT APPROACHABLE FOR FIRST-TIME READERS. ACCOMPLISHING BOTH THOSE THINGS AT ONCE PROVED CHALLENGING. I MADE THE TITLE PAGE RED TO GIVE IT A DIFFERENT MOOD. AREN'T SIDECARS WEIRDLY ADORABLE?

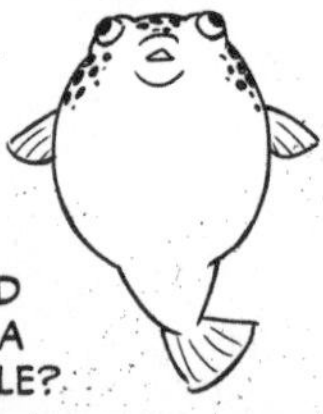

SPY×FAMILY

EXTRA MISSION 2

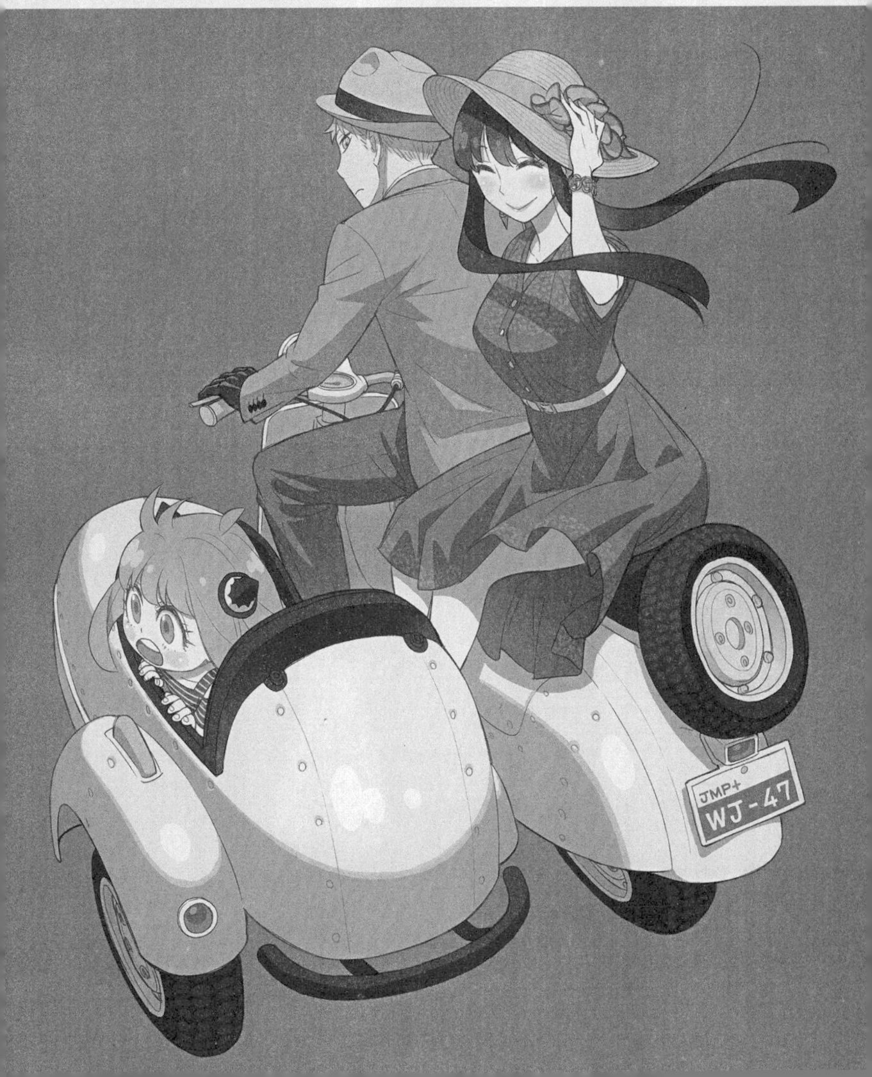
JMP+
WJ-47

TOP SECRET (BONUS)

YOR'S WEEK IN FASHION

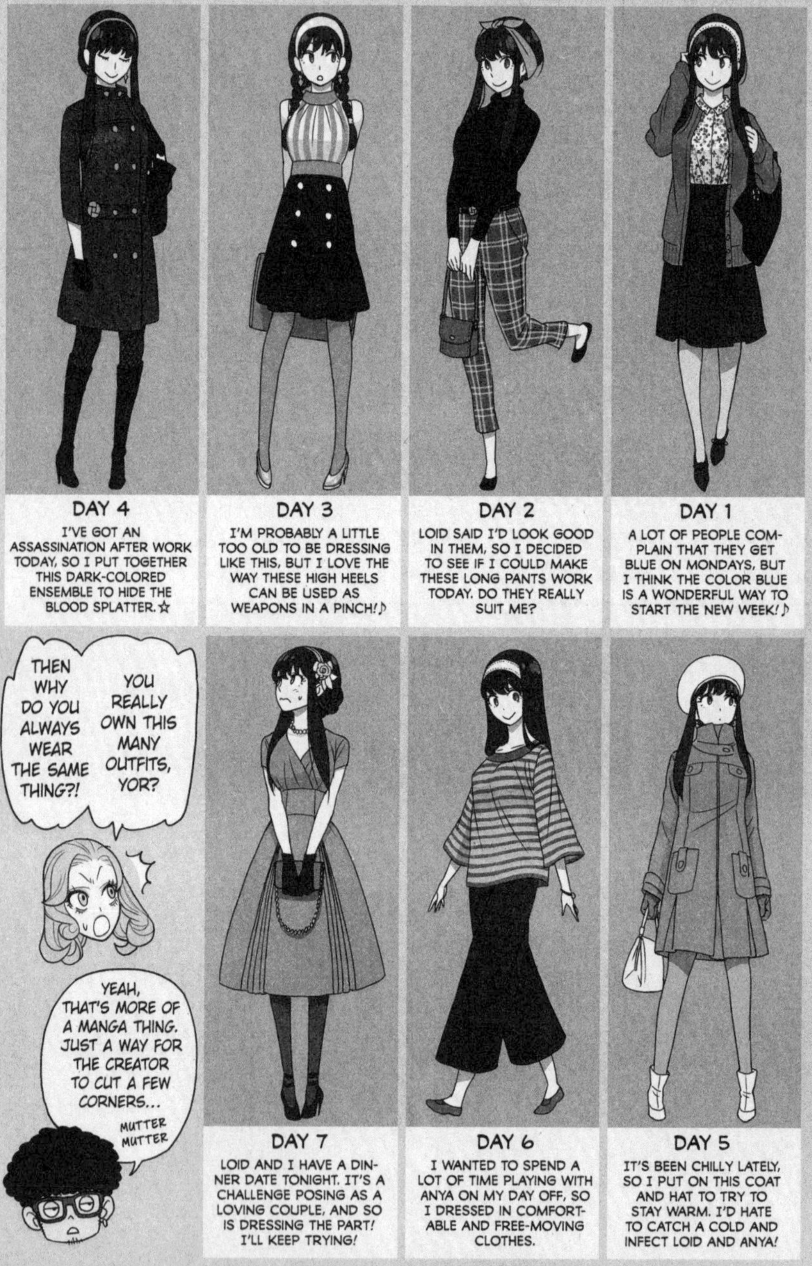
DAY 1
A LOT OF PEOPLE COMPLAIN THAT THEY GET BLUE ON MONDAYS, BUT I THINK THE COLOR BLUE IS A WONDERFUL WAY TO START THE NEW WEEK!♪
DAY 2
LOID SAID I'D LOOK GOOD IN THEM, SO I DECIDED TO SEE IF I COULD MAKE THESE LONG PANTS WORK TODAY. DO THEY REALLY SUIT ME?
DAY 3
I'M PROBABLY A LITTLE TOO OLD TO BE DRESSING LIKE THIS, BUT I LOVE THE WAY THESE HIGH HEELS CAN BE USED AS WEAPONS IN A PINCH!♪
DAY 4
I'VE GOT AN ASSASSINATION AFTER WORK TODAY, SO I PUT TOGETHER THIS DARK-COLORED ENSEMBLE TO HIDE THE BLOOD SPLATTER.☆
DAY 5
IT'S BEEN CHILLY LATELY, SO I PUT ON THIS COAT AND HAT TO TRY TO STAY WARM. I'D HATE TO CATCH A COLD AND INFECT LOID AND ANYA!
DAY 6
I WANTED TO SPEND A LOT OF TIME PLAYING WITH ANYA ON MY DAY OFF, SO I DRESSED IN COMFORTABLE AND FREE-MOVING CLOTHES.
DAY 7
LOID AND I HAVE A DINNER DATE TONIGHT. IT'S A CHALLENGE POSING AS A LOVING COUPLE, AND SO IS DRESSING THE PART! I'LL KEEP TRYING!
YOU REALLY OWN THIS MANY OUTFITS, YOR?
THEN WHY DO YOU ALWAYS WEAR THE SAME THING?!
YEAH, THAT'S MORE OF A MANGA THING. JUST A WAY FOR THE CREATOR TO CUT A FEW CORNERS...
MUTTER MUTTER

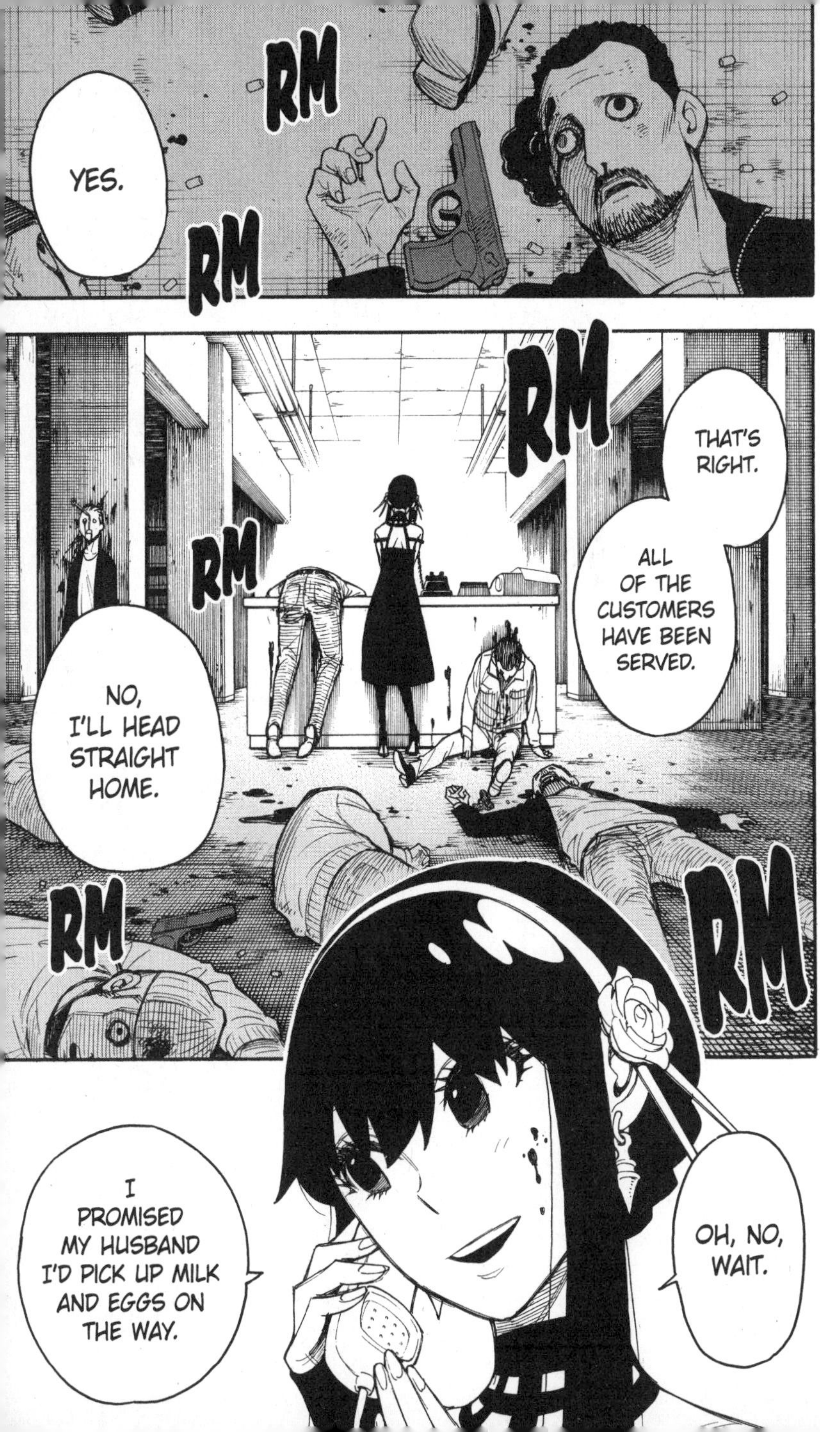
RM
YES.
RM
RM
THAT'S RIGHT.
ALL OF THE CUSTOMERS HAVE BEEN SERVED.
RM
NO, I'LL HEAD STRAIGHT HOME.
RM
RM
OH, NO, WAIT.
I PROMISED MY HUSBAND I'D PICK UP MILK AND EGGS ON THE WAY.

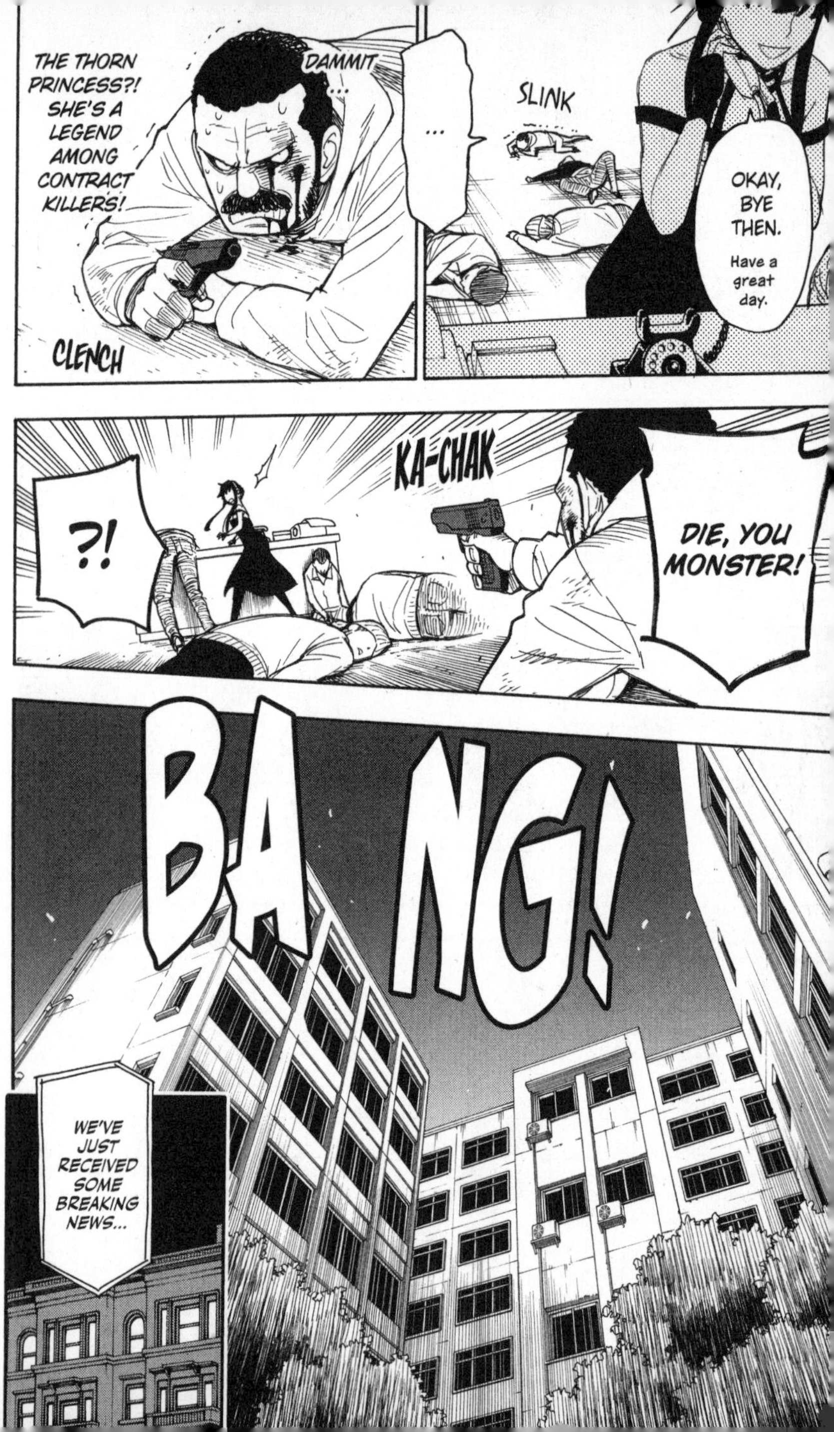
OKAY, BYE THEN.
Have a great day.
SLINK
...
DAMMIT...
THE THORN PRINCESS?! SHE'S A LEGEND AMONG CONTRACT KILLERS!
CLENCH
DIE, YOU MONSTER!
KA-CHAK
?!
BANG!
WE'VE JUST RECEIVED SOME BREAKING NEWS...

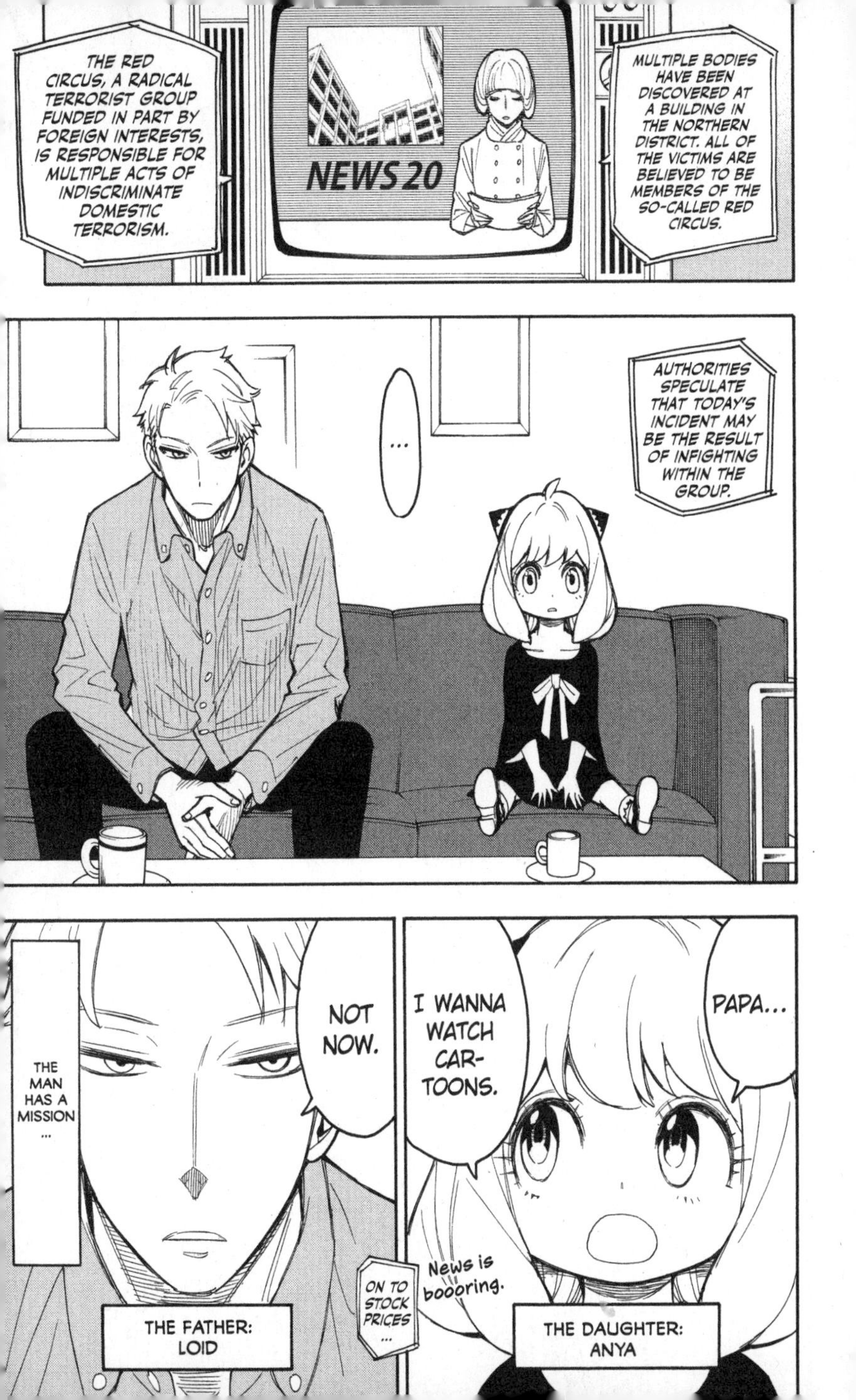
NEWS 20
MULTIPLE BODIES HAVE BEEN DISCOVERED AT A BUILDING IN THE NORTHERN DISTRICT. ALL OF THE VICTIMS ARE BELIEVED TO BE MEMBERS OF THE SO-CALLED RED CIRCUS.
THE RED CIRCUS, A RADICAL TERRORIST GROUP FUNDED IN PART BY FOREIGN INTERESTS, IS RESPONSIBLE FOR MULTIPLE ACTS OF INDISCRIMINATE DOMESTIC TERRORISM.
AUTHORITIES SPECULATE THAT TODAY'S INCIDENT MAY BE THE RESULT OF INFIGHTING WITHIN THE GROUP.
...
PAPA...
I WANNA WATCH CAR-TOONS.
News is boooring.
THE DAUGHTER: ANYA
NOT NOW.
THE MAN HAS A MISSION ...
ON TO STOCK PRICES ...
THE FATHER: LOID

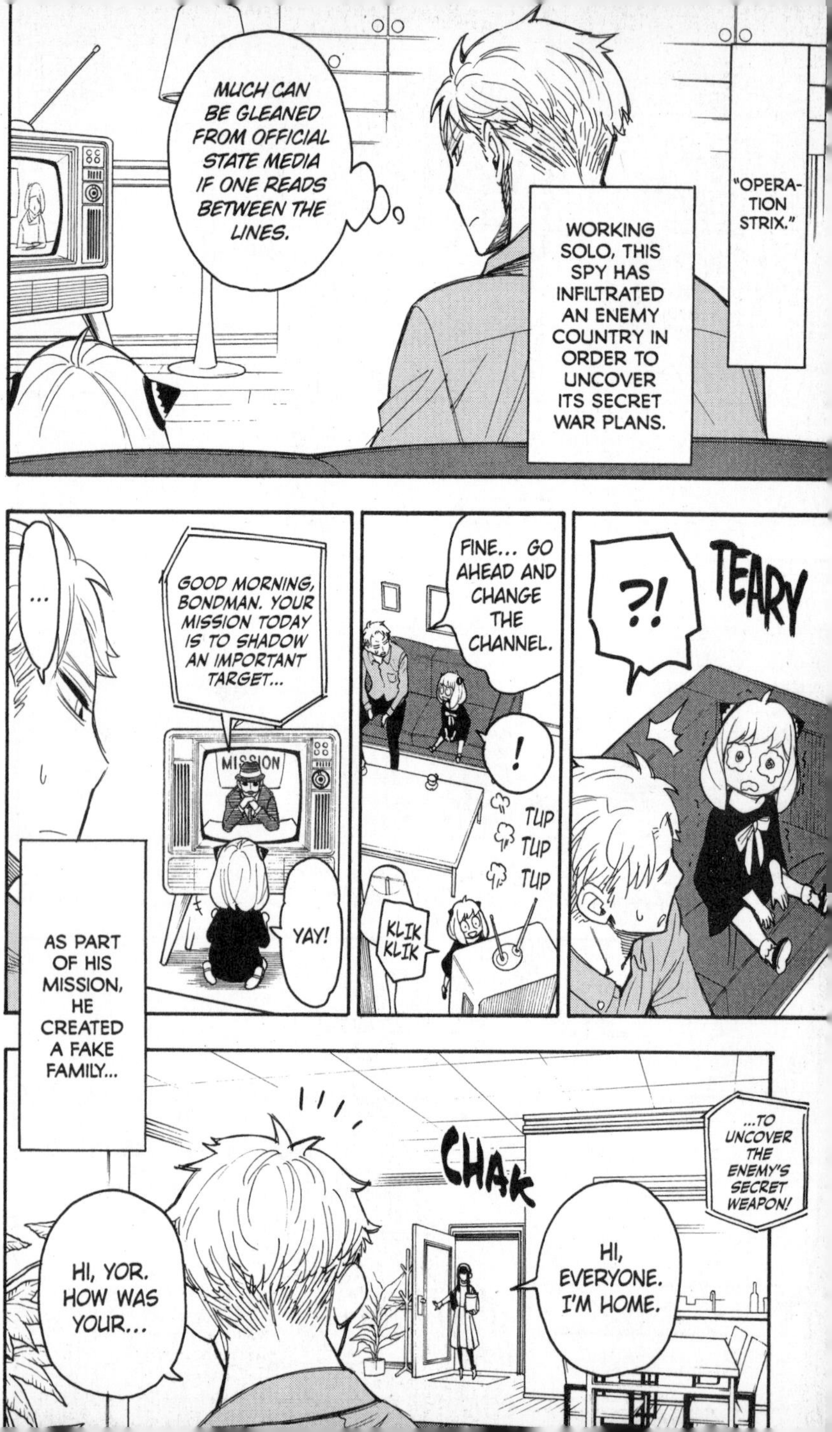

"OPERATION STRIX."
WORKING SOLO, THIS SPY HAS INFILTRATED AN ENEMY COUNTRY IN ORDER TO UNCOVER ITS SECRET WAR PLANS.
MUCH CAN BE GLEANED FROM OFFICIAL STATE MEDIA IF ONE READS BETWEEN THE LINES.
?!
TEARY
FINE... GO AHEAD AND CHANGE THE CHANNEL.
!
TUP TUP TUP
KLIK KLIK
GOOD MORNING, BONDMAN. YOUR MISSION TODAY IS TO SHADOW AN IMPORTANT TARGET...
MISSION
YAY!
...
AS PART OF HIS MISSION, HE CREATED A FAKE FAMILY...
...TO UNCOVER THE ENEMY'S SECRET WEAPON!
CHAK
HI, EVERYONE. I'M HOME.
HI, YOR. HOW WAS YOUR...

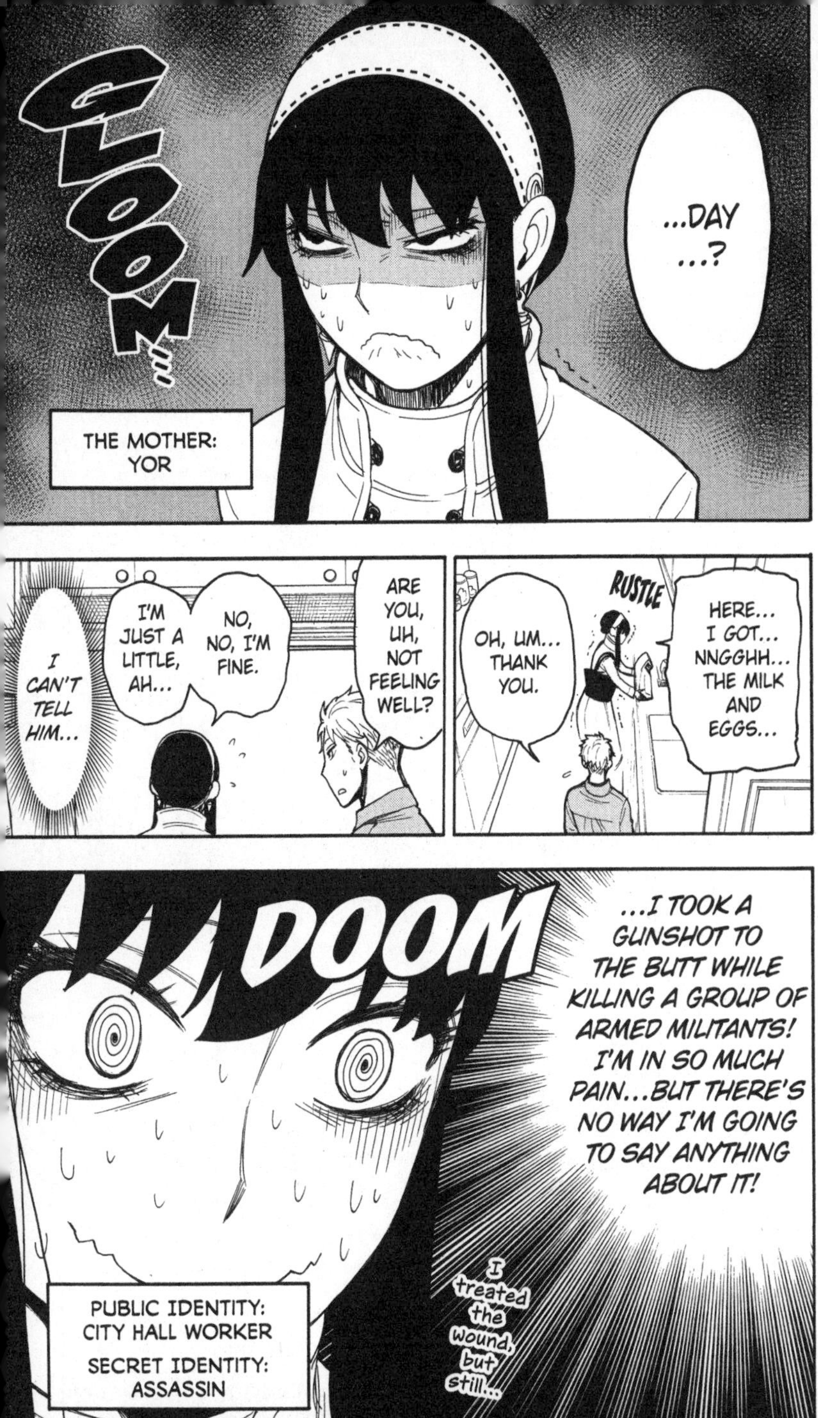
...DAY ...?
GLOOM...
THE MOTHER: YOR
RUSTLE
HERE... I GOT... NNGGHH... THE MILK AND EGGS...
OH, UM... THANK YOU.
ARE YOU, UH, NOT FEELING WELL?
NO, NO, I'M FINE.
I'M JUST A LITTLE, AH...
I CAN'T TELL HIM...
...I TOOK A GUNSHOT TO THE BUTT WHILE KILLING A GROUP OF ARMED MILITANTS! I'M IN SO MUCH PAIN...BUT THERE'S NO WAY I'M GOING TO SAY ANYTHING ABOUT IT!
DOOM
I treated the wound, but still...
PUBLIC IDENTITY: CITY HALL WORKER
SECRET IDENTITY: ASSASSIN

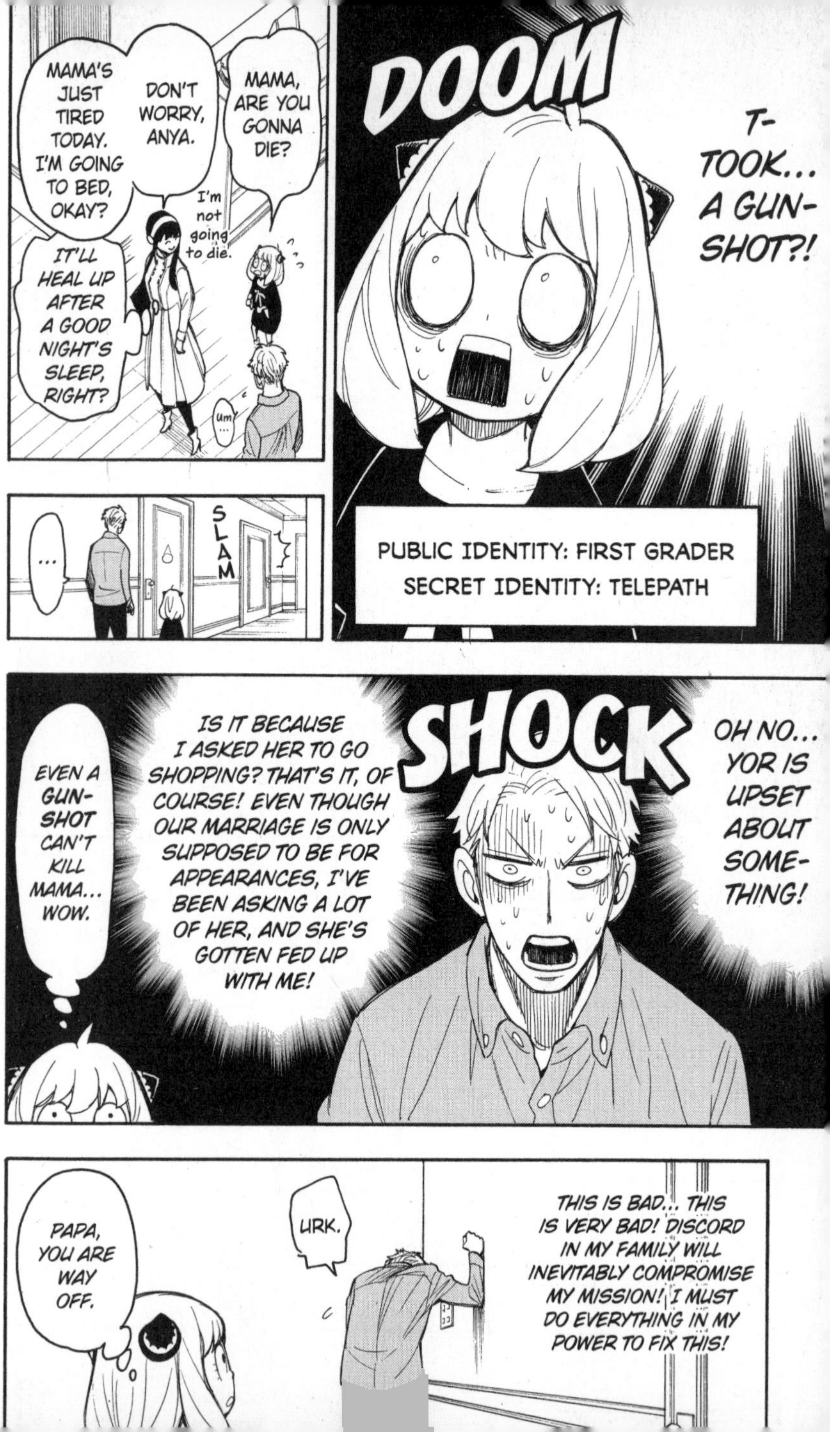
DOOM
T-TOOK... A GUN-SHOT?!
PUBLIC IDENTITY: FIRST GRADER
SECRET IDENTITY: TELEPATH
MAMA, ARE YOU GONNA DIE?
DON'T WORRY, ANYA.
MAMA'S JUST TIRED TODAY. I'M GOING TO BED, OKAY?
I'm not going to die.
IT'LL HEAL UP AFTER A GOOD NIGHT'S SLEEP, RIGHT?
um...
SLAM
...
SHOCK
OH NO... YOR IS UPSET ABOUT SOME-THING!
IS IT BECAUSE I ASKED HER TO GO SHOPPING? THAT'S IT, OF COURSE! EVEN THOUGH OUR MARRIAGE IS ONLY SUPPOSED TO BE FOR APPEARANCES, I'VE BEEN ASKING A LOT OF HER, AND SHE'S GOTTEN FED UP WITH ME!
EVEN A GUN-SHOT CAN'T KILL MAMA... WOW.
THIS IS BAD... THIS IS VERY BAD! DISCORD IN MY FAMILY WILL INEVITABLY COMPROMISE MY MISSION! I MUST DO EVERYTHING IN MY POWER TO FIX THIS!
URK.
PAPA, YOU ARE WAY OFF.

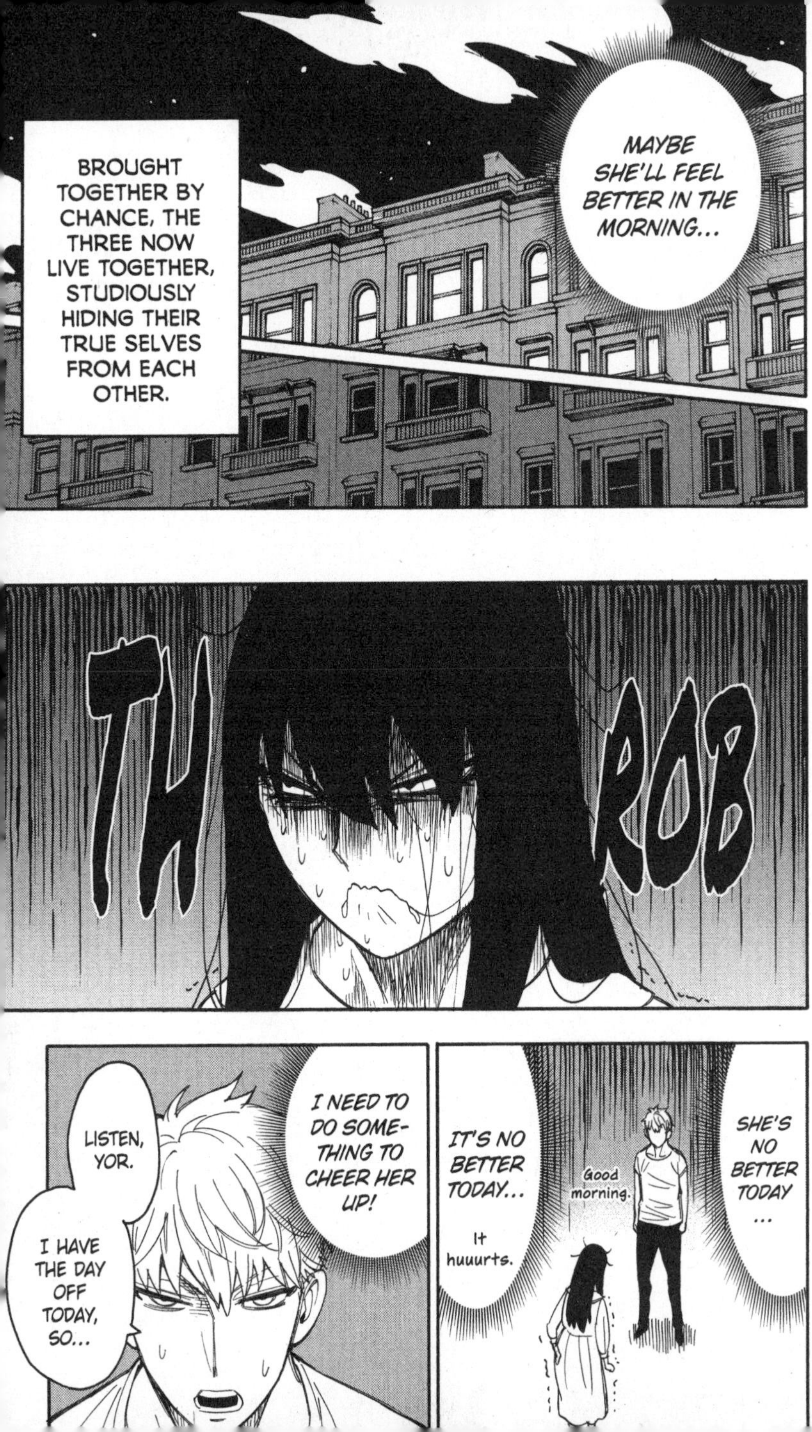
MAYBE SHE'LL FEEL BETTER IN THE MORNING...
BROUGHT TOGETHER BY CHANCE, THE THREE NOW LIVE TOGETHER, STUDIOUSLY HIDING THEIR TRUE SELVES FROM EACH OTHER.
THROB
SHE'S NO BETTER TODAY ...
Good morning.
IT'S NO BETTER TODAY...
It huuurts.
I NEED TO DO SOME-THING TO CHEER HER UP!
LISTEN, YOR.
I HAVE THE DAY OFF TODAY, SO...

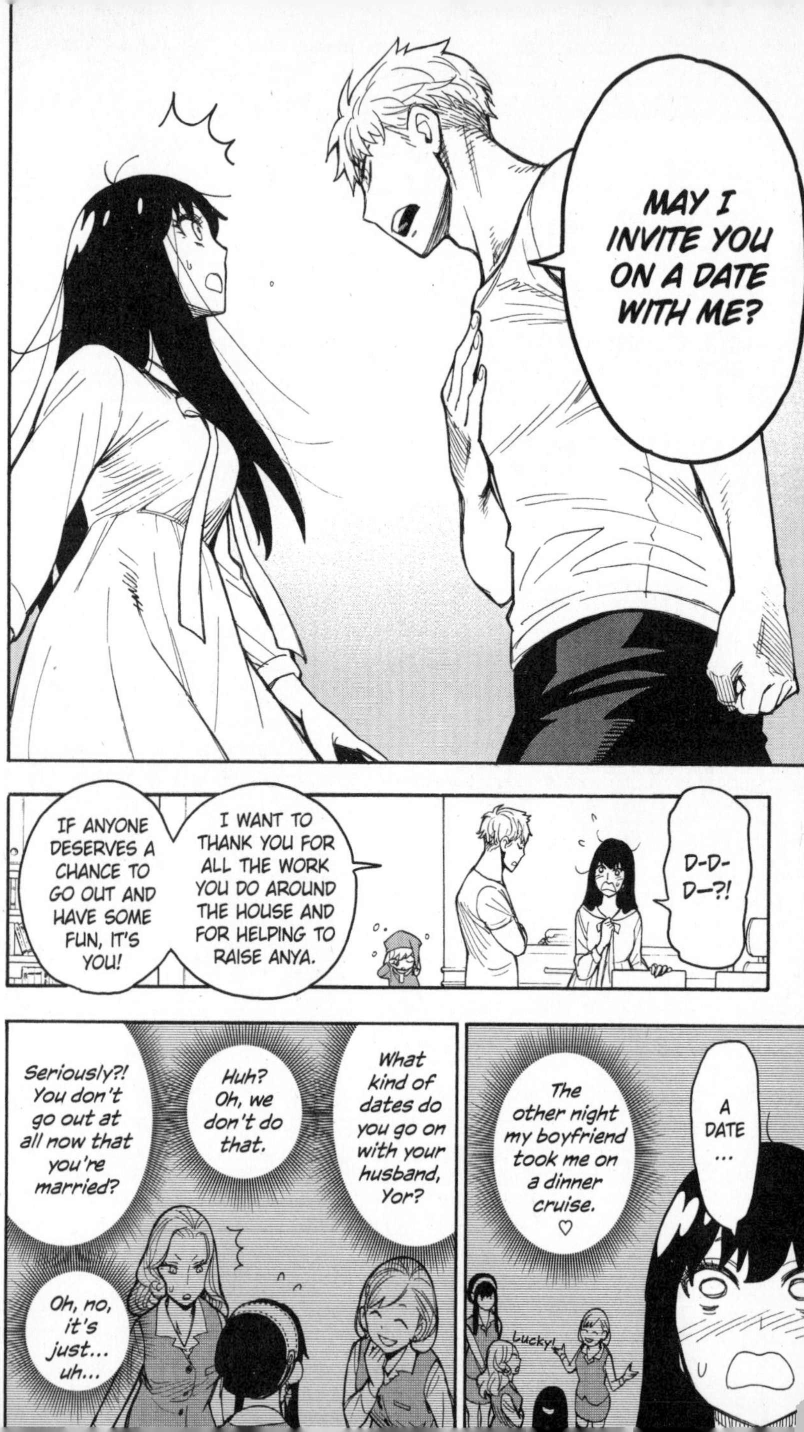
MAY I INVITE YOU ON A DATE WITH ME?
D-D-D—?!
I WANT TO THANK YOU FOR ALL THE WORK YOU DO AROUND THE HOUSE AND FOR HELPING TO RAISE ANYA.
IF ANYONE DESERVES A CHANCE TO GO OUT AND HAVE SOME FUN, IT'S YOU!
A DATE ...
The other night my boyfriend took me on a dinner cruise. ♡
Lucky!
What kind of dates do you go on with your husband, Yor?
Huh? Oh, we don't do that.
Seriously?! You don't go out at all now that you're married?
Oh, no, it's just... uh...

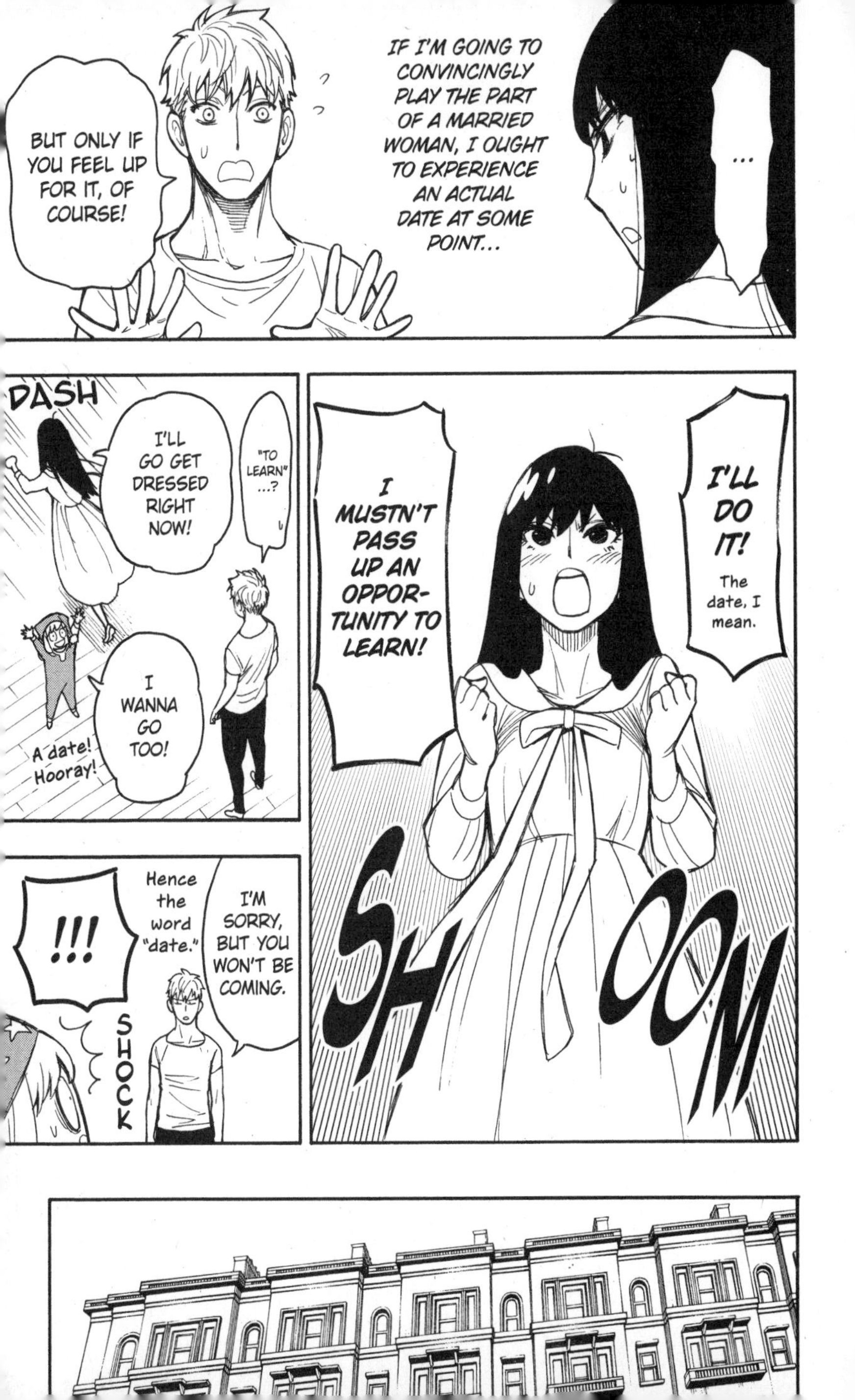
...
IF I'M GOING TO CONVINCINGLY PLAY THE PART OF A MARRIED WOMAN, I OUGHT TO EXPERIENCE AN ACTUAL DATE AT SOME POINT...
BUT ONLY IF YOU FEEL UP FOR IT, OF COURSE!
I'LL DO IT!
The date, I mean.
I MUSTN'T PASS UP AN OPPOR-TUNITY TO LEARN!
SHOOM
"TO LEARN" ...?
I'LL GO GET DRESSED RIGHT NOW!
DASH
I WANNA GO TOO!
A date! Hooray!
I'M SORRY, BUT YOU WON'T BE COMING.
Hence the word "date."
!!!
SHOCK

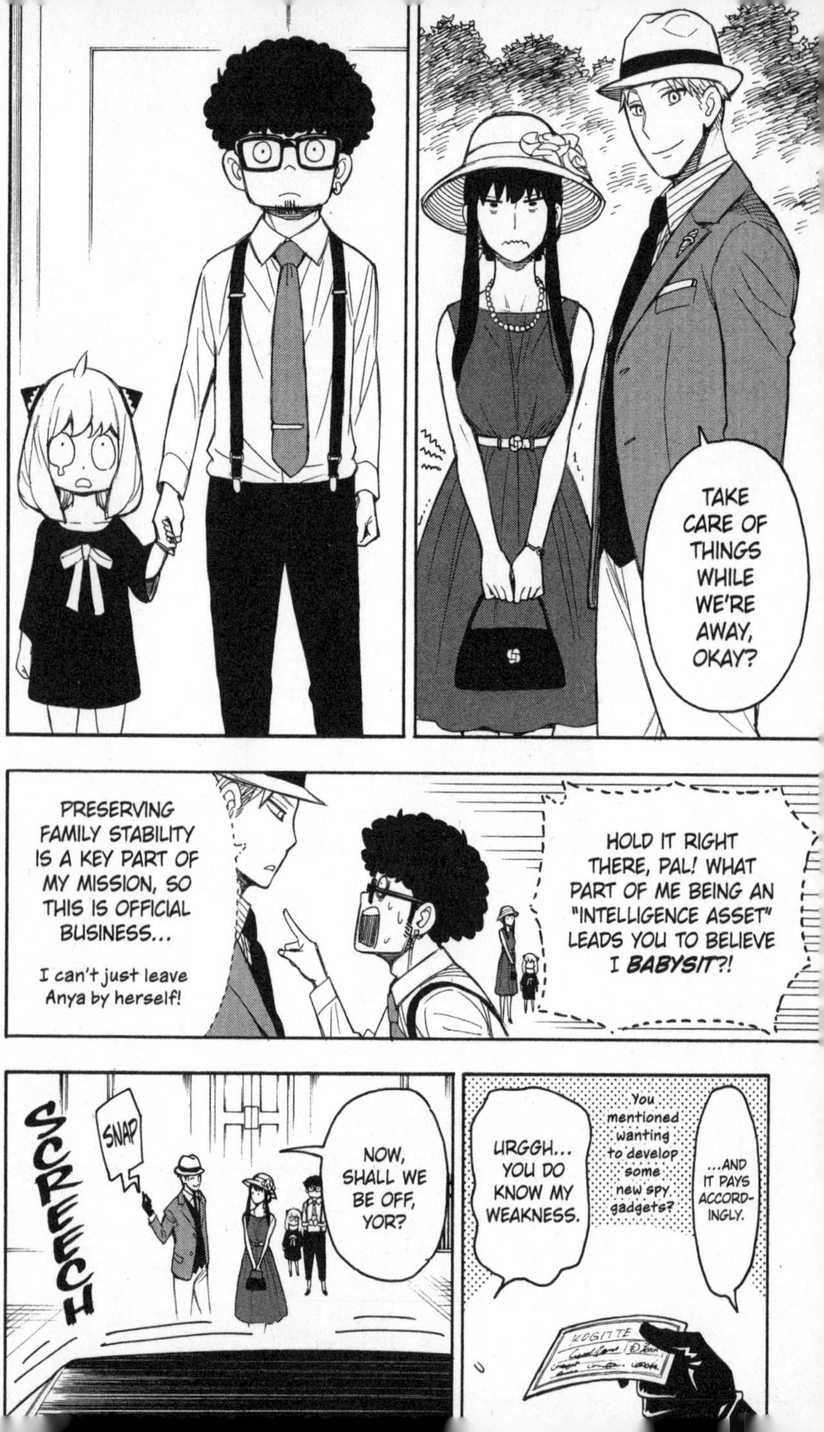
TAKE CARE OF THINGS WHILE WE'RE AWAY, OKAY?
HOLD IT RIGHT THERE, PAL! WHAT PART OF ME BEING AN "INTELLIGENCE ASSET" LEADS YOU TO BELIEVE I *BABYSIT*?!
PRESERVING FAMILY STABILITY IS A KEY PART OF MY MISSION, SO THIS IS OFFICIAL BUSINESS...
I can't just leave Anya by herself!
...AND IT PAYS ACCORDINGLY.
You mentioned wanting to develop some new spy gadgets?
URGGH... YOU DO KNOW MY WEAKNESS.
NOW, SHALL WE BE OFF, YOR?
SNAP
SCREECH

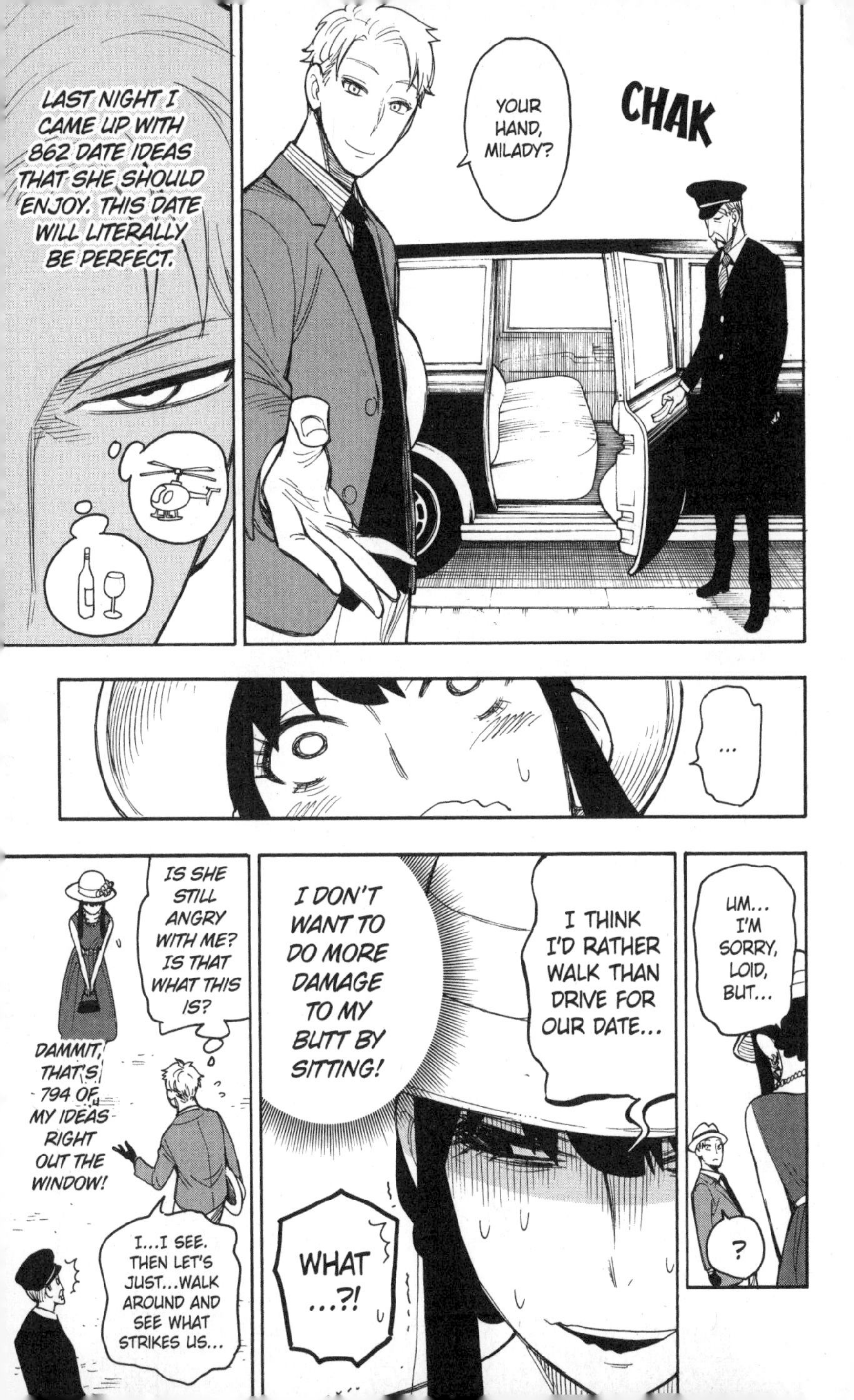
CHAK
YOUR HAND, MILADY?
LAST NIGHT I CAME UP WITH 862 DATE IDEAS THAT SHE SHOULD ENJOY. THIS DATE WILL LITERALLY BE PERFECT.
...
UM... I'M SORRY, LOID, BUT...
?
I THINK I'D RATHER WALK THAN DRIVE FOR OUR DATE...
I DON'T WANT TO DO MORE DAMAGE TO MY BUTT BY SITTING!
WHAT ...?!
IS SHE STILL ANGRY WITH ME? IS THAT WHAT THIS IS?
DAMMIT, THAT'S 794 OF MY IDEAS RIGHT OUT THE WINDOW!
I...I SEE. THEN LET'S JUST...WALK AROUND AND SEE WHAT STRIKES US...

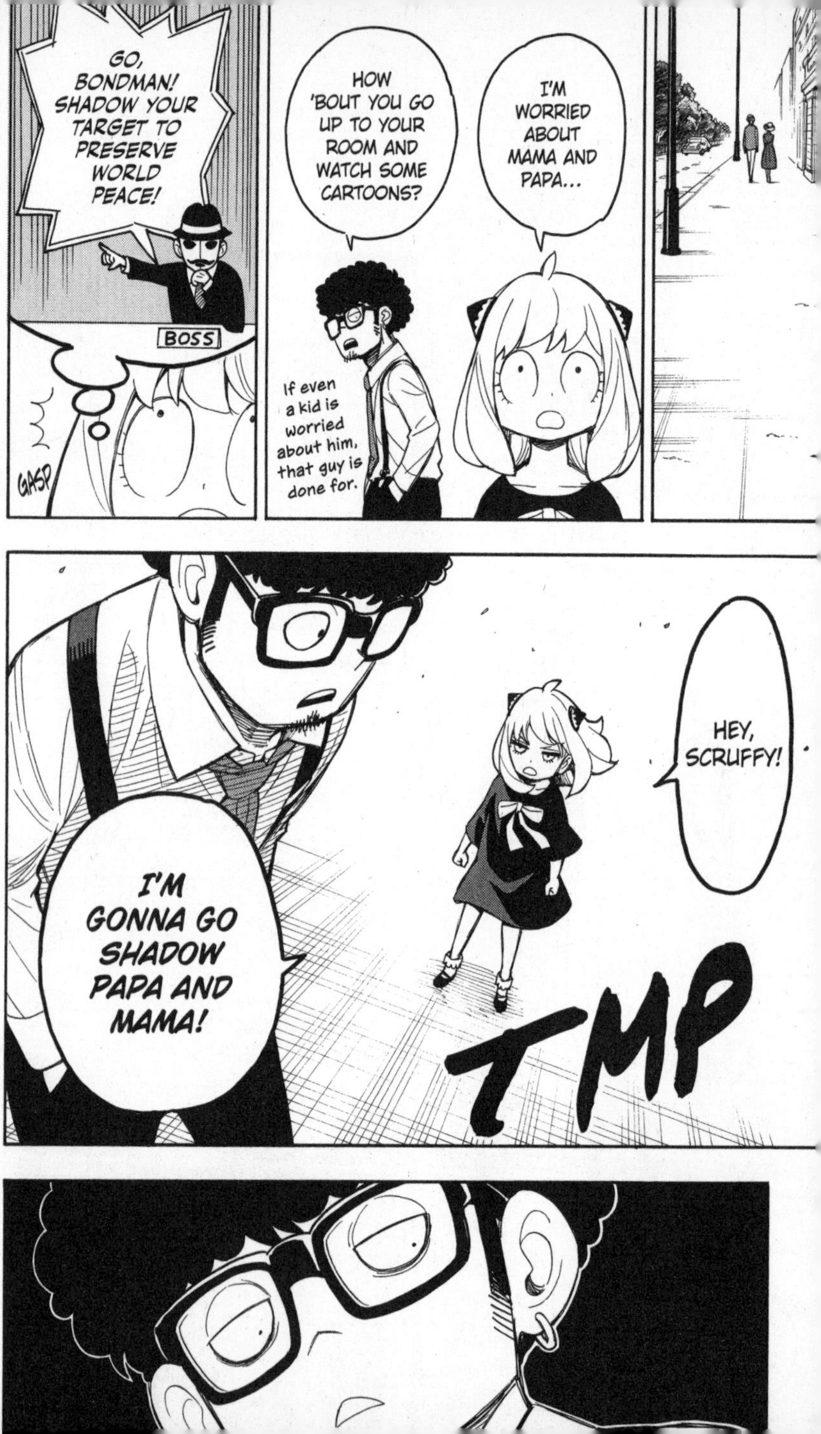
I'M WORRIED ABOUT MAMA AND PAPA...
HOW 'BOUT YOU GO UP TO YOUR ROOM AND WATCH SOME CARTOONS?
If even a kid is worried about him, that guy is done for.
GO, BONDMAN! SHADOW YOUR TARGET TO PRESERVE WORLD PEACE!
BOSS
GASP
HEY, SCRUFFY!
TMP
I'M GONNA GO SHADOW PAPA AND MAMA!

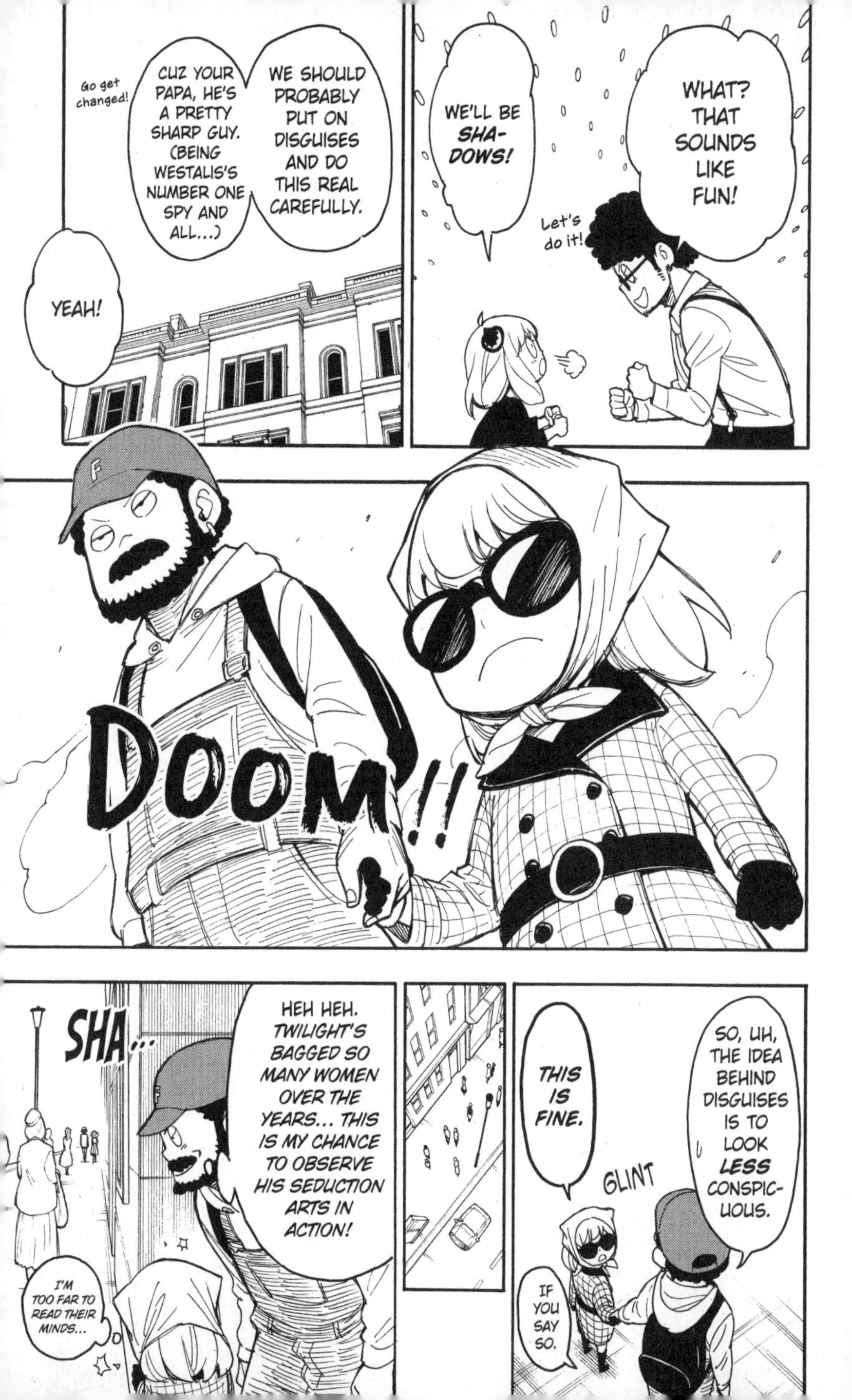
WHAT? THAT SOUNDS LIKE FUN!
Let's do it!
WE'LL BE SHADOWS!
WE SHOULD PROBABLY PUT ON DISGUISES AND DO THIS REAL CAREFULLY.
CUZ YOUR PAPA, HE'S A PRETTY SHARP GUY. (BEING WESTALIS'S NUMBER ONE SPY AND ALL...)
Go get changed!
YEAH!
DOOM!!
SO, UH, THE IDEA BEHIND DISGUISES IS TO LOOK LESS CONSPICUOUS.
THIS IS FINE.
GLINT
IF YOU SAY SO.
SHA...
HEH HEH. TWILIGHT'S BAGGED SO MANY WOMEN OVER THE YEARS... THIS IS MY CHANCE TO OBSERVE HIS SEDUCTION ARTS IN ACTION!
I'M TOO FAR TO READ THEIR MINDS...

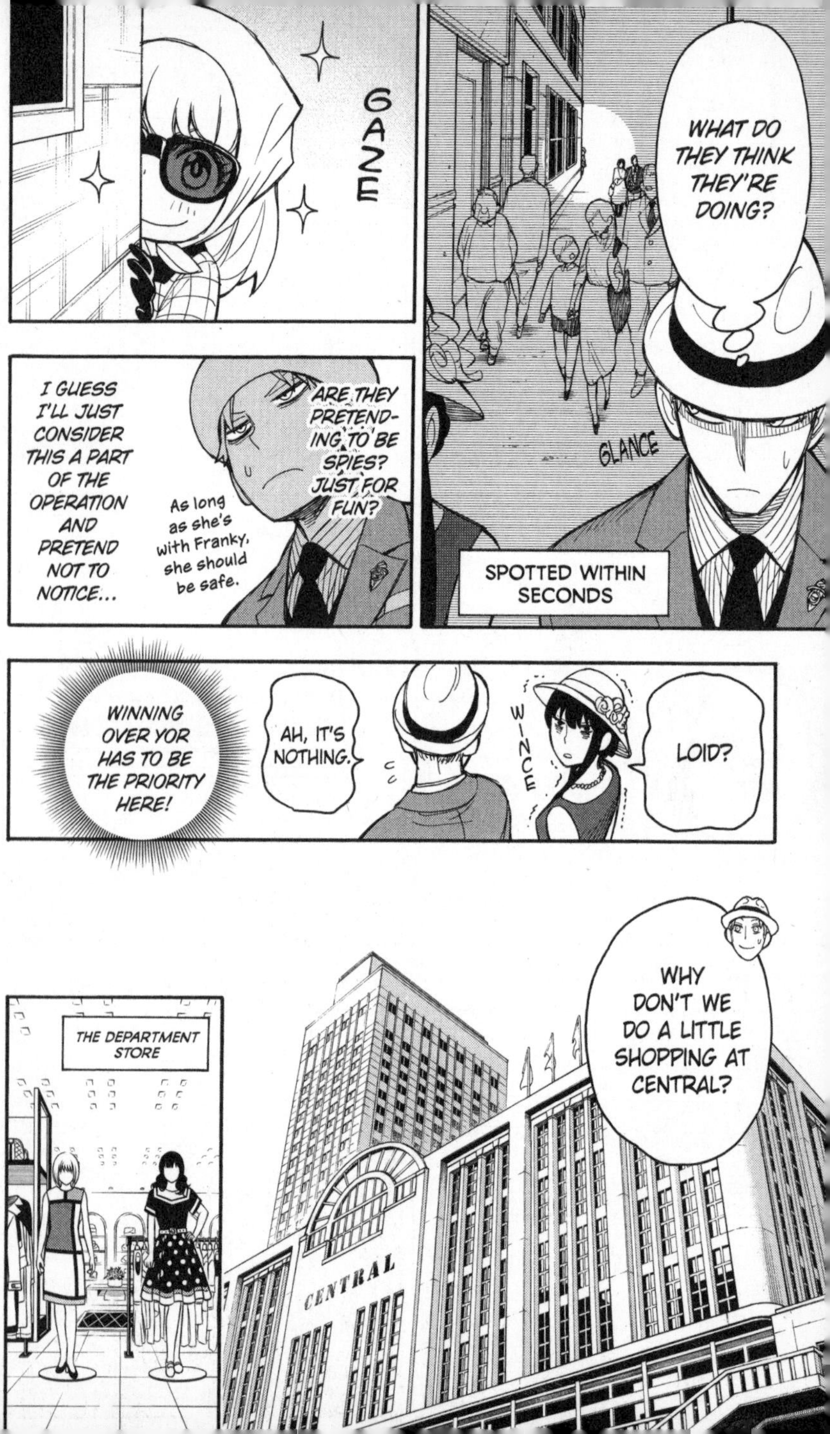
WHAT DO THEY THINK THEY'RE DOING?
GLANCE
SPOTTED WITHIN SECONDS
GAZE
ARE THEY PRETEND-ING TO BE SPIES? JUST FOR FUN?
As long as she's with Franky, she should be safe.
I GUESS I'LL JUST CONSIDER THIS A PART OF THE OPERATION AND PRETEND NOT TO NOTICE...
LOID?
WINCE
AH, IT'S NOTHING.
WINNING OVER YOR HAS TO BE THE PRIORITY HERE!
WHY DON'T WE DO A LITTLE SHOPPING AT CENTRAL?
CENTRAL
THE DEPARTMENT STORE

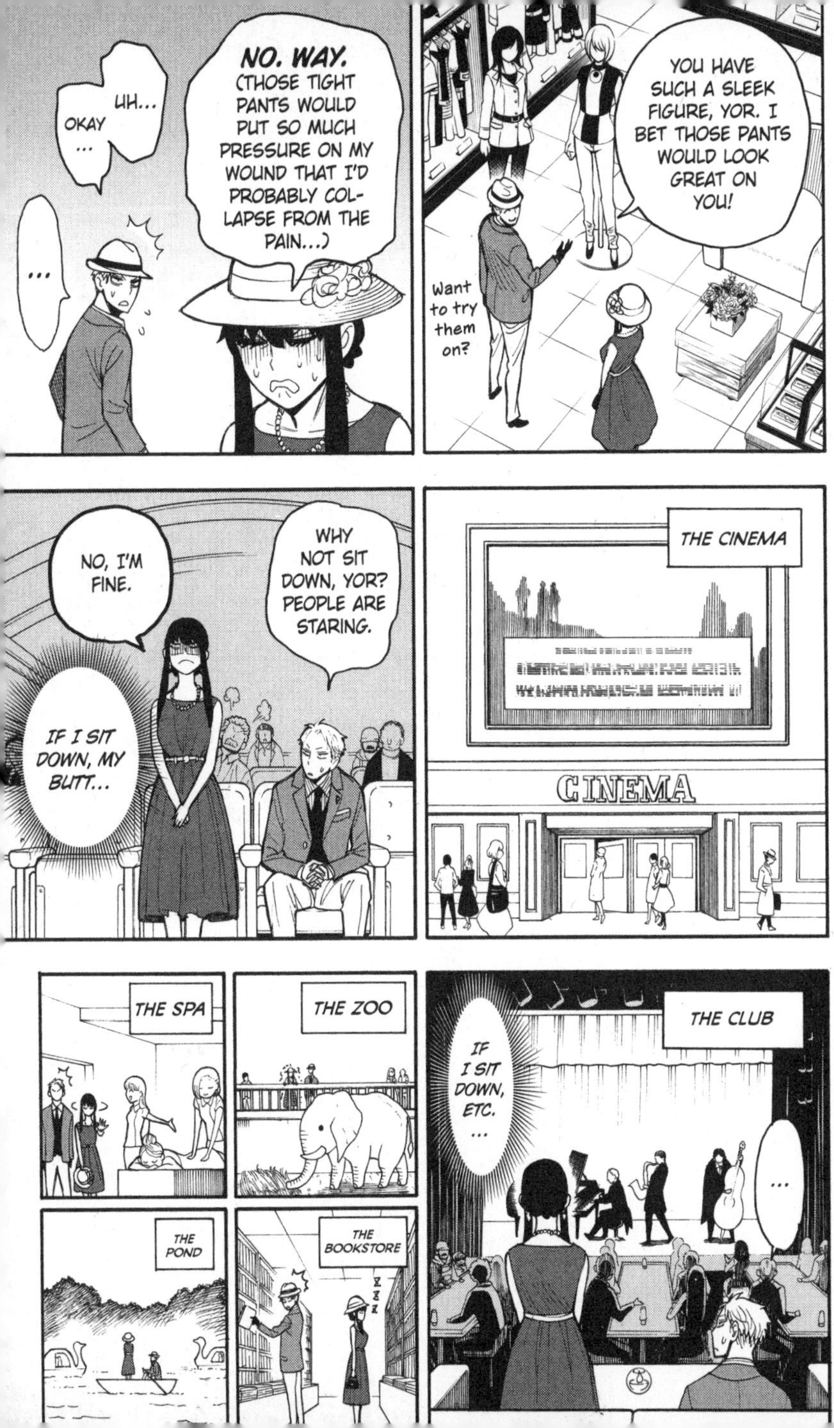
YOU HAVE SUCH A SLEEK FIGURE, YOR. I BET THOSE PANTS WOULD LOOK GREAT ON YOU!
Want to try them on?
NO. WAY. (THOSE TIGHT PANTS WOULD PUT SO MUCH PRESSURE ON MY WOUND THAT I'D PROBABLY COL-LAPSE FROM THE PAIN...)
UH... OKAY...
...
THE CINEMA
CINEMA
WHY NOT SIT DOWN, YOR? PEOPLE ARE STARING.
NO, I'M FINE.
IF I SIT DOWN, MY BUTT...
THE CLUB
IF I SIT DOWN, ETC. ...
...
THE ZOO
THE SPA
THE BOOKSTORE
THE POND

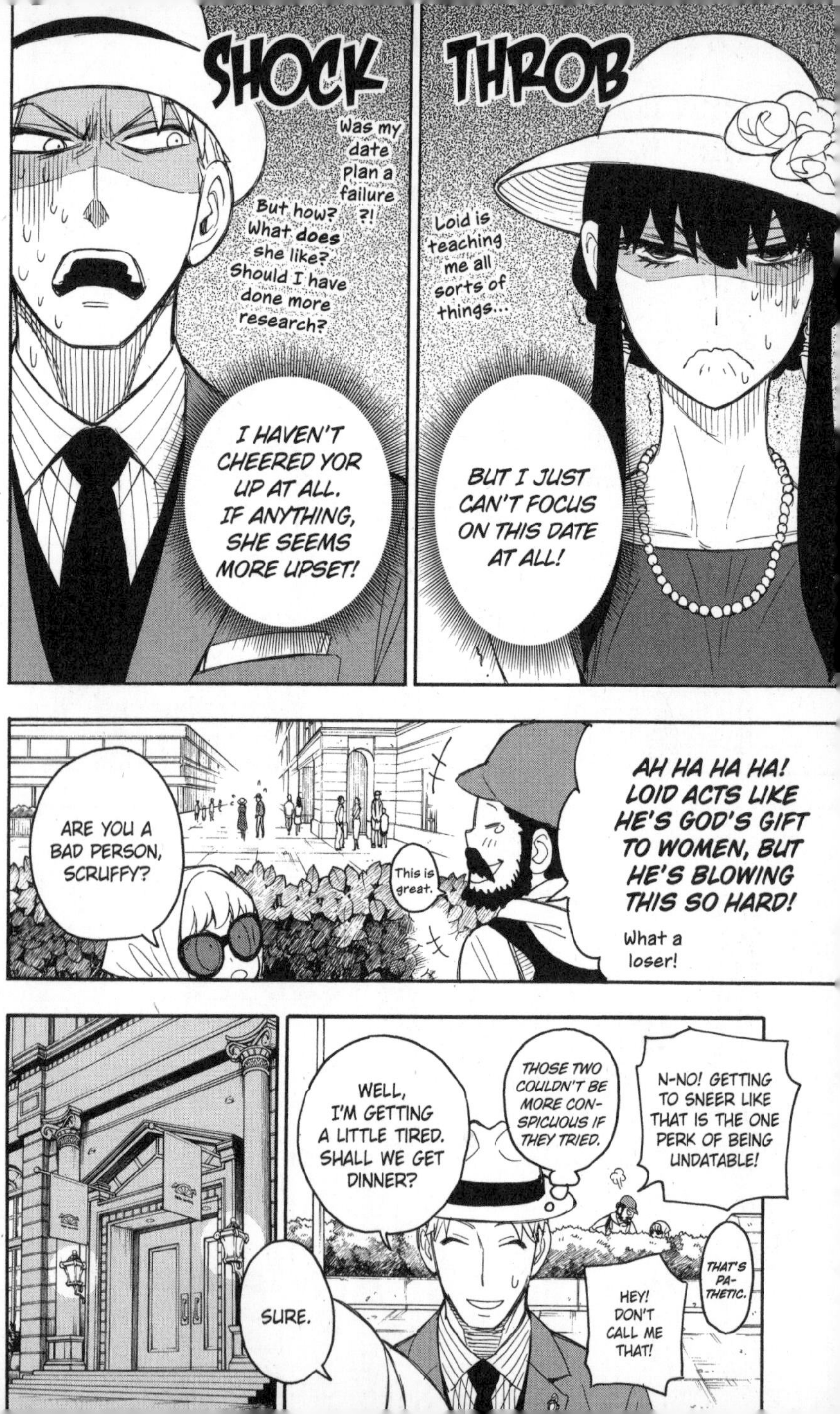
THROB
Loid is teaching me all sorts of things...
BUT I JUST CAN'T FOCUS ON THIS DATE AT ALL!
SHOCK
Was my date plan a failure ?!
But how? What does she like? Should I have done more research?
I HAVEN'T CHEERED YOR UP AT ALL. IF ANYTHING, SHE SEEMS MORE UPSET!
AH HA HA HA! LOID ACTS LIKE HE'S GOD'S GIFT TO WOMEN, BUT HE'S BLOWING THIS SO HARD!
What a loser!
This is great.
ARE YOU A BAD PERSON, SCRUFFY?
N-NO! GETTING TO SNEER LIKE THAT IS THE ONE PERK OF BEING UNDATABLE!
THOSE TWO COULDN'T BE MORE CON-SPICUOUS IF THEY TRIED.
WELL, I'M GETTING A LITTLE TIRED. SHALL WE GET DINNER?
THAT'S PA-THETIC.
HEY! DON'T CALL ME THAT!
SURE.

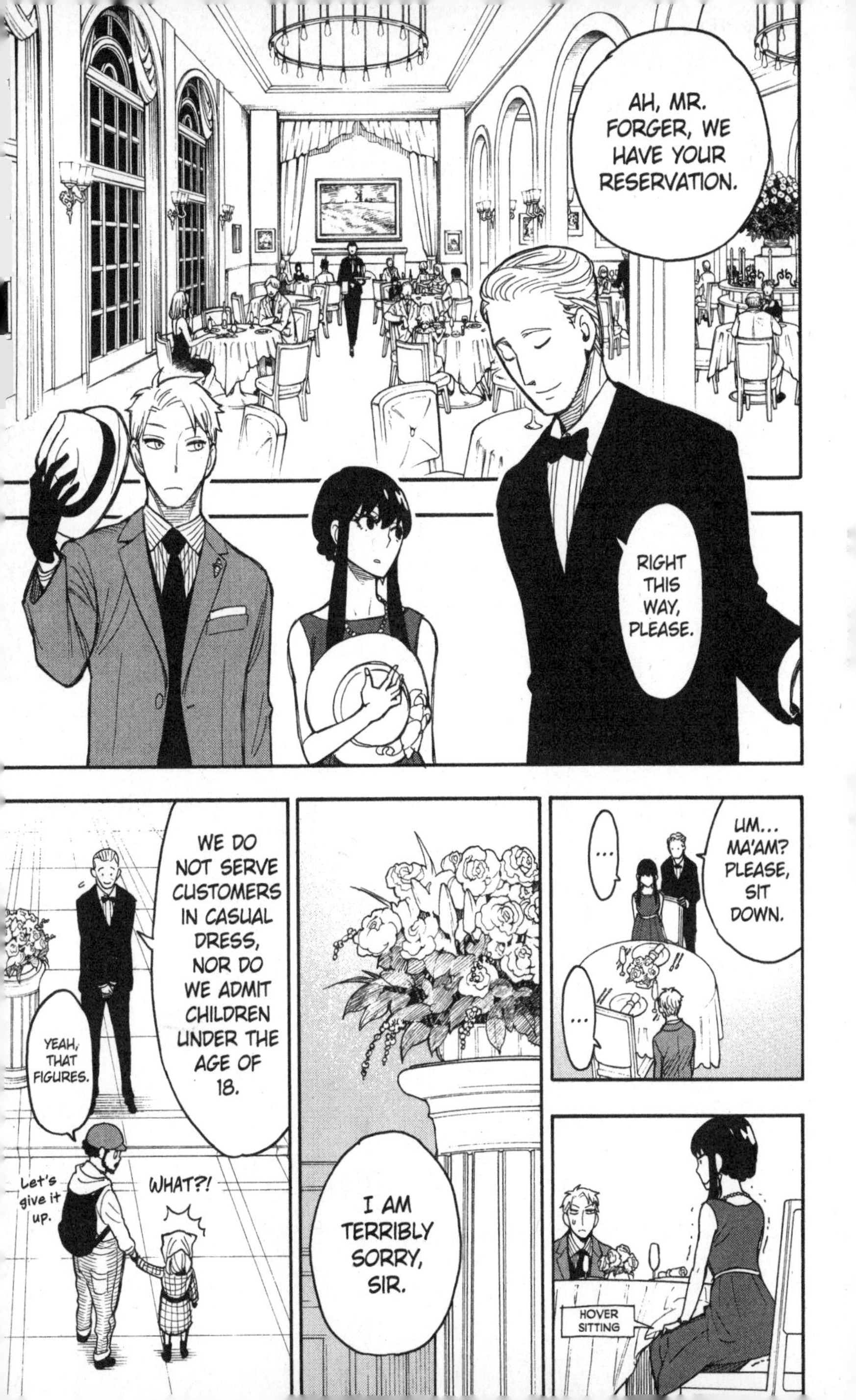
AH, MR. FORGER, WE HAVE YOUR RESERVATION.
RIGHT THIS WAY, PLEASE.
UM... MA'AM? PLEASE, SIT DOWN.
...
...
HOVER SITTING
I AM TERRIBLY SORRY, SIR.
WE DO NOT SERVE CUSTOMERS IN CASUAL DRESS, NOR DO WE ADMIT CHILDREN UNDER THE AGE OF 18.
YEAH, THAT FIGURES.
WHAT?!
Let's give it up.

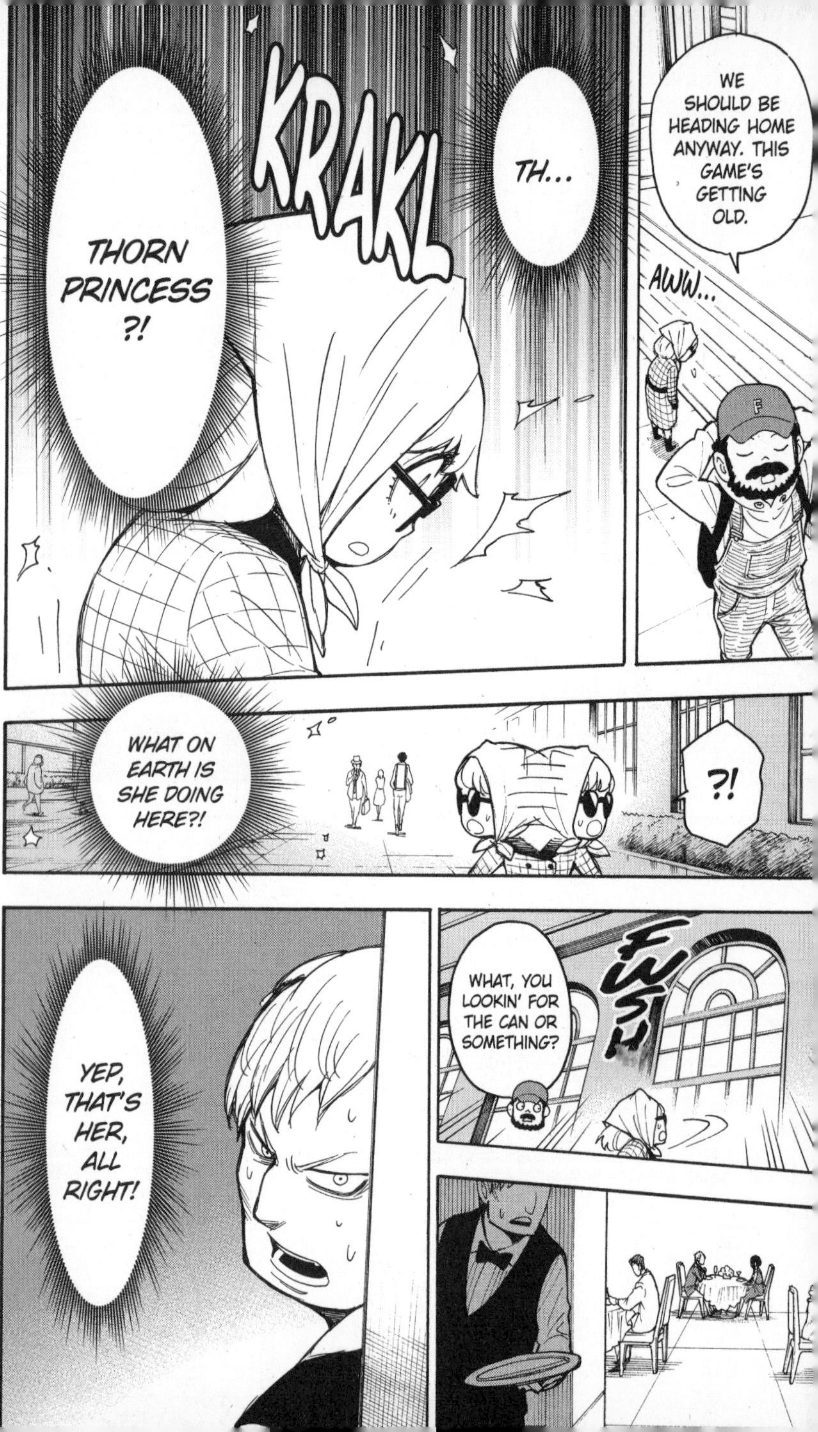
WE SHOULD BE HEADING HOME ANYWAY. THIS GAME'S GETTING OLD.
AWW...
TH...
KRAKL
THORN PRINCESS ?!
?!
WHAT ON EARTH IS SHE DOING HERE?!
WHAT, YOU LOOKIN' FOR THE CAN OR SOMETHING?
FWSH
YEP, THAT'S HER, ALL RIGHT!

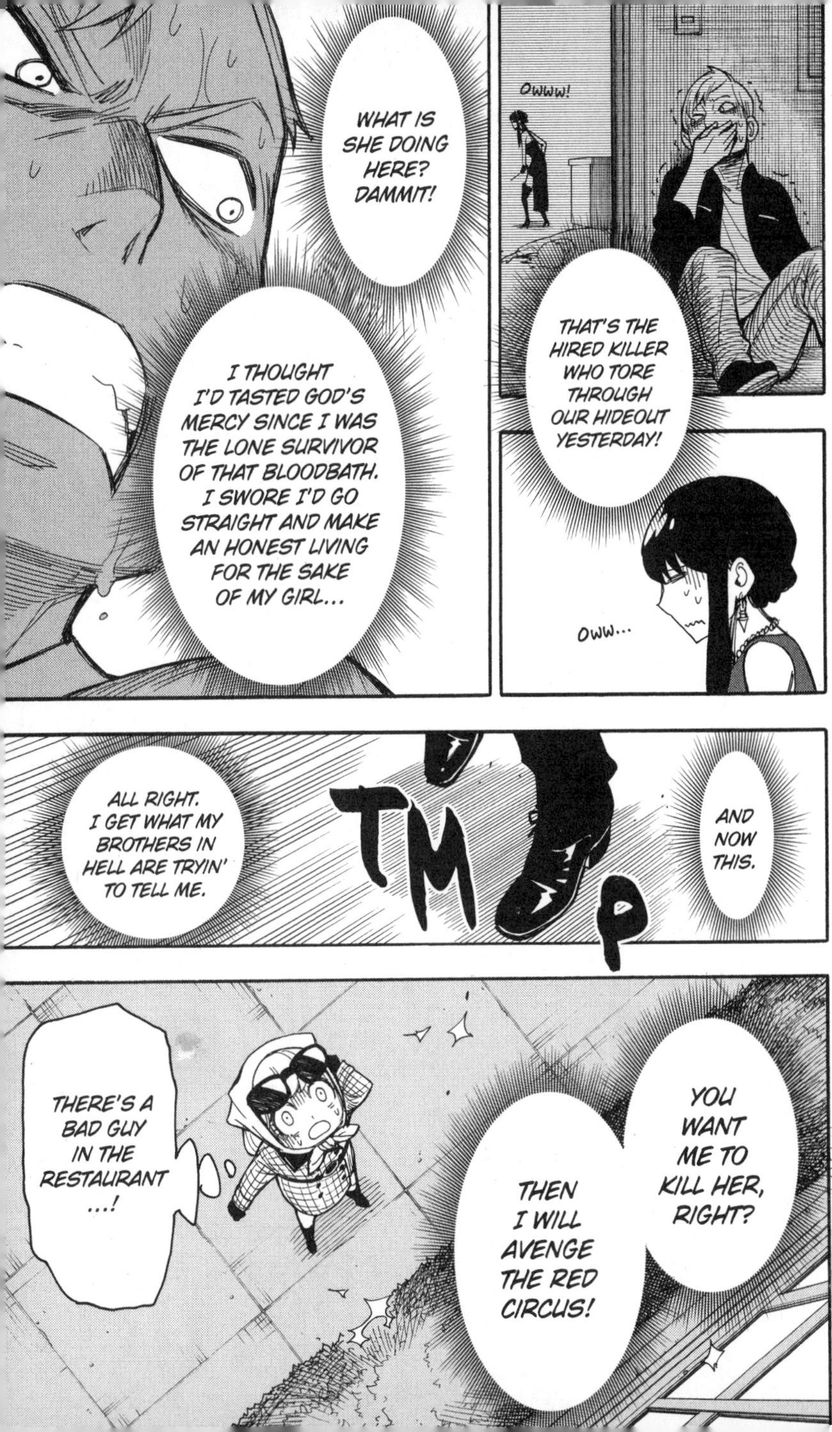
OWWW!
THAT'S THE HIRED KILLER WHO TORE THROUGH OUR HIDEOUT YESTERDAY!
OWW...
WHAT IS SHE DOING HERE? DAMMIT!
I THOUGHT I'D TASTED GOD'S MERCY SINCE I WAS THE LONE SURVIVOR OF THAT BLOODBATH. I SWORE I'D GO STRAIGHT AND MAKE AN HONEST LIVING FOR THE SAKE OF MY GIRL...
AND NOW THIS.
TMP
ALL RIGHT. I GET WHAT MY BROTHERS IN HELL ARE TRYIN' TO TELL ME.
YOU WANT ME TO KILL HER, RIGHT?
THEN I WILL AVENGE THE RED CIRCUS!
THERE'S A BAD GUY IN THE RESTAURANT ...!

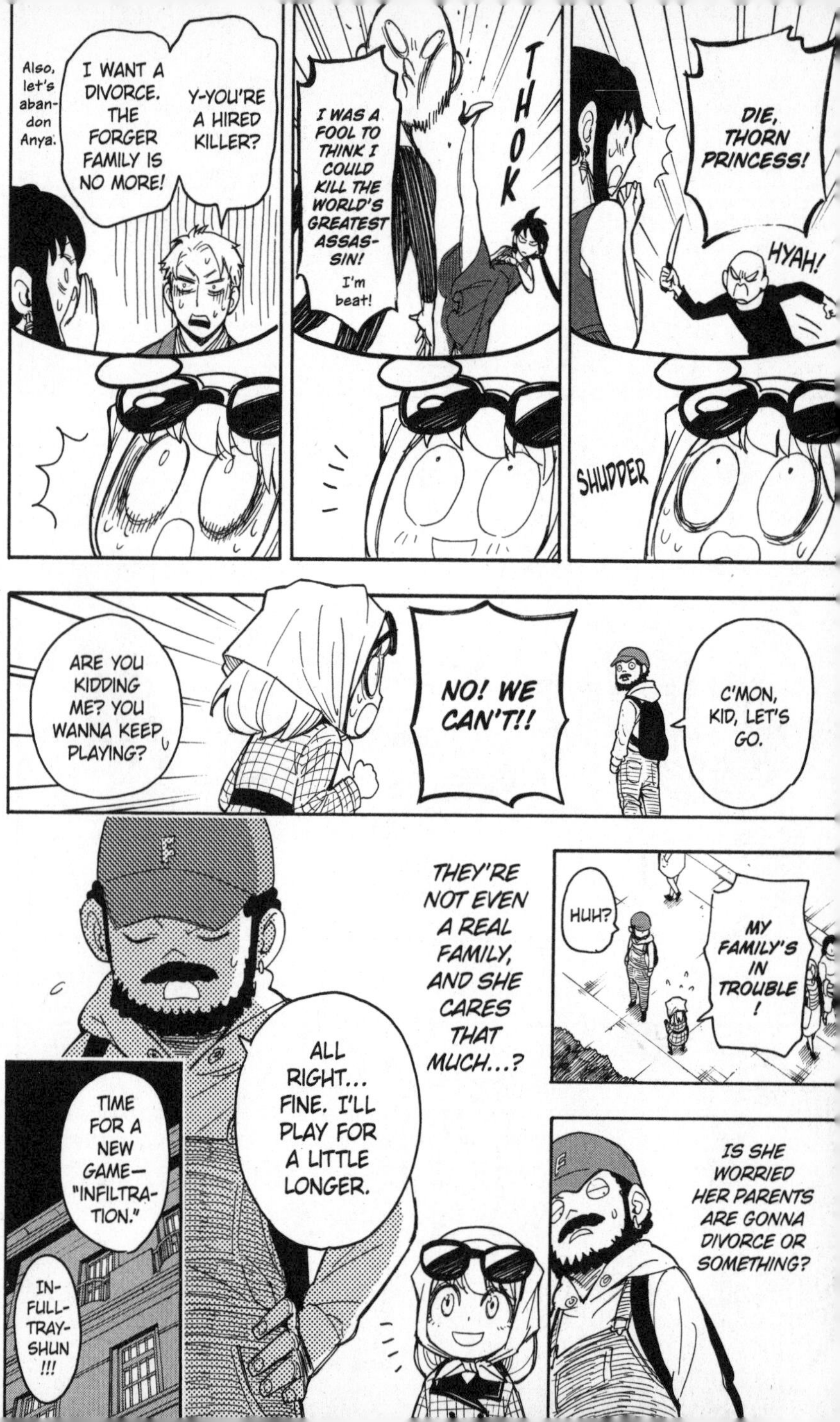
DIE, THORN PRINCESS!
HYAH!
SHUDDER
THOK
I WAS A FOOL TO THINK I COULD KILL THE WORLD'S GREATEST ASSAS-SIN!
I'm beat!
Y-YOU'RE A HIRED KILLER?
I WANT A DIVORCE. THE FORGER FAMILY IS NO MORE!
Also, let's aban-don Anya.
C'MON, KID, LET'S GO.
NO! WE CAN'T!!
ARE YOU KIDDING ME? YOU WANNA KEEP PLAYING?
HUH?
MY FAMILY'S IN TROUBLE!
IS SHE WORRIED HER PARENTS ARE GONNA DIVORCE OR SOMETHING?
THEY'RE NOT EVEN A REAL FAMILY, AND SHE CARES THAT MUCH...?
ALL RIGHT... FINE. I'LL PLAY FOR A LITTLE LONGER.
TIME FOR A NEW GAME—"INFILTRA-TION."
IN-FULL-TRAY-SHUN!!!

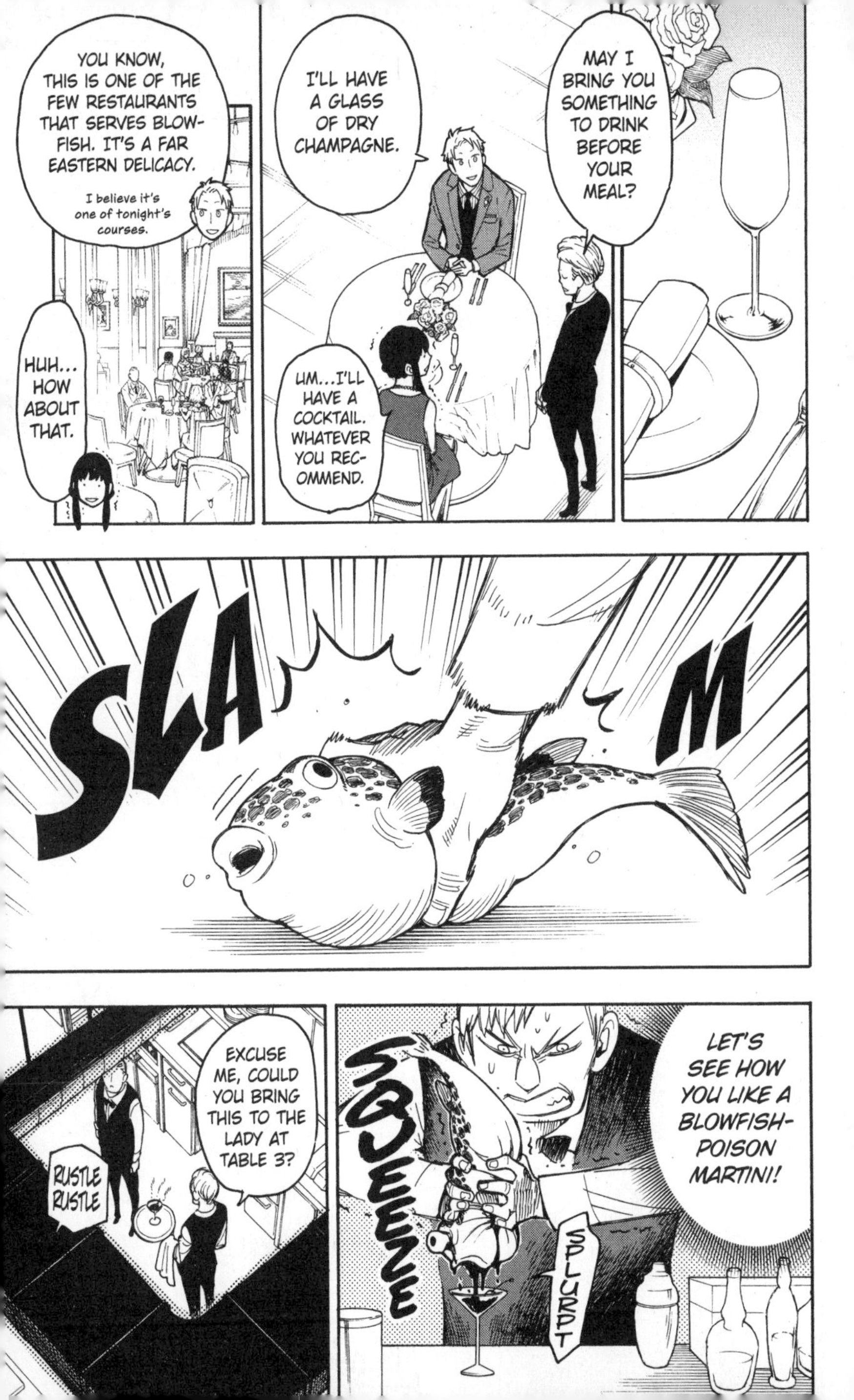
MAY I BRING YOU SOMETHING TO DRINK BEFORE YOUR MEAL?
I'LL HAVE A GLASS OF DRY CHAMPAGNE.
UM...I'LL HAVE A COCKTAIL. WHATEVER YOU RECOMMEND.
YOU KNOW, THIS IS ONE OF THE FEW RESTAURANTS THAT SERVES BLOW-FISH. IT'S A FAR EASTERN DELICACY.
I believe it's one of tonight's courses.
HUH... HOW ABOUT THAT.
SLAM
LET'S SEE HOW YOU LIKE A BLOWFISH-POISON MARTINI!
SQUEEZE
SPLURPT
EXCUSE ME, COULD YOU BRING THIS TO THE LADY AT TABLE 3?
RUSTLE RUSTLE

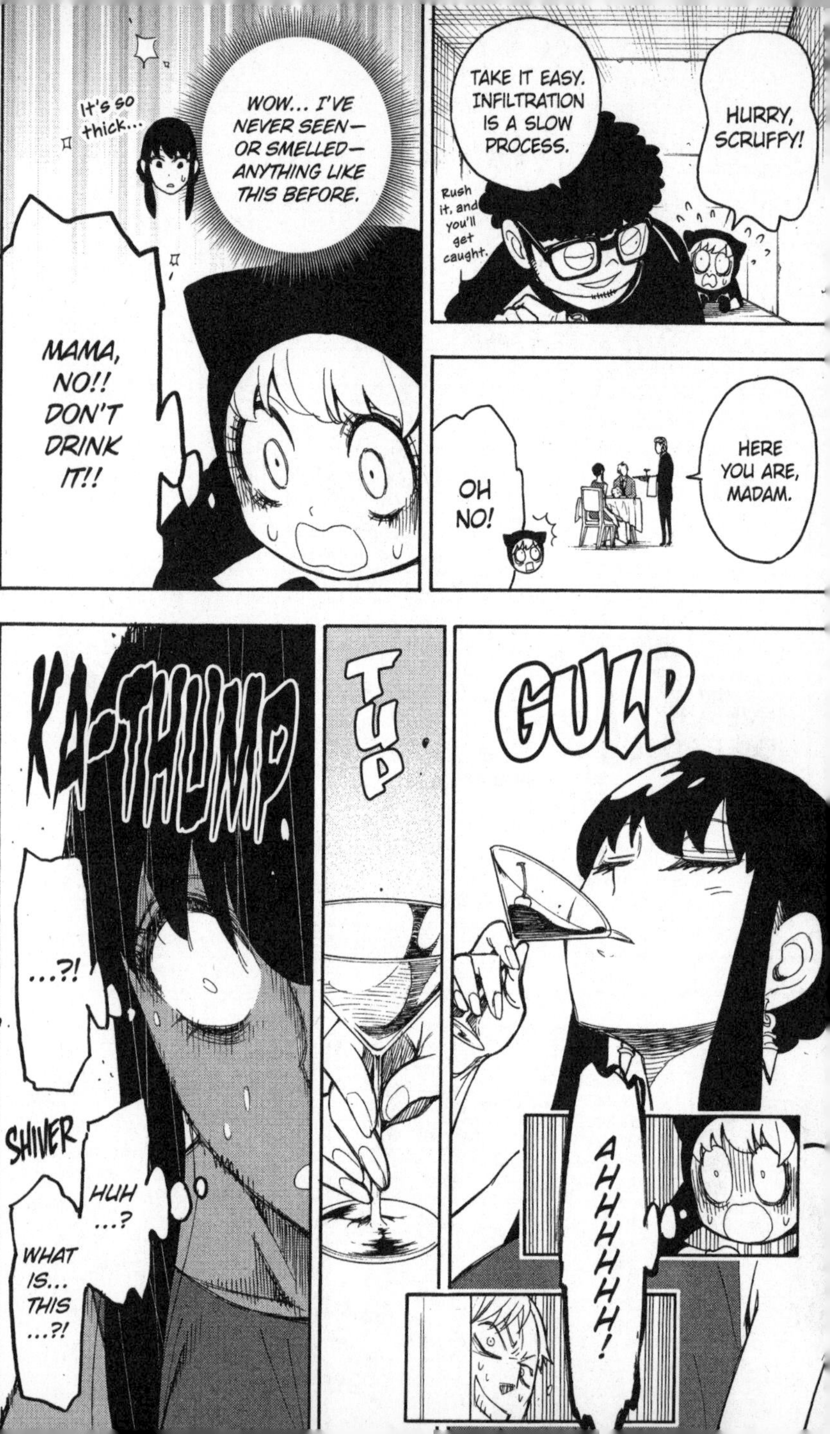
HURRY, SCRUFFY!
TAKE IT EASY. INFILTRATION IS A SLOW PROCESS.
Rush it, and you'll get caught.
HERE YOU ARE, MADAM.
OH NO!
WOW... I'VE NEVER SEEN—OR SMELLED—ANYTHING LIKE THIS BEFORE.
It's so thick...
MAMA, NO!! DON'T DRINK IT!!
GULP
AHHHHHH!
TUP
KA-THUMP
...?!
SHIVER
HUH ...?
WHAT IS... THIS ...?!

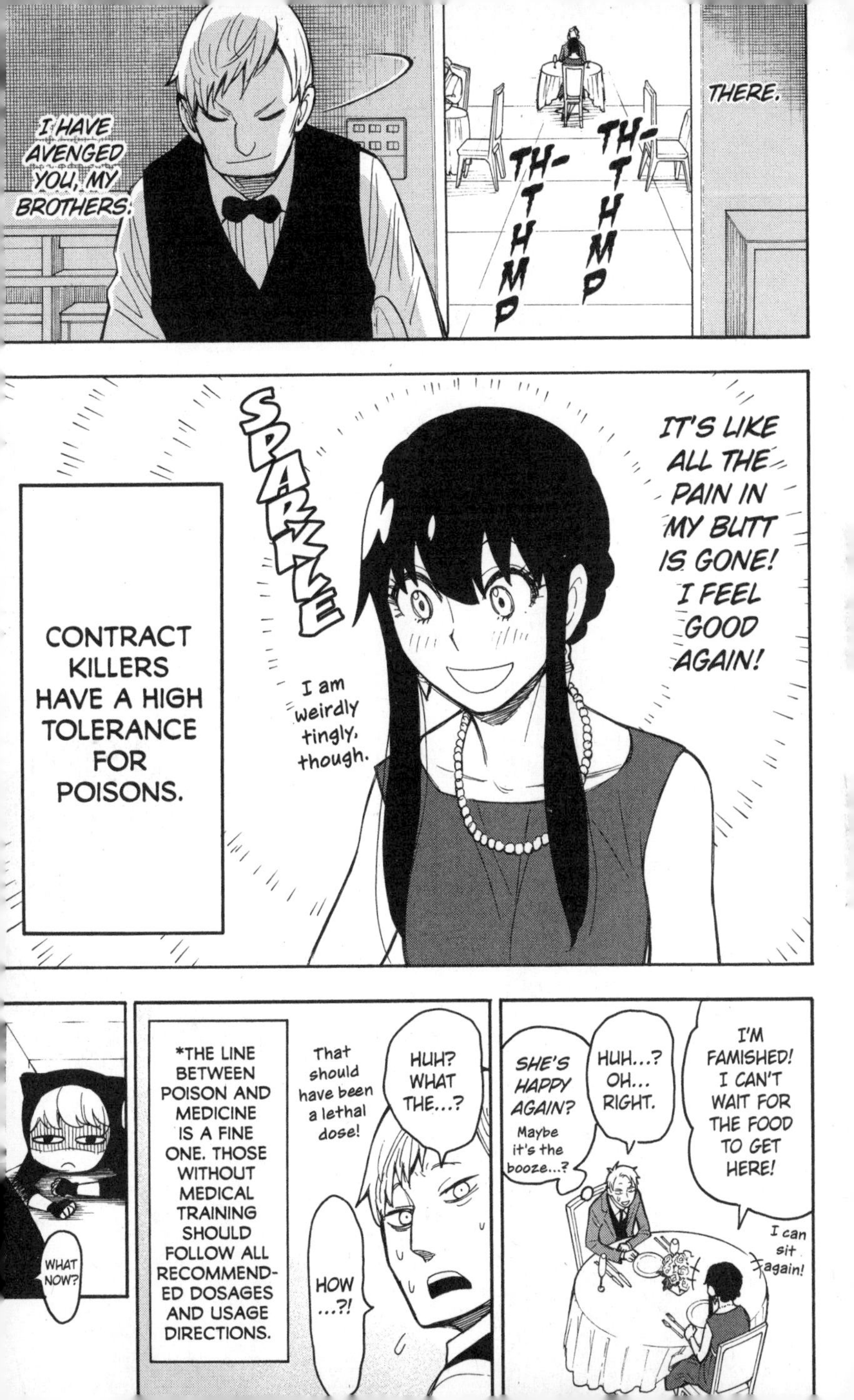
THERE.
TH-THUMP
TH-THUMP
I HAVE AVENGED YOU, MY BROTHERS.
IT'S LIKE ALL THE PAIN IN MY BUTT IS GONE! I FEEL GOOD AGAIN!
SPARKLE
I am weirdly tingly, though.
CONTRACT KILLERS HAVE A HIGH TOLERANCE FOR POISONS.
I'M FAMISHED! I CAN'T WAIT FOR THE FOOD TO GET HERE!
I can sit again!
HUH...? OH... RIGHT.
SHE'S HAPPY AGAIN?
Maybe it's the booze...?
HUH? WHAT THE...?
That should have been a lethal dose!
HOW ...?!
*THE LINE BETWEEN POISON AND MEDICINE IS A FINE ONE. THOSE WITHOUT MEDICAL TRAINING SHOULD FOLLOW ALL RECOMMENDED DOSAGES AND USAGE DIRECTIONS.
WHAT NOW?

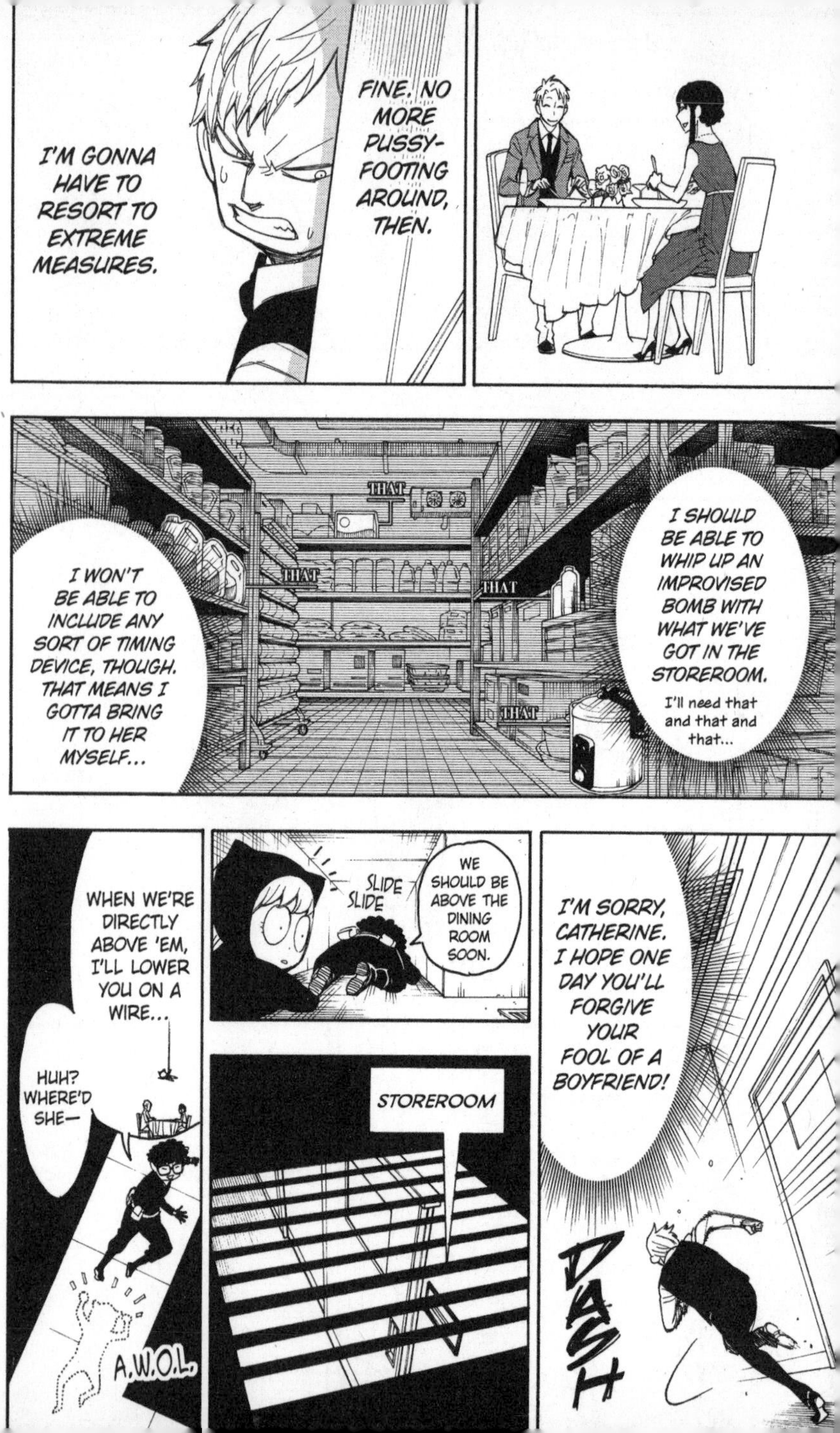
FINE. NO MORE PUSSY-FOOTING AROUND, THEN.
I'M GONNA HAVE TO RESORT TO EXTREME MEASURES.
I SHOULD BE ABLE TO WHIP UP AN IMPROVISED BOMB WITH WHAT WE'VE GOT IN THE STOREROOM.
I'll need that and that and that...
THAT
THAT
THAT
THAT
I WON'T BE ABLE TO INCLUDE ANY SORT OF TIMING DEVICE, THOUGH. THAT MEANS I GOTTA BRING IT TO HER MYSELF...
I'M SORRY, CATHERINE. I HOPE ONE DAY YOU'LL FORGIVE YOUR FOOL OF A BOYFRIEND!
DASH
WE SHOULD BE ABOVE THE DINING ROOM SOON.
SLIDE SLIDE
STOREROOM
WHEN WE'RE DIRECTLY ABOVE 'EM, I'LL LOWER YOU ON A WIRE...
HUH? WHERE'D SHE—
A.W.O.L.

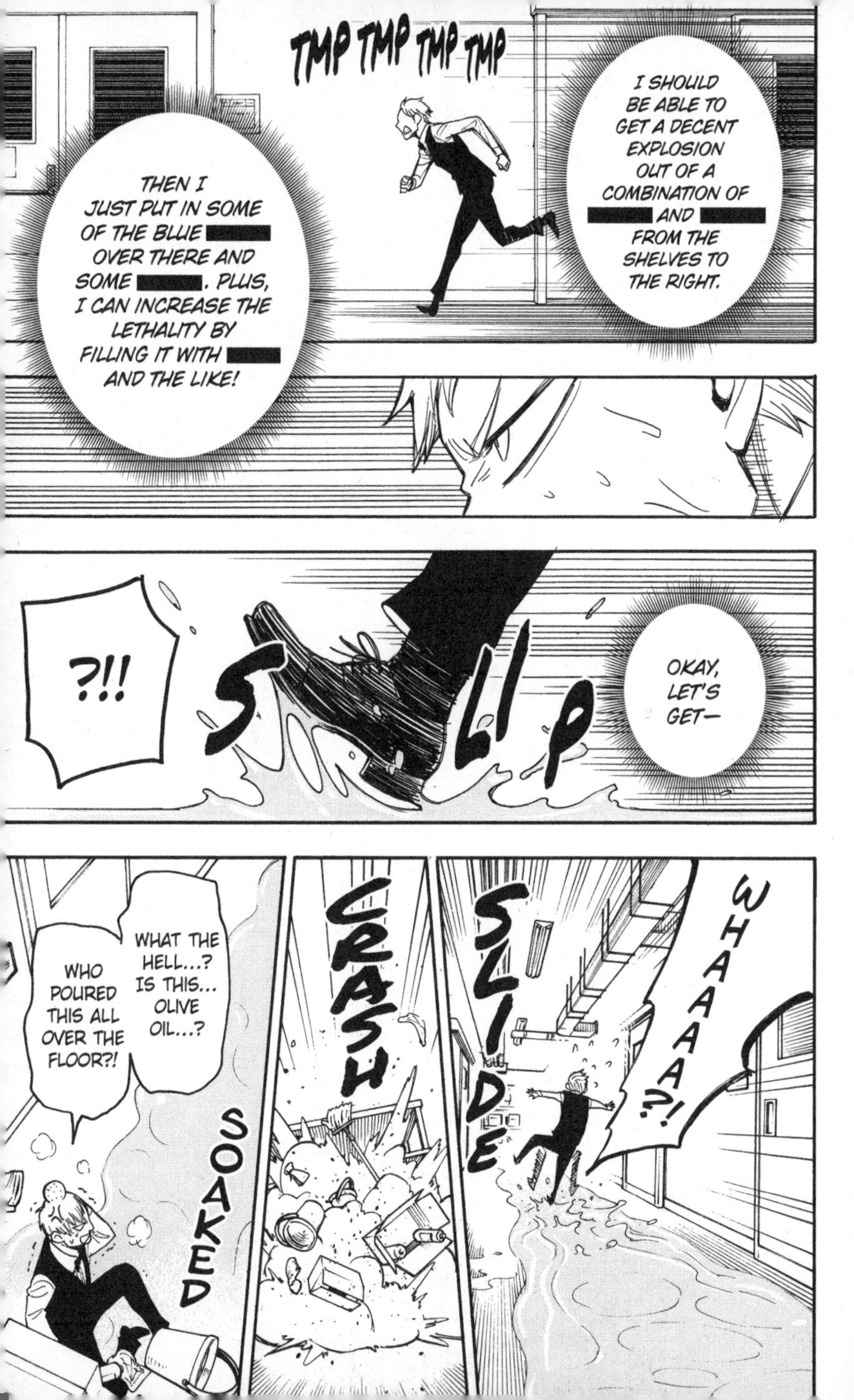
TMP TMP TMP TMP
I SHOULD BE ABLE TO GET A DECENT EXPLOSION OUT OF A COMBINATION OF [redacted] AND [redacted] FROM THE SHELVES TO THE RIGHT.
THEN I JUST PUT IN SOME OF THE BLUE [redacted] OVER THERE AND SOME [redacted]. PLUS, I CAN INCREASE THE LETHALITY BY FILLING IT WITH [redacted] AND THE LIKE!
OKAY, LET'S GET—
SLIP
?!!
WHAAAAA?!
SLIDE
CRASH
WHAT THE HELL...? IS THIS... OLIVE OIL...?
WHO POURED THIS ALL OVER THE FLOOR?!
SOAKED

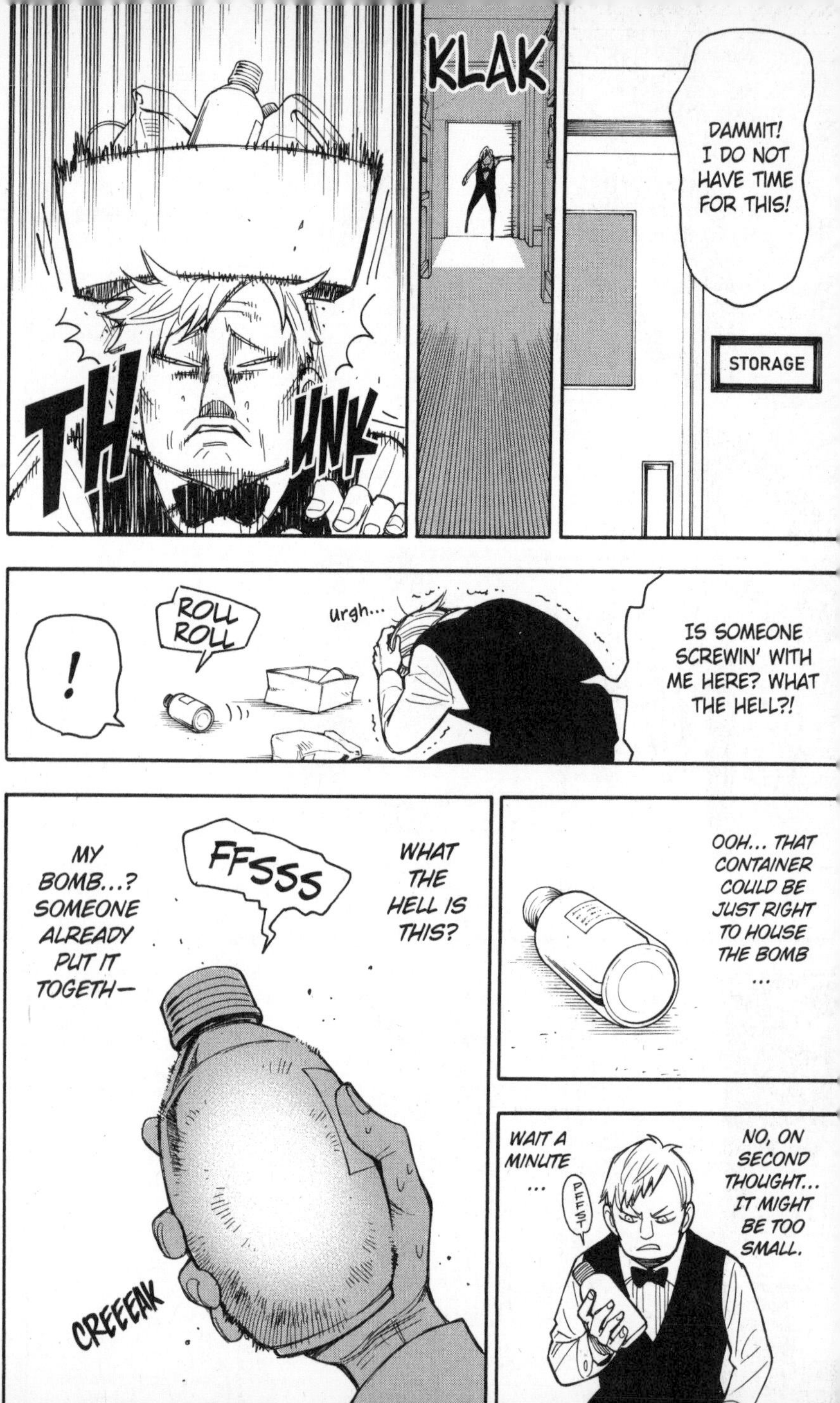
DAMMIT! I DO NOT HAVE TIME FOR THIS!
STORAGE
KLAK
THUNK
IS SOMEONE SCREWIN' WITH ME HERE? WHAT THE HELL?!
urgh...
ROLL ROLL
!
OOH... THAT CONTAINER COULD BE JUST RIGHT TO HOUSE THE BOMB ...
NO, ON SECOND THOUGHT... IT MIGHT BE TOO SMALL.
PFFST
WAIT A MINUTE ...
WHAT THE HELL IS THIS?
FFSSS
MY BOMB...? SOMEONE ALREADY PUT IT TOGETH—
CREEEAK

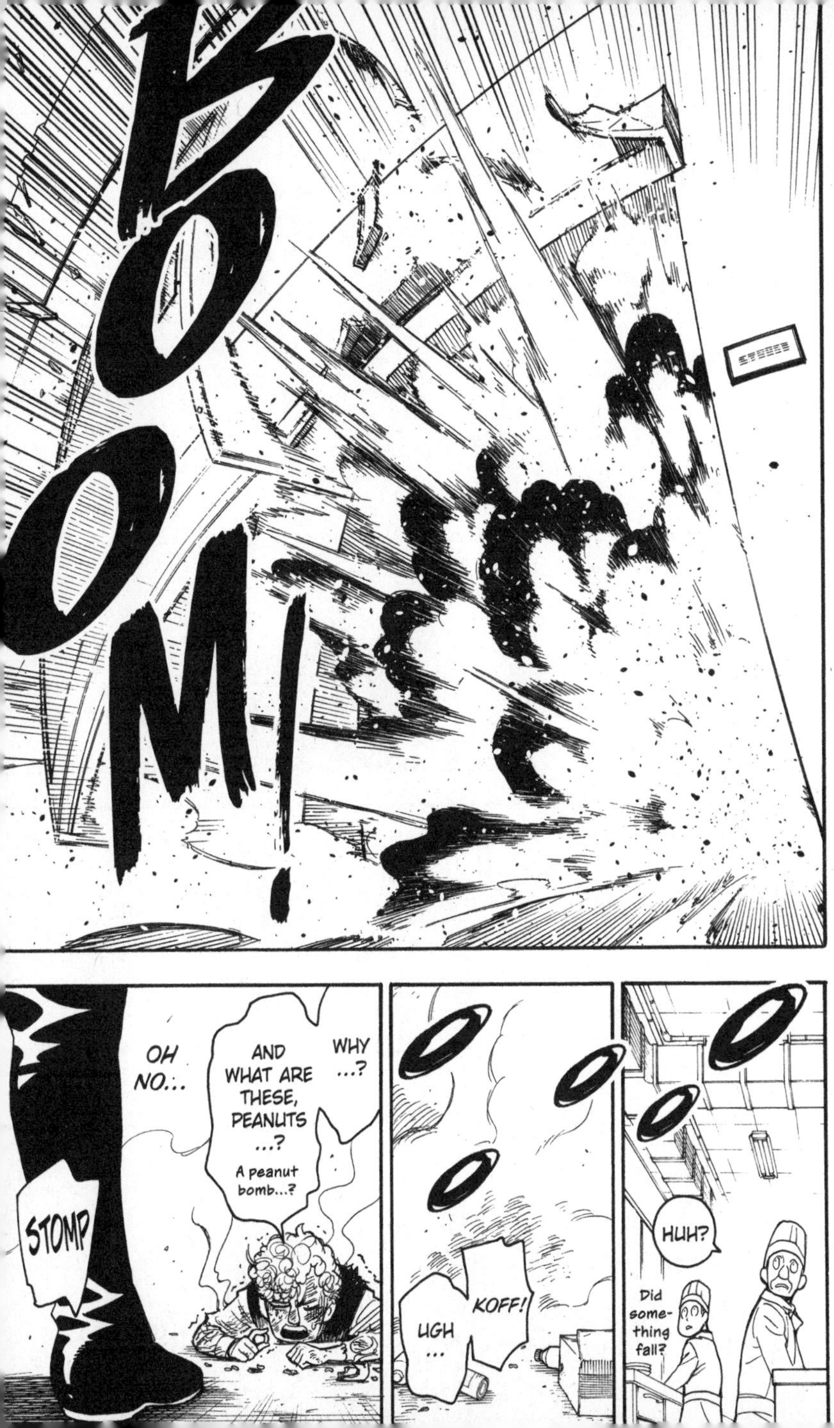
BOOM!
HUH?
Did something fall?
KOFF!
UGH...
WHY...?
AND WHAT ARE THESE, PEANUTS...?
A peanut bomb...?
OH NO...
STOMP

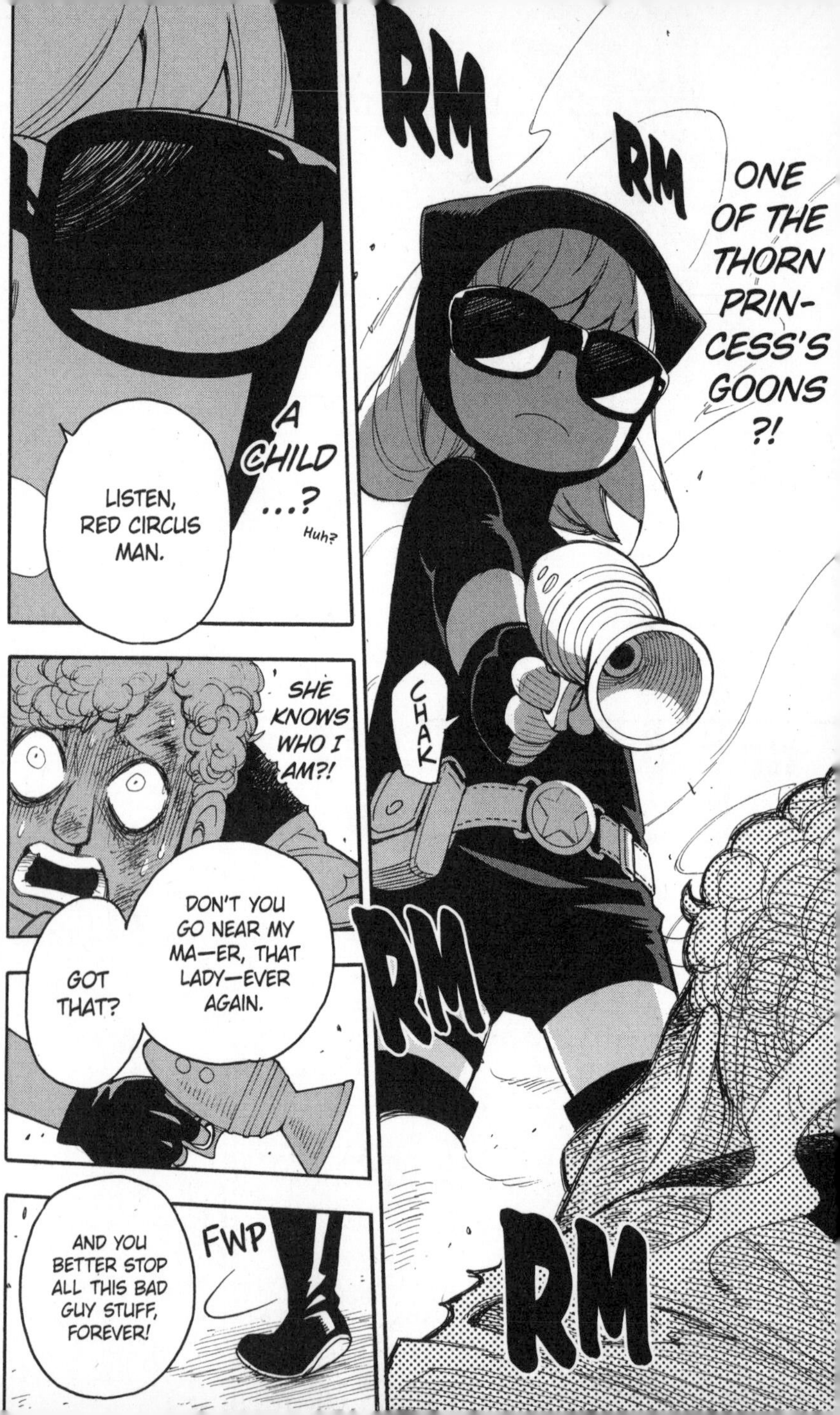
RM
RM
ONE OF THE THORN PRIN-CESS'S GOONS ?!
CHAK
RM
RM
A CHILD ...?
Huh?
LISTEN, RED CIRCUS MAN.
SHE KNOWS WHO I AM?!
DON'T YOU GO NEAR MY MA—ER, THAT LADY—EVER AGAIN.
GOT THAT?
FWP
AND YOU BETTER STOP ALL THIS BAD GUY STUFF, FOREVER!

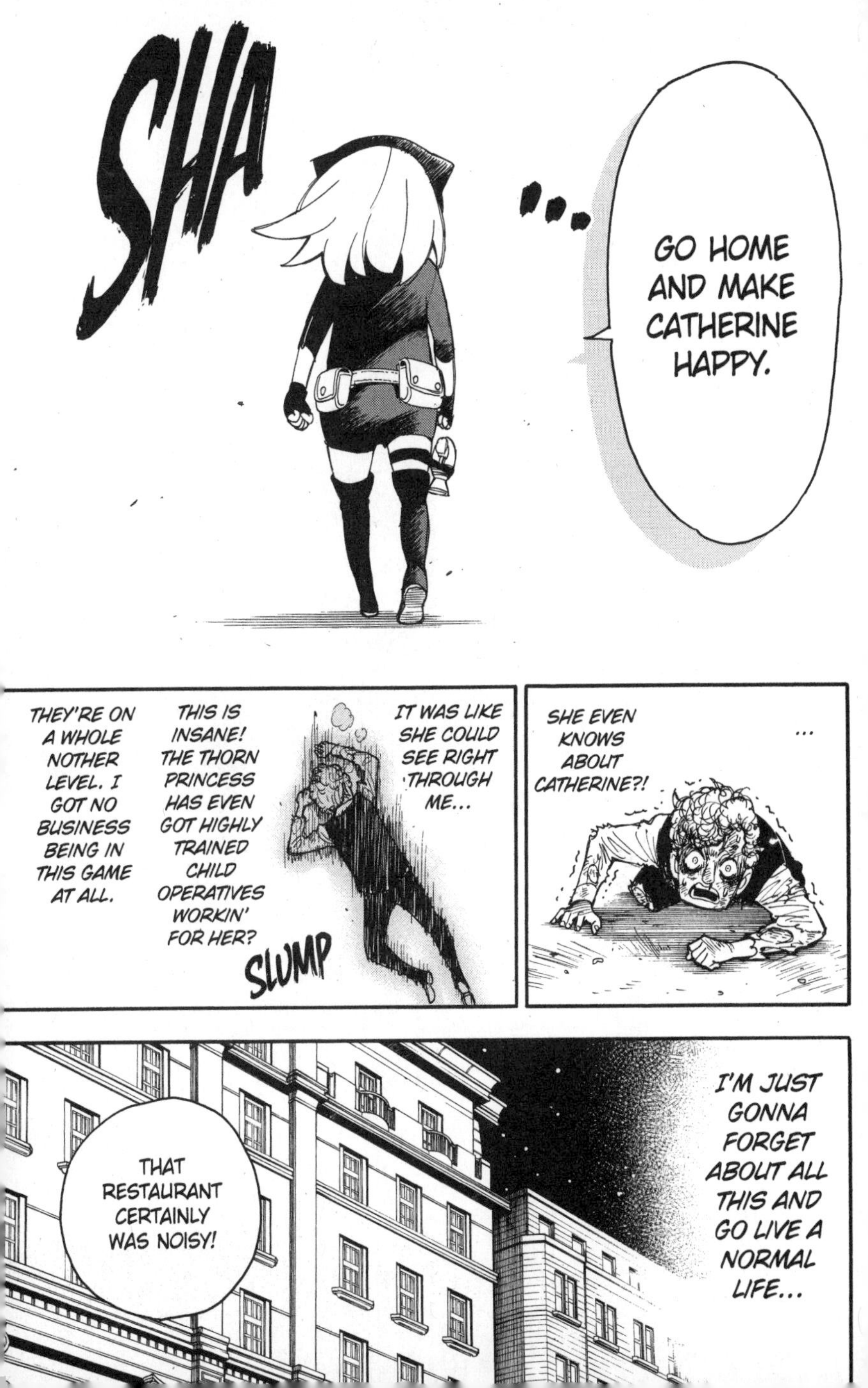
GO HOME AND MAKE CATHERINE HAPPY.
...
SHA
...
SHE EVEN KNOWS ABOUT CATHERINE?!
IT WAS LIKE SHE COULD SEE RIGHT THROUGH ME...
THIS IS INSANE! THE THORN PRINCESS HAS EVEN GOT HIGHLY TRAINED CHILD OPERATIVES WORKIN' FOR HER?
THEY'RE ON A WHOLE NOTHER LEVEL. I GOT NO BUSINESS BEING IN THIS GAME AT ALL.
SLUMP
I'M JUST GONNA FORGET ABOUT ALL THIS AND GO LIVE A NORMAL LIFE...
THAT RESTAURANT CERTAINLY WAS NOISY!

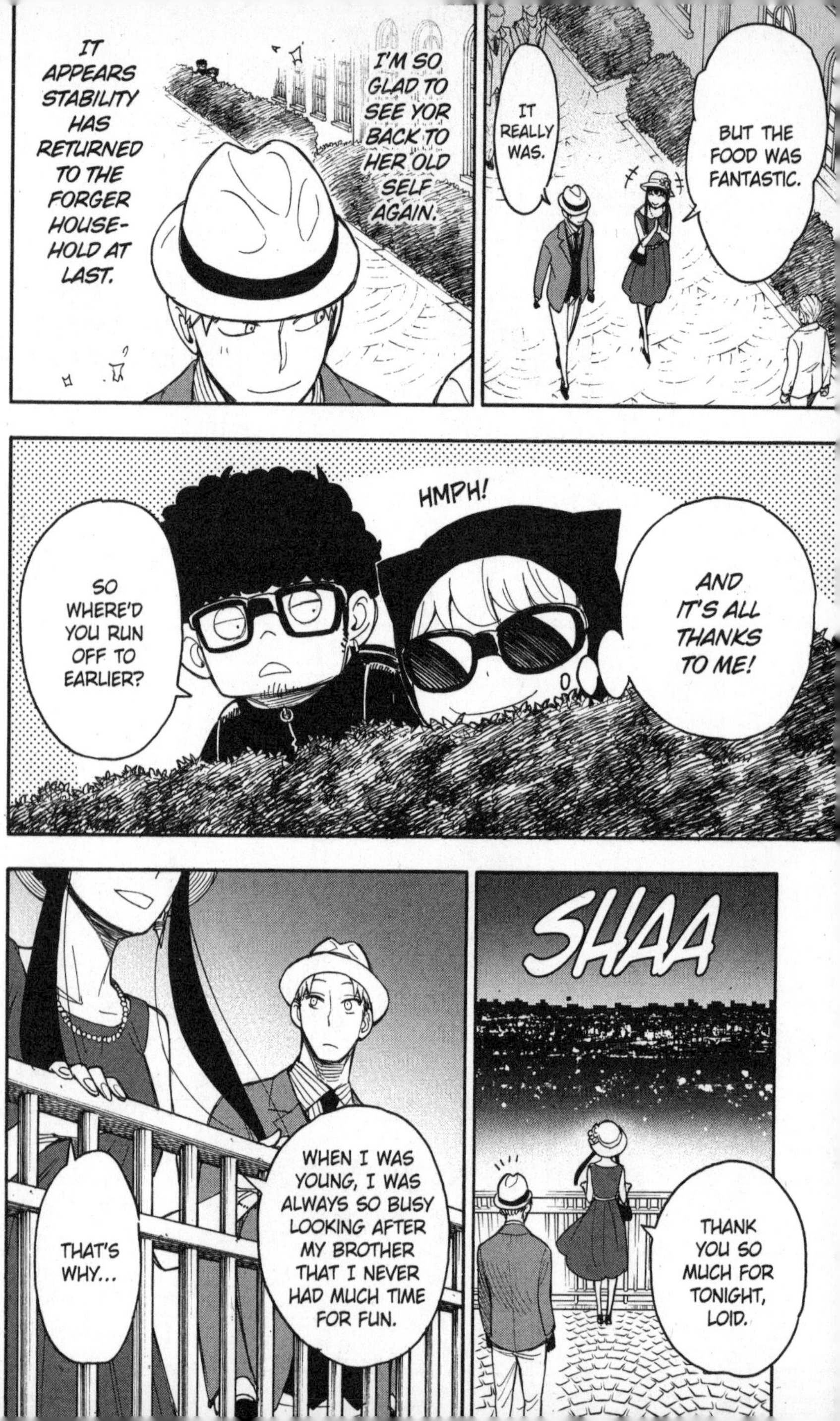
BUT THE FOOD WAS FANTASTIC.
IT REALLY WAS.
I'M SO GLAD TO SEE YOR BACK TO HER OLD SELF AGAIN.
IT APPEARS STABILITY HAS RETURNED TO THE FORGER HOUSE-HOLD AT LAST.
HMPH!
AND IT'S ALL THANKS TO ME!
SO WHERE'D YOU RUN OFF TO EARLIER?
SHAA
THANK YOU SO MUCH FOR TONIGHT, LOID.
WHEN I WAS YOUNG, I WAS ALWAYS SO BUSY LOOKING AFTER MY BROTHER THAT I NEVER HAD MUCH TIME FOR FUN.
THAT'S WHY...

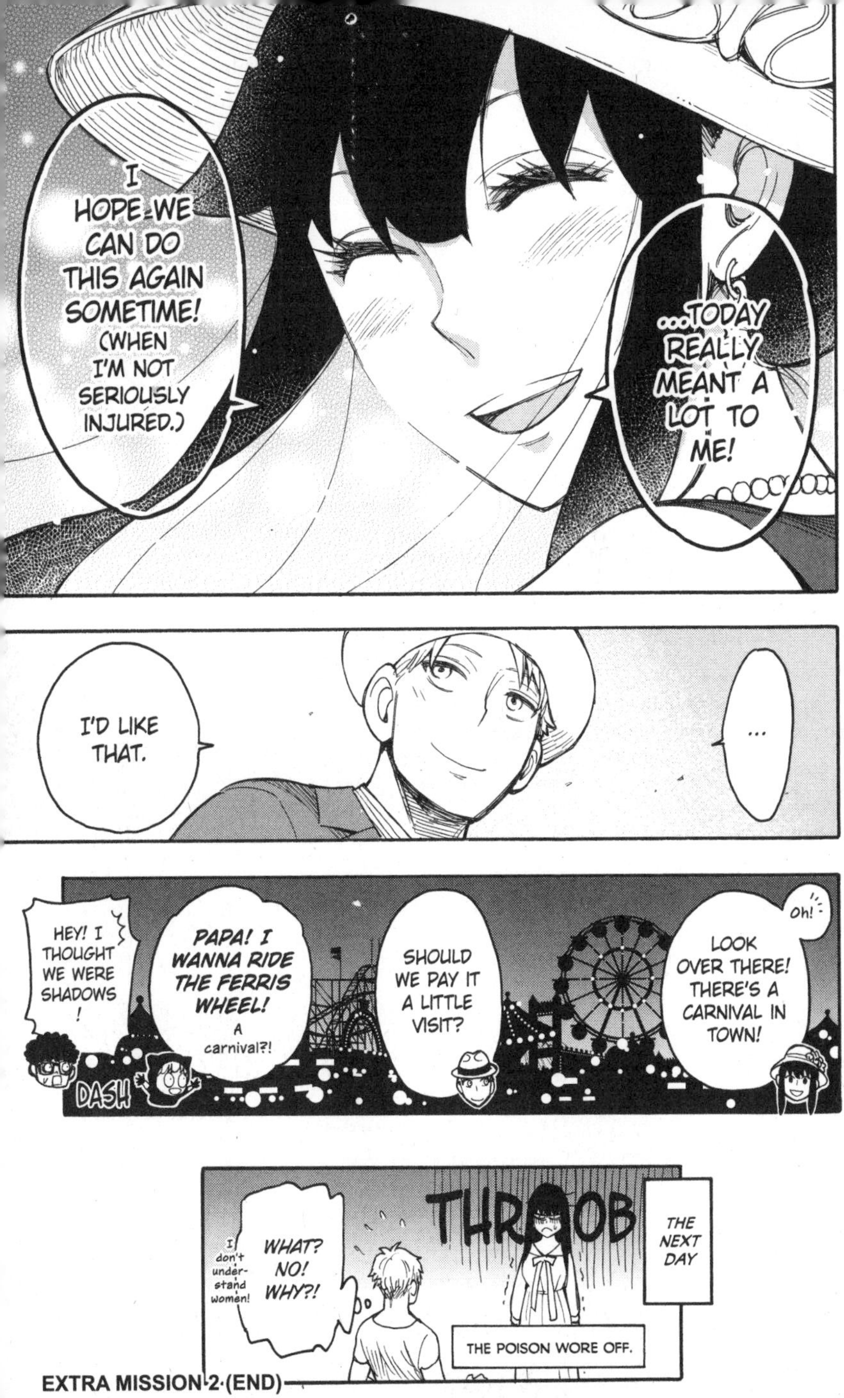
...TODAY REALLY MEANT A LOT TO ME!
I HOPE WE CAN DO THIS AGAIN SOMETIME! (WHEN I'M NOT SERIOUSLY INJURED.)
...
I'D LIKE THAT.
Oh!
LOOK OVER THERE! THERE'S A CARNIVAL IN TOWN!
SHOULD WE PAY IT A LITTLE VISIT?
PAPA! I WANNA RIDE THE FERRIS WHEEL!
A carnival?!
HEY! I THOUGHT WE WERE SHADOWS!
DASH
THE NEXT DAY
THROB
THE POISON WORE OFF.
WHAT? NO! WHY?!
I don't under-stand women!

EXTRA MISSION 2 (END)

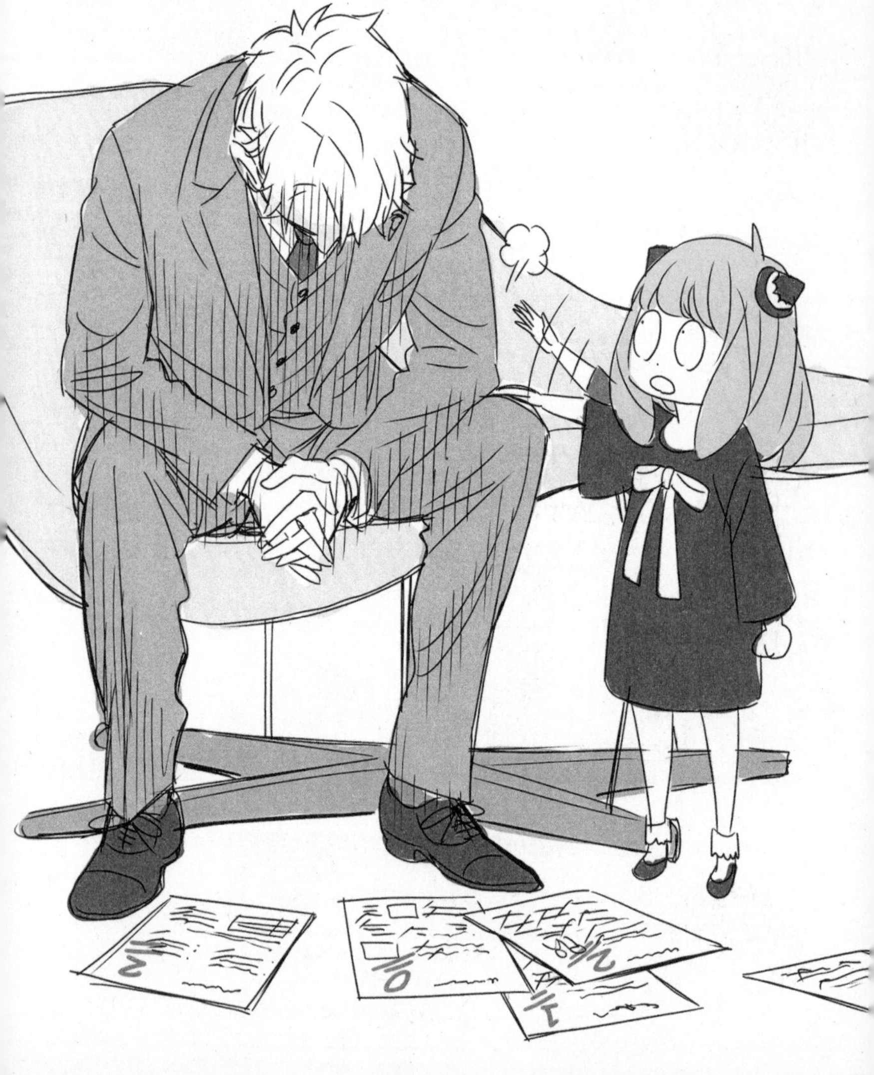

HOW YOR DOES HER HAIR: REVEALED!

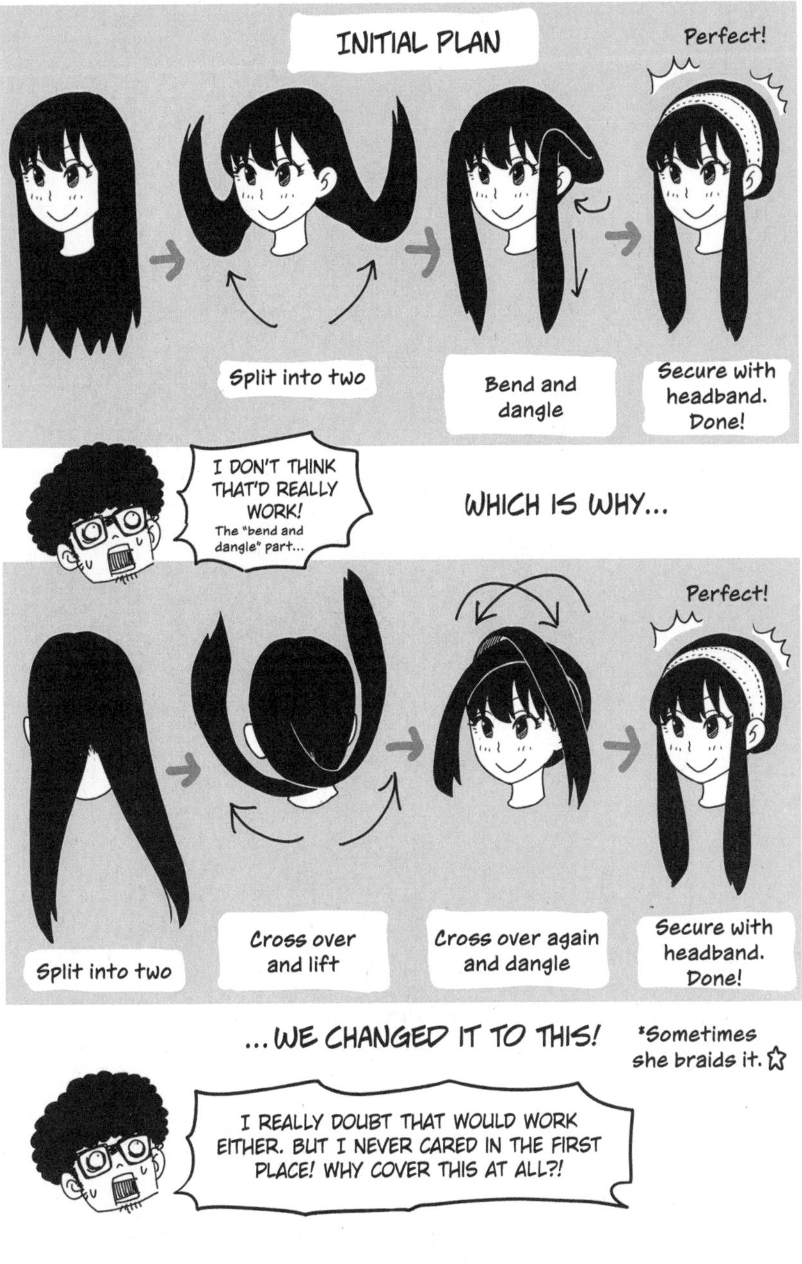
INITIAL PLAN
Perfect!
Split into two
Bend and dangle
Secure with headband. Done!
I DON'T THINK THAT'D REALLY WORK!
The "bend and dangle" part...
WHICH IS WHY...
Perfect!
Split into two
Cross over and lift
Cross over again and dangle
Secure with headband. Done!
...WE CHANGED IT TO THIS!
*Sometimes she braids it. ☆
I REALLY DOUBT THAT WOULD WORK EITHER. BUT I NEVER CARED IN THE FIRST PLACE! WHY COVER THIS AT ALL?!

Outside of the occasional autobiography, we typically only hear about spies when they fail. When they do their jobs flawlessly, leaving no traces behind, there are no public records of their deeds at all.

Spying is an occupation where you're only recognized when you fail—I couldn't handle that. I'm the type that wants to be lavished with praise!

—TATSUYA ENDO

Tatsuya Endo was born in Ibaraki Prefecture, Japan, on July 23, 1980. He debuted as a manga artist with the one-shot "Seibu Yugi" (Western Game), which ran in the Spring 2000 issue of *Akamaru Jump*. He is the author of *TISTA* and *Gekka Bijin* (Moon Flower Beauty). *Spy x Family* is his first work published in English.

SPY x FAMILY 3

SHONEN JUMP Edition

STORY AND ART BY **TATSUYA ENDO**

Translation **CASEY LOE**

Touch-Up Art & Lettering **RINA MAPA**

Design **JIMMY PRESLER**

Shonen Jump Series Editor **AMY YU**

Graphic Novel Editor **JOHN BAE**

First published in Japan in 2019 by SHUEISHA Inc., Tokyo.
English translation rights arranged by SHUEISHA Inc.

Printed in Italy

Published by VIZ Media, LLC
P.O. Box 77010
San Francisco, CA 94107

10 9 8 7
First printing, December 2020
Seventh printing, June 2022

RATED T+ OLDER TEEN ratings.viz.com

PARENTAL ADVISORY
SPY x FAMILY is rated T+ for Older Teen and is recommended for ages 16 and up. This volume contains realistic violence.

VIZ MEDIA
viz.com

SHONEN JUMP

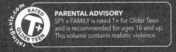

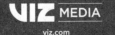

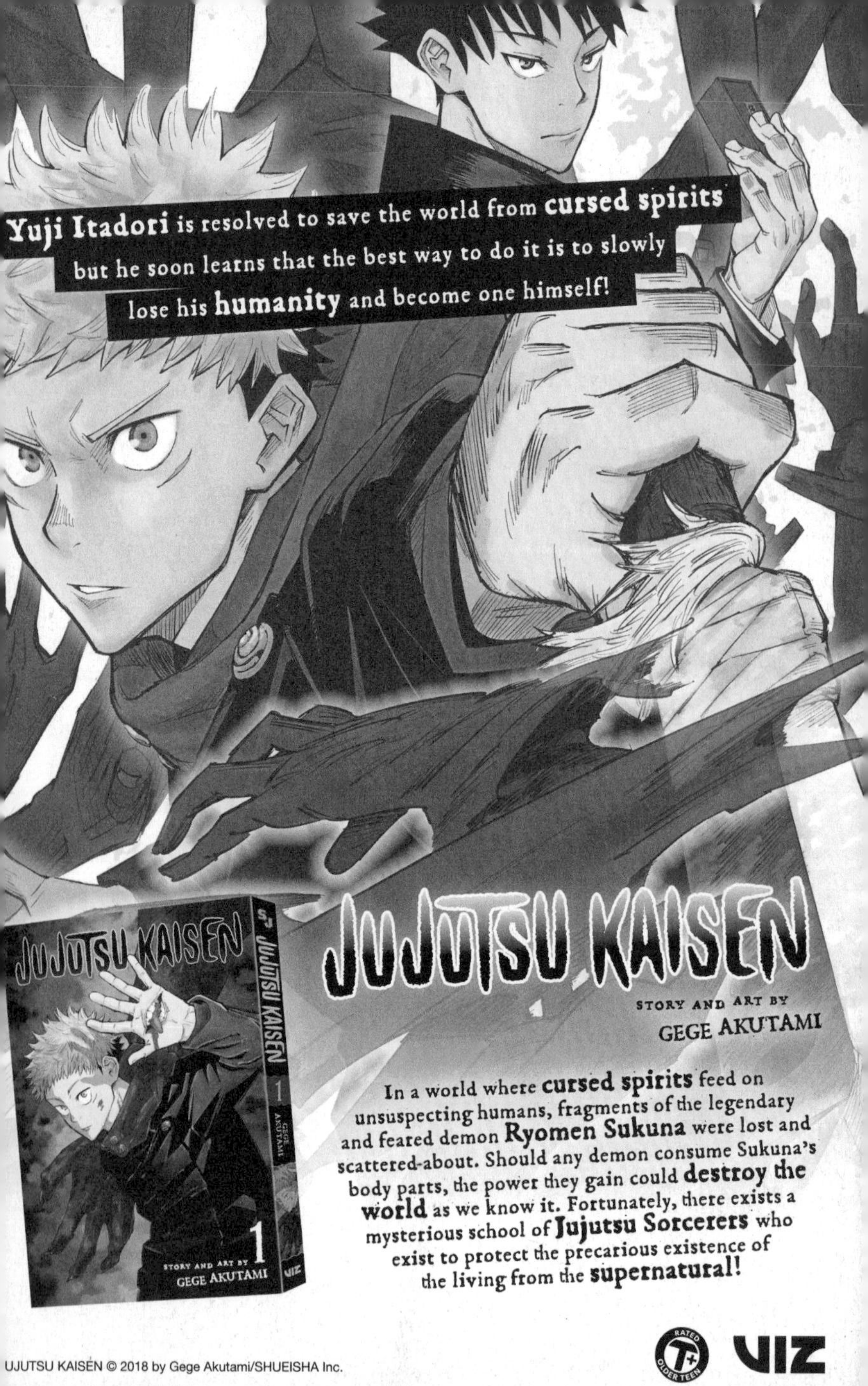

Yuji Itadori is resolved to save the world from cursed spirits
but he soon learns that the best way to do it is to slowly
lose his humanity and become one himself!
JUJUTSU KAISEN
SJ
JUJUTSU KAISEN
1
GEGE AKUTAMI
STORY AND ART BY
GEGE AKUTAMI
VIZ
JUJUTSU KAISEN
STORY AND ART BY
GEGE AKUTAMI
In a world where cursed spirits feed on
unsuspecting humans, fragments of the legendary
and feared demon Ryomen Sukuna were lost and
scattered-about. Should any demon consume Sukuna's
body parts, the power they gain could destroy the
world as we know it. Fortunately, there exists a
mysterious school of Jujutsu Sorcerers who
exist to protect the precarious existence of
the living from the supernatural!
RATED T+ OLDER TEEN
VIZ

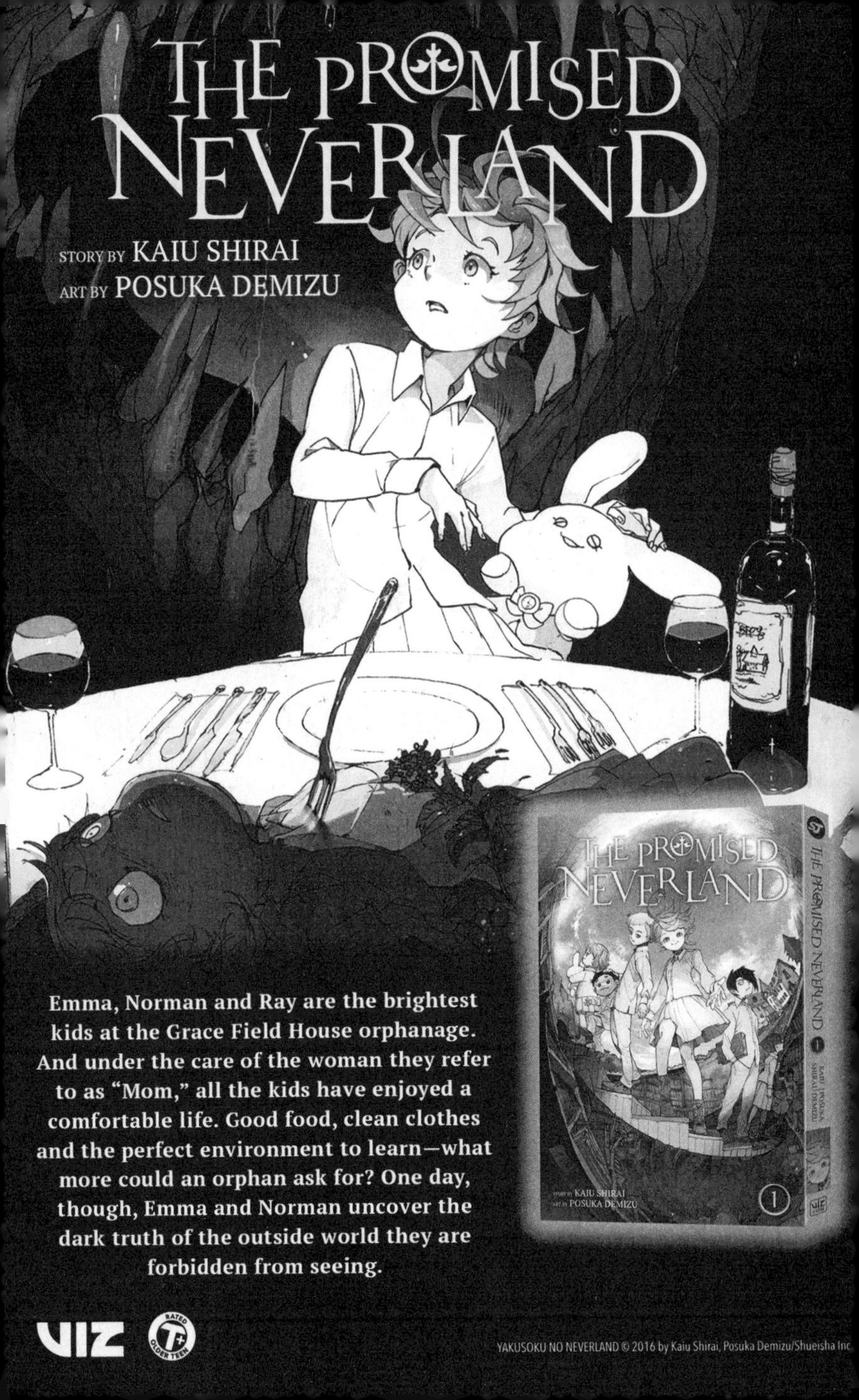
THE PROMISED NEVERLAND
STORY BY KAIU SHIRAI
ART BY POSUKA DEMIZU
Emma, Norman and Ray are the brightest kids at the Grace Field House orphanage. And under the care of the woman they refer to as "Mom," all the kids have enjoyed a comfortable life. Good food, clean clothes and the perfect environment to learn—what more could an orphan ask for? One day, though, Emma and Norman uncover the dark truth of the outside world they are forbidden from seeing.
VIZ
RATED T+ OLDER TEEN
YAKUSOKU NO NEVERLAND © 2016 by Kaiu Shirai, Posuka Demizu/Shueisha Inc.

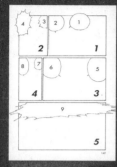

YOU'RE READING THE WRONG WAY!

SPY x FAMILY reads from right to left, starting in the upper-right corner. Japanese is read from right to left, meaning that action, sound effects and word-balloon order are completely reversed from English order.